Cross Cultural Awareness
and Social Justice
in Counseling

Cross Cultural Awareness and Social Justice in Counseling

Edited by
Cyrus Marcellus Ellis and Jon Carlson

Routledge
Taylor & Francis Group
New York   London

Routledge
Taylor & Francis Group
711 Third Avenue,
New York, NY 10017

Routledge
Taylor & Francis Group
27 Church Road, Hove
East Sussex, BN3 2FA

International Standard Book Number-13: 978-0-415-95452-5 (Softcover)

Library of Congress Cataloging-in-Publication Data

Cross cultural awareness and social justice in counseling / edited by Cyrus Marcellus
    Ellis and Jon Carlson.
        p. ; cm.
    Includes bibliographical references and index.
    ISBN 978-0-415-95452-5 (hardbound : alk. paper)
    1. Cross-cultural counseling--United States. I. Ellis, Cyrus Marcellus. II. Carlson,
Jon.
        [DNLM: 1. Counseling--methods--United States. 2. Cross-Cultural
Comparison--United States. 3. Cultural Competency--United States. 4. Mental
Disorders--therapy--United States. 5. Minority Groups--psychology--United States. 6.
Social Justice--United States. WA 305 C9508 2008]

BF636.7.C76C76 2008
158'.3--dc22   2008010749

Visit the Taylor & Francis Web site at
http://www.taylorandfrancis.com

and the Routledge Web site at
http://www.routledge.com

CONTENTS

PREFACE

The evil that is in the world almost always comes of ignorance, and good intentions may do as much harm as malevolence if they lack understanding.

—Albert Camus, Nobel Prize winner

The profession of health and human services has been engaged in the work of social justice for a very long time. Social justice has also evolved into a variety of definitions. It is a wonderful evolution of thought and practice within our society when people begin to recognize that we are better off living together from a position of understanding as opposed to one of suspicion and fear.

Social justice has been tackled from a variety of perspectives. It has advocates in the world of economics, educational leadership, and religion as well as psychology and counseling. Social justice, in a global sense, is an ideology of balancing the recompense of our society against the disadvantages of our society. As one rap star once said, social justice can be the difference between "joy and pain." Social justice brings into the light the historical context of issues such as race, gender, ability, and class while simultaneously removing the veil and displaying the resulting negative emotions and lived experience of people who are on intimate terms with the sting of living inside an ism.

What is social justice? Social justice can be thought of in terms of one's internal sense of conscience or spiritual responsibility as well as one's sense of righteousness for the world. Whether your sense of social justice comes from your faith, your spirit, or your religious conviction, social justice can be equated to the harmonious nature by showing love, goodness, or kindness to your fellow being because you are a recipient of blessings and precious love yourself. Social justice can be seen as the purest form of altruism because you are doing well toward others for goodness sake. Social justice is, for us, a spiritual connection because it recognizes everybody's right to live and that we are active participants in the force of nature. Social justice is when individuals stand up for what is right and act in community with like-minded people to hold our society accountable for violations of the common good. We ought not use our social justice posture to bolster the self; social justice is a posture that provokes its followers to maintain a solid and real connection to everyday people and their resulting lived conditions of injustice.

Our thoughts on the etiology of social justice match that of Rev. Dr. Martin Luther King who said, "Like life, racial understanding is not something that we find but something that we must create. And so the ability of Negroes and whites to work together, to understand each other, will not be found readymade; it must be created by the fact of contact" (King, 1983, p.33). Although Dr. King was speaking of Whites and Blacks, the recognition that personal contact with people who are under the thumb of oppression, bigotry, racism, and White supremacy ought to fuel our desires to be true advocates of social justice and be on guard for the pitfalls of becoming ideologues.

Entering into a project on culture and social justice has been stressful and enlightening. Constructing a book involving a wide range of issues forced us to look carefully at ourselves. We have been colleagues and friends for several years but have avoided looking carefully at who we really are.

We conceived the idea to create a text for the various human service disciplines that not only addresses diversity but also what it means to be an advocate for our society. As we discussed the various aspects of the book, our cross-cultural awareness began to grow and we noticed the many societal changes that have occurred in our own lives. We realized that this book would not have been written 40 years ago. On the surface, there are some very obvious but stark contrasts between the editors. At every glance we (Drs. Carlson and Ellis) are as different (pardon the pun) as night and day.

Dr. Ellis was born in 1967. Dr. Carlson's first child was born one year later in 1968. Dr. Ellis has civil rights–era parents from Louisiana and Mississippi and began life as a member of a supportive Black middle class that abounded in music, education, art, and religious faith. Dr. Carlson was born of privilege in a far western Chicago suburb. His family was White and upper class. Things changed for Dr. Ellis in his late childhood when his father and mother divorced and the family lived in housing projects and humble conditions. Dr. Ellis' father had been a truck driver and his mother was a service worker helping out in kitchens and cleaning offices to make ends meet. His upbringing was not full of extravagant vacations to national amusement parks or trips to famous places. Dr. Ellis' life was filled with the ideas and promises of a better future for himself and his people through the hard work and example of many people in the civil rights movement. Dr. Ellis was groomed to understand what came before him and how the deaths of notables in the African American community (i.e., Medgar Evers, Martin Luther King, Malcolm X) were not to go unnoticed. Additionally, the deaths of John Kennedy and Robert Kennedy were also family lessons of how his community of African Americans bears a mark that is long lasting and deeply entrenched in this country. It was taught that his life must be a testament to the people who did not make it to the other side of the mountain and never to forget that his life is not his own but connected to a rich tradition of people who suffered for his pleasures today.

Dr. Carlson grew up in a large house on the "right side" of the Fox River in Elgin, Illinois. He had a large group of friends and didn't want for much. His father was a hard-working contractor and his mother a well-educated community leader. He was raised with extensive travel, cultural opportunities, and even had private voice and dance lessons. He spent his summers at the family's home on Lake Geneva, Wisconsin, where he fished, sailed and drove the mahogany Chris-Craft.

Dr. Ellis' dad was an Army veteran from the Korean Conflict era. Dr. Ellis' father served as his hero, then and now. He became a truck driver and was known as the "Alka Seltzer" on the citizens band radio (CB) in the '70s and '80s. Whereas some kids saw Disneyland and other places on summer vacation, Dr. Ellis saw the nation on the Eisenhower Interstate Highway System from the left side of a red-and-white International flat-nose semi.

Dr. Carlson's father was also an Army veteran serving in World War I. He graduated from the 8th grade, worked a couple of years, and enlisted. He never spoke about his experiences but just felt appreciative that he survived. He vowed to never sleep in a tent again!

Dr. Ellis grew up in the American South on the West Bank of New Orleans as opposed to Dr. Carlson's upbringing in the Midwest. The American South has a lot of beauty as well as a lot of ugliness. The South taught Dr. Ellis that freedom has many layers and that poverty and race really impact how much position in life one can have.

Dr. Carlson clearly grew up on the other side of town from where Dr. Ellis described. There were people of color in Elgin, but they kept to themselves and didn't interact much with the White culture.

During Dr. Ellis' humble life he decided to join the U.S. Army. Dr. Ellis spent 20 years of his life in uniform for his country. He began his career as an enlisted man and obtained the rank of sergeant. He was awarded a scholarship while on active duty then went back to college and enrolled in Reserve Officer Training Corps (ROTC). He was commissioned and served for the next 12 years as an Army officer retiring as a captain. He was willing to deploy to any place in the world if ordered to do so.

Dr. Carlson did not seek military service and was never drafted. He agonized, along with many others of his generation, as to whether he would actually serve his country in the war in Vietnam.

Dr. Ellis was educated as an undergraduate mainly at Rider University in Lawrenceville, New Jersey. Rider is a private school that was attended by many privileged White kids and it was located in a suburb of Trenton, New Jersey, just 30 miles south of Princeton. Dr. Ellis earned his commission in the U.S. Army, his BA degree, and his MA degree from this school. He received his PhD from the Curry School of Education at the University of Virginia. His professional work has focused on those people who fall into some of the unfair categories of addicts and "crazy people." These are the people who suffer with mental health and addiction issues but do not possess a great deal of resources to always get the best care.

Dr. Carlson, on the other hand, attended all "blue collar" public colleges. He received his BS and MS degrees from Southern Illinois University in Carbondale and his EdD from Wayne State University in Detroit.

The last 40 years have shown a great deal of societal changes. It is interesting to note that this text is being written by a multitude of authors and professionals all of whom are primarily being coordinated by Dr. Ellis, who is a junior faculty member at Governors State University and who serves as the lead editor. Higher education has taken on many of the challenges that our society has been attempting to address over the same period of time. Higher education, as an establishment representative of our culture, has many of the same pitfalls that our society possesses. In large part, educated White males have constructed the nature of higher education and have developed the manner by which people gain access or are shut out of receiving education. Over the past 40 years significant changes have occurred to remove the oppressive institutional, cultural, and political values of higher education.

Pop culture also reflects the significance of these cultural changes. Modern television has a myriad of shows that address homosexuality, biracial couples, people with different abilities, and many other topics that were only viewed as abnormal (if not sick!) in the days of *Chico and the Man, All in the Family,* and *Good Times.* African Americans, Latino Americans, and Americans of different ability are headlining shows as the primary characters and, in some cases, are the producers and directors of their own television shows.

The editors are, at times, on different sides of pop culture as well. Dr. Carlson has recently read *DO YOU* by Russell Simmons, the rap and fashion mogul from New York who founded Def Jam records, which produced such artists as LL Cool J, Run DMC, and the Beastie Boys. In contrast, Dr. Ellis has thoroughly enjoyed concerts where Randy Travis, the famous country singer, and the Southern rock band known as the Marshall Tucker Band have performed. It is an interesting phenomenon to experience and recognize when two men of different backgrounds are openly engaging in activities that, on the surface, are not germane to their racial and cultural foundation. Who would have thought, 40 years ago, that top entertainers and athletes (including golf and tennis) would be Black?

The past 40 years have shown that things can and will change. Although we have significant changes in the appearance of our nation, we still have issues with legislative, political, and the cultural dimensions of our society. The attitudes of many toward racially different people, the economically challenged, the ability challenged as well as the divide among gender, sexual orientation, and immigrants still exist within our society and, at times, make their way into and influence local, regional, and national debates concerning those who wish to maintain power and those seeking access to the nation's resources. The resulting thoughts, attitudes, feelings, and beliefs that are derived from this imbalance enter the counseling environment and it is that set of issues that tends to confound the helpers as they try to work through issues with the culturally diverse population. This text is designed to illuminate the issues that enter into the helping relationship so that professional helpers can be aware of the silent and expressed lived conditions of people trying to gain equity and legitimacy in our society.

We begin this book with recognizing the reason and the need for social justice and providing the reader with some developmental and personally reflective information on the editors to illuminate our society from a tangible perspective. Chapter 1 opens the book with Rebecca Toporek's account of how the helping profession became aware and developed a knowledge and skill set to recognize diversity. Her chapter involves identifying major figures who demonstrated advocacy through their professional work and scholarly activities. Chapter 2 is written by Amie Manis, Shunda Brown, and Matthew Paylo and is intended to help the reader understand the process of becoming an advocate.

The chapter is arranged to help the reader recognize advocacy for the helping professions, illuminate key concepts related to advocacy, the roles and characteristics of helping professionals as advocates in terms practice and research, and lists resources available to helping professionals and educators for enhancing our advocacy competence. Chapter 3 is written by Rebecca Farrell to assist the reader in recognizing the importance of developing a diverse counseling posture. Her chapter focuses on how counselors can take an active role in creating an environment to receive clients in a cultural context. Her work forces the reader to recognize the importance of not allowing hidden or inappropriate theoretical approaches to enter into the counseling context.

Chapters 4 through 12 are dedicated to the work of helping culturally diverse clients using a social justice perspective. Chapter 4 begins with Shunda Brown and Kathleen May's work on counseling with women. In this chapter, they review the historical context of women in society and in the helping profession. Their work uncovers present-day struggles women face from continuing oppression and discrimination. The impact of violence on women is also illuminated as well as suggestions that helping professionals can use to work with women from a social justice perspective. Chapter 5 is written by Matt Englar-Carlson and is dedicated to the cultural issues facing helping professionals when working with men. Although men's work has been around for some time, textbooks including men's issues have been rare. This chapter focuses on the socialization of men and how this impacts their intrapersonal and interpersonal relationships as well as how men's overall socialization impacts the development of their masculinity. Multiple suggestions are provided to the helping professional to assist them when working with men from a social justice perspective by addressing gender-based ideals of masculinity, removing sexist attitudes toward men, and assisting young boys and men as they have been negatively impacted by society. Chapter 6 is the contribution of Marc Grimmett and Don Locke on counseling with African Americans. This chapter provides insight into a group of people often misunderstood and tagged with a variety of social ills. Key to this chapter is the illumination of the legislative and cultural oppression levied against this group. The authors give a comprehensive view of the cultural context of this group and how it impacts the overall development of the African American community.

Chapter 7 is written by Anneliese Singh and is on the topic of counseling with Asian Americans. This chapter challenges helping professionals to view Asian Americans through a sociopolitical lens in an attempt to have the reader consider the history of Asians and Asian Americans in the American context. The author challenges the notion

of Asians as the "model minority" and how these and other myths add
to the experience and mental health of Asian Americans. Chapter 8 is
written by Robert Smith and R. Esteban Montilla and covers counseling with Spanish-speaking clients. This chapter provides an overview
of counseling Spanish-speaking clients. The authors provide a scholarly review of issues affecting the mental health of Spanish-speaking
clients. Their work addresses the issues of acculturation and counselor
preferences as factors to consider when working with Spanish-speaking
clients. The authors conclude this chapter with important concepts that
assist the helping professional when working with this population from
a social justice posture. Chapter 9, written by Sherri Turner and Mark
Pope, is about counseling with North America's indigenous people. The
authors explore how helping professionals can counsel North America's
indigenous people or Native Americans under the umbrella of social
justice. Social justice for Native Americans may be a debatable topic, but
Turner and Pope emphasize the social justice construct of equal rights,
security, and social benefits toward a population who lives within the
veil of their history as it is viewed through the lens of American history
and White–Indian relationships. Chapter 10 provided by Toni Tollerud
and Linda Slabon concerns counseling with gay, lesbian, bisexual, and
transgender (GLBT) people. The authors' work underscores the call
of social justice to see everyone as a person of worth and value. This
chapter reveals to the helping professional the need to understand the
intricate nature of oppression and hatred that complicates the adaptive
development of the GLBT population. The authors provide a cadre of
words and phrases that provoke the soul and provide enlightenment to
helping professionals on how complex the issues are for people attempting to be validated for who they are and how they love. The cross-cultural awareness and social justice suggestions provided in this chapter
provide a sound framework for understanding the external impact and
internalized responses of the GLBT population to our society. Chapter
11 is written by Adam Zagelbaum concerning a most relevant topic of
counseling with new citizens. Zagelbaum's work provides an in-depth
look at the lure of the United States to others around the world and how
our way of life is so attractive to people yearning for a better way of life.
The reality of entering into our culture is often a difficult adjustment to
make and this chapter reveals the hardships and struggles faced by people immigrating to the United States. Social justice practices on behalf
of new citizens are explained in a comprehensive manner to assist helping professionals recognize the social and political impediments of
immigrants attempting to find legitimacy in the new land. Chapter 12
is provided by Leon Caldwell and it involves counseling the poor and

disenfranchised. The author provides the reader a perspective to helping professionals that provide services to those in poverty. Poverty, as a construct, is defined so that helpers can understand the impact of poverty on individuals and communities. Viewing the etiology of poverty and its impact on individuals living in poverty are crucial determinants of helpers who need to examine their own biases to the abilities of people who live in a state of financial poverty.

In addition to all of the contributing authors providing salient and practical suggestions to become more culturally aware and socially just, in chapter 13 we provide some closing remarks to help frame the mind, body, and soul concerning cultural awareness and social justice practices. Training recommendations and experiences are provided as well as additional resources so that everyone can gain access to cross-cultural information for the growth of the helping profession and the improvement of our world.

SUGGESTIONS FOR THE READER

The task for the users of this text is to examine their internal reactions to the chapters presented in this book so that they can begin to determine their level of cross-cultural awareness and social justice toward people in society. The work in this text is designed so readers can examine the nature of their cross-cultural awareness and social justice activity to date and then begin to strategize on how it can be increased to positively affect persons who traditionally receive the sting of disadvantaging conditions from within our society. Each chapter is intended to inform and create a sense of mental dissonance for readers in order to initiate the process of tearing down one's comfort zone. Each chapter is intended to introduce societal and environmental values that have created the conditions of partiality and bias on a variety of groups.

Cyrus Marcellus Ellis
Jon Carlson

REFERENCE

King, Coretta Scott. (1983). *The words of Martin Luther King Jr.* (2nd ed). New York: Newmarket Press.

ACKNOWLEDGMENTS

As we complete a work like this, there are many, many people deserving of acknowledgment. Jon has allowed me to take the lead in offering acknowledgements so I would like to acknowledge God, which some call the Great Spirit for his grace and mercy on me. As a father of two beautiful daughters, Courtney Lynn and Morgan Crystina Ellis, I need to acknowledge them as a constant source of joy and the truest sign in my life that I am special. Each of those little girls has my heart and they increase the value of my life every day. My journey into the professorate was not a solo effort; there are many who aided in that journey. Atop the list is Deirdre M. Ellis, thank you. To my mother, Augustine Ellis, the memory of my sister Anastasia Maria "Stacey" Ellis, and my brothers Gerard Joseph Ellis and Lionel A. Ellis, Jr., go my love and appreciation.

I acknowledge my mentors from Rider University's psychology program: Dr. John Suler, Dr. Anne Law, and Dr. Ruth Simpkins. From Rider University's graduate counseling program I give special attention to my mentor and most trusted example of what it means to be a member of the professorate, Dr. Jesse DeEsch. I have had the honor of attending and graduating from the University of Virginia. To the faculty of the counselor education program at UVa from 1997 to 2000, who helped shape and challenge me throughout my program, I offer my thanks and wish to recognize Dr. Ken Lafleur, Dr. Joan Franks, Dr. Kathleen May, and Dr. Claudia Sowa. I must give special thanks for continued mentorship and support from Dr. Spencer "Skip" Niles. One of my greatest joys of my time at Mr. Jefferson's University is my relationship with a man I consider to be equal to the love and respect of my father, Dr. Robert H. Pate, Jr. From me, Dr. Pate has a son's love.

I have been blessed to have a wonderful array of friends and family over the course of my life that also plays a role in the completion of this work. For my friends who stretch from the West Bank of New Orleans to the East Coast of the USA, I thank you for being a part of me. To my friends, who are also colleagues, our years of thinking out loud and "conferencing" have been a joy to me.

The only sadness in the completion of this work is the absence of one voice and one phrase of congratulations coming from my father, Lionel A. Ellis, Sr. My father lived and died as my hero. He still serves me daily as my standard for what strength, valor, and perseverance ought to be. I miss him daily and wish he could hold this work and see his name on the cover.

Jon and I would like to offer special thanks to the community of scholars, staff members, and members of the Governors State University community. We are appreciative of their support of our scholarly activity. To the grad assistants of Dr. Ellis-Tiffany Bernard, Georgia Smith, and Tina Musselman, your assistance in the production of this book is greatly appreciated.

EDITORS

Cyrus Marcellus Ellis, PhD, is an Associate Professor in the Division of Psychology and Counseling at Governors State University. Dr. Ellis received his BA in psychology from Rider College, his MA in counseling from Rider University, and a PhD in counselor education from the University of Virginia. He is the 1995 recipient of the Lincoln Scott Walter Award in Counseling from Rider University, the 1999 recipient of the William Van Hoose Memorial Award from the Curry Foundation at the University of Virginia, and a 2004 recipient of the OHANA award from Counselors for Social Justice. Dr. Ellis' scholarly activity includes work in race relations, self-concept, social justice, and counselor training. Dr. Ellis has a professional history of treating the mentally ill and the chemically addicted. He has been a counseling professional at group homes, inpatient hospitals, and outpatient clinics and has been a consultant for community services.

Jon Carlson, PsyD, EdD, ABPP, is a Distinguished University Professor in the Division of Psychology and Counseling at Governors State University and a psychologist at the Wellness Clinic in Lake Geneva, Wisconsin. In 2004, the American Counseling Association named Dr. Carlson a Living Legend in Counseling. He was the founding editor of *The Family Journal*, a long-time editor of the *Journal of Individual Psychology*, the author of more than 40 books, and has been the creator and host of more than 200 training video/DVD productions for the American Psychological Association.

CONTRIBUTORS

Shunda L. Brown, PhD, is an Assistant Professor of Counselor Education at the University of North Florida in Jacksonville, Florida. Dr. Brown is a graduate of the counselor education program at the University of Virginia. She has an extensive background as a mental health counselor and has provided services to children, adolescents, and families in Florida, Tennessee, and Virginia. Dr. Brown is a member of the American Counseling Association, the Association for Multicultural Counseling and Development, and the Association for Counselor Education and Supervision. Dr. Brown's service to the profession encompasses leadership positions in various professional organizations. She is the president of the Florida Association for Spiritual, Ethical, and Religious Values in Counseling and serves on the Florida Counseling Association's Delegate Assembly and the Legislative Platform. She is the faculty adviser for the Sigma Phi Epsilon Chapter of Chi Sigma Iota Counseling Honor Society and past president of the Jefferson Counselors Association, a chapter of the Virginia Counselors Association. She was recognized as an Emerging Leader by the Southern Association for Counselor Education and Supervision and is the recipient of awards and scholarships from the University of Virginia, the Virginia Counselors Association, and the Rho Beta Chapter of Chi Sigma Iota Counseling Honor Society. Dr. Brown recognizes the importance of multicultural counseling and social justice, and believes that this awareness positively affects what she brings to teaching, supervision, mentoring, scholarship, and professional service.

Leon D. Caldwell, PhD, is a Research Associate Professor in the Division of Social Work in the School of Public Policy and Urban Affairs at the University of Memphis. Dr. Caldwell received his doctorate in counseling psychology from Pennsylvania State University and an MEd and BA from Lehigh University. He develops and directs community-based mental health interventions for underserved and underrepresented populations with a particular focus on youth. His work primarily focuses on mental health promotion for African American youth and families. He has published and presented about mental health service delivery and the need for alternative forms of service delivery to vulnerable populations. Dr. Caldwell convenes the African American Male Empowerment Summit and is the executive director of the Think Tank for African American Progress.

Matt Englar-Carlson, PhD, is an Associate Professor of counseling at the California State University at Fullerton. He holds graduate degrees in health psychology education and counselor education and received his PhD in counseling psychology from the Pennsylvania State University. A former elementary school counselor, his main areas of scholarly interest focus on training counselors to understand how masculinity influences well-being, interpersonal relationships, and the process of counseling men. An additional theme in his scholarly work is exploration of the positive psychology of men and the integration of masculinity with social justice work. He is the coeditor (with Mark A. Stevens) of *In the Room with Men: A Casebook of Therapeutic Change* (APA Books, 2006) and coeditor (with Mark Kiselica and Andy Horne) of *Counseling Troubled Boys: A Guidebook for Professionals* (Routledge, 2008). Dr. Englar-Carlson resides in Huntington Beach, California, with his wife, Alison, and son, Jackson.

Rebecca L. Farrell, PhD, is an Assistant Professor of Counselor Education at Morehead State University in Morehead, Kentucky. She teaches and supervises in the school counseling (master's) and mental health (EdS) programs. Dr. Farrell is a graduate of Virginia Polytechnic Institute and State University. She is a member of the American Counseling Association, the Association for Counselor Educators and Supervisors, Kentucky Counseling Association, and the Kentucky School Counseling Association. Dr. Farrell also serves on the executive committee for the Professional Counseling Fund, a political action committee for the counseling profession.

Marc A. Grimmett, PhD, is an Assistant Professor of Counselor Education at North Carolina State University in Raleigh, North Carolina, where he is the coordinator of the community counseling program. Dr. Grimmett earned his doctorate in counseling psychology from the University of Georgia and is a health services provider psychologist. His research focuses on the development of an empowerment model and program for the career development of African American boys titled Brothers in Excellence (BE), "Don't just talk about it, BE about it!"

Don C. Locke, EdD, Distinguished Professor Emeritus of Counselor Education at North Carolina State University, is a graduate of Ball State University in Muncie, Indiana. He is an active life member of the American Counseling Association serving as a past chair of the Strategic Planning Committee. He served as president of Chi Sigma Iota, the Association for Counselor Education and Supervision; and chair of the ACA Foundation. He is the recipient of the ACA Professional Development Award and the North Carolina Counseling Association Ella Stevens Barrett Award. Dr. Locke is a past editorial board member for the *Journal of the Association for Counselor Education and Supervision*, the *Journal of the American Mental Health Association*, and the *International Journal for the Advancement of Counselling*. He is the author of 6 books and more than 100 journal articles, focusing on diversity and multiculturalism.

Amie A. Manis, MA, NCC, is a doctoral candidate in the Counselor Education Program at the University of Virginia. She is also a college counselor at the Virginia Military Institute. Ms. Manis has 15 years experience as a client advocate and administrator in nonprofit organizations serving at-risk children, adults, and families in inner-city Boston and the mountains of southwest Virginia, her adopted home. Her scholarship and service reflect her long-standing interest in and the promotion of multicultural awareness and social justice. These passions are rooted in and have been sustained by her family, her clients, and the opportunity to learn at Harvard University, Virginia Tech, and the University of Virginia. Ms. Manis has been privileged to serve on the Governing Council of the American Counseling Association and on the Board of the Virginia Association for Counselor Education and Supervision. Her work has been recognized for excellence by the American Counseling Association, the Virginia Counselors Association, the Curry Foundation of the University of Virginia, and the Rho Beta Chapter of Chi Sigma Iota.

Kathleen M. May, PhD, is an Associate Professor Emeritus of Counselor Education at the University of Virginia in Charlottesville, Virginia. She joined the faculty in 1990 and retired in 2008. Dr. May is a graduate of the Counselor Education Program at the University of Florida. She was a practicing counselor in Florida for 10 years before joining the academy. Dr. May was active in various state and national professional organizations and served in various leadership positions. Dr. May's scholarship has centered on women's issues, feminist multicultural teaching, pedagogy, and supervision and human sexuality. She is the recipient of several awards including the Media Award from the International Association of Marriage and Family Counselors. Dr. May plans to spend her retirement years in Costa Rica.

R. Esteban Montilla is an Assistant Professor of Counseling Education with the Department of Counseling and Human Services at St. Mary's University, San Antonio, Texas. He is a graduate of Texas A&M University and a professional member of the American Counseling Association. Dr. Montilla is one of the founders of the Sociedad Interamericana de Counseling and has established counseling training and centers in Venezuela and Nicaragua. Dr. Montilla is well recognized for his ability to integrate spirituality into the practice of counseling and psychotherapy. He is the author of several books, including *Pastoral Counseling with Latinos and Latinas* (2005) and *Viviendo la Tercera Edad* (2004).

Matthew J. Paylo, PhD, is the Director of Mental Health Services at the Virginia Department of Corrections Fluvanna Correctional Center for Women in Troy, Virginia.

Mark Pope, EdD, is a Professor and Chair of the Division of Counseling and Family Therapy at the University of Missouri–Saint Louis. Dr. Pope is an elder of St. Francis River Band of Cherokees and a senior trial judge of the Southeastern Cherokee Tribal Court. He also served as the director of Psychological Services for the American Indian AIDS Institute and the Native American AIDS Project in San Francisco. He received the 1996 Human Rights Award given by the state of California's professional counseling association, the 2001 Human Rights Award given by the American Counseling Association of Missouri, and the 2002 Kitty Cole Human Rights Award awarded nationally by the American Counseling Association. Dr. Pope is a past president of both the American Counseling Association and National Career Development Association.

Linda S. Slabon, MDiv, MSW, LCSW, MA, has worked as a dual career professional for over 20 years as an ordained minister and as a clinical social worker. She received her divinity degree from the Lutheran School of Theology in Chicago and her master's degrees in social work and American culture studies from the University of Iowa. She currently serves the Unitarian Universalist congregation in DeKalb, Illinois, is on the staff of the DeKalb County Hospice, and is in private practice at the Center for Creative Healing. Rev. Slabon has served on many boards and organizations, including the DeKalb Area Women's Center, and as president of the Central Midwest District UU Minister's Association. She formed an advocacy group to support gay, lesbian, bisexual, and transgender students in the local schools. She enjoys making music with her partner, Toni, spiritual retreats, peace work, and watching the birds at the feeders in her yard.

Anneliese A. Singh, PhD, LPC, NCC, is an Assistant Professor in the Counselor and Human Development Services Department at the University of Georgia in Athens, Georgia, with teaching responsibilities in the school counseling program. Dr. Singh's clinical and research interests are Asian American counseling and psychological issues, resilience and coping strategies of historically marginalized people (e.g., people of color, LGBT, immigrants), qualitative methodology, feminist theory and practice, and working with survivors of trauma. Dr. Singh is a graduate of Georgia State University in counseling psychology. She is the president-elect of the Association of Lesbian, Gay, Bisexual, and Transgender Issues in Counseling of the American Counseling Association and is an active member within the Asian American Psychological Association, serving on the board of the Division of Women. Dr. Singh is the recipient of the Courtland Lee Multicultural Excellence Award and is active in the national movement to end child sexual abuse.

Robert L. Smith, PhD, FFPR, is Chairperson and Professor of the Counseling Doctoral Program and Educational Psychology Department in the College of Education of Texas A&M University–Corpus Christi. He is also the executive director of the International Association of Marriage and Family Counseling. Dr. Smith's interests include the integration of teaching, research, and service; the integration of school, community, and family services; and outcome research in the counseling profession. Dr. Smith is an active researcher and is the editor or author of 6 books and over 60 articles. Dr. Smith's counseling program was the 2007 recipient of the Outstanding Counselor Education Program Award presented by the Association of Counselor Educators and Supervisors.

Toni R. Tollerud, PhD, has been a Professor in the Department of Counseling, Adult and Higher Education at Northern Illinois University for over 18 years. Currently, she is the director of training at the Center for Child Welfare and Education in the College of Education, where she works in partnership with the Department of Children and Family Services to advocate for the educational needs of children and adolescents in care. She has held numerous American Counseling Association divisional offices at the state and regional level. She has been the recipient of many awards, including the C.A. Michaelman Outstanding Counselor of the Year and the Illinois Mental Health Counselors Outstanding Service Award. Her passion includes supervision, school counseling, women's issues, and GLBT issues. She lives with her partner, Linda, and together they enjoy traveling, performing and singing, and Italian food.

Rebecca L. Toporek, PhD, is the Coordinator of the Career Counseling Specialization and Assistant Professor in the Counseling Department at San Francisco State University. She has been a career and community college counselor for 20 years and a counselor educator for 4 years. Dr. Toporek has published numerous articles on career counseling, and multicultural and advocacy competence, and has coedited two books on multicultural counseling and social justice. She received her doctorate degree from the University of Maryland, College Park, and has received the Ohana and the Mary Arnold Smith Anti-Oppression Award from Counselors for Social Justice, the Kitty Cole Human Rights Award from the Association for Multicultural Counseling and Development, and research awards from the National Career Development Association and the Society for Vocational Psychology for research on multicultural career assessment.

Sherri Turner, AT, BA, MA, MDiv, PhD, is an Associate Professor at the University of Minnesota in the American Psychological Association–approved Counseling and Student Personnel Psychology Program. Her research is in counseling strategies for Native American people, and in the educational and career development of Native American and inner-city adolescents. She is an active member of the American Psychological Association, and has served as a member of the Society of Vocational Psychology's Social Action Committee, the co-chair of the Division of Counseling Psychology's Social Action Group on Welfare and Homelessness, a member of the University of Minnesota's Diversity Leadership Council for Keeping Our Faculties of Color, and the chair of the University of Minnesota's College of Education and Human Development's Multicultural and Diversity Committee.

Adam Zagelbaum, PhD, NCC, completed his doctoral study at Ball State University's Counseling Psychology Program and currently is an Assistant Professor in the Counseling Program at Governors State University with primary teaching responsibilities in school counseling courses. He has served as the president of the Illinois Association for Counselor Education and Supervision, and various offices within the Illinois School Counseling Association. Dr. Zagelbaum is an active member of the American Counseling Association, American School Counseling Association, Association for Counselor Education and Supervision, and the American Psychological Association. He has served as a guest editor for the *Illinois Counseling Association Journal*, and has been a recipient of the Governors State University Faculty Excellence Award. Dr. Zagelbaum's research interests include conflict management, career decision-making issues for children and adolescents, and mentoring issues for young professionals.

1

COUNSELING FROM A CROSS-CULTURAL
AND SOCIAL JUSTICE POSTURE

Rebecca L. Toporek

Paul, a counselor in a university counseling center, disclosed to his colleague that he was having trouble understanding and maintaining empathy for one of his clients. He was concerned because in the past he had looked to clinical issues to explain a lack of connection and typically understood these impasses to be due to unresolved issues of the client. But this time, that strategy didn't seem to work. After some discussion, Paul's colleague recommended that he review his case notes from the past couple of years to identify cases in which Paul experienced a lack of connection with the client or where clients seemed to have left counseling prematurely. After doing this, Paul was disturbed to discover that there did seem to be a pattern across clients that included difficulty empathizing with clients of a particular ethnic background. His notes also indicated that he felt that many of these clients were not taking responsibility for their own distress and instead blamed external sources. Although this was not true in all cases, the pattern was striking and these clients typically did not continue in counseling. He was unsure how to interpret this and what to do.

The Multicultural Counseling Competencies (Sue, Arredondo, & McDavis, 1992) and the *Guidelines on Multicultural Education, Training, Research, Practice, and Organizational Change for Psychologists* (American Psychological Association [APA], 2002), hereafter referred to as the Multicultural Guidelines, were designed to help counselors, psychologists, and trainees examine their ability to provide services equitably and competently to their clients. These documents offer structures that address multiple areas such as awareness, knowledge, and skill regarding cultural issues, attitudes, and beliefs and interventions.

Since the early 1900s, individual counselors, psychologists, and consumers have raised concerns about the adequacy of mental health provision for individuals who differed from the dominant culture (see Guthrie, 1978; Hall, 1997; Jackson, 1995; Katz, 1985; S. Sue, 1977; Wade, 1993). However, formal recognition of the need to attend to the place of culture in health, wellness, and psychological service has been a decades-long, almost century-long, process. This chapter will provide a historical context for the development of the Multicultural Competencies (D. W. Sue et al., 1992) and the Multicultural Guidelines (APA, 2002). One important aspect of these documents is the attention to sociopolitical and contextual barriers to well-being. Recently, another set of competencies, the American Counseling Association Advocacy Competencies (Lewis, Arnold, House, & Toporek, 2002), acknowledge that systemic and institutional barriers (for example, racism, sexism, heterosexism, ableism, poverty, etc.) influence clients' well-being and provide clearer guidance regarding counselors' roles that extend beyond intrapsychic interventions to address client concerns at a more systemic level. Because the ACA Advocacy Competencies extend this important aspect of the Multicultural Competencies, I will include a brief discussion of these. Paul's situation can then be revisited in light of the Competencies and Guidelines, along with recommended self-assessment questions and activities.

WHAT IS *COMPETENCE?*

Before embarking on an exploration of multicultural competencies, multicultural guidelines, and advocacy competencies, professional counselors need to consider the term *competence* to help establish some parameters for this discussion. "Competence is a set of skills or attributes that allow one to effectively intervene on the demands of a particular situation or circumstance" (Daniels & Pack-Brown, 2006, p. 5). This general definition reflects the spirit of efforts to identify specific multicultural competencies. Recognizing the complexity and expanse of cultural information and awareness, Parham (2004) suggested a three-tiered competence framework that describes varying levels of competence beginning at a *pre-competent level*, moving to a *competent level*, and then a *proficient level*. In this framework, he described pre-competent as a professional who is aware that competence is important but does not have the skills to implement this cultural awareness, knowledge, and skill in practice. Competent professionals demonstrate skills to effectively intervene in culturally appropriate ways in a particular circumstance. Parham further suggested that professionals who demonstrate a more stable set of skills, awareness, and knowledge consistently over time and circumstances could be considered proficient. Although research has not specifically investigated the implementation of this three-tiered framework for multicultural competence, the recognition that professionals may be at varying levels with respect to competence is useful for considering competence as an ongoing journey.

The metaphor of a journey reflects the nature of professional development. "There can be little doubt that even the best present education and training will become obsolete within a relatively short period of time, unless the psychologist makes a very determined effort to refurbish and to expand *his* [sic] professional base of knowledge and technique" (Lewinsohn & Pearlman, 1972, p. 48). This classic statement reflects the contemporary need for intentional continuous development of one's knowledge and skills generally. Similarly, an assumption of the Multicultural Competencies (D. W. Sue et al., 1992) and the Multicultural Guidelines (APA, 2002) is that initial training provides a foundation for practice but that the professional must pursue ongoing development. This is particularly true given the breadth of cultural backgrounds presented by clients, the dynamic nature of cultural information, and the influence of historical events on the experience of individuals and communities. Given these definitions and assumptions of competence as a global construct, I'd like to turn the focus more specifically to the concept of cultural competence.

WHAT IS *CULTURAL COMPETENCE*?

Cultural competence has been defined in numerous ways with most definitions including some element of cultural knowledge as well as self-awareness. D. W. Sue and D. Sue (2003) described the following three characteristics of a culturally competent counselor. First, a culturally skilled counselor actively works toward increasing her or his awareness regarding her or his cultural assumptions, values, and biases. Second, a culturally skilled counselor works toward understanding the client's worldview without negative judgments, has relevant culture-specific knowledge, and understands that culture is complex and dynamic. Third, a culturally skilled counselor actively works toward appropriate, relevant, and sensitive intervention strategies and skills. It is important to note that the language of this definition affirms that the process of becoming culturally competent requires that counselors continuously reflect on their own perspectives and limitations as well as the need for ongoing growth.

Addressing cultural competence from a slightly different perspective, S. Sue (1998) defined cultural competence as "the belief that people should not only appreciate and recognize other cultural groups but also be able to work effectively with them" (p. 440). He asserted that there are three characteristics of cultural competency: (a) being scientifically minded, (b) having skills in dynamic sizing, and (c) culture-specific expertise. Scientific mindedness, according to S. Sue, is demonstrated by therapists who form hypotheses using cultural and individual information, develop creative ways to test their hypotheses, and then appropriately act based on the information they have gathered. Dynamic sizing refers to the skills necessary for distinguishing when it is appropriate to generalize learned cultural information and when individual factors may be more relevant. In addition, dynamic sizing also refers to the ability to determine when to generalize from one's own experience and how to do it appropriately. Culture-specific expertise includes such knowledge as cultural practices and values, immigration trends, family roles and expectations, and help-seeking norms, as well as culturally relevant interventions. It is not assumed that counselors and psychologists would be experts in all cultural backgrounds, but that they consider this knowledge as relevant to their clients and know enough to determine when cultural expertise is needed. For example, if the practitioner is working with clientele that is largely represented by a particular ethnic group, they have a responsibility to gain culture-specific knowledge that is relevant for that group. These definitions are generally representative and as such have been shaped throughout the developmental process of the field of multicultural counseling. Having a sense of this history and the growing pains associated with transformation is important in order to gain a sense of how complex and protracted this evolutionary process has been. The development toward a cultural competent profession is far from complete, yet important progress has been made.

THE NEED FOR MULTICULTURAL COMPETENCIES AND THE TRANSFORMATION OF ORGANIZATIONS

Comprehending the history of the Multicultural Competencies (D. W. Sue et al., 1992) and the Multicultural Guidelines (APA, 2002) involves understanding the growth of the professional literature that identified the need for such documents as well as recognizing the evolution of professional organizations and their response to diversity and cultural competence. Beginning as early as 1932, Sanchez (as cited in Kiselica & Robinson, 2001) raised concerns regarding the use of general psychological theories and tools with diverse populations. Some of the criticisms of traditional counseling theories and practices have been that they define concepts such as health and normalcy in terms of the dominant culture and that they serve to maintain the dominant power structures (D. W. Sue & D. Sue, 2003); that they do not address concerns adequately enough to be relevant to changing communities (Hall, 1997); and that general counseling theories and tools are not sufficient to understand the complexities and significance of a person's experience given their cultural context (Pedersen, 1997). In addition, researchers and advocates have also discussed the role of bias in counseling and mental health diagnosis and treatment (Atkinson et al., 1996; Burkard & Knox, 2004; Constantine & Gushue, 2003; Lott, 2002; Rosenthal, 2004; Schnitzer, 1996; Whaley, 1998).

By 1999, a sufficient body of empirical literature regarding the importance of culture in health and well-being had been accumulated to bring this issue to the attention of the United States surgeon general and was summarized in that office's 1999 report:

> More often, culture bears on whether people even seek help in the first place, what types of help they seek, what types of coping styles and social supports they have, and how much stigma they attach to mental illness. Culture also influences the *meanings* that people impart to their illness. Consumers of mental health services, whose cultures vary both between and within groups, naturally carry this diversity directly to the service setting. ... What becomes clear is that culture and social contexts, while not the only determinants, shape the mental health of minorities and alter the types of mental health services they use. Cultural misunderstandings between patient and clinician, clinician bias, and the fragmentation of mental health services deter minorities from accessing and utilizing care and prevent them from receiving appropriate care. (U.S. Department of Health and Human Services, 1999, chap. 2)

Although the professional literature continued to highlight these issues, advocacy for change made slow inroads into professional organizations. Initial organizational changes paralleled the civil rights movement and reflected increased inclusion of diverse members. With greater representation of diversity came greater advocacy for the recognition of culture as an important part of counseling and psychology. In

1972, the Association of Non-White Concerns in Personnel and Guidance (now the Association of Multicultural Counseling and Development [AMCD]) was created as a division of the American Counseling Association (ACA, then known as the American Personnel and Guidance Association) to address the needs of culturally diverse groups and individuals. Within the American Psychological Association (APA) the Office of Ethnic Minority Affairs (OEMA) was established in 1979 as a demonstration of a commitment within APA resources for efforts related to ethnic minority issues and concerns. In the mid-1980s, the Society for the Psychological Study of Ethnic Minority Issues (Division 45 of APA) was created. The establishment of these organizations was an essential step in recognizing the critical influence of culture in counseling and psychology, and acknowledging the need for specific attention and advocacy for these issues and populations. In addition, these organizations provided support and coordination for researching and articulating how culture could be addressed in counseling more appropriately.

MULTICULTURAL COMPETENCIES

The Multicultural Counseling Competencies (D. W. Sue et al., 1992) grew out of decades of research regarding the need for cultural sensitivity, culturally appropriate interventions, bias, and inappropriate service. They were designed to provide a standard for curriculum and training of counselors and other helping professionals as well as to facilitate culturally relevant services across a wide range of culturally diverse groups.

The eventual ACA endorsement of the Multicultural Competencies (D. W. Sue et al., 1992) in 2002 was preceded by a long and arduous journey illustrating the influence of evolution and advocacy. In 1981, Allen Ivey, the president of APA's Society of Counseling Psychology (Division 17) charged its Professional Standards Committee with the task of identifying issues related to cross-cultural counseling. As a result of this work, in 1982, D. W. Sue and colleagues published a call to the profession asserting the need for a change in the way services were provided and the way that competence was conceptualized within the counseling profession. In this call, they identified the need to recognize the relevance of culture in clients' lives and counseling concerns. Further, they asserted that in order to function effectively as a counselor, the professional needs to understand the biases, values, and assumptions that she or he brings into counseling. This report clearly asserted the need for change as well as a specific set of recommendations for improved service; however, little organization action was taken for close to 10 years.

Then, in 1991, the president of AMCD, Thomas Parham, commissioned its Professional Standards Committee to review and revise the competencies proposed by D. W. Sue et al. (1982) integrating research, practice, and input from multicultural professionals (Arredondo & Perez, 2006). The resulting document outlined 31 multicultural counseling competencies, including three dimensions: counselor awareness of own attitudes and beliefs, counselor understanding of the client's worldview, and culturally relevant interventions. Within each of these domains, D. W. Sue and his colleagues (1992) identified the need for awareness, knowledge, and skill. The resulting document strongly encouraged the American Counseling Association (then known as the American Association for Counseling and Development). In 1992, the Multicultural Counseling Competencies were published in ACA's *Journal of Counseling and Development* (Sue, Arredondo, & McDavis, 1992).

Even after the second proposal of the Multicultural Competencies in 1992, the necessary support for endorsement was not present in the ACA governance structure. Four years later, in response to claims that the competencies needed to be more specific and concrete before they could be considered for adoption, the Professional Standards Committee of AMCD convened to draft an "operationalizing" document to further elaborate each of the 31 competencies providing explanations and examples of strategies for each (Arredondo et al., 1996). In addition, the document introduced the Personal Dimension of Identity Model to emphasize the integration of multiple aspects of cultural identity that influence everyone's worldview. This model suggests that everyone's identity is a compilation including an "A" dimension (individual characteristics or aspects that are not readily changeable, such as age, gender, ethnicity, race, sexual orientation, etc.); "B" dimension (contextual dimensions, such as educational background, relationship status, etc.); and "C" dimension (historical influences). It is important to recognize the significance of the inclusion of this model contrary to later criticism charging that the multicultural competencies exclude other aspects of identity or specific ethnicities (e.g., Weinrach & Thomas, 1996).

These documents formed the cornerstone of Multicultural Competencies. Since then, a few authors have extended the Multicultural Competencies (D. W. Sue et al., 1992) to facilitate application, training, and service. One such elaboration was proposed by Toporek and Reza (1996, 2001) to help counselors create a professional development plan for increasing cultural competence. They suggested that each of the 31 competencies could be viewed in terms of personal competence, professional competence, and institutional competence. For example, a counselor would need to examine her or his attitudes and beliefs from a personal level, a professional level, and an institutional level. Within this framework, self-assessment questions might include, what are my personal beliefs? What are my beliefs as a counselor? And, what are my beliefs as a member of my institution? Because Toporek and Reza's model was designed to facilitate counselors in developing their competence, they also suggested that effective growth should attend to affective, cognitive, and behavioral learning or growth.

Two other significant publications have enhanced the Multicultural Competencies (D. W. Sue et al., 1992) and its implementation. In 1998, D. W. Sue and colleagues published a volume elaborating multicultural competence and adding three new competencies to the original 31 to address organizational and structural issues. This book also introduced the concept of ethnocentric monoculturalism and reinforced the importance of recognizing cultural competence within organizations. In 2003, AMCD published a book exploring each area of multicultural competence using a case approach (Roysircar, Arredondo, Fuertes, Ponterotto & Toporek, 2003). These documents provided additional support and resources in the service of greater cultural competence and facilitated implementation.

The 2002 ACA endorsement of the Multicultural Counseling Competencies (D. W. Sue et al., 1992) affirmed the profession's commitment to recognizing culture as an important part of practice. These competencies remain in place as the standard for the profession of counseling and continue to provide guidance for practice, training, and research. In addition, numerous assessment instruments have been developed to assess multicultural competence (e.g., Kim, Cartwright, Asay, & D'Andrea, 2003; Holcomb-McCoy, 2000; Ponterotto et al., 1996; Sodowsky, 1996) and research has been conducted on variables related to multicultural competence (e.g., Fuertes, Stracuzzi, & Bennett, 2006; Pope-Davis & Coleman, 1997). These competencies have served as an important resource for other guidelines such as that developed within APA.

GUIDELINES ON MULTICULTURAL EDUCATION, TRAINING, RESEARCH, PRACTICE, AND ORGANIZATIONAL CHANGE FOR PSYCHOLOGISTS

Recognizing different roles and demands for psychologists, a task force of members from APA's Society of Counseling Psychology (Division 17) and Society for the Psychological Study of Ethnic Minority Issues (Division 45) was created to develop a specific set of guidelines for psychologists. Although the resulting Multicultural Guidelines were presented and endorsed in 2002, their development spanned 22 years and numerous committees, task forces, and boards. Fortunately, this extensive professional and political evolution is chronicled in the introduction to the Multicultural Guidelines providing a historical context and foundation for readers (APA, 2002).

The objectives of the Multicultural Guidelines are to address issues that are pertinent to the work of psychologists and to present recommendations for addressing culture in psychological services, teaching, and research.

> The specific goals of these Guidelines are to provide psychologists with: (a) the rationale and needs for addressing multiculturalism and diversity in education, training, research, practice, and organizational change; (b) basic information, relevant terminology, current empirical research from psychology and related disciplines, and other data that support the proposed guidelines and underscore their importance; (c) references to enhance on-going education, training, research, practice, and organizational change methodologies; and (d) paradigms that broaden the purview of psychology as a profession. (APA, 2002, p. 1)

Of the six guidelines in the document, the first two guidelines are intended to apply to all psychologists regardless of the type of work or setting, and focus on the need for psychologists to demonstrate an understanding of themselves, their beliefs, their assumptions, and their attitudes as well as the role that cultural issues play in psychological service. The remaining four guidelines address implications for specific roles or settings, namely, teaching and education in psychology, research, practice, and organizational change. The six guidelines are:

Guideline #1: Psychologists are encouraged to recognize that, as cultural beings, they may hold attitudes and beliefs that can detrimentally influence their perceptions of and interactions with individuals who are ethnically and racially different from themselves (APA, 2002, p. 17).

Guideline #2: Psychologists are encouraged to recognize the importance of multicultural sensitivity/responsiveness, knowledge, and understanding about ethnically and racially different individuals (APA, 2002, p. 25).

Guideline #3: As educators, psychologists are encouraged to employ the constructs of multiculturalism and diversity in psychological education (APA, 2002, p. 30).

Guideline #4: Culturally sensitive psychological researchers are encouraged to recognize the importance of conducting culture-centered and ethical psychological research among persons from ethnic, linguistic, and racial minority backgrounds (APA, 2002, p. 36).

Guideline #5: Psychologists strive to apply culturally appropriate skills in clinical and other applied psychological practices (APA, 2002, p. 43).

Guideline #6: Psychologists are encouraged to use organizational change processes to support culturally informed organizational (policy) development and practices (APA, 2002, p. 50).

Since their publication, the Multicultural Guidelines (APA, 2002) have been referred to as a resource for cultural competence with various populations (e.g., Fouad & Arredondo, 2007; Hinrichsen, 2006; Nicolas, DeSilva, & Grey, 2006; Vasquez, Han, & De Las Fuentes, 2006), for work in different settings (e.g., Resnick, 2006), and for integrating multiculturalism in training programs (e.g., Constantine & Sue, 2005; Fouad, 2006).

The story of the development of the Multicultural Competencies (D. W. Sue et al., 1992) and the Multicultural Guidelines (APA, 2002) are case studies of organizational change reflecting research findings and practical knowledge in response to the needs of clients and consumers. Although research has investigated many aspects regarding cultural sensitivity and inclusion in mental health services, the direct question of the meaning of cultural competence from the consumer perspective is an important one to consider.

CULTURAL COMPETENCE AND THE CONSUMER PERSPECTIVE

In 2001, Pope-Davis, Liu, Toporek and Brittan-Powell highlighted the need for more research that directly asked clients about their perceptions of multicultural competence, whether it was important, and how it might be related to general competence of their counselor. After conducting focus groups with clients, the authors found that clients were unsure what multicultural competence was and, therefore, had some difficulty responding to the question. Consequently, Pope-Davis and his colleagues (2002) embarked on a grounded theory qualitative study to explore clients' experiences in multicultural counseling more generally and to discover how multicultural competence, or lack thereof, was experienced by clients. The model that emerged from their interviews did not provide simple answers. Rather, the model presented a complex and holistic picture of the variables that clients identified as central to their experience in multicultural counseling. These variables moderated when and how multicultural competence was important and the relationship between multicultural competence and general counseling competence.

In the model described by Pope-Davis et al. (2002), the clients indicated that the extent to which the counselor met the clients' concerns was most important. This was the core construct around which all other variables related. In other words, if the client felt that her or his need was being met by the counselor, the expectations of cultural competence were tempered. It is important to note that cultural competence was still identified as important; however, clients were willing to forgive slight cultural misunderstandings. If the client felt that her or his need was not being met in counseling, cultural misunderstandings and shortfalls on the part of the counselor were amplified. This was especially the case when the client identified her or his need as being related to cultural issues or oppression.

Pope-Davis and his colleagues (2002) identified four domains that interacted with the client's perceived needs and influenced her or his experiences in counseling. Two of these referred to perceptions the client either brought into counseling (Client Characteristics) or took away from counseling (Client Appraisal of Counseling). *Client Characteristics* referred to dimensions brought to counseling by the client such as their reasons for seeking and continuing in counseling, expectations of the counselor and counseling process, the client's cultural awareness of her- or himself and the effect of culture on counseling, and the role of family and other support systems in coping with cultural concerns. *Client Appraisal of Counseling* included the client's feelings about future counseling and their assessment of their counseling experience. Two other domains reflected dynamics or processes that took place within the context of counseling. The first one, *Client Processes,* referred to internal processes clients used to make meaning of the counseling interaction and the actions they took to deal with the counselor, including how they managed culture in counseling, their perceptions of having to educate the counselor, their decisions to confront (or not confront) cultural insensitivity in counseling, and the ways they explained their counselor's cultural understanding or lack thereof. The other internal domain was the *Client–Counselor Relationship*, which referred to the client's perceptions of what occurred in the interactions between the client and counselor and included the client's willingness to disclose (uncertainty about confidentiality counseling style, self-image management), perceptions of the counselor's behavior and approach, and perceived equity and power in the counseling relationship. It is important to emphasize that clients reflected the complexity of culture and indicated that cultural competence was important, although the way in which it was important and the extent of importance varied across a number of different variables. Similar results were found in Ward's (2005) qualitative exploration of African American women's experiences in counseling, confirming the complex interplay of cultural variables and the effect of these on the counseling process and the influence of cultural competence.

For counselors and psychologists, the findings of these studies are useful in interpreting and applying the Multicultural Competencies and Multicultural Guidelines. Using the constructs identified in the study, practitioners are able to identify areas to assess with regard to culture as well as possible processes that might influence the client–counselor relationship. With the inclusion of these two studies, the literature provides us with ample research on cultural variables in counseling as well as client voices regarding the impact of culture and cultural competence in counseling. One of the issues that was raised by client voices was the importance of the counselor acknowledging the oppression and discrimination felt by clients in marginalized cultural groups. The relevance of these systemic factors on the counseling process highlighted the need for counselors and psychologists to be able to address issues beyond the intrapsychic level through sociopolitical awareness, empowerment, and advocacy.

MULTICULTURAL COMPETENCE, ADVOCACY, AND THE ADVOCACY COMPETENCIES

Through the Multicultural Competencies (D. W. Sue et al., 1992), it was clear that individuals and communities who had been institutionally and systemically oppressed struggle with more than what intrapsychic interventions can alleviate. Oppression, discrimination, inequitable policies, and lack of access and resources create environmental barriers that permeate mental health and well-being. Because many clients face structural barriers, counselors and psychologists ethically must, at the very least, be able to distinguish the role of these barriers in clients' health and well-being from intrapsychic barriers (Prilleltensky & Prilleltensky, 2003). When the client's distress is attributed to the client alone, and interventions focus on client change, without acknowledging and addressing the external systems, numerous problems occur (Toporek & Pope-Davis, 2005). First, the client comes to believe that she or he is the cause of the problem, when, in fact, she or he is the recipient of the problem. Second, the counselor inadvertently colludes with the oppressive system to maintain the status quo. Ideally, counselors and psychologists should be able to facilitate the removal of these barriers. However, until recently there were only a few that have provided guidance for counselors and psychologists to ethically and appropriately intervene on behalf of clients (see Atkinson, Thompson, & Grant, 1993; Lewis, Lewis, Daniels, & D'Andrea, 1998).

Although there has been a history of inadequate service for marginalized populations and a lack of attention to systemic barriers within the professions of counseling and psychology, there are numerous examples of individuals and institutions that have served to address inequities in society and in the profession. This has been referred to as social action or social justice advocacy (Lee & Walz, 1998; Toporek, Gerstein, Fouad, Roysircar & Israel, 2006). There have been some attempts to organizationally facilitate counselors in taking advocacy roles. In 1998, Courtland Lee defined his term as president of the American Counseling Association with a focus on the role of social action in counseling (Lee & Walz, 1998). Loretta Bradley, in 2000, distinguished her presidency through an emphasis on advocacy and commissioned a series of papers (later published as a book) describing advocacy in counseling with a variety of populations (Lewis & Bradley, 2000). Later, in 2001, Jane Goodman strengthened this by creating a Presidential Task Force to establish a set of advocacy competencies that was later adopted by the Governing Council of ACA (Lewis, Arnold, House, & Toporek, 2002). These competencies not only provided guidance for advocacy in counseling but also drew attention to systemic barriers as noted in the Multicultural Competencies (D. W. Sue et al., 1992) and Multicultural Guidelines (APA, 2002), and included multicultural competence as a necessary condition for ethical advocacy.

The ACA Advocacy Competencies (Lewis et al., 2002) are organized around two dimensions: the nature of client involvement (advocacy with the client and advocacy on behalf of the client) and level of intervention (individual, community, and public or societal). At the individual level, advocacy with the client or student was identified as *empowerment*, whereas advocacy on behalf of the client was termed *client/student advocacy*. At the community/school level, advocacy with the client or community was identified as *community collaboration*, whereas advocacy on behalf of the community was termed *community advocacy*.

Finally, at the public or societal level, advocacy with the client or community was identified as *public information*, and advocacy on behalf of the client or community was described as *social action*. Implementing the ACA Advocacy Competencies (Lewis et al., 2002) requires assessing the situation and client objectives, determining the appropriate levels of intervention, understanding sociopolitical contexts considering cultural congruence of the interventions, building collaborative partnerships with the client, and establishing allies. The full set of Advocacy Competencies may be found at ACA's Web site (www.counseling.org). The Advocacy Competencies add an important dimension because it provides specific guidelines for implementation of systemic interventions for oppression, discrimination, and cultural injustice.

The Multicultural Competencies (D. W. Sue et al., 1992), Multicultural Guidelines (APA, 2002), and the Advocacy Competencies (Lewis et al., 2002) have several common threads, including the need for continuous professional development; understanding and respect for culture in wellness; the role of systemic forces in positive or negative development and coping; and the appropriateness of a range of helping roles for counselors and psychologists. To illustrate how these competencies and guidelines may help guide counselor self-assessment and change, I would like to go back to the case of Paul and examine his case in light of the material described in this chapter.

REVISITING PAUL

At the beginning of this chapter, we learned that Paul discovered a disturbing trend across his relationships with clients. First, it is commendable that Paul has been willing, and insightful enough, to recognize this trend. Second, it is important that he is willing to seek consultation to address this issue. If we were providing consultation with Paul, we might suggest that he examine the issue from three aspects noted by the Multicultural Competencies (D. W. Sue et al., 1992) and ask himself a number of questions. When considering these questions, it is important to acknowledge the intragroup differences that exist based on variables such as racial and ethnic identity, immigration, acculturation, socioeconomic status, gender, sexual orientation, disability status, religion, and a host of other variables. Having noted these variations, it may be worthwhile for Paul to look at the trends he has found and consider whether there are other significant dimensions of identity that characterize these clients. For example, do these clients represent a socioeconomic class, religion, or sexual orientation in addition to the noted ethnicity?

Having integrated a more complex view of identity regarding his clients, we may suggest that Paul begin a self-assessment. First, what are his beliefs and attitudes regarding the clients from the ethnicity he has identified? Is there a pattern that characterizes the way he has conceptualized these clients? When thinking about this ethnicity, what are some beliefs he may have learned as a child? How much exposure and what type of exposure has he had to people from this ethnicity? These are examples of questions that might help Paul to begin to consider how his attitudes and beliefs may be influencing the way he sees these clients, thus influencing the way he interacts with these clients. His responses to these questions may help him identify potential areas for growth as well as possible activities to facilitate that growth. For example, if Paul discerns that his main contact with individuals of this particular ethnicity and social status is through his work as a substance abuse counselor, he may want to engage in some cultural immersion activities in which he interacts with a community of that ethnicity that does not involve substance abuse and in which he is not in a position of power. In this way, he would have the opportunity to engage with a less "selective" portion of the identified ethnicity and begin to challenge his attitudes and stereotypes. It would be most beneficial for the immersion activity to be one in which Paul may engage with people of the community over time and in a way that allows for the development of mutual relationships.

The second set of questions reflects the extent of his knowledge regarding this ethnic group and the other dimensions of identity. For example, it may be helpful for Paul to consider the sociopolitical and historical context for that ethnicity, particularly for individuals of the identified socioeconomic status. How much understanding does he have of the systemic barriers that face clients from this ethnic and economic identity stratum? In addition, he may assess the extent of his knowledge regarding natural help-giving systems and help-seeking behavior in this particular ethnicity. It is important to consider his understanding of the historical point of contact for the group, in other words, the historical relationship and initial contact of the group with the dominant society. Generally, how much does Paul know about cultural values, norms, family systems, community support, and traditions of this ethnic group? It is worth reemphasizing S. Sue's (1998) principles of being scientific minded and dynamic sizing throughout this process. Specifically, the cultural knowledge can provide some information that would allow Paul to make more accurate hypotheses regarding his clients as well as have an ability to distinguish cultural attributes or situations that allow for generalizing and individualizing.

The third set of questions reflects Paul's level of skill intervening in a culturally competent way. In this case, Paul is a practitioner, and thus he may utilize Multicultural Guideline #5 (APA, 2002) as well as the Multicultural Competencies (D. W. Sue et al., 1992). If he were teaching or conducting research, he would be advised to consider Multicultural Guidelines #3 and #4, respectively. In terms of practice, a number of questions may be helpful for Paul. How comfortable is he in addressing ethnic and cultural differences with his clients? How well is he able to integrate referral to natural healing systems when appropriate? How well is he able to distinguish when an issue should be addressed at the individual level, community level, or institutional or policy level? How well developed are his advocacy skills? APA's Multicultural Guideline #6 can be helpful for considering how Paul may proceed if he finds that he needs further development of interventions skills at the organizational level.

The questions presented here for Paul only begin to explore possible areas for growth and are intended to stimulate thought and action. There are numerous other questions that may be appropriate for Paul and the involvement of a consultant or mentor would be invaluable in identifying relevant areas for inquiry. The point is that the Multicultural Competencies (D. W. Sue et al., 1992), the Multicultural Guidelines (APA, 2002), and the ACA Advocacy Competencies (Lewis et al., 2002) are tools that are meant to be applied to facilitate growth and increase our ability to serve our clients competently. As noted earlier, the recognition of the centrality of culture in all counseling relationships and the acknowledgement of systemic barriers have been acts of advocacy and, in a sense, revolutionary. Although the field has come a long way, there is still much work to be done.

SUMMARY AND FUTURE DIRECTIONS

Although there was extensive research regarding the need to address cultural aspects within counseling and psychology, traditionally the assumption has been that if psychological practice was practiced competently, there would not be a need for culture-specific guidelines. The 1999 surgeon general's report summarizes these issues succinctly:

> Key elements of therapeutic success depend on rapport and on the clinicians' understanding of patients' cultural identity, social supports, self-esteem, and reticence about treatment due to societal stigma. Advocates, practitioners, and policymakers, driven by widespread awareness of treatment inadequacies for minorities,

began to press for a new treatment approach: the delivery of services responsive to the cultural concerns of racial and ethnic minority groups, including their languages, histories, traditions, beliefs, and values. This approach to service delivery, often referred to as cultural competence, has been promoted largely on the basis of humanistic values and intuitive sensibility rather than empirical evidence. Nevertheless, substantive data from consumer and family self-reports, ethnic match, and ethnic-specific services outcome studies suggest that tailoring services to the specific needs of these groups will improve utilization and outcomes. (U.S. Department of Health and Human Services, 1999, chap. 2)

As noted in this quote, the need for culture-specific interventions is present; at the same time there are clear directions for growth. Research and conceptual literature regarding multicultural competence and advocacy has become more complex and sophisticated as evidenced by the increase of articles and books addressing multiple life contexts, identities, and variability across and within populations (e.g., Ponterotto, Casas, Suzuki, & Alexander, 2001; Pope-Davis & Coleman, 1997; D. W. Sue et al., 1998). Along with these advances, a number of areas are in need of further attention including accountability of practitioners, educators, and researchers; increased understanding of the complexities of multicultural and advocacy competence; more advanced research examining empirically supported interventions; more increased community engagement and participatory scholarship; and research examining psychology and counseling as social change catalysts.

Much work remains to solidify and integrate multicultural and social justice understanding throughout theory, research, and practice so that professional competence is conceptualized as demonstrating cultural competence. Bringing cultural competence into the core of counseling and psychology has been a critical evolutionary step toward maintaining relevance in a diverse world. Knowing the evolution and foundation on which monumental progress has been built can strengthen our resolve and pursuit of greater cultural competence as a profession.

REFERENCES

American Psychological Association. (2002). *Guidelines on multicultural education, training, research, practice, and organizational change for psychologists.* Retrieved October 20, 2007, from http://www.apa.org/pi/multiculturalguidelines/formats.pdf

Arredondo, P., & Perez, P. (2006). Historical perspectives on the multicultural guidelines and contemporary applications. *Professional Psychology: Research and Practice, 37*(1), 1–5.

Arredondo, P., Toporek, R., Brown, S., Jones, J., Locke, D., Sanchez, J., & Stadler, H. (1996). Operationalization of multicultural counseling competencies. *Journal of Multicultural Counseling and Development, 24*(1), 42–78.

Atkinson, D. R., Brown, M. T., Parham, T. A., Matthews, L. G., Landrum-Brown, J., & Kim, A. U. (1996). African American client skin tone and clinical judgments of African American psychologists and European American psychologists. *Professional Psychology: Research and Practice, 27*, 500–505.

Atkinson, D. R., Thompson, C. E., & Grant, S. K. (1993). A three-dimensional model for counseling racial/ethnic minorities. *The Counseling Psychologist, 21*(2), 257–277.

Burkard, A. W., & Knox, S. (2004). Effect of therapist color-blindness on empathy and attributions in cross-cultural counseling. *Journal of Counseling Psychology, 51*(4), 387–397.

Constantine, M. G., & Gushue, G. V. (2003). School counselors' ethnic tolerance attitudes and racism attitudes as predictors of their multicultural case conceptualization of an immigrant student. *Journal of Counseling & Development, 81*(2), 185–190.

Constantine, M. G., & Sue, D. W. (Eds.). (2005). *Strategies for building multicultural competence in mental health and educational settings.* Hoboken, NJ: Wiley.

Daniels, J., & Pack-Brown, S. (2006). *ACA Taskforce on Exemplary Practices: Multicultural counseling and advocacy competencies.* Symposium presented at the American Counseling Association National Conference Montreal, Canada.

Fouad, N. A. (2006). Multicultural guidelines: Implementation in an urban counseling psychology program. *Professional Psychology: Research and Practice, 37*(1), 6–13.

Fouad, N. A., & Arredondo, P. (2007). *Becoming culturally oriented: Practical advice for psychologists and educators.* Washington, DC: American Psychological Association.

Fuertes, J. N., Stracuzzi, T. I., & Bennett, J. (2006). Therapist multicultural competency: A study of therapy dyads. *Psychotherapy: Theory, Research, Practice, Training, 43*(4), 480–490.

Guthrie, R. V. (1978). *Even the rat was white: A historical view of psychology.* New York: Harper & Row.

Hall, C. C. I. (1997). Cultural malpractice: The growing obsolescence of psychology with the changing U.S. population. *American Psychologist, 52,* 642–651.

Hinrichsen, G. A. (2006). Why multicultural issues matter for practitioners working with older adults. *Professional Psychology: Research and Practice, 37*(1), 29–35.

Holcomb-McCoy, C. C. (2000). Multicultural counseling competencies: An exploratory factor analysis. *Journal of Multicultural Counseling & Development, 28*(2), 83–97.

Jackson, M. (1995). Multicultural counseling: Historical perspectives. In J. G. Ponterotto, J. M. Casas, L. A. Suzuki, & C. M. Alexander (Eds.), *Handbook of multicultural counseling* (pp. 3–16). Thousand Oaks, CA: Sage.

Katz, J. H. (1985). The sociopolitical nature of counseling. *The Counseling Psychologist, 13,* 615–624.

Kim, B. S. K., Cartwright, B. Y., Asay, P. A., & D'Andrea, M. J. (2003). A revision of the Multicultural Awareness, Knowledge, and Skills Survey—Counselor edition. *Measurement & Evaluation in Counseling & Development, 36*(3), 161–180.

Kiselica, M. S., & Robinson, M. (2001). Bringing advocacy counseling to life: The history, issues, and human dramas of social justice work in counseling. *Journal of Counseling & Development, 79*(4), 387–397.

Lee, C. C., & Walz, G. R. (Eds.). (1998). *Social action: A mandate for counselors.* Alexandria, VA: American Counseling Association and ERIC Counseling and Student Services Clearinghouse.

Lewinsohn, P. M., & Pearlman, S. (1972). Continuing education for psychologists. *Professional Psychology, 3*(1), 48–52.

Lewis, J., Arnold, M. S., House, R., & Toporek, R. L. (2002). *ACA Advocacy Competencies.* Advocacy Task Force, American Counseling Association. Retrieved January 15, 2007, from http://www.counseling.org/Content/NavigationMenu/RESOURCES/ADVOCACYCOMPETENCIES/advocacy_competencies1.pdf

Lewis, J., & Bradley, L. (Eds.). (2000). *Advocacy in counseling: Counselors, clients, and community,* Greensboro, NC: Caps Publications.

Lewis, J. A., Lewis, M. D., Daniels, J. A., & D'Andrea, M. J. (1998). *Community counseling: Empowerment strategies for a diverse society* (2nd ed.). Pacific Grove, CA: Brooks/Cole.

Lott, B. (2002). Cognitive and behavioral distancing from the poor. *American Psychologist, 57*(2), 100–110.

Nicolas, G., DeSilva, A. M., & Grey, K. S. (2006). Using a multicultural lens to understand illnesses among Haitians living in America. *Professional Psychology: Research and Practice, 37*(6), 702–707.

Parham, T. (2004). Raising the bar on what passes for competence. *The California Psychologist, 37*(6), 20–21.

Pedersen, P. B. (1997). *Culture-centered counseling interventions: Striving for accuracy.* Thousand Oaks, CA: Sage.

Ponterotto, J. G., Casas, M., Suzuki, L. A., & Alexander, C. M. (Eds.). (2001). *Handbook of multicultural counseling.* Thousand Oaks, CA: Sage.

Ponterotto, J. G., Rieger, B. T., Barrett, A., Harris. G., Sparks, R., Sanchez, C. M., & Magids, D. (1996). Development and initial validation of the Multicultural Counseling Awareness Scale. In G. R. Sodowsky & J. C. Impara (Eds.), *Multicultural assessment in counseling and clinical psychology* (pp. 247–282). Lincoln, NE: Buros Institute of Mental Measurement.

Pope-Davis, D. B., & Coleman, H. L. K. (Eds.). (1997). *Multicultural counseling competencies: Assessment, education and training, and supervision.* Thousand Oaks, CA: Sage.

Pope-Davis, D. B., Liu, W. M., Toporek, R. L., & Brittan-Powell, C. S. (2001). What's missing from multicultural competency research: Review, introspection, and recommendations. *Cultural Diversity and Ethnic Minority Psychology, 7*(2), 121–138.

Pope-Davis, D. B., Toporek, R. L., Ligiero, D., Ortega, L., Bashshur, M. L., Brittan-Powell, C. S., Liu, W. M., Codrington, J., & Liang, C. (2002). A qualitative study of clients' perspectives of multicultural counseling competence. *The Counseling Psychologist, 30*(3), 355–393.

Prilleltensky, I., & Prilleltensky, O. (2003). Synergies for wellness and liberation in counseling psychology. *The Counseling Psychologist, 31*(3), 273–281.

Resnick, J. L. (2006). Strategies for implementation of the multicultural guidelines in university and college counseling centers. *Professional Psychology: Research and Practice, 37*(1), 14–20.

Rosenthal, D. A. (2004). Effects of client race on clinical judgment of practicing European American vocational rehabilitation counselors. *Rehabilitation Counseling Bulletin, 47*(3), 131–141.

Roysircar, G. S., Arredondo, P. A., Fuertes, J., Ponterotto, J., & Toporek, R. L. (2003). *Multicultural counseling competencies 2003: AMCD.* Alexandria, VA: Association of Multicultural Counseling and Development.

Schnitzer, P. K. (1996). "They don't come in": Stories told, lessons taught about poor families in therapy. *American Journal of Orthopsychiatry, 66*(4), 572–582.

Sodowsky, G. R. (1996). The Multicultural Counseling Inventory: Validity and applications in multicultural training. In G. R. Sodowsky & J. C. Impara (Eds.), *Multicultural assessment in counseling and clinical psychology* (pp. 283–324). Lincoln, NE: Buros Institute of Mental Measurement.

Sue, D. W., Arredondo, P., & McDavis, R. J. (1992). Multicultural counseling competencies and standards: A call to the profession. *Journal of Counseling and Development, 70*, 477–486.

Sue, D. W., Bernier, Y., Durran, A., Feinberg, L., Pedersen, P. B., Smith, E. J., & Vasquez-Nuttal, E. (1982). Position paper: Cross-cultural counseling competencies. *The Counseling Psychologist, 10*, 45–52.

Sue, D. W., Carter, R. T., Casas, J. M., Fouad, N. A., Ivey, A. E., Jensen, M., et al. (1998). *Multicultural counseling competencies: Individual and organizational development.* Thousand Oaks, CA: Sage.

Sue, D. W., & Sue, D. (2003). Counseling the culturally diverse: *Theory and practice (4th ed.)*. New York: John Wiley & Sons.

Sue, S. (1977). Community mental health services to minority groups: Some optimism, some pessimism. *American Psychologist, 32*, 616–624.

Sue, S. (1998). In search of cultural competence in psychotherapy and counseling. *American Psychologist, 53*(4), 440–448.

Toporek, R. L., Gerstein, L. H., Fouad, N. A., Roysircar, G. S., & Israel, T. (2006). *Handbook for social justice in counseling psychology: Leadership, vision, & action*. Thousand Oaks, CA: Sage.

Toporek, R. L., & Pope-Davis, D. B. (2005). Exploring the relationships between multicultural training, racial attitudes, and attributions of poverty among graduate counseling trainees. *Cultural Diversity and Ethnic Minority Psychology, 11*(3), 259–271.

Toporek, R. L., & Reza, J. V. (1996, April). *Complexity of confluence in multicultural competence*. Paper presented at the Annual Meeting of the American Counseling Association, Pittsburgh, PA

Toporek, R. L., & Reza, J. V. (2001). Context as a critical dimension of multicultural counseling: Articulating personal, professional, and institutional competence. *Journal of Multicultural Counseling and Development, 29*(1), 13–30.

U.S. Department of Health and Human Services. (1999). *Mental health: A report of the surgeon general—Executive summary*. [Electronic version]. Rockville, MD: Author. Available at http://www.surgeongeneral.gov/library/mentalhealth/home.html

Vasquez, M. J. T., Han, A. L., & De Las Fuentes, C. (2006). Adaptation of immigrant girls and women. In J. Worell & C. D. Goodheart (Eds.), *Handbook of girls' and women's psychological health: Gender and well-being across the lifespan* (pp. 439–446). New York: Oxford University Press.

Wade, J. C. (1993). Institutional racism: An analysis of the mental health system. *American Journal of Orthopsychiatry, 63*, 536–544.

Ward, E. C. (2005). Keeping it real: A grounded theory study of African American clients engaging in counseling at a community mental health agency. *Journal of Counseling Psychology, 52*(4), 471–481.

Weinrach, S. G., & Thomas, K. R. (1996). The counseling profession's commitment to diversity-sensitive counseling: A critical reassessment. *Journal of Counseling and Development, 74, 472–477.*

Whaley, A. L. (1998). Racism in the provision of mental health services: A social-cognitive analysis. *American Journal of Orthopsychiatry, 68*(1), 47–57.

2

THE HELPING PROFESSIONAL AS AN ADVOCATE

Amie A. Manis, Shunda L. Brown, and Matthew J. Paylo

A major focus of the helping professions has been to promote intra-psychic change in clients, often with an implicit goal of facilitating clients' adaptation to the social environment. While assisting clients to change is indeed within the realm of the helping professional, advocacy aimed at eliminating injustices in the social environment is as well. The advent of multicultural counseling, rooted in the civil rights movement in the United States and recognized as the fourth force in counseling, challenged the helping professions to examine their own theories and practices for dominant cultural prejudices and biases. This internal examination has not only led to helping professionals reclaiming our role as advocates, but also to important clarifications about that role.

Specifically, researchers and practitioners have begun to explore and better grasp the impact of the social environment on mental health relative to a wide array of bio-psycho-social characteristics, such as race, ethnicity, gender, sexual orientation, ability, age, religious/spiritual orientation, and socioeconomic status (SES). Sadly, these bio-psycho-social characteristics have often contributed to the social marginalization of individuals and groups as a result of prejudice and oppression. An advocacy orientation encompasses an understanding of the dynamics of oppression, the importance of environmental context and change with respect to mental health, and the role of both the client and the helping professional as agents of environmental change (Toporek, 2001).

This chapter explores the role of the helping professional as an advocate for social justice. The chapter is divided into five major segments.

The first section provides a snapshot of advocacy in the helping professions. The second section defines key concepts related to advocacy. The third section presents and discusses the advocacy and social justice competencies. The fourth section discusses the multiple roles and characteristics of helping professionals as advocates in terms of practice and research. The fifth and last section identifies resources available to helping professionals and educators for enhancing our advocacy competence.

ADVOCACY TRADITIONS IN THE HELPING PROFESSIONS
Turn-of-the-Century Pioneer

The story of Clifford Beers reminds us that advocacy has been an integral part of the counseling profession since its inception. In the early 1900s, Beers became an avid social justice advocate for individuals who suffered from mental illnesses. As a result of being committed to a psychiatric hospital, Beers was able to personally identify with the inhumane treatment suffered by individuals with mental illness while in the care of mental health professionals. This profound experience compelled him to advocate on behalf of those who didn't have a voice by writing a book in 1909 titled *A Mind That Found Itself: An Autobiography* (Kiselica & Robinson, 2001). Trailblazers such as Clifford Beers remind us that social justice is part of our professional heritage and that as helping professionals we must expand our roles to include environmental change.

The Fourth Force: Reclaiming Advocacy as a Helping Role

Like the social justice initiatives at the turn of the last century, the civil rights movement in the United States was a powerful catalyst for challenging oppression and illuminating the rationalization of social injustices on the basis of the bio-psycho-social characteristics that reflect our humanity, namely race. Multicultural counseling, now recognized as the fourth force in counseling, grew out of that heightened consciousness of prejudice and a collective self-examination within the helping professions. This self-examination is an ongoing process, initiated by the courage of professionals, like our forebear Beers, whose lived experiences of prejudice fueled their passion and commitment to reclaiming advocacy as the province of the helping professional.

ADVOCACY: KEY CONCEPTS

Diversity, social justice, and advocacy may be most accurately understood as the discrete, yet interrelated concepts and practices that embody multicultural counseling. Examining each of these concepts and the relationships among them is essentially an exploration of the birth of multicultural counseling and its evolution as a major force within the helping professions to this point (Arredondo & Perez, 2003). At the heart of the fourth force, and indeed the birth of the helping professions, was an awareness of oppression as a social dynamic that negatively impacts the mental health of marginalized populations.

Oppression

Oppression encompasses a variety of isms, such as racism, heterosexism, ableism, sexism, ageism, and anti-Semitism. Hardiman and Jackson (1992) purport:

> Oppression exists when one social group exploits another social group for its own benefit. Oppression is distinct from a situation of simple brute force or control. It is first and foremost a systematic phenomenon that involves ideological domination, institutional control, and the promulgation of the dominant group's ideology of domination and culture on the oppressed. Oppression is simply a set of beliefs that asserts one group's superiority over another. Nor is it random acts of discrimination or harassment towards members of the subordinate group. It is a *system* of domination with many interlocking parts. (p. 2)

Implicit in the above description of oppression is the assertion that the United States is socially stratified by group membership based on race/ethnicity, religion, age, sex, sexual orientation, SES, religious/spiritual orientation, and disability status. Thus, access to resources is often unfairly dispersed. This social stratification system often causes discrimination, social injustices, and exploitation and may consequently contribute to mental health complications such as depression, low self-esteem, crime, drug and alcohol problems, and relationship issues (Ratts, D'Andrea, & Arredondo, 2004).

Diversity

Prominent literature reflects varied approaches to defining multiculturalism and the more recent adoption of the term diversity. At the core, there are two historically rooted perspectives on defining multiculturalism, an exclusive and inclusive perspective. The exclusive perspective reflects the birth of the multicultural movement in the context of the civil rights movement in that it emphasizes the importance of focusing social justice initiatives exclusively on race and ethnicity (Stone, 1997). The inclusive definition emphasizes the importance of including the full range of bio-psycho-social dimensions of identity that are subject to the dynamics of power, privilege, and oppression. These include dimensions of identity such as race and ethnicity, as well as gender, SES, sexual orientation, religious/spiritual orientation, age, ability, and region of origin.

The current usage of the term *multiculturalism* is frequently synonymous with *diversity*. In fact, the American Psychological Association (APA, 2003) clarifies the usage:

> The terms *multiculturalism* and *diversity* have been used interchangeably to include aspects of identity stemming from gender, sexual orientation, disability, socioeconomic status, or age. Multiculturalism, in an absolute sense, recognizes the broad scope of dimensions of race, ethnicity, language, sexual orientation, gender, age, disability, class status, education, religious/spiritual orientation, and other cultural dimensions. (p. 380)

This shift in definition is consistent with other evidence in the literature that the fear that a much-needed and long-advocated consideration of race and ethnicity would be diluted by the adoption of an inclusive approach (Helms, 1994) has waned. The debate regarding an exclusive approach to advocacy versus an inclusive approach has given way in the face of pragmatic considerations and a desire to promote social justice for all marginalized groups (Sue, Bingham, Porché-Burke, & Vasquez, 1999).

Clearly, a collective self-examination of the counseling profession relative to discrimination and oppression on the basis of race and ethnicity continues to be important, particularly from the standpoints of theory, research, and their implications for practice. Helms (1994) also voiced this assertion when citing the results of a content analysis of 1,800 published articles. Her study illustrated trends including a lack of focus on racial and ethnic minority groups as well as a lack of empirical studies, which still rings true according to a recent content analysis of the *Journal of Counseling and Development* (Arredondo, Rosen, Rice, Perez, & Tovar-Gomero, 2005). Yet, there is also increasing clarity among leaders of the multicultural movement that the inclusive approach to multicultural counseling is not only more pragmatic, but also represents a consistent valuing of bio-psycho-social diversity and social justice for all (K. M. May, personal communication, September

2006; Sue et al., 1999). Sue et al. (1999) identify this shift and clarify the rationale behind it:

> Because race, culture, ethnicity, gender, and sexual orientation are characteristics of each and every one of us, psychologists must work to understand, value, and study multiple worldviews as they relate to major biological, cultural, ethnic, and other sociodemographic groupings ... It became apparent ... that the term *multiculturalism* must include the broad range of significant differences (race, gender, sexual orientation, ability and disability, religion, class, etc.) that so often hinder communication and understanding among people. Otherwise, groups feel excluded from the multicultural debate, find themselves in opposition to one another, and engage in a "who's more oppressed" game. (p. 1063)

Adopting an inclusive definition of culture necessarily means that the focus of theory development and research are diversified beyond race and ethnicity. Therefore, it is necessary to collectively harness the power of constituent groups within the multicultural movement around common goals. Chief among these is the promotion of social justice, through advocacy, for all individuals who are marginalized by the dominant culture.

Social Justice

It is the desire to relieve suffering that is at the heart of counseling, and the recognition that some suffering is the result of conditions outside of an individual that bring us into the realms of social justice and advocacy. In fact, although there are definitional variations in the literature with respect to social justice as a goal of advocacy, the common root is grounded in a quest for the equitable distribution of advantages among people regardless of bio-psycho-social characteristics (Constantine, Hage, Kindaichi, & Bryant, 2007; Fouad, Gerstein, & Toporek, 2006; Goodman et al., 2004).

Berger (2007) produced a commentary on social justice by asking, quite simply, what is it? Her answer came from the spiritual strivings of Catholicism and the Jewish faith. Berger states that in the Christian tradition, social justice and social charity form the horizontal and vertical axes (as in the sign of the cross) to bring about harmony for people and communities by loving God and by also loving thy neighbor as you love yourself. What is interesting is that her concept of social justice is more humanistic than academic. Social justice for her is when individuals stand up for what is right and act in an organized manner with like-minded people to "hold social institutions accountable—whether government or private—to the common good" (p. 37). Berger also warns that social justice can be an idea in name only if the believers of social justice lose contact and a personal touch with everyday people and their experiences.

There is a synergetic relationship between diversity and social justice, the driving concepts of the fourth force of counseling, and the brackets for advocacy. Oppression on the basis of bio-psycho-social diversity moves helping professionals to advocate for a more socially just society. Sue et al. (1999) describe this synergy in their own terms:

> Our own stand on this matter, however, is quite clear. Multiculturalism is not only about understanding different perspectives and worldviews but also about social justice. As such it is not value neutral: Multiculturalism stands against beliefs and behaviors that oppress other groups and deny them equal access and opportunity. (p. 1064)

Advocacy

Although diversity and social justice are most aptly conceptualized as central concepts of the fourth force, advocacy may be most accurately conceptualized as a central practice of the fourth force of counseling. Cheatham et al. (2002) propose that the practice of advocacy is appropriate regardless of a helping professional's theoretical approach. They discuss multicultural counseling and therapy (Sue, 1995) as a metatheory that may be useful in guiding helping professionals with incorporating multicultural awareness and multiculturally sensitive interventions in their practice.

The term *advocacy* means many things to many people. Advocacy refers to the endeavor or process of "arguing or pleading for a cause or proposal" (Lee, 1998, p. 8). Lewis, Lewis, Daniels, and D'Andrea (2003) contend that advocacy serves two primary purposes: (1) increasing clients' sense of personal power and (2) fostering environmental changes that reflect greater responsiveness to their personal needs. Advocacy is an encompassing continuum with empowerment of the client at one end of the continuum and social action on the other end. This umbrella theory of advocacy inclusively comprises the multiple facets of advocacy, ranging from the empowerment of an individual or group, which "assist in recognizing and addressing sociopolitical barriers to well-being" (Toporek, 2000, p. 7), to action that is taken in the form of societal interventions. Definitions of advocacy that build upon either empowerment or social action or both follow.

The most comprehensive definition of empowerment is McWhirter's (1991) five-part definition. She defines empowerment as:

The process by which people, organizations, or groups that are powerless or marginalized: (a) become aware of the power dynamics at work in their life context, (b) develop the skills and capacity for gaining reasonable control over their lives, (c) which they exercise, (d) without infringing on the rights of others, and (e) which coincides with actively supporting the empowerment of others in their community. (p. 12)

Empowerment builds upon the awareness of the power imbalance to the extent that individuals take ownership, challenge, and combat that power while not going to the extreme sense of infringing on others' rights in the process. This endeavor requires a tremendous amount of support and courage, eventually allowing the helping professional and the client to move past the limited mind-set of just remaining on the individual level to an ecological mind-set.

The other end of the continuum is social action. Social action is the implementation of an intervention constructed by the client and/or counselor toward the larger, more public arena on the group, institutional, state, federal, or societal level that inhibits access or growth and development. These actions influence the social structure, which some scholars argue is the only way helping professionals can assist oppressed and marginalized clients achieve lasting mental health (Goodman et al., 2004).

ADVOCACY AND SOCIAL JUSTICE COMPETENCIES

In response to a call to action issued during the 1999 presidency of Loretta Bradley, the American Counseling Association (ACA) endorsed a set of advocacy competencies to clarify the roles and responsibilities of counselors as advocates, and therefore proponents of social justice. The Advocacy Competencies were created in 2002 by a task force consisting of leaders and scholars (Judy Lewis, Mary Smith Arnold, Reese House, and Rebecca Toporek) who were members of ACA's professional division, Counselors for Social Justice (CSJ). The Advocacy Competencies were finalized in January 2003 and were subsequently endorsed by the ACA Governing Council at the 2003 ACA National Convention.

Advocacy Competencies

The Advocacy Competencies serve as a framework for addressing issues of oppression from individual to systemic levels. The Advocacy Competencies state:

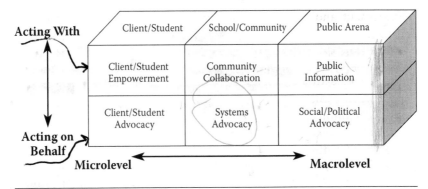

Figure 2.1 Advocacy Competency Framework.

Advocacy-oriented counseling recognized the impact of social, political, economic, and cultural factors on human development. They also help their clients and students understand their own lives in context. This process lays the groundwork for self-advocacy. (Lewis et al., 2002, Advocacy Competencies link, para. 1)

The task force that developed the Advocacy Competencies contends that helping professionals may advocate in three domains: (1) the client/student level, (2) the school/community level, and (3) the larger public arena. This committee further suggests that each domain can be broken down in two subsets. Each subset is contingent on whether the counselor acts with the client or on behalf of the client. This model of advocacy competency domains is presented visually in Figure 2.1.

Client/Student Advocacy Level The client/student level, the microlevel, consists of client/student empowerment or client/student advocacy. The movement within this subsystem is on a continuum dependent on whether the helping professional acts with the client/student or the helping professional acts on the behalf of the client/student. The first subset of the client/student domain addresses the implementation of empowerment strategies occurring in the direct counseling scope. The counselor assists clients'/students' development by aiding clients/students in understanding their lives in the context of a sociopolitical, economic, and cultural world. This implementation brings awareness and support to the client/student, which is the "groundwork for self-advocacy" (Lewis et al., 2002, p. 2). The second subset within the client/student domain addresses counselors' ability to advocate on the behalf of clients/students. This level of intervening occurs when a counselor becomes aware of external barriers that impeded a client's/student's development and the client/student lacks the access to resources or services.

School/Community Advocacy Level The next domain of advocacy competency is the macrolevel or school/community level. The first subset within this domain is community collaboration. The authors define community collaboration as alerting or allying with community organizations that are already working toward change, assisting in the recognition of difficulties within the community that impede clients'/students' development. The second subset in the domain of school/community is system advocacy. Changing the "status quo" takes maintaining a vision, through collaboration and systems analysis, along with a helping professional's ability to assume a leadership role.

Public Arena Advocacy Level The last domain of advocacy competency is the public arena or the macrolevel. The first subset within this domain is public information. The authors define public information as the disseminating of information that helping professionals have due to their training in human development, attempting to raise the consciousness of society to the macro systems' issues regarding human dignity. The second subset within the domain of the larger public arena is social/political advocacy. Lewis et al. (2002) define social/political advocacy as the helping professional's ability to act as a change agent in the larger more public arena, bringing shared client concerns to the masses. This subset relates to the influences that public policy has on the public as a whole.

Lewis et al. (2002) theorize a number of competencies within all the previously mentioned domains. These competencies add to the existing list of advocacy characteristics, creating an even fuller potential for dialogue of the characteristics needed to facilitate advocacy counseling.

In light of the increased ownership of advocacy as a domain of the helping professional, exploring social justice from a number of perspectives is occurring in the helping professions. It is important to note that just as there have been multiple perspectives on what the term multicultural means as a collective vision evolved, so there are too with respect to the terms advocacy and social justice. Although we present social justice as the goal of advocacy, others see social justice from the perspective of action. For example, Constantine et al. (2007) have proposed a set of social justice competencies. As scholars and researchers in the helping professions proceed to clarify these concepts and practices and reach consensus, it is clear at this point that both the Advocacy

Competencies and the social justice competencies reflect the core intent and values of the fourth force of counseling.

Social Justice Competencies

Constantine et al. (2007) recently proposed nine social justice competencies for counselors. They are: (1) gain knowledge of how social injustices are manifested and experienced at the individual, cultural, and societal levels; (2) participate in active self-reflection on issues concerning race, ethnicity, oppression, power, and privilege; (3) when interacting with clients and community organizations, maintain ongoing self-awareness of how your personal positions of power and privilege may unintentionally parallel experiences with oppression and injustice; (4) promote the well-being of individuals and groups by challenging interventions that seem exploitive; (5) gain knowledge about indigenous models of health and healing and work alongside these entities to promote culturally relevant, holistic interventions; (6) expand awareness of global issues and injustices; (7) conceptualize and implement preventive therapeutic interventions; (8) collaborate with community organizations to provide culturally relevant services to the identified groups; and (9) hone systemic and advocacy skills to facilitate social change within institutions and communities.

These social justice competencies reflect the key components of the Multicultural Counseling Competencies—namely knowledge, awareness, and skill—and the systemic perspective of the Advocacy Competencies (Lewis et al., 2002). They are clearly embedded in the tenets of multicultural counseling theory (Cheatham et al., 2002; Fuertes & Gretchen, 2001) and represent a unique perspective on adding flesh to the key concepts of counseling's fourth force. A step back to view our full professional evolution helps illuminate the multicultural movement and its evolution in terms of a culmination of multiple perspectives:

All professions start out with an idea … So, too, counseling started out with an idea: talking and/or testing can help people with a variety of issues … As professions grow from their initial idea, they begin to develop competing ideas … Counseling, too, developed opposing camps. In the personal counseling arena, psychodynamic advocates squared off against Skinnerians who opposed cognitive behaviorists … As professions mature, they seem to learn that many approaches have a piece of the puzzle. The question changes from "Who is right and who is wrong" to "What works best in a given situation." It is not so much that each theory is a different animal as that each paradigm is touching a different part of the elephant. (Kaplan & Cogan, 2005, p. 17)

REAUTHORING THE ROLE OF THE HELPING PROFESSIONAL: ADVOCACY PRACTICE AND RESEARCH

Advocacy, including empowerment and social action, is an essential component of counseling according to the ACA Code of Ethics (American Counseling Association, 2005), the ASCA Code of Ethics (American School Counselor Association, 2004), and the CACREP Accreditation Standards (Council for Accreditation of Counseling and Related Educational Programs, 2001). Therefore, because counselors are responsible for competently advocating on behalf of clients, counselor educators are responsible for educating and instructing counselors on how to be advocates. In this section we offer best practices and research concerning the characteristics of advocates in counseling and present implications for future research efforts.

Advocacy Practice

Advocacy practice entails adopting roles that will require leaving the comfort of our offices to conduct our work in other settings, such as the client's home or school, recreational and community centers, churches, local agencies, and the offices and meeting places of policymakers (such as school board members, legislators, and government administrators). Indirect forms of helping that involve influencing the people and institutions that affect clients' lives complement the provision of direct services to clients (Kiselica & Robinson, 2001).

Conceptualizing and Selecting Helping Roles   Current perspectives regarding the types of roles helping professionals (Constantine et al., 2007; Kiselica & Robinson, 2001; Romero & Chan, 2005) may be compelled take to effectively meet the needs of a rapidly diversifying population and globally oriented society are provided in the professional literature. Constantine et al. cite the 1993 work of Atkinson, Thompson, and Grant with respect to eight potential helping roles "in relation to working with diverse cultural populations" (p. 26).

These roles, clearly reflective of multicultural counseling and therapy (Sue, 1995) are: (1) facilitator of indigenous healing methods, (2) facilitator of indigenous support systems, (3) adviser, (4) advocate, (5) change agent, (6) consultant, (7) counselor, and (8) psychotherapist. Constantine et al. (2007) go on to present three "client-based factors" (p. 26) that help counselors determine which of the roles to adopt:

(1) client's level of acculturation, (2) internal versus external etiology of the client's problem, and (3) goals of intervention. So, for example, if the goal of a helping professional is social justice for an African American client experiencing racism in the public school system, the helping professional may choose to adopt one or more of the roles, perhaps an advocate, adviser regarding self-advocacy, and change agent within the school system. Which role(s) would you choose?

Using Professional Privilege to Educate and Empower   Helping professionals are in positions of institutional power and privilege in relation to clients. Counselors have access to institutional policies and resources in ways that are different from those available to clients. Practicing as an ethical helping professional implies that we use our professional stature and our institutional involvement to influence policy and practice by empowering an individual client to influence public health initiatives (Kiselica & Robinson, 2001; Toporek, 2000).

Of critical importance is the need for helping professionals to examine the role power plays in the helper–client relationship. This process entails an understanding of the ways in which race, ethnicity, gender, sexual orientation, and other dimensions of identity influence the therapeutic alliance. Additionally, it involves an understanding that helping professionals and clients are often members of both oppressor and oppressed social groups. In reality, a significant number of helping professionals are members of the dominant group and have been the recipients of fewer social injustices and greater privilege (Toporek, 2000).

For example, the current demographic composition of professional counselors primarily consists of educated, middle class, heterosexual individuals of European descent (Bradley, Sexton, & Smith, 2005). Though the majority of professional counselors are European American women, they are prone to experience gender bias. Conversely because of their identity with the dominant culture, European American women are characteristically the recipients of privilege in society and within the profession.

Mindfulness and the Multicultural Counseling Competencies   Viewing the world through the lens of oppressor and oppressed group statuses requires consideration of all of the various bio-psycho-social aspects that make up human identity. This perspective allows helping professionals and researchers to recognize that their roles may shift and change when working with clients and the larger community. For example, helping professionals may need to draw on their roles as parents, sexual minorities, or men and women to assist clients. Given this perspective, it is critical for helping professionals to recognize how their "multiple selves" can influence the helping process.

A developmental milestone in the multicultural counseling movement was the official adoption of the Multicultural Counseling Competencies in 2002. The competencies underscore the critical importance of attending to culture in helping relationships through the cultivation of cultural awareness, knowledge, and skill (Arredondo et al., 1996). Ongoing cultivation of these competencies is critical to ethical and effective advocacy practice.

Research in the helping professions has demonstrated that positive outcomes for clients rest mostly in the therapeutic alliance established by the professional. In essence, the helping professional may be conceived of as the instrument of change. Like any instrument, calibration is required prior to use. Thus, in adopting the role of advocate, best practice begins with the cultivation of our own cultural awareness.

Kiselica and Robinson (2001) reflect on the importance of the cultivation of self-awareness and its relationship to advocacy:

> Perhaps the most important step we all must take in advocacy work is to look deep within ourselves and try to discover what forms of human suffering move us to the point that we want to get up and fight—each of us in our own unique way—for other human beings. (p. 395)

They speak to our motivation as agents of change as residing in our lived experience, as well as our awareness of the lived experiences of others with respect to positions of privilege, power, and oppression relative to our bio-psycho-social characteristics.

Lago (2006) also underscores the importance of practicing cultural awareness and contends that helping professionals need to

> enhance their own understanding of their own stereotypes, assumptions, and judgments; appreciate the very different psychological and cultural frameworks by which other people live; inform their own processes of self-monitoring in relation to negative attitudes; and help them avoid imposing their own frame of reference upon clients. (p. 127)

In addition, developing a cultural knowledge and skill base as a means of better anticipating and understanding the lived experiences of our clients is critical to the best practice of advocacy. Building this competency must be viewed as is an ongoing process, which may occur through continuing education; supervision; consultation; reviewing professional publications; and consulting with clients, colleagues, and cultural informants. It is important that helping professionals treat this knowledge and skill base as a resource and a framework for conceptualization and intervention, and avoid its use as a stereotypical treatment protocol.

Practicing from the Bio-Psycho-Social Model   The shift to embracing an inclusive definition of diversity (APA, 2003) reflects an inherent recognition of humans as bio-psycho-social organisms (Sue et al., 1999). The legacy of the fourth force may be the counseling profession's reflexive incorporation of well-informed, individual and systemic attention to the biological, social, and political aspects of being (Watts, 2004), as well as the psychological aspects. Kaplan and Cogan (2005) propose that this type of practice is embodied in the **bio-psycho-social model**, which they define as

> a comprehensive, integrative, and elegant model that allows us to address all major areas of the presenting issue across three spheres: physical, psychological, and sociocultural. It allows (and actually encourages) us to holistically examine the interactive and reciprocal effects of environment, genetics, and behavior. (pp. 18–19)

This model guides us in holistic approaches to helping and represents an embracing of an integrated professional identity that is our professional birthright (Kiselica & Robinson, 2001)

Applying the bio-psycho-social framework to training and, ultimately, research and practice, like the development of the Multicultural Counseling Competencies (Arredondo & Perez, 2003), may represent the manifestation or newest evolution of more than a century of advocacy work in the counseling profession (Hill, 2003). It may also signify a multidisciplinary reconceptualization of human development. Watts (2004) identifies the imperative to social justice as an important component of this reconceptualization, also reflected in the profession's Code of Ethics (ACA, 2005).

So, in wielding the power and privilege of the helping position ethically, we must remember that clients also exist in the context of multiple selves, and as such may also be advocates. Just like each helping professional, each client possesses bio-psycho-social characteristics that may encompass positions of oppression and power simultaneously. Depending upon the goals of clients, arriving at an understanding of their own bio-psycho-social positionality may be a co-constructed therapeutic end, whereas taking steps toward self-advocacy at a local level or for marginalized groups at a community level may also be a co-constructed therapeutic end.

Current and Future Directions in Research

Theoretical and conceptual treatment of diversity, social justice, and advocacy abounds in the literature. In particular, a great deal has been written about the characteristics of advocates in helping settings. This next segment describes existing research using both qualitative and quantitative methodologies.

Qualitative Research on Characteristics of Advocates   Jennings (1996) conducted a qualitative research study involving 39 human rights advocates, and implemented focus groups to examine central themes leading to advocacy behaviors. Two central themes emerged: (1) a critique of societal structures and values; and (2) a description of self. Jennings states that from the critiques of society, advocates embrace a global and systems perspective, and have a moral obligation and responsibility to respond with integrity to others. In addition, the interviewees "moved between observations of society, beliefs about self, and the tension between the two" (p. 80). Therefore, the interaction between self-concept and social perspective occurs simultaneously, affecting the advocate's ability to make sense of the incongruence. Advocates are motivated through moral conviction to "preserve the self-concept by maintaining a sense of integrity between self-concept and personal behavior" (p. 80), which leads to advocating behavior.

This qualitative research study presents a number of characteristics needed for helping professionals who wish to advocate on behalf of clients. The characteristics are primarily focused on the advocate's ability to be aware of society, with all its oppression and unbalance of power, along with an awareness of the self, in the sense of how an individual can live an authentic life. This study significantly adds to literature about the characteristics needed to advocate for clients, providing a research-based conceptualization of the motivation behind advocacy.

A qualitative research study conducted by Field and Baker (2004) involved nine school counselors. They implemented a focus group methodology to examine how counselors defined advocacy, their perceptions of essential behaviors of advocates, the value of advocacy, and how they learned to be advocates. The researchers suggest that from the focus groups, three distinct themes or behaviors emerged: (1) being flexible and having a broad range of skills in dealing with different people in different situations; (2) authentic acceptance of others while simultaneously being aware of own values and beliefs; and (3) having realistic expectations for the advocacy work. Field and Baker suggest that two other themes or behaviors were discussed, but because they were only mentioned by one individual, they were not placed with the three other themes or behaviors. The two additional themes or behaviors were being a voice for students individually and collectively to parents, administrators, and teachers; and the maintaining of a sense of humor.

This study presents a number of considerations for the characteristics of an advocate, although the focus of the study was not primarily an exploration of the characteristics of an advocate. The study adds to the discussion of the needed characteristics to advocate for clients.

Quantitative Research on Characteristics of Advocates   In an empirical quantitative study, Nilsson and Schmidt (2005) examined the hypothesized variables that contribute to graduate counseling students' desired and actual involvement in social advocacy. The authors' inquiry explored the influence of problem-solving skills, worldview, social concern, number of courses taken, and political interest in an attempt to identify possible predictors of social justice advocacy among counseling students. The variables of age, gender, ethnicity, religious orientation, sexual orientation, and political orientation also were explored to determine if significant differences occurred in the sample population of graduate students. The sample population was composed of 134 counseling graduate students from a Midwestern university. One early limitation of the study was the low representation compared to the parameter population concerning the demographic variables (e.g., sexual orientation, ethnicity, religious affiliations, and gender). The participants were primarily Caucasian females identifying themselves as heterosexual Christian Democrats. The researchers measured the constructs of desired and actual social advocacy by the use of the following instruments: the Activity Scale (ACT; Kerpelman, 1969), the Problem-Solving Inventory (PSI; Heppner, 1988), the Social Interest Scale (SIS; Crandall, 1975), the Scale to Assess World Views (SAWV; Ibrahim & Kahn, 1987), and a researcher-constructed demographic survey.

Nilsson and Schmidt (2005) contend that the variables of age, number of courses taken, political interest, and problem solving predicted the desire to engage in social advocacy. The only variable that individually predicted desired social advocacy was political interest. This quantitative study adds to the dialogue of needed characteristics to advocate for clients. Political interest and involvement appear to be linked to advocacy, but the results from this study need to be interpreted with caution. Along with the sampling limitation of the study, one of the instruments may not have adequately measured the construct the researchers set out to measure. The researchers used an instrument, the Social Activity Scale, which was constructed in the 1960s. Decades have passed and the cultural, political, and social landscapes are qualitatively and quantifiably different.

The paucity of research that studies attributes that are essential to becoming an effective advocate has begun to be addressed with research aimed at quantifying measurable aspects of advocacy characteristics (Paylo, 2007). As stated earlier, the growing body of literature suggests that the counseling profession is beginning to acknowledge the importance of recognizing systemic injustices and promoting social justice as an essential element of the working alliance. Notwithstanding, the majority of social justice counseling publications are either position pieces or self-reflections on social justice.

Therefore, more empirical research studies need to be conducted if we are to better understand the impact of social justice and advocacy in the profession. This call for more research is echoed by social justice scholars who have questioned how social justice principles are incorporated into counselor training programs (Goodman et al., 2004). Future research will need to focus on developing a means of measuring systemic injustice in order to improve the understanding and training of future counselor educators in social justice and advocacy.

RESOURCES FOR BUILDING ADVOCACY COMPETENCE

All helping professionals have an opportunity, if not a responsibility, to be an advocate for both their clients and themselves. To be an advocate for one and not the other undermines success with either. Notwithstanding, many helping professionals do not have adequate information or resources related to building advocacy competence, particularly at the social action end of the advocacy continuum.

The most basic way to gain advocacy knowledge and resources is to be a member of professional organizations. Most professional organizations offer workshops, trainings, and publications that address multicultural counseling issues relative to culturally appropriate and empowering helping practices with specific populations. In addition, many professional organizations have developed advocacy initiatives. For example, ACA is very committed to social justice through advocacy and provides education and assistance to individuals who are interested in this topic. On its Web site (www.counseling.org), ACA has a wealth of information concerning various up-to-date legislative issues. In particular, the ACA Public Policy and Legislation Initiative is guided by an annual legislative agenda that is adopted by leaders in the helping profession.

ACA's Office of Government Relations offers a digest of publications on effective ways to communicate with legislators. In addition, it provides legislative training sessions at state and national levels. Two days prior to the ACA annual conference, ACA conducts a Learning Institute that offers more than 40 training workshops on various topics, including social justice and advocacy. Counselors for Social Justice (CSJ), a division of ACA, also hosts a Social Justice Conference annually that provides a forum whereby helping professionals and community members can explore the role of collaborating between diverse communities to better serve clients and the community alike.

The American Mental Health Counselors Association (AMHCA) is another professional organization that advocates for social justice through its Office of Public Policy and Legislation (PP&L). The PP&L Office works to educate policymakers about the role of mental health counselors and to increase lawmakers' awareness about mental illness and its effects on people's lives. In addition, the PP&L Office manages the Federal Legislative Advocacy Network (FLAN), which provides grassroots support for the association's advocacy initiatives in Congress and state legislatures. More information concerning the aforementioned organizational efforts may be found on the CSJ Web site (www.counselorsforsocialjustice.com), the ACA Web site (www.counseling.org), and the AMHCA Web site (www.amhca.org).

CONCLUSION

Diversity, advocacy, and social justice embody the fourth force in counseling. These concepts and practices both reflect and allow for the expansion of a rich and passionate professional history rooted in an appreciation of human development. The bio-psycho-social model is an apt fit with the ideals of the profession, as well as a powerful means of understanding and treating clients in an ethical and holistic fashion.

The potential of the bio-psycho-social model to put to rest the hard-fought battle for human rights in the field is enormous. The use of the model represents an understanding of and appreciation for cultural dimensions of being and social justice as part and parcel of human development. It seems the relevance of this model is increasingly clear in light of the rapid globalization of society. This change is upon us and must be addressed in our practice and research as helping professionals as we are uniquely positioned to influence not only the clients we serve, but the systems and institutions in which we all travel.

REFERENCES

American Counseling Association (ACA). (2005). *ACA code of ethics.* Washington, DC: Author.

American Psychological Association (APA). (2003). Guidelines on multicultural education, training, research, practice, and organizational change for psychologists. *American Psychologist, 58*(5), 377–402.

American School Counselor Association (ASCA). (2004). *Ethical standards for school counselors.* Retrieved January 7, 2007, from http://www.school-counselor.org/content.asp?contentid=173

Arredondo, P., & Perez, P. (2003). Expanding multicultural competence through social justice leadership. *The Counseling Psychologist, 31*(3), 282–289.

Arredondo, P., Rosen, D. C., Rice, T., Perez, P., & Tovar-Gomero, Z. G. (2005). Multicultural counseling: A 10-year content analysis of the *Journal of Counseling & Development. Journal of Counseling & Development, 83*(2), 155–161.

Arredondo, P., Toporek, R., Brown, S., Jones, J., Locke, D. C., Sanchez, J., et al. (1996). Operationalization of the multicultural counseling competencies. *Journal of Multicultural Counseling and Development, 24*(1), 42–78.

Berger, R. M. (2007, February). What the heck is 'social justice'? *Sojourners Magazine, 36*(2), 37. Retrieved December 2, 2007, from Humanities Module database (Document ID: 1205603931).

Bradley, L. J., Sexton, T. L., & Smith, H. B. (2005). The American Counseling Association Practice Research Network: A new research tool. *Journal of Counseling and Development, 83*(4), 488–491.

Cheatham, H., D'Andrea, M., Ivey, A. E., Bradford Ivey, M., Pedersen, P., Rigazio-DiGilio, S., et al. (2002). Multicultural counseling and therapy I: Metatheory—taking theory into practice. In A. E. Ivey, M. D'Andrea, M. Bradford Ivey, & L. Simek-Morgan (Eds.), *Theories of counseling and psychotherapy: A multicultural perspective* (5th ed.). Boston: Allyn and Bacon.

Constantine, M. G., Hage, S. M., Kindaichi, M. M., & Bryant, R. M. (2007). Social justice and multicultural issues: Implications for the practice and training of counselors and counseling psychologists. *Journal of Counseling & Development, 85*(1), 24–29.

Council for Accreditation of Counseling and Related Educational Programs (CACREP). (2001). *Standards.* Retrieved February 10, 2007, from http://www.cacrep.org/print.html

Crandall, J. E. (1975). A scale for social interest. *Journal of Individual Psychology, 31,* 187–195.

Field, J. E., & Baker, S. (2004). Defining and examining school counselor advocacy. *Professional School Counseling, 8,* 56–63.

Fouad, N. A., Gerstein, L. H., & Toporek, R. L. (2006). Social justice and counseling psychology in context. In R. L. Toporek, L. H. Gerstein, N. A. Fouad, G. Roysircar, & T. Israel (Eds.), *Handbook for social justice in counseling psychology* (pp. 1–17). Thousand Oaks, CA: Sage.

Fuertes, J. N., & Gretchen, D. (2001). Emerging theories of multicultural counseling. In J. G. Ponterotto, J. Manuel Cassas, L. A. Suzuki, & C. M. Alexander (Eds.), *Handbook of multicultural counseling* (2nd ed.). Thousand Oaks, CA: Sage.

Goodman, L. A., Liang, B., Helms, J. E., Latta, R. E., Sparks, E., & Weintraub, S. R. (2004). Training counseling psychologists as social justice agents: Feminist and multicultural principles in action. *The Counseling Psychologist, 32*(6), 793–837.

Hardiman, R., & Jackson, B. (1992). Oppression: Conceptual and developmental analysis. In M. Adams, P. Brigham, P. Dalpes, & L. Marchesani (Eds.), *Social diversity and social justice—Diversity and oppression: Conceptual frameworks* (pp. 1–6). Dubuque, IA: Kendall/Hunt.

Helms, J. E. (1994). How multiculturalism obscures racial factors in the therapy process: Comment on Ridley et al. (1994), Sodowsky et al. (1994), Ottavi et al. (1994), and Thompson et al. (1994). *Journal of Counseling Psychology, 41*(2), 162–165.

Heppner, P. P. (1988). *The problem solving inventory (PSI): Manual.* Palo Alto, CA: Consulting Psychologists Press.

Hill, N. (2003). Promoting and celebrating multicultural competence in counselor trainees. *Counselor Education & Supervision, 43*, 39–51.

Ibrahim, F., & Kahn, H. (1987). Assessment of worldviews. *Psychological Reports, 60*, 163–176.

Jennings, T. E. (1996). The developmental dialectic of international human-rights advocacy. *Political Psychology, 17*, 77–95.

Kaplan, D., & Cogan, S. L. (2005). The next advancement in counseling: The bio-psycho-social model [Electronic version]. *Vistas,* 17–25.

Kerpelman, L. C. (1969). Student political activism and ideology: Comparative characteristics of activist and non-activist. *Journal of Counseling Psychology, 16*, 8–13.

Kiselica, M. S., & Robinson, M. (2001). Bringing advocacy counseling to life: The history, issues, and human dramas of social justice work in counseling. *Journal of Counseling & Development, 79*, 387–397.

Lago, C. (2006). *Race, culture, and counseling: The ongoing challenge* (2nd ed). Maidenhead: Open University Press.

Lee, C. C. (1998). Counselors as agents of social change. In C. C. Lee & G. R. Walz (Eds.), *Social action: A mandate for counselors* (pp. 3–14). Alexandria, VA: American Counseling Association and ERIC Counseling and Student Services Clearinghouse.

Lewis, J., Arnold, M. S., House, R., & Toporek, R. L. (2002). *Advocacy competencies: Task Force on Advocacy Competencies.* Alexandria, VA: American Counseling Association. Retrieved February 10, 2007, from http://www.counseling.org/Files/FD.ashx?guid=24135fca-b378-4fe2-ae35-a467487858f7

Lewis, J., Lewis, M., Daniels, J., & D'Andrea, M. (2003). *Community counseling: Empowerment strategies for a diverse society* (3rd ed.). Pacific Grove, CA: Brooks/Cole.

McWhirter, E. H. (1991). Empowerment in counseling. *Journal of Counseling and Development, 69*(3), 22–27.

Nilsson, J. E., & Schmidt, C. K. (2005). Social justice advocacy among graduate students in counseling: An initial exploration. *Journal of College Student Development, 46*(3), 267–279.

Paylo, M. J. (2007). *Characteristics of counselors that advocate.* Unpublished doctoral dissertation, University of Virginia, Charlottesville.

Ratts, M., D'Andrea, M., & Arredondo, P. (2004). Social justice counseling: A "fifth force" in the field. *Counseling Today, 47*(1), 28–30.

Romero, D., & Chan, A. (2005). Profiling Derald Wing Sue: Blazing the trail for the multicultural journey and social justice in counseling. *Journal of Counseling & Development, 83*(2), 202–213.

Stone, G. L. (1997). Multiculturalism as a context for supervision: Perspectives, limitations, and implications. In D. B. Pope-Davis & H. L. K. Coleman (Eds.), *Multicultural counseling competencies: Assessment, education, training and supervision* (pp. 263–289). Thousand Oaks, CA: Sage.

Sue, D. W. (1995). Toward a theory of multicultural counseling and therapy. In J. Banks & C. Banks (Eds.), *Handbook of research on multicultural education.* New York: Macmillan.

Sue, D. W., Bingham, R. P., Porché-Burke, L., & Vasquez, M. (1999). The diversification of psychology: A multicultural revolution. *American Psychologist, 54*(12), 1061–1069.

Toporek, R. (2000). Developing a common language and framework for understanding advocacy in counseling. In J. Lewis & L. Bradley (Eds.), *Advocacy in counseling: Counselors, clients, and community* (pp. 5–14). Greensboro, NC: Caps Publications.

Toporek, R. L. (2001). Context as a critical dimension of multicultural counseling: Articulating personal, professional, and institutional competence. *Journal of Multicultural Counseling and Development, 29,* 13–30.

Watts, R. J. (2004). Integrating social justice and psychology. *The Counseling Psychologist, 32*(6), 855–865.

3

DEVELOPING A DIVERSE COUNSELING POSTURE

Rebecca L. Farrell

It takes one kind of mind to absorb facts and another to absorb the presence of another human being.

—Abraham Maslow

Rapid demographic changes in the American society have given impetus to the call for the counseling profession to be cross-culturally competent. Although diversity has always existed, its presence and significance is becoming more difficult to negate as it continuously permeates the dominant, mainstream culture. Yet resistance to acknowledging, tolerating, and even accepting the value of diversified differences still ensues. This is part of human nature. Newness and deviations from the perceived norms are faced with opposition so that individuals do not have to grapple with the fear of losing whatever measure of power, privilege, and status they possess. The covert and overt development, implementation, and enforcement of societal, institutional, and individually based rules help maintain and/or enhance the sense of the cultural environment as well as the personhood through the use of power and control.

Within the United States, the Jim Crow Laws (1876–1965), the internment of Japanese Americans during World War II, immigration and illegal alien laws, and the Patriot Act (2001) illustrate societal (i.e., government) edicts in which discrimination and oppression were and are both intentional and unintentional. The institution of marriage, while healthy and respected in many cultures, can also be used to oppress

45

others when applied through a particular religious or cultural lens. On a more individualized level, the disparities between the poor and wealthy, the haves and have-nots continue to escalate. Furthermore, interethnic (e.g., African Americans and Caucasians, African Americans and Korean Americans) and intraethnic (e.g., gangs, SES, education, attractiveness) relations still encompass conflicts and tension that are often incited by rivalry, which is embedded in power and control.

Perhaps in the struggle to maintain and/or obtain power, privilege, and status individuals, regardless of group membership, are disconnecting from each other. The inability to recognize and value the humanness in others allows for the creation, internalization, and perpetuation of stereotypes, prejudice, discrimination, oppression, and racism. Even though these are often rationalized as a means for understanding differences and ensuring societal and personal protection and purity, the impact of the generated outcomes are negative and profound.

It is imperative, then, that counselors assume the responsibility to actively address oppressive, discriminatory, and ism-based practices, beliefs, attitudes, and values within the process of therapy. From an ethical perspective, the preamble of the American Counseling Association's (ACA) *Code of Ethics* (2005) specifically states that "association members recognize diversity and embrace a cross-cultural approach in support of the worth, dignity, potential, and uniqueness of people within their social and cultural contexts" (p. 4). In order to embody a diverse counseling posture, counselors must be willing to analyze their own cultural existence and contributions to the therapeutic relationship while being openly receptive to the diversity of their clients. Such behavior is also ethically mandated. Essentially, every person holds, to some extent, prejudicial, oppressive, racist, and stereotyped attitudes and beliefs. These are learned from being encapsulated in one's own cultural world, insubstantial interethnic interactions, and/or the propensity to classify for a clearer comprehension (Ponterotto, Utsey, & Pedersen, 2006).

Wrenn (1962) recognized the dehabilitating impact of ethnocentrism in the counseling profession and called for changes. Approximately 30 years later Sue, Arredondo, and McDavis (1992) went beyond the rhetoric and answered the call with the introduction of the multicultural counseling competencies. The extensive literature on cross-cultural counseling centered primarily on the characteristics of diversified populations, the "how to" effectively counsel members (e.g., diagnosing, assessing, treatment planning, using interventions and techniques, and establishing therapeutic relationships), and examining cultural competencies. One area that seemed to be neglected and in which a dearth in information remains is that of counselors as diverse individuals. So much of the literature assumes an external focus on others and how counselors need to be aware of their biases, values, and beliefs and obtain knowledge and skills to be cross-culturally competent. Very little attention is given to how counselors begin to explore, address, and even challenge who they are as diverse beings. If the counseling process is to commence with counselors, then it only seems natural and sensible that cross-cultural training also begins with counselors engaging in comprehensive examinations of their personal cultural identity.

PREPARING TO ADDRESS DIVERSITY

If establishing a therapeutic framework that is culturally inclusive is of paramount importance to the profession, a stronger emphasis ought to be placed on the exploration of the counselor in relation to self, others, and environments. This requires a commitment from counselors to become more self-actualized by challenging established worldviews and understanding their own existence. However, gaining self-insight to personal ideological views is anything but easy or simplistic (Collins & Pieterse, 2007). Individuals entering counselor training programs bring with them at least 20 years of life experiences, values, and beliefs that have shaped their worldviews. How feasible is it then for students to truly develop a diverse counseling posture in the 2 or more years of training? Is there enough time to delve beyond the surface level, to question established worldviews, to adequately address the myriad of emotions that might result, to unlearn what has been learned, and adopt new frames of reference?

It would be a great disservice not only to the public, but the counseling profession to believe that cross-cultural competence and complete self-awareness are obtainable within a defined time period. Most counseling programs, especially those with CACREP accreditation, only require one course in multiculturalism. The insufficient emphasis is blatant. However programs frequently claim that multiculturalism is infused throughout the remaining coursework, thereby preparing students more fully to work with diversity issues. Research provides a contrasting picture by indicating that multicultural counseling courses, workshops, and trainings within counselor training programs and professional development-based conferences do not inadequately prepare counselors to be cross-culturally competent (Holocomb-McCoy & Myers, 1999). One plausible explanation for such findings is that formal educational forums serve primarily as catalysts for awareness and knowledge rather than skill development. Even though the cross-cultural competence tripartite model calls for awareness, knowledge, and skills, counselor training programs seem to place a stronger emphasis on awareness and knowledge throughout the coursework.

Awareness and Knowledge

More specifically, Hulnick's (1977) advice for counselors to be self-aware seems to serve as the infrastructure. Students are quite frequently asked to examine their reasons for becoming counselors. Their exploration of values and beliefs allows for a deeper personal awareness and understanding of the self. Practicum courses and internships challenge students to examine who they are as counselors and how they interact with clients. Each opportunity tends to promote surface-level growth. Yet, professional competence requires an intentional act of personal growth. How then does the counseling profession and in particular its training programs ensure that members are addressing the personal growth needs of their students along with building competence in their knowledge and skills?

Naturally, it would behoove the profession if all members were invested in assuming a robust cross-cultural counseling framework. Despite the ethical responsibility, interest has to be captured first and then maintained. Take a moment to contemplate on conferences and professional development workshops in which attendees have choices about which sessions to attend. Now describe the audience for diversity presentations. What have you noticed? From my experience and the experience of many of my colleagues, individuals who are more apt to attend presentations on diversity seem to represent the minority, whether this is by race or ethnicity, sexual orientation, gender, and other factors of diversity. Thus the presenters are most likely "preaching to the choir." Absenteeism or minimal participation by members of the dominant cultures could invoke frustration, anger, and confusion in members of the nondominant cultures. Rather than being consumed with negativity, these individuals could examine the situation from the dominant members' worldview and advocate for cultural awareness and inclusion.

Cross-cultural significance in terms of inherent value must be effectively communicated. In addition to speaking the rhetoric, counselors' identities and lives must also epitomize a cross-cultural framework. Drawing from key concepts of feminist theory, they need to live by the principles in which they espouse. Perhaps through this type of modeling, more counselors would commit to becoming more culturally knowledgeable, skilled, and immersed. Oftentimes the unknown, incomplete understanding, and fear of loss hinders individuals in being receptive to different ideologies. Thus, the recognition of others embracing their cultural identity and infusing it as an integral aspect of their everyday functioning might help lessen the risk of examining and comprehending one's own cultural identity.

Ridley (2005) proposed in his guiding principles for becoming cross-culturally inclusive that counselors understand their own cultural being. Collins and Pieterse (2007) suggested that counselors understand how they have contributed to their "racial reality" (p. 16) by engaging in out-of-comfort-zone experiences, which help to uncover hidden perspectives. Through the experiential activities, counselors, according to these two authors, will recognize that race influences everything and thus cannot be ignored. Counselors will also obtain a clearer understanding of how realities are formed and that they share commonalities and differences with the realities of others. However, these experiences are meaningless unless counselors commit to becoming more cognizant of their attitudes and behaviors that could impact their rendering of counseling services (Toporek, 2001). Personal experiences need to be understood in order to grow personally. Some suggestions to assist counselors in increasing their self-awareness include:

- Increasing interpersonal and intrapersonal relationships from within one's own culture and outside of one's culture
- Exposing yourself to cross-cultural information for personal/professional development
- Creating counseling space that is inviting to a variety of people
- Becoming intentional with practices that increase the salience of your practice

Counselor educators can be instrumental in the process of self-exploration. Students' sense of cultural identity can be addressed throughout the program beginning with the exploration of wanting to be a counselor. Consider the following hypothetical case example.

Case Example

As an only child, Damian grew up in a loving, Christian home with both parents in an affluent suburban, predominantly Caucasian neighborhood. He believed his family and upbringing were typical. During his undergraduate work, Damian student-taught in a preschool for low-income families. A routine lice check resulted in the dismissal of some of the preschoolers. The next day, one female child who was dismissed returned with a shaved head. Damian couldn't understand the parent's behavior or inability to love the child. This experience compelled Damian to become a counselor because he did not want children to have to endure what he perceived to be unloving and negligent care.

Damian, as many other students, appeared to have a straightforward reason for wanting to be a counselor. He knew his own agenda and reality of family. Yet in counseling, it is not about the counselors' agenda and worldview, but rather those of their clients. How do students begin to learn this concept from divulging their reasons for seeking a career in counseling?

Most often classroom sharing only encompasses the students' reasons, which allows them to maintain surface-level awareness of the reason itself. This approach does not provide students such as Damian with opportunities to synthesize and process their reasons from a more personal stance. What values, beliefs, and life experiences influenced the reason? At what point would students be asked to examine them? How might such examination provide students with the necessary abilities to comprehend their cultural being? These are the types of questions that counselor training programs could strive to introduce, explore, and process so that students are provided with a basis for continued exploration upon graduation. Other points to ponder for this type of activity include the following questions:

- What values, beliefs, and life experiences help to shape your reason for wanting to be a counselor?
- In what ways do these values, beliefs, and life experiences shape who you are?
- How are these values, beliefs, and life experiences reflective of your cultural, racial, and/or ethnic identity?
- How might these values, beliefs, and life experiences enhance your ability to counsel?
- How might these values, beliefs, and life experiences hinder your ability to counsel?
- What are you willing to do to begin growing and/or making changes?

Utilizing a more robust framework will enable counselors and students to become more self-aware of how their "personal identity is cultural identity" (Jones Thomas & Schwarzbaum, 2006, p. 1) or racial and/or ethnic identity as well. Furthermore, recognition of the behaviors they are currently engaging in as well as those they will need to strive for to become more effective and competent will be facilitated.

Students might struggle at first to answer questions that are thought provoking and challenging. They will most likely require time for deeper contemplation. Thus questions ought to be posed early on in the program and continuously processed. In Damian's case, identifying a Caucasian racial identity might be more difficult as this is the case for most Caucasians. He might require more time even beyond his program to truly understand his racial identity. Rather than solely focusing on the racial aspect of his identity, Damian could examine other factors that shape him, such as family, socioeconomic status, geographical location, religion, and sex. He could address how these factors were influential in his decision to become a counselor. Further exploration of his worldviews could help him begin to understand the meaning of being Caucasian in terms of privilege, biases, and values. Perhaps then his cultural identity might be inclusive of his race.

If Damian was of another race or ethnicity, he would still be encouraged to address how his worldviews influenced his decision. His ability to identify a racial or ethnic identity could provide a more complete picture of his decision as well as how he perceives the counseling process. Several scholars (e.g., Brinson & Kottler, 1995; Ivey, D'Andrea, Bradford, & Simek-Morgan, 2007; Sue & Sue, 1990) would agree that Damian's perception of reality and identity are rooted in his experiences as a member of minority status. Although culture is significant, issues presented in counseling are not always rooted in it. Determining when the issue is just the issue and when it is rooted in culture can be difficult and is an acquired skill. Understanding the issue from the client's frame of reference will be of assistance. Counselors must also remain cognizant of being color conscious and strive to assume an opened-minded and flexible counseling approach. Assuming an approach that recognizes individuality within group membership is not only beneficial but crucial. Worldviews do differ among members of the same group (Brinson, 1996) because growth and development are unique to each individual. Thus, cultural identity differs as well.

Although the racial identity models are merely hypotheses on individuals' identity development within their group, it is important that counselors are able to apply the appropriate models to their own cultural identity before assisting their clients through their journey or cultural identity quest. Another key component of exploring placement in the models involves privilege and denial. Understanding the impact of both on development is essential. Counselors will be able to more fully recognize the individuality of the experience as well as the shared group characteristics. Upon this recognition and acquisition of knowledge, counselors will more likely be able to develop a culturally appropriate counseling approach that is void of negative labeling and inaccurate perceptions (Brinson, 1996).

Scholars for cross-cultural counseling (e.g., Hardiman, 1982; Helms, 1984; McIntosh, 1988; Ponterotto, 1988; Sue, 2003) postulated that the privilege of being members of the dominant culture keeps Caucasians from truly seeking their racial or cultural identity. Members of minority cultures are not granted the same luxury. In fact, it may be safe to postulate that in addition to assuming a racial, ethnic, or cultural identity within their group membership, they also must learn the dominant culture to be accepted. Privilege and power are used to maintain distance and reinforce ethnocentric values, beliefs, and lifestyles. Consider how often members of the dominant culture truly become immersed in other cultures. What is their motivation for doing so?

Implicit and Explicit Development of Racism and Prejudice

The pursuit of establishing an awareness and knowledge of cultural identity involves an assessment of how worldviews shape counselors' sense of self, goals, and interpersonal interactions (Ridley, 2005). The evaluation requires counselors to examine how prejudices, stereotypes, and racism are embedded in their worldviews. The ease with which racism and prejudice can be openly discussed rarely exists. The failure to examine one's self, including prejudicial and racist perspectives, could prove to be quite harmful to clients. More specifically, counselors who lack awareness of their own being are more likely to dismiss or lack appreciation for their clients' experiences, which would be unethical (Constantine, Hage, Kindaichi, & Bryant, 2007).

It is of paramount importance that counselors seek to discover their limitations on issues of differences. Personal time must be dedicated to consider if your development has within it a developed sense of superiority, fear, anger, or suspicion of others based on environmental misgivings. Inquiries about racism, prejudices, and stereotypes may usually occur during the multicultural course because it seems the most obvious place to start. Conversations about racism and prejudice outside of "that course" can be perceived as being risky because individuals may react defensively. The multicultural course makes it safer to broach the subject even though the element of risk remains present.

In order to become more culturally inclusive, counselors must be willing to take more risks and are challenged to do so. Addressing issues of racism, prejudice, and stereotypes that are discriminatory and oppressive, and one's own perpetuation of these requires each individual to become accountable and responsible for their actions at every level of society. In the Tony Award-winning Broadway play *Avenue Q* (Oremus, 2003), the musical number "Everyone's a Little Bit Racist" points out that racism exists in all individuals. It brings to light how ethnic and racial jokes, exclusion based on appearance, preconceived and faulty perceptions of others, derogatory terms to describe racial and ethnic groups, and the push for assimilation are all indicative of racist behaviors. This song could be used to broach the subject, facilitate discussions, and enable individuals to examine the purpose and meaning of their defensive attitudes in an environment of safety. As individuals begin to examine these topics, the *Color of Fear* film trilogy (Mun Wah, 1994, 1997, 2006), *Last Chance for Eden* (Mun Wah, 2002, 2003), out-of-comfort-zone experiences, and interviews could lead to more in-depth conversations while challenging individuals to address their discomfort with being prejudicial and racist.

The statement that all individuals are racist has been a source of controversy and debate especially since racism has been predominantly associated with the dominant mainstream culture. How can members of the minority be racist? Perhaps they cannot be if racism is perceived to be solely on race. Sue (2003) posited that only the members of the "White" culture could be racist due to power and privilege. However, racism exists internationally. Take for example, the Okinawans in Japan. Although they might have Japanese physical characteristics, their culture differs from that of mainland Japan and this has been a source of conflicts. Mainland Japan would like to see Okinawa assimilate due to ethnocentric views.

Racism seems to be driven by privilege, power, and control and thus can assume a more global approach. For example, is a heterosexual, Christian, and patriarchic society indicative of racism? Individuals often reply that they are prejudicial not racist. Thus, how is racism differentiated from prejudice? Scholars such as Allport (1979), Ponterotto et al. (2006), and Ridley (2005) have delineated the two concepts in terms of action and thoughts. Racism is action based, whereas prejudice encompasses faulty, misconstrued, or incomplete thoughts and feelings. When prejudices are acted on, the behaviors, actions, and outcomes lead to racism. Jones (1997) was a bit more elaborative, stating that racism could occur on three levels: (a) personally, (b) bureaucratically, and (c) culturally. Personal racism involves asking how one has power and privilege over those who are not considered group members. A heterosexist society often impedes nonmembers from enjoying the same and equal rights. On a bureaucratic level, racism is perpetuated in policies, standards, and regulations. The pervasiveness of the dominant culture in that assimilation is desired is culturally rooted racism. More specifically, comments made about individuals who immigrate to the United States having to accept the American culture because they live here illustrates ethnocentric and thus racist views.

In reviewing the aftermath of September 11, 2001, as well as the most recent campus shooting at my alma mater, Virginia Polytechnic Institute and State University, there are some stark contrasts that need to be noted in order for all of us not to have a sense of amnesia about the culture we live in. While these incidents can shake the core of our humanity, as well as bring us closer together, it ought to be noted that following the Virginia Tech shooting the president of the Republic of South Korea (in what is considered culturally appropriate action) issued a formal apology while requesting compassion toward Koreans and Korean Americans (Jie-Ae, 2007). Following that tragic day on September 11, we called for calm as Arab-looking individuals were targeted for reprisals. Now take a look at events such as the Oklahoma City bombings and the Columbine school shooting. Think for a moment what it would have been like for our president to issue a warning against White males between the ages of 18 and 35? In these race-related events, the concept of White privilege proposed by McIntosh (1988) was displayed. What was the response by those in power in the United States toward domestic terrorism and international terrorism? When we view these incidents, what is our "reactionary" response along race and class lines? Does it mirror the recognition of differences or does the fear of the unknown rule our psyche.

Case Example

Jasmin, an Arab Muslim American, and Natalia, an African American, have known each other since they were in kindergarten. Their parents were close friends. Then the 9/11 attacks occurred and everything changed. The relationship between the families became estranged. Invitations to outings dissipated and the conversations were terse. Natalia's family began to lock their doors while scrutinizing Jasmin's family's purchases and gatherings. It seemed to Natalia and her parents that Arab Muslim families were visiting Jasmin and her family more frequently, which was disconcerting while raising suspicion.

It seems as though, based on the information provided, that Natalia and her family engaged in racist behaviors. They might have held prejudices about Arab Americans, however, an assumption could be made that these were not acted upon due to the friendship before the attacks. Before labeling the scenario as racist or prejudicial, it would be beneficial for counselors to understand the intent behind the actions as well as other factors that might not be evident so that the issues can be adequately addressed and resolved. Failure to do so leads to a narrow focus and thus conclusions (Ridley, 2005).

Counselors need to be attentive to use of color consciousness and blindness, which are racist. The ability to decrease engaging in these behaviors is twofold. Coming to terms with the personal sense of cultural being and group membership, and actively seeking and engaging in cultural experiences that differ from their own culture are required (Arredondo, 1999). Out-of-comfort-zone activities are prime examples of enriching personal experience with diversity. These can occur both within training programs as well as upon graduation. Perhaps counselors will be more likely to continue seeking these experiences if they are encouraged to do so while they are students and are able to truly process the significance of the event. Concerted efforts to seek diversified experiences that extend outside of the personal comfort level need to be made. Aspects to consider when engaging in and processing out-of-comfort-zone experiences include the following:

- How the events were unique or different as a result of the culture of the organizing group
- Describing emotions and responses to being a minority in relation to the specific event
- Examining what was learned about the culture that was experienced
- Ability to interact with members
- Examining what was learned about oneself and how differences are approached (focus on this from intellectual, affective, and behavioral lenses)
- Identifying skills that you would like to either develop or further develop and explore, and how you will work on these skills, and
- Explaining how the identified skills will assist in becoming more cross-culturally competent

These experiences are meant to challenge counselors to examine their own biases while gaining factual information and firsthand accounts in order to become more receptive and responsive to diversity (Brinson, 1996).

Interviewing and exposure to diverse clients in the counseling setting serve as other opportunities for growth. It is not uncommon to hear students, in particular, express their fears of offending individuals when they are required to interact with members belonging to different cultural groups. The significance and impact of the actual experience is often limited by the fear because individuals may become extremely paralyzed as they grapple with what to say next. The privilege of being able to wear blinders might be more apparent as students and counselors begin to recognize how they are inadequately prepared to mingle with a wide variety of individuals.

Prior to participation, students and counselors would benefit immensely by contemplating what they are hoping to obtain through the interactions. Exploring personal perceptions and then evaluating how these were challenged or affirmed is an integral part of the process. Additionally, examining intentions is crucial as is reframing the fear of offending. How might avoidance limit learning as well as the ability to be culturally responsive? What is the possibility that individuals will recognize the desire to learn and thus not be offended, but rather embrace the exchange as a teachable moment? Are counselors willing to be taught?

Take some time to ruminate upon these questions. Students and counselors must remember that remaining surface level and avoiding the elephant in the room in both the interviews and counseling does not lead to the acquisition of robust knowledge or change no matter how much these are willed. Avoiding questions that cause discomfort limits the scope to which counselors are able to examine their interactions from intellectual, behavioral, and emotional lenses. Risks are an inherent part of counseling and counselors will surely benefit from taking some time to promote personal and professional growth as well as cultural sensitivity.

Theoretical Approaches

The counselor's theoretical approach is one component that helps establish a counseling environment that is culturally inviting and sensitive. It can seem daunting to learn several theories within a short amount of time. Having to identify a personal theoretical approach can be quite stressful especially when counseling experiences are limited. The easiest solution is to draw from favorite theories that have already been established. Yet counselors must remain cognizant that the Western-based theories are imperfect in the area of cultural inclusiveness (Ridley, 2005). Whether a personal theoretical orientation is formulated or established theories are used, counselors must ask how their approach is inclusive and exclusive of diversity as to avoid engaging in cultural ambivalence. They must be willing to ask: To what extent is my personal orientation culturally appropriate? Additionally, it is important for counselors to examine the extent to which their theoretical approach has (a) residual effects of their biases, beliefs, and values; (b) an openness to the worldviews and realities of clients; (c) an acceptance of multiple truths; (d) the ability to adapt and be flexible in the process of change; and (e) ways to draw on the diversity of both the counselor and client to help establish the therapeutic relationship (Ivey, D'Andrea, Bradford Ivey, & Simek-Morgan, 2007). From an ethical perspective, counselors ought to recognize how their approaches reflect values that are culture- and class-bound and are mono- or multilingual.

From an inclusive framework, multiculturalism is no longer about race and ethnicity even though these concepts still remain the crux. A more global approach encompasses gender, sexual orientation, age, geography, religion, disabilities and abilities, education, socioeconomic status, health and well-being, and life experiences; all of which will only serve to provide a robust and comprehensive image and understanding of individuals. Thus it would be beneficial to counselors to assume a theoretical approach that recognizes the aforementioned factors.

The multicultural–feminist–social justice theory and the RESPECT-FUL acronym is used to illuminate the following (Ivey et al., 2007, p. 33):

Religious/spiritual identity
Economic class background
Sexual identity
Psychological maturity
Ethnic/racial identity
Chronological/developmental challenges
Traumatic experiences and other threats to one's well-being
Family identity and history
Unique physical characteristics
Location of residence and language differences

Consider integrating Bronfenbrenner's (1989) ecological model with other theories:

- Individual characteristics
  - Sex, gender, cognition, behaviors, genetics/biological factors
- Microsystem
  - Family, friends, works, church, etc.
- Mesosystem
  - Relationships among microsystems
- Exosystem
  - Public policy, politics, etc.
- Macrosystem
  - Gender roles, cultural values, SES, religion, etc.
- Chronosystem
  - Interconnectedness between people and environment

Implementing the approach requires the skills of assessing and diagnosing in a culturally appropriate manner.

Constantine et al. (2007) integrated nine social-justice related guidelines into a cross-cultural framework.

INSTITUTIONAL DISCRIMINATION

Case Example

Sarah, an 18-year-old college freshman of Asian descent, was enrolled in a precalculus course. Math had never been her strong forte and after weeks of struggling to grasp the concepts, Sarah decided to seek assistance from the professor during office hours. The professor answered Sarah's request for help by stating that she should not need any additional help because all Asians excelled in mathematics. Despite her protests, the professor refused to provide further assistance.

Counselors must recognize that the development of one's individual identity is continuously evolving through interactive exchanges with the environment. Additionally, counselors aspire to be advocates for systemic changes within society, politics, government, institutions, communities, and families. The framework encompassing principles of social justice will enhance the counseling mission of promoting mental, social, and emotional well-being. There must be a shift in paradigm to become culturally inclusive.

Questions to ponder: Who are you as a cultural being? What privilege, power, and control do you possess? How are you prejudicial, racist, oppressive, and discriminatory? What are the reasons why? How competent are you when counseling from a culturally inclusive framework? How do you hold yourself responsible for developing a diverse counseling posture? How will you advocate for cross-cultural counseling?

REFERENCES

Allport, G. W. (1979). *The nature of prejudice* (25th anniversary ed.). Reading, MA: Addison-Wesley.

American Counseling Association. (2005). *Code of ethics*. Alexandria, VA: Author.

Arredondo, P. (1999). Multicultural counseling competencies as tools to address oppression and racism. *Journal of Counseling & Development, 77*(1), 102–108.

Brinson, J. A. (1996). Cultural sensitivity for counselors: Our challenge for the twenty-first century. *Journal of Humanistic Education & Development, 34*, 195–206.

Brinson, J. A., & Kottler, J. A. (1995). Minorities' underutilization of counseling centers' mental health services: A case for outreach and consultation. *Journal of Mental Health Counseling, 17*, 371–385.

Collins, N. M., & Pieterse, A. L. (2007). Critical incident analysis based training: An approach for developing active racial/cultural awareness. *Journal of Counseling Development, 85*(1), 14–23.

Constantine, M. G., Hage, S. M., Kindaichi, M. M., & Bryant, R. M. (2007). Social justice and multicultural issues: Implications for the practice and training of counselors and counseling psychologists. *Journal of Counseling & Development, 85*(1), 24–29.

Hardiman, R. (1982). *White identity development: A process oriented model for describing the racial consciousness of White Americans.* Unpublished doctoral dissertation, University of Massachusetts, Amherst.

Helms, J. E. (1984). Toward a theoretical explanation of the effects of race on counseling: A Black and White model. *Counseling Psychologist, 12,* 153–165.

Holocomb-McCoy, C. C., & Myers, J. E. (1999). Multicultural competence and counselor training: A national survey. *Journal of Counseling & Development, 77,* 294–302.

Hulnick, R. (1977). Counselor: Know thyself. *Counselor Education and Supervision, 17,* 69–72.

Ivey, A. E., D'Andrea, M., Bradford Ivey, M., & Simek-Morgan, L. (2007). *Theories of counseling and psychotherapy: A multicultural perspective* (6th ed.). Boston: Allyn & Bacon.

Jie-Ae, S. (2007). South Korea shocked by U.S. shooting link. *CNN.* Retrieved May 8, 2007, from http://www.cnn.com

Jones, J. M. (1997). *Prejudice and racism* (2nd ed.). New York: McGraw-Hill.

Jones Thomas, A., & Schwarzbaum, S. (2006). *Culture & identity: Life stories for counselors and therapists.* Thousand Oaks, CA: Sage.

McIntosh, P. (1988). *White privilege and male privilege: A personal account of coming to see correspondences through work in women's studies* (Working Paper Series No. 189). Wellesley, MA: Wellesley College Center for Research on Women.

Oremus, S. (2003). Everyone's a little bit racist. On *Avenue Q* [CD]. New York: BMG Music.

Mun Wah, L. (Director). (1994). *The color of fear* [Documentary]. (Available from Stirfry Seminars, 2311 8th St., Berkeley, CA 94710, http://www.stirfryseminars.com)

Mun Wah, L. (Director). (1997). *The color of fear 2: Walking each other home* [Documentary]. (Available from Stirfry Seminars, 2311 8th St., Berkeley, CA 94710, http://www.stirfryseminars.com)

Mun Wah, L. (Director). (2002). *Last chance for Eden: Part 1* [Documenary]. (Available from Stirfry Seminars, 2311 8th St., Berkeley, CA 94710, http://www.stirfryseminars.com)

Mun Wah, L. (Director). (2003). *Last chance for Eden: Part 2* [Documenary]. (Available from Stirfry Seminars, 2311 8th St., Berkeley, CA 94710, http://www.stirfryseminars.com)

Mun Wah, L. (Director). (2006). *The color of fear 3* [Documenary]. (Available from Stirfry Seminars, 2311 8th St., Berkeley, CA 94710, http://www.stirfryseminars.com)

Ponterotto, J. G. (1988). Racial consciousness development among White counselor trainees: A stage model. *Journal of Multicultural Counseling and Development, 16,* 146–156.

Ponterotto, J. G., Utsey, S. O., & Pedersen, P. B. (2006). *Preventing prejudice: A guide for counselors, educators, and parents* (2nd ed.). Thousand Oaks, CA: Sage.

Ridley, C. R. (2005). *Overcoming unintentional racism in counseling and therapy: A practitioner's guide to intentional intervention* (2nd ed.). Thousand Oaks, CA: Sage.

Sue, D. W. (2003). *Overcoming our racism: The journey to liberation.* New York: Wiley.

Sue, D. W., Arredondo, P., & McDavis, R. J. (1992). Multicultural counseling competencies and standards: A call to the profession. *Journal of Multicultural Counseling and Development, 20,* 64–88.

Sue, D. W., & Sue, D. R. (1990). *Counseling the culturally different* (2nd ed.). New York: Wiley.

Toporek, R. (2001). Context as a critical dimension of multicultural counseling: Articulating personal, professional, and institutional competence. *Journal of Multicultural Counseling and Development, 29*(1), 64–88.

Wrenn, C. G. (1962). The culturally encapsulated counselor. *Harvard Educational Review, 32,* 444–449.

4

COUNSELING WITH WOMEN

Shunda L. Brown and Kathleen M. May

A book chapter on counseling women has the potential to be harmful to women of color and other women who are marginalized if such a chapter proposes a monocultural perspective. A monocultural perspective would entail the historical feminist perspective that promotes gender to the exclusion of other salient dimensions of a woman's identity, such as race, class, ability, attractiveness, and sexual orientation. Our perspective is an integration of feminism and multiculturalism as the underpinnings of a therapeutic approach for counseling women. While we recognize the tensions in this integration, we propose that such integration promotes social justice.

Feminist therapy has its roots in the predominately White, upper middle-class feminist therapy movement that grew out of political activism in the United States in the 1970s (Comas-Diaz, 1994) and the lived experiences of women in psychology and counseling training programs (Rampage & May, 2001). "Women of color have historically—and justifiably—viewed feminism as ethnocentric and class bound and have challenged the centrality of gender oppression espoused by many Euroamerican feminists" (Morrow, Hawxhurst, Montes de Vegas, Abousleman, & Castaneda, 2006, p. 234). Unfortunately, women of color, lesbian and bisexual women, and women from other marginalized groups were included sporadically and unevenly in the early feminist therapy movement.

Similarly, multicultural counseling perspectives emerged from the social and political unrest of the 1960s and from criticism by multicultural scholars and practitioners regarding the racist underpinnings of traditional therapies. The movement was initially characterized by the importance of racial and ethnic identity and oppression to the exclusion of other salient aspects of identity and their associated oppressions, such as gender and class. Multicultural scholars, like feminists, rejected the biases in traditional therapies with their emphasis on intrapsychic forces as the etiology of problems and their assumptions that all individuals have equal access to power and choice (Atkinson & Hackett, 2004).

Whatever the historical roots of feminist counseling and multicultural counseling, both perspectives now recognize that individuals have multiple identities with implied positionality. However, this commonality does not imply that further integration will be without challenge or controversy.

> A core challenge to this integration is to resolve a multicultural commitment to respect diversity of cultural values while simultaneously holding a feminist value that women's subservience to men is something to be overcome. The complexity of working to empower women when their cultural or religious beliefs dictate certain limits on their behavior is something that needs to be addressed continually to continue the dialogue. (Morrow et al., 2006, p. 234)

An integrative feminist multicultural therapeutic approach holds promise for counseling women and involves a commitment to social justice (Comas-Diaz, 1994; May, 1998; Morrow et al., 2006).

In this chapter, we review the historical context of women in our society and in counseling. Present-day barriers women continue to face and the resulting oppression and discrimination are then explored. We also consider violence against women. Women's identity development is examined. We then propose a feminist multicultural approach for counseling women. In addition, we provide a case example from our work as feminist multicultural advocates for social justice.

HISTORICAL CONTEXT

Patriarchy is a major part of our country's origins and our social world is constructed on a premise of male superiority. Under patriarchy, males tend to be dominant in positions of power and women are subordinate. It is a system that privileges men over women and also men over other men. Patriarchy is about gender order imposed through individual, collective, and institutional behaviors. Gender interacts with other aspects of identity such as ethnicity and social class.

The culture of counseling and therapy does not have a privileged location outside of the culture at large; it is not exempt from the structures and ideologies of the dominant culture. The culture of therapy is not exempt from the politics of gender, race, class, age, ethnicity, and heterosexuality. Awareness of the extent to which the culture of therapy reproduces the dominant culture can assist counselors in their search for a therapeutic posture. The sexist oppression that is the reality for women in our culture has been reproduced in our counseling theories and practices.

Although tremendous progress has been made, gender inequities are built into the very fabric and structures of society. Even the multicultural movement privileged men of color over women of color.

> Historically, the role of women in multicultural counseling has not been explored in great depth in the literature. Therapists have traditionally taken a unidimensional approach to counseling that negates the female experience by failing to see how gender interacts with other identities and oppressive forces such as racism, sexism, class elitism, and homophobia. (Robinson, 2005, p. 252)

We demonstrate the historical place of women in our society, the gains that have been realized, and the progress that has yet to be made through a brief exploration of the suffrage and feminist movements.

Women's Suffrage

Although the women's suffrage movement—the right of women to vote—was a distinct struggle, its catalyst was another social movement of the time. In 1840, female abolitionist activists were delegates to the World's Anti-Slavery Convention in London. However, the male anti-slavery faction of the convention that opposed women's activism was in control (Keyssar, 2000). Female delegates, including Lucretia Mott and Elizabeth Cady Stanton, were relegated to a segregated women's section. This experience prompted Mott, Stanton, and others to take up the cause of women's rights (Frost & Cullen-Dupont, 1992). Eight years later, they held the first women's rights convention in the United States in Seneca Falls, New York.

The richness and complexity of the women's suffrage movement cannot be given justice in this chapter. The suffrage movement was not always unified; the arguments for giving women the right to vote were varied and, at times, in conflict; the methods and strategies for success were debated; and the movement's leaders came from diverse backgrounds and had unique experiences. Most women in the suffrage movement started as activists in the antislavery or temperance movements, and many came from the Quaker philosophy and were from working- to wealthy-class backgrounds. Others were freed slaves or activists working to alleviate poverty. Some leaders formed organizations to advance the cause, whereas others traveled and gave speeches (Keyssar, 2000).

The Seneca Falls Convention was considered the beginning of the women's suffrage movement. The movement came to an end 72 years later on August 26, 1920, when, following ratification by the necessary 36 states, the 19th Amendment to the Constitution was adopted.

Activism did not end with the passage of the 19th Amendment. The Equal Rights Amendment, which would have eliminated discrimination on the basis of gender, was introduced to Congress 3 years later (Keyssar, 2000). It has never been ratified. Women are not equal to men under the Constitution. The women's suffrage movement was in fact the first wave of feminism.

Feminism

In its simplest form, feminism might be defined as an alternative vision for a just world. However, feminism is anything but simple and there is considerable controversy about what feminism is. Feminists and scholars disagree on whether feminism is an historical movement, a political movement, a belief system, or an intellectual movement. Furthermore, feminism has been divided into many camps, such as liberal feminism, Marxist feminism, lesbian feminism, and radical feminism.

Feminism also has been defined in waves. The first wave consisted of the women's suffrage movement. The second wave occurred during the 1960s and 1970s and the struggle was for greater equality for women across all aspects of life. The third wave consists of today's multicultural feminists who define identity as the site of the struggle.

Third-wave feminists grew up with greater expectations of gender equality and freedom from oppression than their first- and second-wave counterparts. They also have a greater awareness and appreciation of diversity. According to Rubin and Nemeroff (2001), third-wave feminists "aim to disrupt, confuse, and celebrate current categories of gender, sexuality, and race" (p. 93). They encourage activism directed toward diverse forms of injustice and they use personal stories to reveal the complexity and contradictions involved in women's lives (Sinacore & Enns, 2005). To this end, third-wave feminists' commitment to advocacy and activism supports the feminist multicultural framework we propose for counseling women. Although there is no systemic unity in what counts as feminism, there is agreement that it encompasses sexist oppression and it considers the role of gender and power in the explanation of injustice:

> Feminism is grounded on the belief that women are oppressed or disadvantaged by comparison with men, and that their oppression is in some way illegitimate or unjustified. Under the umbrella of this general characterization there are, however, many interpretations of women and their oppression, so that it is a mistake to think of feminism as a single philosophical doctrine, or as implying an agreed political program. (James, 2000, p. 576)

As bell hooks argues, we take the position that sexist oppression does exist, but that it does not exist in isolation:

> Feminism, as liberation struggle, must exist apart from and as a part of the larger struggle to eradicate domination in all its forms. We must understand that patriarchal domination shares an ideological foundation with racism and other forms of group oppression, and that there is no hope that it can be eradicated while these systems remain intact. This knowledge should consistently inform the direction of feminist theory and practice. (1989, p. 22)

And Spelman further explains:

> No woman is subject to any form of oppression simply because she is a woman; which forms of oppression she is subject to depend on what "kind" of woman she is. In a world in which a woman might be subject to racism, classism, homophobia, anti-Semitism, if she is not so subject it is because of her race, class, religion, sexual orientation. So it can never be the case that the treatment of a woman has only to do with her gender and nothing to do with her class or race. (1988, pp. 52–53)

For feminism to have any relevance, we believe that a position of intersectionality (Crenshaw, 1991) must be adopted. Each woman has to be seen in context and her multiple identities must be acknowledged. The strategy to isolate sexist oppression would mean that feminism is only for the most privileged woman—the White, wealthy, young, beautiful, able-bodied, heterosexual woman. Such a position supports women with privilege as the oppressors and all other women as the oppressed. As the philosophical underpinnings for feminist counseling and therapy, such a stance would be unconscionable.

BARRIERS FACED BY WOMEN

In a patriarchal system, women are disadvantaged in most aspects of life and their lived experiences are neither valued nor honored. In this section, we examine some of the barriers women face in major life arenas and the resulting oppression from such barriers.

The Gender Pay Gap and Career Choices

Women have made progress toward gaining economic parity since the feminist movement began. However, Lips (2003) conducted an exhaustive review of the research on the gender pay gap and concluded:

> The gap appears within groupings of race/ethnicity and nationality; it is not diminished at higher levels of education; it cannot be explained easily or completely by women's and men's choices with respect to occupation; and *if* it is closing, it is doing so at a glacial pace. *It seems an inescapable conclusion that the gap reflects, in large part, a continuing tendency to undervalue women and the work they do* [italics added]. Even when women predominate in an occupational domain and perform at least as well as men, their work is valued less than men's. (p. 100)

And at the rate of progress attained between 1989 and 2002, women will not achieve wage parity for another 50 years (Urban Institute, 2004). Women who work full time throughout the year earn 76.2% of what men earn (U.S. Department of Labor, 2006). If part-time and part-year workers are included, the ratio would be much lower, as women are more likely than men to work these reduced schedules in order to manage child-rearing and other caregiving work.

Women of color do not fare as well as women from the dominant group in pay and status. Asian American, African American, American Indian, and Hispanic women continue to earn less than their European counterparts and less than ethnic minority men (Worell & Goodheart, 2006). They are less likely to work in professional and managerial jobs than European American women. Lesbians earn less than heterosexual European American women (Yoder, 1999). Therefore, lesbian couples are doubly affected by the gender pay gap.

The disadvantages of women's lower wages follow women into retirement, especially women who live alone or are primary household earners. Lower incomes make it challenging for women to financially support their families. Moreover, this predicament prevents women from accruing assets, such as buying a home and participating in pension programs, which could assist with maintaining financial security when they become older. These financial difficulties may contribute to the decline of women's mental health and could place a strain on personal and professional relationships.

Lips (2003) offers four broad recommendations that fit with our feminist multicultural counseling framework for counseling women and promoting social justice that can be used to impact the gender earnings gap. Her recommendations are: (1) lobbying for comparable-worth legislation; (2) advocating for family-friendly workplace policies; (3) leading efforts to increase the status, pay, and benefits of part-time workers; and (4) educating employers, other stakeholders, and the public about the often unconscious biases that influence the evaluation of women's work.

Sexual Harassment

According to the U.S. Department of Labor (2006), some 50% to 80% of women in the United States experience some form of sexual harassment during their academic or work lives. In nontraditional jobs, the percentage is even higher. Many offenses remain unreported because it is considered taboo to bring the harassment to light in many workplaces. Additionally, many women do not report their victimization because of fear—fear of tainted personal and professional reputations, humiliation, discrimination, and termination from their jobs.

Recent research asserts that minority women are harassed more often than women who are perceived as part of the dominant culture, meaning White and heterosexual. Women who are visible minorities face a double dose of harassment in the workplace, based on sex and ethnicity or perceived sexual orientation. Gender, sexual orientation, and ethnicity are not independent aspects of women's identities and minority women (racial and sexual) face compounded harassment (Berdahl & Moore, 2006). Sexist stereotypes affect all women but racialized sexual harassment intensifies and complicates the experience for women of color.

Other Harassment Challenges

Women of color also experience harassment without blatant sexual overtones in the workplace. African American women, in particular, continue to be stereotyped as "lazy, welfare-dependent, and incompetent" (Jones & Shorter-Gooden, 2003, p. 151). Asian American women are subjected to the "model minority myth," which, despite its "positive" connotations, is harmful. This blatant racism is very damaging financially and psychologically for ethnic minority women as it influences their career paths. Such realities strongly indicate that career development for women of color must be a crucial component of a feminist multicultural therapeutic approach.

Lesbians also experience unique challenges in the work world. It is true that in the last 15 years, major businesses have instituted nondiscrimination policies and/or have extended health policy benefits to the partners of lesbians as have some local governments and other institutions. Yet these laws and policies do not cover all employers. Working for a religious organization, some government agencies, or even school systems can pose high risks for lesbians. Given the negative stereotype of the "lesbian lifestyle" that is promoted by conservative political and religious organizations, being "out" in such work environments may cause a substantial amount of fear and stress.

Multiple Roles

The multiple roles that women perform are, in many ways, another barrier that they face. Many women devote greater levels of responsibility and commitment to some roles outside of their careers than men do and invest differently in roles that men also assume (Tang & Tang, 2001). Some of these roles include engaging in at least two of the following domains: committed relationships (marital or intimate partner), parenting, caregiver relationships, community activities, friendships, and academic endeavors. There is now recognition that although juggling multiple roles can positively influence the mental health of women, there is a greater acknowledgment that these roles also can have negative consequences for women's physical, emotional, spiritual, and mental well-being. How women manage these roles is influenced by their positionality in relationship to the dominant culture, the resources available to them, and their support systems.

Women's relationship status can greatly impact the roles that are most salient to them and the stress that accompanies the performance of these roles. Single mothers, women in heterosexual relationships, and women in committed same-sex relationships face many of the same challenges but they also experience unique concerns.

Single motherhood continues to be a primary cause of women's persistently high poverty rates. Forty-one percent of families headed by single women live in poverty (Kantrowitz & Wingert, 2001). Single mothers who are poor constantly face the struggle to make ends meet, and there is an ever-present fear that they won't. They aren't able to spend sufficient amounts of quality time with their children or simply enjoy life because of this struggle and lack of financial resources. They are disadvantaged by limited employment opportunities and unavailable or unaffordable services such as child care and transportation. Daily they are faced with increased exposure to pestiferous environmental stressors such as violent communities, substandard housing, potential homelessness, and dehumanizing jobs or welfare's malicious cycle. The insecurity and shame of being poor also burden them and all these stressors can contribute to a negative self-image and resulting mental health concerns. However, income does not protect single mothers from all stressors. They are still burdened by society's negative stereotypes of single mothers and women, and, in particular, mothers of any socio-economic background typically place their personal needs last or they simply lack the energy and time necessary to address these issues.

Marriage for women does not necessarily mean protection from oppressive systems; in fact, marriage itself can be oppressive. We examine one aspect of a women's experience in marriage—the work that is done to maintain the home and family. Following a review of the literature consisting of more than 200 scholarly articles and books on household labor, Coltrane (2000) concluded that "most men still do much less housework than women do, with married men creating about as much demand for household labor as they perform" (p. 1208). He found that spouses' employment hours and relative earnings, gender and family ideology, and a host of other factors, such as life stage and ethnicity, influence the division of household labor. What is important in these studies for counseling women is that the research has also consistently found more balanced divisions of household tasks positively impact women's marital satisfaction, their perceptions of fairness, and rates of depression. And as Coltrane stated:

> Because most housework continues to be performed by women, wives, and daughters, and because most women buy out of onerous domestic tasks when they can afford to, we ought not lose sight of the fact that domestic labor allocation is embedded in social arrangements that perpetuate class, race, and gender inequities. (pp. 1225–1226)

Lesbians in committed relationships experience many of the everyday problems in living that heterosexual couples do; however, the sociopolitical climate toward lesbian partnerships is hostile and discriminatory. In most states, same-sex marriages and/or civil unions are not recognized and lesbians are not afforded the rights and benefits that married, heterosexual couples are.

There are unique aspects about women loving each other that influence the way human issues and women's issues are experienced and understood. Lesbian couples tend to build relationships on intimacy, mutuality, equality, and interdependence. This interdependence and intimacy often extends to the lesbian community, if a community is available.

In traditional theories, the very qualities that two women bring to a relationship are pathologized. Many traditional family theoretical approaches are loaded with heterosexual bias: concepts such as boundaries, enmeshment, and fusion exemplify this bias. Therapists and counselors must adopt a therapeutic approach that is affirmative of lesbians' ways of knowing, and that encompasses knowledge and awareness of their unique strengths and challenges (Fassinger, 2000). The real oppression and discrimination that lesbians in committed relationships face must be understood and validated by the therapist. Chapter 10 of this text provides greater detail into the issues surrounding lesbian women.

CULTURAL CONSIDERATIONS

The cultural messages women receive are barriers to their well-being—their emotional, spiritual, and physical health. In this section, we demonstrate how these cultural messages contribute to societal oppression of women.

Sex and Violence

Women are faced with entrenched misogyny, which is partially due to the sexist depictions of women and the exploitative and violent way in which they are represented in the media. Women are portrayed as highly sexualized objects in movies, songs, and videos alike. This proliferation of misogyny is not genre specific and it is widespread across many cultures (hooks, 2000). It is commonplace to drive down the street and hear passers-by blasting music with lyrics that refer to women as bitches and whores. Regardless of a woman's level of self-worth, this blatant form of disrespect could negatively affect any female's psyche.

Women of color struggle with being seen as anything other than a sexualized object. African American and Hispanic women, in particular, are often perceived as being extremely promiscuous and having loose morals. On the other hand, Asian American women are ostracized and seen as "China dolls" or geisha girls. Such blatant stereotypes place ethnic minority women at a disadvantage, which in turn, may lead to self-defeating behavior and internalized oppression.

Standards of Attractiveness

The stereotyped standards of beauty expressed through advertisement and the mass media have had an impact on the health and self-esteem of girls and women. Societal pressure for females to be thin has led to the internalization of an unrealistic body shape as the ideal and has resulted in body dissatisfaction and disordered eating patterns and diet-ing (Stice, Shaw, & Nemeroff, 1998). It is estimated that 35% of women engage in disordered eating.

Cases of eating disorders among diverse racial ethnic groups are often underreported because studies typically do not include ethnically diverse populations. Perhaps, consequently, many people believe that women of color are immune to the pressure to be thin. This lack of awareness is partially due to the assumption that African American and Hispanic cultures are more accepting of diverse body sizes and seem to favor a broader beauty ideal (Dounchis, Hayden, & Wilfley, 2001). Although this tolerance may help protect some ethnic minor-ity females from body dissatisfaction and low self-image, studies sug-gest that as ethnic minority females reach adolescence, they experience social pressure to be thin and express the same type of body dissatisfac-tion and drive for thinness as girls from the dominant culture (Perez & Joiner, 2003)

Affective Disorders

Society continues to be plagued with misconceptions about the nature of women's mental health, and the media provides a forum for the per-petuation of gender bias. Gender bias is manifested in advertisements for psychotropic medications. These advertisements covertly purport that women lack emotional stability more than men and women need psychotropic medications. Alarmingly, physicians have contributed to the stigmatization of women and they prescribe more psychotropic medications to women than men (Travis & Compton, 2001). Approxi-mately 70% of antidepressants are prescribed for women, often with improper diagnosis and monitoring.

Gender bias itself may be a contributing cause of depression among women. In addition, women's depression may result from being socialized to maintain relationships and place the needs of others at the cost of their own. And ethnic minority women are even more vulnerable due to higher rates of exposure to racism, discrimination, violence, poverty, incarcera-tion, and homelessness. These factors can lead to feelings of isolation, weak-ness, and shame—external societal oppression becomes internalized.

Substance Abuse

According to the *National Survey on Drug Use and Health* (Substance Abuse and Mental Health Services Administration, 2005), men are twice as likely as women to be classified with substance dependence. Though alcohol and substance abuse is less prevalent for women, they experience a unique myriad of concerns that are associated with their substance use.

Females are more likely to initiate substance use as a result of experiencing a traumatic life event, which can include the following: lack of economic, professional, and social parity; physical or sexual assault or abuse; childhood trauma; disturbance in the family environment, such as divorce, sudden physical illness; and accidents (Ashley, Marsden, & Brady, 2003). In response to these challenging predicaments, women may self-medicate by indulging in alcohol or by abusing prescription drugs or illicit drugs.

Many cultural factors are associated with substance dependence in females. These cultural variables must be understood if outreach, intervention, education, and treatment services for women are to be effective. These characteristics include but are not limited to age, race/ethnicity, sexual orientation, socioeconomic status, geographical region of residence, perceptions of harm, and drug availability (Substance Abuse and Mental Health Services Administration, 2005).

For example, when considering age as a cultural factor, older women are at greater risk of self-medicating with alcohol and prescriptions drugs than older men as a means to deal with loneliness, feelings of being invisible, financial insecurity, or spousal loss (National Center for Addiction and Substance Abuse at Columbia University, 2006). In addition, older women face age discrimination and are negatively stereotyped more than men; there are limited positive images of older women. As older women age, they are likely to lose their autonomy and are forced to depend on others, mainly their children, for caretaking; thereby causing them to feel as though they are a burden to others.

In addition to these challenges, older women of color may feel heightened psychological distress due to racial discrimination and oppression, which can lead to increased feelings of powerlessness and hopelessness (Curtis-Boles & Jenkins-Monroe, 2000). All of these external conditions can influence the use of substances among older women and can engender stress, loneliness, and depression.

Mental health disorders and substance abuse/addiction oftentimes occur together. Although the disorders have different causes, the presence of one puts an individual at higher risk for developing the other. Scholars posit that co-occurring mental health and substance addiction disorders are correlated with increased risk of depression, suicide, violence, incarceration, and, more emergently, HIV/AIDS and other sexually transmitted diseases (Institute of Medicine, 1999).

Women with mental health and substance abuse/addiction disorders face numerous obstacles when attempting to access treatment.

Few programs are designed to address the needs of women who have co-occurring disorders. Further, in comparison to men, women may have a more difficult time seeking treatment because they face a greater social stigma. Women who abuse substances are perceived as having compromised society's standard for female morality because they are no longer seen as the stabilizing force in the family (Covington, 2002). If they are mothers, viable child care arrangements may not be available if they were to seek treatment.

In addition, the recovery models (i.e., medical model, biopsychosocial model, and cognitive-behavioral model) were normed on men and demonstrate a dearth of relevance to the lived experiences of women, thereby failing to provide effective treatment interventions for women. Moreover, the first step in the Alcoholics Anonymous (AA) Twelve Step Recovery Program is for the alcoholic to acknowledge that she is "powerless over alcohol." Notwithstanding the acknowledged importance of this first step for some individuals, it does not take into consideration that women are marginalized and many already feel powerless in some aspect of their lives. Therefore, women don't need to be humbled; they need to be supported to find their own strength within themselves.

Effective substance abuse prevention and treatment programs for women require an understanding of the factors that contribute to substance use among women and intervention approaches that address women's needs. Treatment programs should provide comprehensive services that entail prenatal and gynecological care, sexual or physical abuse counseling, and career counseling and training (Ashley et al., 2003). Moreover, service providers should be mindful that many women substance abusers, ethnic minority women in particular, have strong family and community relationships and rely on a religious/spiritual community. These communities can provide invaluable support to women while they are in treatment.

VIOLENCE AGAINST WOMEN

"One of the most damaging manifestations of sexism in any society is the physical, sexual, and emotional abuse of women that results from virulent misogynist attitudes intertwined with women's relative powerlessness" (Atkinson & Hackett, 2004, p. 105). Violence against girls and women occurs throughout the lifespan. It directly or indirectly affects the lives of most women. Forms of violence against women include but are not limited to intimate-partner violence, sexual assault, and dating violence. Violence against women, whether physical, emotional, psychological, or sexual, is used to intimidate and control women.

In 2006, 18 million women reported being raped or physically assaulted by a spouse, intimate partner, or date in their lifetime (Tjaden & Thoennes, 2006). Men were the perpetrators in over 90% of these incidents. In 2005, intimate-partner violence made up 43% of all non-fatal cases of violent crime experienced by *women*. An estimated 18% to 30% of women will experience domestic violence during their lifetime.

There is no significant statistical difference in the prevalence of violence in relationships between women of color and women from the dominant culture (Mahoney, Williams, & West, 2001; Tjaden & Thoennes, 2006). However, ethnic minority women are more likely to be portrayed as victims of abuse and intimate-partner violence than White women, contributing to the stereotype that there is more violence among communities of color. Although violence against women is not linked specifically to racial/ethnic factors, it is linked to socioeconomic status. Women living in households with an annual household income of less than $10,000 and whose husbands are unemployed, experience intimate-partner violence at significantly higher rates than women in households with annual incomes of $10,000 or more. Therefore, access to autonomous economic resources, including welfare, plays a pivotal role in abused women's decision making and safety planning.

Most research, 80% to 95%, has focused on violence by men against women, but violence also occurs in same-sex relationships and women can be the perpetrators. Lesbians are subjected to identical levels of abuse as heterosexual women, but their predicament can be more emotionally and mentally distressing because they face additional challenges that are due to their sexuality. For example, an abusive partner can make threats to out the victim to her family, friends, or coworkers as to make the victim comply to her demands, as well as prevent the victim from leaving the relationship. It is also possible that the abuser may change the story and claim that she is the one being abused, which can confuse or tear apart the support network that the victim may have.

Moreover, if the individual's family doesn't acknowledge her lesbian relationship or doesn't even know that she has a same-sex partner, family support may not be an option. Within the work environment, if the woman needs to take time off to tend to mental health issues or physical injuries that result from the abuse, she may find it difficult to do so. Although lesbians who have experienced intimate-partner violence may seek counseling, they are less likely to seek traditional legal, medical, and social services because of homoprejudice, the stigma associated with being a lesbian, and the fear that they will not be perceived as legitimate victims (Mahoney et al., 2001). Predicaments such as these make it difficult for women to admit they are being abused and to seek support to help them end the relationship.

Contrary to primitive myths, women do not freely choose to be victimized. In reality, the socialization of men and women, and the pervasive powerlessness of women in society serve as significant causative factors in violence toward women (Atkinson & Hackett, 2004). The helping profession has made a concerted effort to address the unique challenges of these women. However, we must continue to advocate at the individual, societal, and political levels to ensure that all women live free from violence. Counselors must make certain that women who are survivors of violence have access to the services and programs that will aid in their healing and that their economic status and diverse backgrounds will not hinder their ability to live independently.

WOMEN'S IDENTITY DEVELOPMENT

The new era of multiculturalism has encouraged the profession to embrace the "belief" that many variables contribute to identity formation. An individual should not be defined by any one characteristic; a combination of several factors may be salient to the individual. Some of these elements include race and ethnicity, sexual orientation, gender, and feminism. How individuals define themselves on these factors influences their overall sense of identity. Moreover, it is the cumulative effect of the different characteristics of the self that determines identity.

Historically, research on women's development was portrayed through a European, middle class, male-dominant lens. When scholars began to consider the psychological development of women, they posited that women were not fully developed based on standards established with men (Marcia & Friedman, 1970). Many researchers responded to this criticism and began to redefine the norms of identity for women, thus allowing women to create healthy patterns of identity development on their own terms (Josselson, 1996). However, these identity development theories rarely examined the multiple layers of female identities and instead offered a one-dimensional view of racially and culturally diverse groups.

Womanist identity development was developed out of the exclusion of women of color in the feminist movement and in women's research. Scholars posit that many ethnic minority women are less likely than women of European descent to subscribe to a feminist identity (Boisnier, 2003). Although many women of color may support the principles of the women's movement, they may not ultimately identify with being a feminist because the movement failed to capture and address the unique experiences and issues that were of importance to them. Instead, many ethnic minority women subscribe to a womanist identity, a response to the historic and continued invisibility (and exclusion) of African American women in European American, middle-class feminist movements.

Helms' womanist identity model provides an understanding of how women move from external, societal definitions of womanhood to an internal, personally salient definition of womanhood (Boisnier, 2003). This model draws on Cross' (1971) Black racial identity development model and other identity models for women (Downing & Roush, 1985), and focuses on within-group differences among women in their experiences of womanhood. The womanist identity model is applicable to women across racial and ethnic groups because the emphasis is placed on how a woman comes to value herself as a woman without pressure to conform to society's normed roles of womanhood. Moreover, it does not require that women self-identify as feminists and/or espouse feminist beliefs.

The womanist identity model is comprised of four stages that outline a progression toward "abandoning passive acceptance of external definitions of womanhood to the active synthesis of one's own vision of womanhood" (Carter & Parks, 1996, p. 484). In stage one, pre-encounter, the woman consciously and unconsciously conforms to societal values concerning traditional sex roles and denies that there is prejudice and discrimination against women. She thinks and behaves in ways that devalue women and privilege men. Contact with new experiences that may challenge her initial worldview may result in movement into the second stage, encounter. During this stage, women become more aware of sexism and identify more with womanhood. Women begin to question societal values and beliefs and begin exploring alternative ways to conceptualize the roles of women and men. The third stage, immersion–emersion, has two phases. During the first phase, women idealize other women and actively reject male supremacist definitions of womanhood. During the second phase, women are in search of positive self-affirmation and definitions of womanhood and seek affiliation with other women. In the fourth and final stage, internalization, women integrate a personally defined, positive view of womanhood into their identity and refuse to be constrained by or dependent on external definitions.

Scholars have asserted that the womanist identity development model may be an effective tool in mental health counseling because healthy development is marked by a positive view of womanhood along with personal and ideological flexibility regarding one's role and identity as a woman (Carter & Parks, 1996). Researchers assert that there is a positive correlation between womanist development and self-esteem, perceptions of environmental bias, and gender role expectations. Clearly, as with any other therapeutic goal and conceptualization, this is a value-laden endeavor. Thus, it is essential that therapists be clear about their own motivations for such goals and act according to the best interest of their clients.

A FEMINIST MULTICULTURAL APPROACH TO COUNSELING WOMEN

A feminist multicultural approach to counseling women must include a commitment to social justice. This commitment requires therapists to question the dominant practices in the field from assessment and diagnosis, to the therapeutic relationship, to treatment interventions and techniques.

Assessment and Diagnoses

Feminist multicultural therapists working for social justice do not accept the *Diagnostic and Statistical Manual of Mental Disorders* (DSM-IV; American Psychiatric Association, 1994) as the mental health bible (Morrow et al., 2006). They question the cultural and gender biases contained within the manual and within other traditional diagnostic models. Feminist multicultural counselors and therapists recognize that clients' presenting "symptoms" may be healthy reactions to very unhealthy situations and are careful not to assume intrapsychic causes.

Sinacore-Guinn (1995) proposed a model of diagnoses that is culture and gender sensitive and reduces the possibility that clients will be misdiagnosed or diagnosed inappropriately. Counselors who adopt such a framework are working for social justice for all women. Four broad categories are contained within the model and are used to understand the client's presenting concern: (1) cultural systems and structures, (2) cultural values, (3) gender socialization, and (4) trauma (Sinacore-Guinn, 1995, pp. 21–22).

In Sinacore-Guinn's model, "community structure, family, school, interaction styles, concepts of illness, life stage development, coping patterns, and immigration history" (1995, p. 21) are relevant factors to consider in addressing the client's cultural systems and structures. It is essential that they are explored broadly as part of assessment. The second category in this model requires a thorough understanding of the client's cultural values and five value orientations are used to assist in this process: time, activity, relational orientation, person–nature orientation, and the basic nature of people. The insight into the client's worldview gained by such exploration helps avoid misdiagnosis when the client's concern is best explained by her cultural context. Gender socialization, the third category, involves examining what is considered to be gender-appropriate behavior within the client's culture and the ways nonadherence to gender norms are pathologized. The final category in Sinacore-Guinn's model, trauma, entails consideration of acute forms of trauma, such as sexual abuse and domestic violence, as well as more chronic and insidious forms of trauma, such as racism or ageism.

Conducting an assessment similar to the one recommended by Sinacore-Guinn will aid therapists in avoiding misdiagnoses and lessen the possibility that they are perpetuating oppression or injustice. Such an approach helps ensure that sex stereotyping and sex bias in the diagnosis of psychopathology will be avoided and that intrapsychic causes will not be attributed to problems explained by external factors.

Other important considerations for feminist multicultural therapists are acute awareness of their own biases and a holding of the belief that the client is the expert about her own lived experiences. Questions are framed from a not-knowing position and place the client within the context of her family, community, and culture.

The Therapeutic Relationship

The therapeutic relationship is based on a collaborative approach. The counselor views the client as an expert on her own story and acknowledges that the client is an active partner in the assessment and treatment process. Feminist multicultural counselors do not claim a neutral or objective therapeutic stance; such a posture means leaving the patriarchal system implicit and unchallenged. Feminist multicultural therapists are consciously and deliberately active in presenting their feminist multicultural perspective.

Feminist multicultural therapists work to flatten the hierarchy in the therapeutic relationship and to demystify the counseling process.

> Thus, differing statuses related to privilege and power in the therapy dyad—those related to gender, race/ethnicity, culture, class, sexual orientation, and so on, as well as those related to the therapist-client hierarchy itself—are raised by the therapist in order to provide a context for understanding how dynamics of oppression may operate in the therapy relationship. (Morrow et al., 2006, p. 240)

Feminist multicultural therapists working toward social justice do not replicate the power imbalances found in our society; they actively analyze power dynamics in the therapeutic relationship and in clients' lives.

Treatment Interventions and Techniques

"The personal is political" is very relevant to the feminist multicultural framework that we propose for counseling women. The approach is about transforming the individual, the family, and society—not about helping women adjust to an unjust world. Collaboration between the therapist and client is assumed in this model; activism is required of the therapist and the client. Morrow et al. (2006) described how these two foci of activism can merge into something very powerful. For example, when a therapist from an upper middle-class background and a client from an impoverished background work together to establish safe and affordable child care, the therapist's commitment to social justice is made apparent and the client is "the expert" in the activist work.

This declaration of activism supports a very basic tenet of a feminist multicultural framework for counseling women—empowerment. Empowerment has been defined in many ways from women finding their voice and speaking their truth to "achieving reasonable control over one's destiny, learning to cope constructively with debilitating forces in society, and acquiring the competence to initiate change at the individual and system level" (Pinderhughes, 1995, p. 136). Morrow and Hawxhurst (1998) stress that empowerment involves both analysis and action. They define empowerment as "a process of changing the internal and external conditions of people's lives, in the interest of social equity and justice, through individual and collective analysis and action that has as its catalyst a political analysis" (p. 41).

Consciousness-raising is a critical component in counseling women. Feminist multicultural therapists recognize and make explicit the destructive influences of gendered roles on the expression of women's competence within and outside the family. Sex role analysis and power analysis are two techniques that can assist in consciousness-raising. Both processes involve an educational component that reframes and challenges the client's definition of the problem to include the impact of socialization. Appropriate interventions follow the analysis. Racism, sexism, ageism, and other oppressive practices are acknowledged. Clients are challenged to repossess and develop those aspects of themselves that have been previously ignored because they were not the norms promoted by the dominant culture.

With its emphasis on consciousness-raising and empowerment, it follows that a feminist multicultural perspective would place a high value on group work. Group work has many advantages, including helping to reduce power differentials between the therapist and clients as well as instilling a sense of community. Group members experience the power of universality and have the opportunity to give and and receive support from others. Butler (1985) offered that a group approach to therapy "enables women to (1) validate each other's strengths; (2) develop mutual support systems; (3) break down their isolation from each other; and (4) help each other perceive various possibilities for growth" (p. 36). Morrow et al. (2006) emphasize how groups are microcosms of societal dynamics and provide the opportunity to explore issues of privilege, power, and oppression, with the facilitators modeling open communication and respect.

Ethical Considerations

A major premise of the approach we recommend for counseling women is that the social locations and social identities (e.g., oppressor or oppressed, and race/ethnicity, class, sexual orientation, gender, and age) of therapists and clients contribute substantially to how the therapeutic journey unfolds. These positions must be brought into the therapeutic process. We believe that working toward social justice is both a process and a goal (Toporek & McNally, 2006). The process of attending to the multiple identities of both the therapist and client is social justice intervention in itself; the social action taken as a result of the oppression or discrimination that is uncovered contributes to the goal of a more just society. Ethical practice requires counselors to pay attention to the complexity of women's lives and to the shifting dynamics of the therapeutic relationship. Ongoing reflection is the hallmark of a feminist multicultural approach.

In addition to the guidance offered by our ethical code (American Counseling Association, 2005) and our multicultural competencies (Roysircar, 2003) and advocacy competencies (Lewis, Arnold, Douse, & Toporek, 2005), we recommend that counselors and therapists pay particular attention to feminist perspectives on ethics. These perspectives are delineated in the *Feminist Therapy Code of Ethics* (Feminist Therapy Institute, 2000), Principles Concerning the Counseling and Therapy of Women (American Psychological Association, 1979), and Guidelines for Psychological Practice with Girls and Women (Nutt, Rice, Enns, & Members of the APA Interdivisional Task Force to Develop Guidelines for Counseling/Psychotherapy with Girls and Women, 2003). These perspectives serve as recommendations for counselors and therapists to increase their awareness, knowledge, and skills in providing services to women. They are aspirational in nature and help assure a high level of ethical practice.

A CASE STUDY

Migdalia, "Mindy," was referred by her physician to the mental health clinic. She was experiencing signs of stress, including anxiety, sleeplessness, and headaches. Her physician could find no physical causes for these symptoms and suggested that she consider counseling. Mindy was skeptical that therapy would be helpful but she decided to follow her physician's advice and made an appointment at the local mental health center.

Mindy is a 38-year-old Puerto Rican female who grew up in New York. She is a second-generation Latina woman and has many relatives who have remained in Puerto Rico. Mindy's therapist is Sarah, a White female in her late 40s. Sarah was raised in a predominately White community in the South. Sarah has been with the mental health center for approximately 10 years and she specializes in women's issues.

Mindy works for a nonprofit agency that specializes in environmental concerns. She has been with the company for 5 years and was recently promoted to human resource manager. Though she is very proud of her accomplishments, Mindy finds the position emotionally and physically taxing. She has additional responsibilities and supervises three men and one woman, all of whom are of European descent.

Mindy considers herself bicultural and has learned how to effectively juggle mainstream, dominant values and Latino cultural values. Nevertheless, Mindy is not immune to the pressures she feels to work harder in this role to challenge the negative stereotypes of her ethnic group and to the racist comments she often overhears by her colleagues. She feels isolated on the job because she is the only ethnic minority and feels that her peers fail to acknowledge her as a woman with great intelligence and strengths. Instead, they see her as a Puerto Rican woman who was promoted due to her ethnicity, that is, she is a recipient of affirmative action.

Since assuming this management position, Mindy finds herself working longer hours, which is placing a strain on her familial relationships. Mindy has been married to 40-year-old Miguel for 18 years. Miguel works in construction and is "extremely loving and supportive" of Mindy's professional aspirations. His financial contributions to the family have fluctuated; this fluctuation is attributable to the instability of the construction industry.

Mindy and Miguel have a 16-year-old daughter and 10-year-old son. Mindy has close relationships with her children and they excel in school. Nonetheless, Mindy acknowledged that both children are at critical stages in their development and she feels she needs to devote even more time to them. Most of her extended family migrated to Florida so she does not have an extended support network. Thus, Mindy is feeling isolated both at work and at home. Mindy disclosed that she is a devout Catholic and relies heavily upon a Higher Power for guidance and support. During the initial sessions, Sarah concentrated on building a supportive and collaborative relationship with Mindy. Mindy was encouraged to "tell her story." This telling was punctuated by the therapist pointing out strengths that Mindy demonstrated. Sarah used the womanist identity model to help Mindy reject society's definition of womanhood and to actively integrate a personally defined view of what she feels it means to be a woman. Mindy struggled with the idea of whether what it meant to be a woman is the same thing as what it means to be a Latina woman. To further support Mindy's exploration, Sarah referred Mindy to a Latina professional women's support group. This group work served as an adjunct to individual therapy. Mindy was exposed to the self-definitions of a variety of women and, as importantly, the group openly explored their personal beliefs about gender bias and gender role expectations. Mindy began to discover that she did not want to abandon any of the multiple roles in her life; she wanted to perform each role authentically, while acknowledging and accepting her limitations.

The therapist also devoted time to flattening the therapeutic hierarchy and encouraging Mindy to honor her own voice. For example, Mindy would address Sarah as Mrs. Middleton and Sarah would encourage Mindy to call her Sarah. When this failed, Sarah addressed Mindy as Mrs. Rivera, which invited humor into the room but also contributed to a more equal partnership.

Sarah and Mindy discussed their multiple identities: those that were privileged, those that were marginalized, and how their respective identities coalesced into the power dynamics of their relationship. These conversations helped Mindy to consider the analysis and synthesis of how power plays a role in daily living, as well as how it has contributed to her current personal and professional concerns. Sarah validated Mindy's worries and encouraged Mindy to rediscover and celebrate the parts of her self that she has chosen to keep hidden from her contemporaries (administrators, colleagues, and supervisees). Sarah also helped Mindy to consider her personal expectations to accept primary responsibility for the success of the company/department, maintain the home, avail herself emotionally and physically to her immediate and extended family, and be actively involved and assume a leadership position in her religious community.

Sarah did not pathologize Mindy's need to care for others or assume competing roles. Instead, Sarah helped Mindy to extend this caring and compassion to herself. Sarah's consistent caring for Mindy throughout this process allowed Mindy to discover her own passions and the right to pursue them. Furthermore, Sarah encouraged Mindy to capitalize on her relationship with her Higher Power and validated her religious beliefs as a source of strength rather than a weakness. This work allowed Mindy to renegotiate some of the household responsibilities with her partner and children. Consequently, there was more time to engage in family activities.

Other issues were explored in the same collaborative manner with empowerment as the goal. Mindy began to view herself as someone who demonstrates strength in times of adversity and accepted that many of her concerns were actually externally imposed. She decided to terminate individual therapy while remaining active in her support group and religious community.

CONCLUSION

The voices of all women are not heard within this chapter. What is not included is as crucial to consider as what is included. Gender is one aspect of a woman's multiple identities; its saliency varies from woman to woman. Race/ethnicity, sexual orientation, socioeconomic class, and many other aspects of identity influence a woman's lived experience and the degree of privilege or oppression she experiences.

As coauthors, we share our femaleness. On most other salient aspects of our identities, we differ. Who we are inevitably influenced the writing of this chapter. It is a reflection of the combined lenses through which we view the world. It was a challenge and an opportunity. Our friendship grew and we learned more from each other about being a woman of color and being a woman who lives with White privilege.

We hope to have offered the importance of considering each woman in context and, at the same time, a consideration of the commonalities we may share as women. A feminist multicultural approach for social justice is our recommendation for counseling women.

REFERENCES

American Counseling Association. (2005). *Code of ethics*. Alexandria, VA: Author.

American Psychiatric Association. (1994). *Diagnostic and statistical manual of mental disorders* (4th ed.). Washington, DC: Author.

American Psychological Association. (1979). Principles concerning the counseling and therapy of women. *The Counseling Psychologist, 8,* 21.

Ashley, O., Marsden, M., & Brady, T. (2003). Effectiveness of substance abuse treatment programming for women: A review. *The American Journal of Drug and Alcohol Abuse, 29,* 19–53.

Atkinson, D. R., & Hackett, G. (Eds.). (2004). *Counseling diverse populations* (3rd ed.). Boston: McGraw Hill.

Berdahl, J. L., & Moore, C. (2006). Workplace harassment: Double jeopardy for minority women. *Journal of Applied Psychology, 91,* 426–436.

Boisnier, A. D. (2003). Race and women's identity development: Distinguishing between feminism and womanism among Black and White women. *Sex Roles, 49,* 211–218.

Butler, M. (1985). Guidelines for feminist therapy. In L. B. Rosewater & L. Walker (Eds.), *Handbook of feminist therapy* (pp. 32–38). New York: Springer.

Carter, R. T., & Parks, E. E. (1996). Womanist identity and mental health. *Journal of Counseling and Development, 74,* 484–489.

Coltrane, S. (2000). Research on household labor: Modeling and measuring the social embeddedness of routine family work. *Journal of Marriage and the Family, 62,* 1208–1233.

Comas-Diaz, L. (1994). An integrative approach. In L. Comas-Diaz & B. Greene (Eds.), *Women of color* (pp. 287–318). New York: Guilford.

Covington, S. S. (2002). Helping women recover: Creating gender-responsive treatment. In S. L. Straussner and S. Brown (Eds.), *The handbook of addiction treatment for women: Theory and practice* (pp. 52–72). San Francisco: Jossey-Bass.

Crenshaw, K. (1991). Mapping the margins: Intersectionality, identity politics, and violence against women of color. *Stanford Law Review, 43*(6), 1241–1299.

Cross, W. E. (1971). The Negro-to-Black conversion experience: Toward a psychology of Black liberations. *Black World, 20,* 13–27.

Curtis-Boles, H., & Jenkins-Monroe, V. (2000). Substance abuse in African American women. *Journal of Black Psychology, 26,* 450–469.

Dounchis, J. Z., Hayden, H. A., & Wilfley, D. E. (2001). Obesity, eating disorders, and body image in ethnically diverse children and adolescents. In J. K. Thompson & L. Smolak (Eds.), *Body image, eating disorders, and obesity in children and adolescents: Theory, assessment, treatment, and prevention.* Washington, DC: American Psychological Association.

Downing, N. E., & Roush, K. L. (1985). From passive acceptance to active commitment: A model of feminist identity development for women. *The Counseling Psychologist, 13,* 695–709.

Fassinger, R. E. (2000). Applying counseling theories to lesbian, gay, and bisexual clients: Pitfalls and possibilities. In R. M. Perez, K. A. DeBord, & K. J. Bieschke (Eds.), *Handbook of counseling and psychotherapy with lesbian, gay, and bisexual clients* (pp. 107–131). Washington, DC: American Psychological Association.

Feminist Therapy Institute. (2000). *Feminist therapy code of ethics.* Retrieved June 3, 2006, from http://www.feminist-therapy-institute.org/ethics.htm

Frost, E., & Cullen-Dupont, K. (1992). *Women's suffrage in America: An eyewitness history.* New York: Facts on File.

hooks, b. (1989). *Talking back: Talking feminist, thinking Black.* Boston: South End Press.

hooks, b. (2000). *Feminist theory: From margin to center* (2nd ed.). Boston: South End Press.

Institute of Medicine. (1999). *Broadening the base of treatment for alcohol problems.* Washington, DC: National Academy Press.

James, S. (2000). Feminism in philosophy of mind: The question of personal identity. In M. Fricker & J. Hornsby (Eds.), *The Cambridge companion to feminism in philosophy* (pp. 535–584). Oxford: Oxford University Press.

Jones, C., & Shorter-Gooden, K. (2003). *Shifting: The double lives of Black women in America.* New York: HarperCollins.

Josselson, R. (1996). *Revising herself: The story of women's identity from college to midlife.* New York: Oxford University Press.

Kantrowitz, B., & Wingert, P. (2001, May 28). Unmarried, with children. *Newsweek,* 46–54.

Keyssar, A. (2000). *The right to vote: The contested history of democracy in the United States.* New York: Basic Books.

Lewis, J. A., Arnold, M. S., Douse, R., & Toporek, R. (2005). *ACA's advocacy competencies.* Retrieved September 19, 2006, at http://www.counseling. org/Publications

Lips, H. M. (2003). The gender pay gap: Concrete indicator of women's progress toward equality. *Analyses of Social Science and Public Policy, 3,* 87–109.

Mahoney, P., Williams, L. M., & West, C. M. (2001). Violence against women by intimate relationship partners. In C. M. Renzetti, J. L. Edleson, & R. K. Bergen (Eds.), *Sourcebook on violence against women* (pp. 143–178). Thousand Oaks, CA: Sage.

Marcia, J. E., & Friedman, M. L. (1970). Ego identity status in college women. *Journal of Personality, 38,* 249–263.

May, K. M. (1998). A feminist and multicultural perspective in family therapy. *The Family Journal: Counseling and Therapy for Couples and Families, 6,* 123–124.

Morrow, S. L., & Hawxhurst, D. M. (1998). Feminist therapy: Integrating political analysis in counseling and psychotherapy. *Women and Therapy,* *21*(2), 37–50.

Morrow, S. L., Hawxhurst, D. M., Montes de Vegas, A. Y., Abousleman, T. M., & Castaneda, C. L. (2006). Toward a radical feminist multicultural therapy: Renewing a commitment to activism. In R. L. Toporek, L H. Gerstein, N. A. Fouad, G. Roysircar, & T. Israel (Eds.), *Handbook for social justice in counseling psychology: Leadership, vision, and action* (pp. 231–247). Thousand Oaks, CA: Sage.

National Center on Addiction and Substance Abuse at Columbia University. (2006). *Women under the influence.* Baltimore: Johns Hopkins University Press.

Nutt, R. L., Rice, J. K., Enns, C. Z., & Members of the APA Interdivisional Task Force to Develop Guidelines for Counseling/Psychotherapy with Girls and Women (2003). Appendix: Guidelines for psychological practice with girls and women. In M. Kopala & M. A. Keitel (Eds.), *Handbook of counseling women* (pp. 575–579). Thousand Oaks, CA: Sage.

Perez, M., & Joiner, T. E., Jr. (2003). Body image dissatisfaction and disordered eating in black and white females. *International Journal of Eating Disorders, 33,* 342–350.

Pinderhughes, E. (1995). Empowering diverse populations: Family practice in the 21 century. *Families in Society: The Journal of Contemporary Human Services, 76*(3), 131–140.

Rampage, C., & May, K. M. (2001). An interview with a leading feminist family therapist. In K. M. May (Ed.), *Feminist family therapy.* Alexandria, VA: American Counseling Association.

Robinson, T. L. (2005). *The convergence of race, ethnicity, and gender: Multiple identities in counseling* (2nd ed.). Upper Saddle River, NJ: Pearson Prentice Hall.

Roysircar, G. (Ed.). (2003). *Multicultural counseling competencies: 2003.* Alexandria, VA: Association for Multicultural Counseling and Development.

Rubin, L., & Nemeroff, C. (2001). Feminism's third wave: Surfing to oblivion. *Women and Therapy, 23*(2), 91–104.

Sinacore, A. L., & Enns, C. Z. (2005). Diversity feminisms: Postmodern, women-of-color, antiracist, lesbian, third-wave, and global perspectives. In C. Z. Enns & A. L. Sinacore (Eds.), *Teaching and social justice: Integrating multicultural and feminists theories in the classroom* (pp. 41–68). Washington, DC: American Psychological Association.

Sinacore-Guinn, A. L. (1995). The diagnostic window: Culture- and gender-sensitive diagnosis and training. *Counselor Education and Supervision, 35,* 20–31.

Spelman, E. (1988). *The inessential woman.* Boston: Beacon Press.

Stice, E., Shaw, H., & Nemeroff, C. (1998). Dual pathway model of bulimia nervosa: Longitudinal support for dietary restraint and affect-regulation mechanisms. *Journal of Social and Clinical Psychology, 17,* 129–149.

Substance Abuse and Mental Health Services Administration. (2005). *Summary of Findings from National Survey on Drug Use and Health.* Rockville, MD: Author.

Tang, T. N., & Tang, C. S. (2001). Gender role internalization, multiple roles, and Chinese women's mental health. *Psychology of Women Quarterly, 25,* 181–196.

Tjaden, P., & Thoennes, N. (2006). *Full report of the prevalence, incidence, and consequences of violence against women: Findings from the national violence against women survey.* Washington, DC: National Institute of Justice.

Toporek, R. L., & McNally, C. J. (2006). Social justice training in counseling psychology. In R. L. Toporek, L. H. Gerstein, N. A. Fouad, G. Roysircar, & T. Israel (Eds.), *Handbook for social justice in counseling psychology: Leadership, vision, and action* (pp. 37–43). Thousand Oaks, CA: Sage.

Travis, C. B., & Compton, J. D. (2001). Feminism and health in the decade of behavior. *Psychology of Women Quarterly, 25,* 312–323.

Urban Institute. (2004). *Calculations for the Institute for Women's Policy Research.* Unpublished.

U.S. Department of Labor. (2006, March). Women still underrepresented among highest earners. *Issues in Labor Statistics.* Retrieved July 11, 2006, from http://stats.bls.gov/pub/i/pdf/opbils55.pdf

Worell, J., & Goodheart, C. (2006). *Handbook of girls' and women's psychological health.* Oxford: Oxford University Press.

Yoder, J. D. (1999). *Women and gender: Transforming psychology.* Upper Saddle River, NJ: Pearson Prentice Hall.

5

COUNSELING WITH MEN

Matt Englar-Carlson

Chapters about men do not often appear in books focused on multi-cultural and social justice concerns in counseling. After all, how can a group of people (contextually) who have historically been experienced as oppressors and with substantial privilege be a part of the conversation about multiculturalism and social justice? Over the past 30 years there has been an increased awareness and attention given to men as clients in counseling. This focus has highlighted that there is something unique about being a man (i.e., masculinity) that wholly influences how men experience the world both intrapersonally and interpersonally. Men's socialization into masculine roles contributes to gender identity and ways of thinking, feeling, and behaving, presenting problems, and attitudes and potential fears about counseling. It is the saliency of masculinity for men across all facets of life that has led researchers and counselors alike to question the influence of masculinity upon mental health, well-being, and ultimately counseling itself (Good, Gilbert, & Scher, 1990; Scher, 2001).

One of the greatest shifts in the practice of mental health care has been the increased sensitivity and awareness given to cultural diversity issues, including the influence of gender roles (Sue & Sue, 2007). Among other identity factors, gender is now recognized as salient organizing variable of clients' lives and experiences. Understanding the gendered nature of masculinity is an important cultural competency (Levant & Silverstein, 2005; Liu, 2005; Mellinger & Liu, 2006). Guidelines developed for multicultural counseling competency (American Psychological Association

[APA], 2003) and for practice with girls and women (APA, 2006) offer some direction and considerations in regard to helping counselors work with men. These guidelines and principles highlight the importance of the sociocultural context in tailoring counseling to embrace the diverse identities of clients. A second considerable shift influencing the practice of counseling has been the integration of a social justice approach to counseling. Social justice counseling uses all of the methods of counselors to confront inequality and injustice in society (Mays, 2000). This can include advocating for a client or a social cause, working in the social context in which injustice and a client's problem occurs, and actively working to eliminate social problems such as poverty, multiple forms of prejudice and discrimination, and working to create an equitable and just society (Kiselica & Robinson, 2001; Sloan, 2001). In regard to social justice work with men, component social justice counseling involves blending traditional direct service with an ability to challenge sexist, erroneous, and assumptions about men that exist within greater society, social institutions, and the mental health profession itself (Kiselica & Woodford, 2007). Further, social justice work with men leads counselors to creating consciousness-raising experiences for clients and institutions, advocating for specific populations of boys and men that are neglected and mistreated, and effecting social change.

This chapter focuses on counseling men with an appreciation of cultural and contextual factors that influence men and mental health services. This is a new concept for many books on diversity and will add a clinical focus to the lived experience of men. This chapter will provide an introduction to models of masculinities, address how masculine socialization influences the well-being of men, examine the integration of the new psychology of men research findings into the practice of counseling men, and explore the social justice implications for counseling. Suggestions and observations about ways to create male-sensitive clinical practice are presented.

IS THERE SPACE AT THE MULTICULTURAL TABLE FOR MEN AND MASCULINITY?

Despite the fact that we live in a society that appears to be dominated by men in powerful positions, the reality is that many individual men do not feel empowered in their lives, and large groups of men (e.g., African American boys and young men, teenage fathers, blue-collar males, noncustodial fathers, etc.; Kiselica & Woodford, 2007) are marginalized within greater society. Further, current and historical legacies of multiple forms of oppression affect men and women alike. Painful and often traumatic early experiences of loss and separation overlaid by society's expectations of achievement, strength, and toughness can lead a man to feel conflict, anxiety, and confusion. Because the traditional male role requires men to hide more vulnerable emotions, men often have few socially sanctioned outlets for emotional expression. In comparison to women, men seek psychological help at lower rates (Vessey & Howard, 1993); have higher rates of substance abuse (Kessler et al., 1994); die, on average, close to 7 years younger than women and have higher rates of the 15 leading causes of death (see Courtenay, 2000); are less likely to be diagnosed with anxiety and depression-related disorders (e.g., Sachs-Ericsson & Ciarlo, 2000); and have significantly less healthy lifestyles (Courtenay, 1998). Higher rates of alcoholism and drug addiction, violence, and successful suicide suggest that many men act out rather than verbally share their emotional pain. It is imperative that clinicians who work with men in therapeutic settings understand the "new psychology of men" conceptualizations and research that account for internal emotional dynamics as well as cultural gender role socialization (Levant & Pollack, 1995).

Some may argue that all of psychology is the psychology of men. After all, most writers and researchers about counseling, until more recently, were men. Males have traditionally been viewed as representative of humanity; thus, males and their characteristics have been the object of most psychological research (Levant, 1990). Further, ideas and theories of counseling were created from a Western male view of the world, despite the fact that the majority of clients were, and continue to be, female. In general, knowledge about counseling appeared to be structured from a male perspective about treating women. However, a gender-specific approach to understanding human behavior was proposed by feminist scholars in the 1970s as a way to study women's psychological development. The resulting influence from the feminist movement was the understanding that women needed to be understood within the context of role restrictions and clinically treated with gender-appropriate models that understood, considered, and adapted to the experience of women. One outcome of the women's movement within counseling was the creation of specific therapies and treatments that acknowledged the experience of women and outlined treatment tailored to a woman's way of experiencing the world (Brown, 1986; Enns, 1997). Building on these advances in conceptualizing both gender and counseling, men's studies researchers in the 1980s also began to use a gender-specific approach to look at masculinity as a complex and multilayered construct. The feminist movement, when paired with the multicultural counseling movement within psychology, has led to the acknowledgment in current clinical practice that cultural identity and memberships not only matter but are considered an integral aspect of ethical and effective clinical practice.

Given the enormous changes in the empowering roles of women in North American society, traditional male behaviors can no longer be accepted as a normative standard. When studied from more sophisticated psychological and sociological approaches, male behavior seems to be guided by socially constructed rules that encourage men to take charge in their relationships, at work, and in their roles as fathers and husbands. At the same time, situations that call for cooperation, interdependence, or just "being" can create internal conflict for men. The crossfire of interpersonal and intrapersonal demands that require response flexibility may result in frustration and confusion in many men who have been shaped by traditional cultural expectations of how a man is supposed to act.

For many years an obvious, but historically overlooked, aspect of counseling men was the fact that male clients were first and foremost men. Male clients often present a unique challenge to the counselor. Men are often socialized to fear core components of the therapeutic process: the language of feelings, the disclosure of vulnerability, and the admission of dependency needs. Male clients' discomfort with the developing intimacy of a counseling relationship can manifest as early termination, anger at the counselor, unproductive intellectualizing, and other forms of resistance. The development of the scholarly discipline of the new psychology of men has drawn needed attention to the notion that being a man *matters* to the extent that masculinity is a focal organizing principle for all aspects of a man's life (see Brooks & Good, 2001; Englar-Carlson & Stevens, 2006; Levant & Pollack, 1995; Pollack & Levant, 1998). Masculinity, therefore, can be an influential contributor to why (or why not) a man is in counseling and how counseling is ultimately enacted.

For men, this concerted appreciation of masculinity in terms of mental health and well-being could not come at a better time. There have been vast changes in societal expectations for men. Scholars have documented changing gender roles for men (Bernard, 1981; Cabrera, Tamis-LeMonda, Bradley, Hofferth, & Lamb, 2000; Kilmartin, 2007), often highlighting the difficulties that men have experienced when their own gender role appears "outdated" or out of line with current connotations of recent variations of masculinity. Many (Clare, 2000; Kupers, 1993; Levant, 1997; Levant & Kopecky, 1996) have offered the observation that masculinity is in crisis and in need of "redefinition," "revisioning," or "reconstruction."

WHAT DOES IT MEAN TO BE A MAN?

The question "What does it mean to be a man?" has no answer that applies to all men in all contexts. Most scholars in this area adopt a social learning paradigm to understand masculinity (Addis & Cohane, 2005). This paradigm is based on the assumption that men learn gendered attitudes and behaviors from social environments where cultural values, norms, and ideologies about what it means to be a man are reinforced and modeled. At any given time in our society, there are many forms of masculinity. Masculinity varies between and within cultures (Doss & Hopkins, 1998). It is important to recognize the wide variation within male cultures when multiple identities are considered (Smiler, 2004). It is now common to use the term *masculinities* rather than *masculinity* to reflect the various conceptions of male gender roles that may exist by sexual orientation and geographic regions (Blazina, 1997); among different racial, ethnic, religious, age, and socioeconomic groups (Gibbons, Hamby, & Dennis, 1997); and across developmental periods (Kimmel & Messner, 2004; O'Neil & Egan, 1992). Masculinities accounts for the differing definitions and variations of masculinity that exist among men between and within various cultures (i.e., rural, working-class adult White masculinities may take a different form than urban teenage Mexican American masculinities, etc.).

The idea of a social construction of masculinity suggests that masculinity is malleable depending on the dominant social forces in a society during a certain era. Despite the emphasis on the conceptualizing of multiple masculinities, there is a widespread belief that certain forms of masculinities are more socially central and associated with authority and social power (Connell & Messerschmidt, 2005). In the United States, depending on the era, the dominant ideal of masculinity has moved from an upper-class aristocratic image to a more rugged and self-sufficient ideal (Kimmel, 2005). Thus traditional masculinity can be viewed as the dominant form of masculinity (referred to as hegemonic masculinity) and thus highly influential of what members of a culture take to be normative (e.g., White, middle-class, heterosexual definitions of masculinity in the United States). Connell (1990) defined *hegemonic masculinity* as the "culturally idealized form of masculine character," (p. 83) that emphasizes "the connecting of masculinity to toughness and competitiveness," as well as "the subordination of women" and "marginalization of gay men" (p. 94). One of the benchmarks in masculinity ideology theorizing, Brannon's (1976) *blueprint for man-hood* outlined four guidelines for men within the United States. These guidelines describe how a man should act. These four guidelines suggest that men are socialized to avoid appearing feminine ("no sissy stuff"), to gain status and respect ("the big wheel"), to appear invulnerable ("the sturdy oak"), and to seek violence and adventure ("give 'em hell"). These guidelines represent the socially determined gender role stereotypes (i.e., what a "man" should do) that many men take as their notion of appropriate male behavior and expectations. This socialization supports characteristics such as restriction and suppression of emotions and the valuing of rationality; emphasis on independence and achievement; and avoidance of characteristics associated with femininity (Mahalik, Good, & Englar-Carlson, 2003). These guidelines support both adaptive and maladaptive behavior, cognitions, and affect in men.

Men learn about gender role expectations from parents, peers, media, and through numerous developmental shaping experiences in which one is called to enact expected gender role norms. For example, most young boys get the social message that "big boys don't cry," and learn that crying is an unacceptable avenue of expression. The other part of this message is that "only girls cry," and so boys learn clear distinctions of gender appropriate behavior of separating boys/men from girls/women and gays (Good, Thomson, & Brathwaite, 2005). Specially related to men, activating experiences can include injuring oneself, experiencing pain, crying, and then receiving punitive responses from others for one's tears. Crying and expressing other sensitive emotions becomes an indication of weakness and vulnerability associated with femininity or homosexuality. Men learn that others view repressing and masking emotionality as a sign of strength.

STILL LOOKING FOR A CONSTRUCT OF MASCULINITIES

Whereas the blueprint for manhood is a useful tool for conceptualizing masculinity, a common mistake in understanding men and masculinities is belief that the answer to the question "What does it mean to be a man?" can simply be found by naming hegemonic notions of male gender roles and norms. In many ways, past research about masculinity in the United States has created this illusion by discussing men's experiences in general terms as if all men have similar reactions to dominant male paradigms (Casas, Wagenheim, Banchero, & Mendoza-Romero, 1994; Levant & Pollack, 1995; Liu, 2005; Moore & Gillette, 1991). Liu (2002a) suggested that even though the literature on men and masculinity has grown, the understanding of masculinity among men of color has remained limited. In particular, it seems unclear how men of color navigate expectations of hegemonic masculinity. However, recent conceptualizations of masculinities have explored culturally contextualized notions and experiences of manhood.

The social construction of masculinity suggests that the subscription to a dominant ideal of masculinity is not linear or without resistance. Most men are socialized to adopt certain masculine ideals, behaviors, and attitudes. Yet this dominant ideology of masculinity often has inherent conflicts. For example, dominant masculinity was historically predicated on the exclusion of men who were not White, upper class, able-bodied, and privileged (i.e., normative masculinity; Liu, 2005). Historically, men representing any other diversity were considered marginal figures and not used to define normative masculinity. Therefore, men often find themselves negotiating between dominant masculine ideals that inherently exclude them, or not subscribing to these dominant ideals and thus being marginalized. Yet marginalized men also create their own communities where they develop their own cultural standards, norms, and values that create an alternative against dominant masculinity. For instance, in racial, ethnic, or gay communities, men may develop forms of resistance in action and attitude that challenge the expectations of dominant masculinity. Dominant masculinity is also not immune to the influences of masculine subcultures. Music, dress, and other aspects of marginalized men are often incorporated into dominant masculinity. Thus the social construction of masculinity evolves through a cycle in which dominant masculinity marginalizes and excludes some men, yet then adopts attractive aspects of marginalized subgroups.

Masculinities and Race

Although many men try to maintain a colorblind perspective, America is still racially and culturally divided. It is often difficult for White men to comprehend the subtle harassment that men of color experience on a daily basis. For many men of color who grow up outside mainstream European American, heterosexual, middle-class culture, they are reminded by their experiences of prejudice and oppression on a personal and institutional level that although they are men, they are less privileged and more vulnerable to forces outside of their control (Caldwell & White, 2001). Questionable stares, increased scrutiny, and automatic suspicion by peers, strangers, and police are regular occurrences for these men who work and live in the mainstream culture (Majors & Billson, 1992). Not only are they subjected to the stresses of traditional masculinity, they must also cope with the overlay of subtle and not so subtle racism. A layer of anger related to this cultural predicament is common in many men of color, even those who are trying to live by the rules of mainstream society (Franklin, 1998).

Men of African, Latino, and Asian descent face unique challenges because of racial stereotypes that hardly reflect the realities of most men. Franklin (1999) outlined that understanding African American men requires an appreciation for the influence of racism that persistently marginalizes the status of African American men. He detailed the *invisibility syndrome* as a conceptual model for understanding the inner evaluative processes and adaptive behavior of African Americans in managing experiences of racism. Invisibility is considered a psychological experience wherein the person feels that his personal identity and ability is undermined by racism in a myriad of interpersonal circumstances.

For African American men, the encountering of repeated racial slights can create a feeling of being not seen as a person of worth. This is further reinforced by negative stereotypes of African American men as aggressive, violent, and nihilistic (Johnson, 2006). However, studies of masculinity among African American men do not support these harmful stereotypes nor do they support the idea African American men endorse the same notions of masculinity as White men (Hunter & Davis, 1992, 1994). Hunter and Davis (1992) identified four domains of African American manhood as self-determinism and accountability, family, pride, and spirituality and humanism. Hammond and Mattis (2005) studied the meaning of manhood among African American men and found that being responsible and accountable for one's actions, thoughts, and behaviors was the most endorsed notion of masculinity.

Mexican American men have been traditionally socialized to be the authority or dominant figure in the family (Baruth & Manning, 1999; Paniagua, 2005) with accompanying expectations that Mexican American men are strong, dominant, and the provider for the family (Sue & Sue, 2007). Pleck et al. (1993), however, did not find that being Latino led to an endorsement of traditional masculinity. In terms of Asian American men, Liu (2002a) found that Asian men endorsed traditional masculine ideology, and that some traditional Asian values (such as emotional expression and success for familial recognition) were related to dominant masculine values (Liu & Iwamoto, 2006). Further, Asian American men cope with racist and external pressure against their masculinity (Abreau, Ramirez, Kim, & Haddy, 2003), hegemonic gendered expectations (Chen, 1999; Liu, 2002a, 2005), and traditional male Asian cultural expectations (avoidance of shame, collectivism, conformity to norms, deference to authority, emotional self-control, family recognition through achievement, filial piety, humility, and hierarchical relationships; Kim, Atkinson, & Umemoto, 2001; Kim, Atkinson, & Yang, 1999).

Despite the wide variance of masculine identities within ethnic groups, limited experiences and exposure often leaves more privileged members of society with only a superficial understanding of these groups' worldviews. Counselors are encouraged to not only study the macrolevel of cultures other than their own, but also attend to the many variations that occur within groups (Arredondo et al., 1996; Doss & Hopkins, 1998). When considering how to counsel men from racial groups other than their own, counselors need to pay attention to how masculinity intersects with an individual's cultural, familial, and unique psychological makeup.

Other Masculine Identities

While not as obvious as skin color, there are varieties of cultural identity as well that leave men vulnerable to feelings of alienation. Men who are unemployed or who work in the blue-collar work sector may feel alienated from those in white-collar jobs. Liu (2002b) discussed the social class dimensions of the masculine experience and noted how admonitions to compete and achieve economic success may be particularly salient for men of certain social classes. In particular, Liu suggested that normative masculinity inherently contains class variables such as status ideals and expectations. Hegemonic masculinity refers to being in control, being a self-made man, and being the "breadwinner" or "good provider," all of which relate to social class and status.

In many places in America, many gay and bisexual men are fearful of expressing aspects of their sexual orientation in the presence of their straight counterparts. The abuse that many gay men suffer at the hands of heterosexual boys and men, in early life and beyond, is well documented. The common fear of heterosexual men, or heterophobia, may manifest as avoidance of situations in which heterosexual men are present; stress responses when obliged to interact with heterosexual males, especially in groups; and self-devaluation and shame. Additionally, heterophobia may be expressed as a gay man's wholesale devaluation of heterosexual men and heterosexuality in general (Haldeman, 2001, 2006). Jews, Muslims, Christians, and men from other religious backgrounds also feel ambivalence about how public they should be in acknowledging their religious identities. Men with physical and psychological disabilities can be subject to unwanted scrutiny and judgment from other men. Counselors should be sensitive to the predicaments of men who do not fit the middle-class, Caucasian, heterosexist norms.

For counselors working with all men, it is crucial to note that existing models of masculinity do not always account for all men in terms of who they are and how they behave. Traditional and rigid models do not speak to or necessarily account for invisible populations and groups of men. For example, transgender men may not associate any aspects of masculine ideology with their identity. Furthermore, remaining myopically fixed upon traditional notions of masculinity can lead to overlooking the emotionally strong and available, involved and connected, compassion and nurturing man that exists, but is often ignored and marginalized not only among groups of men, but within society as a whole.

A STRENGTHS-BASED UNDERSTANDING ABOUT DEVELOPMENTAL MODELS OF MEN AND MASCULINITY

The past 30 years have provided a wealth of scholarly activity in regard to men and masculinity. This movement referred to as the "new psychology of men" has dominated much of the scholarly literature pertaining to the psychology of boys, men, and masculinity. According to Levant and Pollack (1995), the new psychology of men provides "a framework for a psychological approach to men and masculinity that questions traditional norms for the male role, such as the emphases on competition, status, toughness, and emotional stoicism," and "views certain male problems (such as aggression and violence, homophobia, misogyny, detached fathering, and neglect of health) as unfortunate but predictable results of the male socialization process" (p. 1). These scholarly contributions have provided an acute lens to understand the social construction of masculinity and the accompanying constrictions imposed by traditional images of masculinity; examined variations in how men from different ethnic and racial backgrounds and sexual orientations define masculinity; empirically researched the help-seeking behaviors of men and the relative reluctance to utilize mental health services; and provided an increased awareness of men's sexism and homophobia and the gender-related problems of boys and men.

This line of scholarly inquiry has clearly raised the level of awareness of mental health professionals about the needs of men, yet in many ways it may also have presented men and masculinity in more restrictive and binding ways by being overly focused on deficits and the darker side of men and masculinity. When the topic of men and mental health is brought in the popular press or in professional forums, it is often focused on the bad things that men do, or about how the male socialization process scars boys and men for life, leaving them chronically flawed and in dire need of fixing (Kiselica, 2006). Kiselica noted that much of the recent scholarly literature about men has overemphasized what is wrong with men and masculinity by focusing on male pathology at the expense of important data highlighting male strengths and the good things that men do. Over time, this focus on male deficits has fostered inaccurate generalizations about boys and men that are linked to potentially harmful practices by counselors working with male clients. A deficit perspective fosters the mindset that men are flawed, need to be fixed, and that they are solely at fault for the problems that bring them to counseling. For example, there is a tendency for mental health professionals to view males as being hypoemotional, even though the existing data on gender differences in emotion challenge the notion that men and women are emotionally different (Wester, Vogel, Pressly, & Heesacker, 2002). Heesacker et al. (1999) found that mental health professionals with hypoemotional stereotypes about men are more likely to blame men for the problems they bring to couples counseling. It is rarely stated that most men are reasonably well-adjusted human beings; that most men recognize, experience, and express emotions within the normal range; and that men have long traditions of acting in a prosocial manner (Kiselica, 2006). To more accurately meet the needs of men, counselors must develop a more complex and rich understanding about the emotional lives, psychological development, and behaviors of all men.

As a way of learning about the healthy aspects of men and masculinity and to incorporate a strength-based framework into counseling, Kiselica, Englar-Carlson, and Fisher (2006) proposed a way of understanding men grounded in positive psychology that added a recognition of strengths and virtue over disease, weakness, and damage. In line with positive psychology, this perspective focused on building in men what is right rather than fixing what is wrong (Seligman & Csikszentmihalyi, 2000). This model extended the work of Levant (1995), who observed that there are several attributes of traditional masculinity that are still valuable (e.g., willingness to set aside his own needs for the sake of his family; ability to withstand hardship and pain to protect others; expressing love by doing things for others; his loyalty, dedication, and commitment; abilities to solve problems; think logically; rely on himself; take risks; stay calm in the face of danger; and assert himself). Kiselica et al. (2006) suggested that counselors include a perspective on understanding men that accentuates healthy behaviors and traditions of men. Though not exhaustive, this perspective would include focusing and exploring male relational styles; generative fatherhood and ways fathers contribute to their children's development in beneficial ways; male ways of caring; male self-reliance; the worker/provider tradition of husbands and fathers; male daring, courage, and risk-taking; the group orientation of boys and men; and the humanitarian service of fraternal organizations.

It is important to acknowledge that many of the qualities and traits associated with traditional masculinity (e.g., courage, bravery, risk taking and daring, self-reliance, personal sacrifice, and protectiveness) are only useful and positive if men apply them under the right conditions and situations, and without uniformity. In that sense, the degree to which these aspects are healthy and optimal depends on the ability of a man to exercise good judgment in knowing when and how to express them (e.g., too much self-reliance can limit a man's ability to ask for help, an overemphasis on risk taking can lead to dangerous and fatal accidents, etc.). One of the difficulties with a purely strengths-based approach is that it can exclusively focus on the fostering of well-being and resiliency at the expense of delineating how to address dysfunction. This is where counselors can intervene to help men. The challenge is developing ways of working with men that identifies and builds upon male strengths while treating dysfunctional aspects of masculinity.

CLINICAL CONCERNS AND PRESENTING PROBLEMS

The wealth of scholarly research and writing in the psychology of men has demonstrated an interesting paradox. Even though most of the theoretical work in counseling, psychology, and psychotherapy is predicated on the lived experiences of men's lives, men themselves may not fully benefit from existing and accepted models of clinical treatment (Liu, 2005). Many men face unique psychosocial and interpersonal challenges associated with masculine socialization experiences and changing cultural expectations of both male behavior and the roles of men (Brooks & Good, 2001). For example, some fathers report social pressure to be the family breadwinner (Doucet, 2004), while at the same increasingly being expected to assume greater interpersonal involvement as fathers, partners, and coworkers in ways that are often not encouraged through traditional masculine socialization experiences (Cabrera et al., 2000; Good & Sherrod, 2001; Levant & Pollack, 1995; Pleck, 1997; Real, 2002). Many men do suffer from depression and anxiety-related disorders, but often it is manifested in the forms of addiction, violence, interpersonal conflict, and general irritability. Though many men experience concerns or difficulties that could be addressed in counseling, many men may also have difficulties seeking assistance. Mahalik et al. (2003) identified that the lack of fit between conceptualizations of masculinity and the popular perception of counseling and mental health services as a likely reason for the lack of mental health utilization by men. Many of the tasks associated with help-seeking, such as relying on others, admitting that one needs help, or recognizing and labeling an emotional problem, are at odds with hegemonic notions of masculinity. For many men, their own psychic pain may not be obvious, and thus when men do come for counseling, many male clients are not sure how to behave, confused about how to enter into a relationship with a counselor (or if they really want or need to), and question how counseling can really make a difference in their life (Englar-Carlson & Stevens, 2006).

It is also possible that counselors themselves hold beliefs about men that restrict their ability to fully benefit from counseling. Within the mental health profession, many see men as reluctant visitors to counseling, coerced by family or legal pressures to attend, and conclude that some men are not good candidates for counseling. Developing therapeutic relationships with male clients can also be perceived as more difficult than with female clients (Vogel, Epting, & Wester, 2003). Counselors can take proactive steps to overcome any potential discrepancy between the male client and the process and potential benefits of counseling.

To the extent that counselors hold biased views of men that label them as "perpetrators," "resistant," or "difficult," the process of developing empathy for men's struggles will be inhibited and the likelihood of forming effective therapeutic alliances will be diminished. Both male and female counselors should have an awareness of the ways in which their own countertransference issues with men might influence their behavior in session (Hayes & Gelso, 2001; Scher, 2001). These reactions may take the more obvious form of negative stereotypes resulting from past experiences with men. They can also take the form of blind spots based on shared assumptions that reinforce traditional masculine expectations, such as emotional restrictiveness. Counselors viewing emotional awareness and expression as gender inappropriate for men are unlikely to successfully assist men in exploring and developing connections to their emotional selves. Counselors should be willing to examine their assumptions about men and masculinity in order to prevent shaming men in ways that prevent them from opening up, being vulnerable, examining their views on what it means to be a man, or making desired changes to improve their lives (Robertson & Fitzgerald, 1990; Scher, 2001). Hence, an important step in working with men involves taking the time to learn about male culture in general and about the specific worldview of individual male clients in particular.

Using Sue, Arredondo, and McDavis' (1992) framework for multicultural competency, counselors can work to understand their own biases, develop an understanding of their client's worldview, and create culturally congruent clinical interventions to develop an awareness of their own biases and worldview so they may more effectively work with male clients from similar and diverse cultural backgrounds. Within each of these three domains, counselors need to cultivate the necessary *awareness* (i.e., interpersonal sensitivity), *knowledge* (i.e., facts), and *skills* (i.e., proficiencies). Using this framework, Liu (2005) outlined different cultural competencies when working with men. In terms of awareness, an important step is being able to identify and work through one's negative assumptions, stereotypes, and value conflicts pertaining to counseling men that might result in inability to understand and empathize with them. For example, a knowledge component in developing culturally congruent interventions might be learning male-centered treatment methods (Brooks, 1998; Rabinowitz & Cochran, 2002), whereas an awareness component in understanding a man's worldview may be to understand how shame and saving face influence an Asian American man's expression of emotions or help-seeking behavior (Liu, 2002a; Liu & Chang, 2007; Park, 2006; Sue, 2001; Zane & Yeh, 2002). As a bridge to developing competency in the necessary awareness, knowledge, and skills of culturally congruent ways of counseling men, the remaining parts of this section will review some of the common concerns men are likely to present in the therapeutic environment, and review the special skills and treatment modalities most effective in making progress with male clients.

Psychological Help-Seeking

Men are less likely than women to seek help for both mental health and physical health concerns (Addis & Mahalik, 2003; Möller-Leimkuehler, 2002; Sandman, Simantov, & An, 2000). Reports consistently indicate that men seek professional help less frequently than women regardless of age (Husaini, Moore, & Cain, 1994), nationality (D'Arcy & Schmitz, 1979), and ethnic and racial backgrounds (e.g., Neighbors & Howard, 1987). Men's relative reluctance to seek professional help stands in stark contrast to the range and severity of the problems affecting them. For example, it is estimated that over 6 million men in the United States suffer from depression every year (National Institute of Mental Health [NIMH], 2003). In terms of physical health, men are more likely than women to have gone at least 2 years since seeing a physician, even though men die, on average, close to 6 years earlier than do women, and have higher rates for 14 of the leading 15 causes of death (Arias,

Anderson, Kung, Murphy, & Kochanek, 2003); have higher levels of stress and higher rates of completed suicides (4 times more; Levant & Pollack, 1995), and suffer from higher rates of heart disease, lung cancer, chronic obstructive pulmonary disease, suicide, and alcoholism than do women (Anderson, Kochanek, & Murphey, 1997; Courtenay, 2000). Health care studies report that men fail to get routine checkups, preventive care and health counseling, and often ignore symptoms or delay getting medical attention when in need (Commonwealth Fund, 1998; Guspers Van Wuk, Kolk, Van Den Bosch, & Van Den Hoogen, 1992; Neighbors & Howard, 1987; Sandman et al., 2000).

Men with more traditional conceptions of masculinity also hold more negative attitudes toward their use of both mental health (Addis & Mahalik, 2003; Good & Wood, 1995; Robertson & Fitzgerald, 1992) and career-related services (Rochlen & O'Brien, 2002). When looking at cultural variables, African American men have been found to be less receptive toward help-seeking than European American men (Neighbors, Musick, & Williams, 1998), men from a working class or lower income are less likely to seek psychological help than middle- to upper-class men (Hodgetts & Chamberlain, 2002), and an increased resistance to seeking help has been found in Asian immigrant (Shin, 2002) and Asian American men (Solberg, Ritsma, Davis, & Tata, 1994).

One way for counselors to understand men's help-seeking behavior and beliefs is to consider help-seeking within the context of masculine gender role socialization. Internalized gender roles may create barriers to help-seeking for men, particularly if help-seeking involves violating important masculine gender roles. Many of the tasks associated with help-seeking, such as relying on others, admitting that one needs help, or recognizing and labeling an emotional problem, are at odds with hegemonic notions of masculinity (i.e., the importance of self-reliance, physical toughness, and emotional control; Brannon, 1976; Good, Dell, & Mintz, 1989; Levant & Pollack, 1995; Real, 1997). Komiya, Good, and Sherrod (2000) linked emotional restriction with a reluctance to seek psychological help, with greater emotional openness predictive of more favorable attitudes toward psychological help-seeking. Men may also perceive a greater public stigma associated with seeking help (Timlin-Scalera, Ponterotto, Blumberg, & Jackson, 2003). In college settings, men have been found to experience more self-stigma than women regarding help-seeking (Vogel, Wade, & Haake, 2006), and men may perceive they will be stigmatized for discussing certain concerns with a counselor (Martin, Wrisberg, Beitel, & Lounsbury, 1997).

Another factor that may restrict mental health service utilization by men is the lack of fit between conceptualizations of masculinity and the popular perception of counseling and mental health services (Mahalik et al., 2003). Traditional models of counseling emphasizing the language of feelings, disclosing vulnerability, and admitting dependency needs can create difficulties for men socialized to adopt traditional masculine roles (Rabinowitz & Cochran, 2002). To address this, counselors can tailor the clinical encounter to initially identify the expectations male clients have of the counselor and counseling, and either correct those that are erroneous or change the structure of counseling to be more congruent for a given male client. To address the needs of men, Addis and Mahalik (2003) recommended enacting changes to clinical environments, such as providing greater opportunities for reciprocity for men (e.g., with other group members or the community); increasing the perception of normativeness for particular problems, training counselors to recognize the ego-centrality of certain problems (e.g., is this problem part of me) in order to be more sensitive to how a male may be perceiving the relevance of the concern; reducing the stigma of seeking help and of experiencing mental health problems; and creating alternative nontraditional forms of assistance more congruent with masculine socialization (e.g., psychoeducational classes in work settings). All of these changes could help men feel more comfortable in seeking help.

Assessment and Treatment

One of the difficulties associated with counseling men is that emotional stoicism (Jansz, 2000), the minimizing of painful experiences (Lisak, 2001), irritability (Pollack, 1998), and a reluctance to seeking mental health services (Addis & Mahalik, 2003) often keeps many men from being appropriately understood, clinically diagnosed, and effectively treated. When it comes to theoretical perspectives and men, there is no one theoretical orientation that appears to be more effective than others in conceptualizing distress or treatment. The range of theoretical perspectives is perhaps most reflective of current practices of counseling men. Many scholars and practitioners have looked to tailor existing theoretical views in accordance with perspectives on male socialization (see Englar-Carlson & Stevens, 2006). The consideration of gender role socialization and a client's "masculinity" in each step of the counseling process is in line with what Good, Gilbert, and Scher (1990) referred to as *gender aware therapy*. In this approach, knowledge and understanding of a client's gender role orientation is placed alongside and in conjunction with a counselor's theoretical orientation.

Stevens (2006) suggested a two-component clinical assessment model for use with men, consisting of classification systems designed to identify male strengths (e.g., male forms of nurturing) and mal-adaptive forms of masculinity (e.g., sexism). The first step in the model would be to acknowledge a male client's strengths and how this ben-efits his life. For example, being responsible can mean that one can be depended upon; clear thinking leads to solutions under pressure; being strong means that others can lean on him; being self-sacrificing lessens the danger for others; physical caring provides security for others; and being practical means that he is time efficient and solution focused. The second step in the assessment would be to recognize that there are often costs associated with his approach to life. For example, the tendency to stuff feelings may contribute to physical health problems; being exclu-sively fixed in a problem-solving mode may lead to disconnection from others; staying "strong" may limit or eliminate opportunities to grieve; not admitting weakness may limit self-learning and the ability to get assistance for himself; and having an emphasis on "male pride" may lead to unnecessary violence and risk taking. This model of assessment can help counselors understand how a male client's enactment of mas-culinity influences his life and those around him.

Counselors assessing boys and male adolescents and adults can strive to be aware of traditional Western masculine gender role characteristics that may mask underlying psychological states. The traditional male gender role ideology stresses the importance of men being stoic in the face of pain, competitive in a cross-section of situations, and in control of their emotions (see Levant & Pollack, 1995). When a man displays these reactions in counseling it may appear normative and that he is coping okay. Counselors are encouraged to ask men and boys questions about mood and affect, and be willing to probe more extensively when faced with brief responses, noting discrepancies between self-expres-sion and the severity of precipitating factors. Further, counselors them-selves may be susceptible to their own gender role biases when assessing and diagnosing boys and men (see Cochran, 2001).

Men and Abuse

Although estimates of the sexual abuse of boys vary widely, Baker and King (2004) noted that 16% of adult men claim that they were the vic-tims of child sexual abuse. Other authorities report that at least 3% and as many as 20% of all boys have been the victim of sexual exploita-tion (Holmes & Slap, 1998). Although clear data on racial and ethnic differences are lacking, the best available evidence indicates that most victims are Whites, followed by African Americans, Latinos, and then Asian Americans (Kenny & McEachern, 2000). Research indicates that men who have been have been verbally, physically, and sexually abused as children are more likely to have higher rates of all types of mental illness, including affective disorders, substance abuse, and certain personality disorders, and are more likely to come to the attention of clinicians (Lisak, 2001; Weeks & Wisdom, 1998). Violence, episodes of depression, and higher rates of suicide are also higher among men who have been abused or witnessed abuse in childhood (Lisak, 1994; Rosenbaum & Leisring, 2003).

For many decades, a widespread, mistaken assumption was that only girls were abused, so the problems of boys who were sexually traumatized went overlooked (Bolton, Morris & MacEachron, 1989). Many reported incidents of abuse of boys were swept under the table by adults responsible for investigating the matter, which was a common response by officials of the Catholic church until the scandal of priests violating boys recently became public knowledge (Plante, 2004). Homophobia is another factor related to underreporting. Many boys who have been violated by other males fear that they will be labeled a "fag" or a "homo" if they reveal the abuse to anyone, so they keep it a secret (Cabe, 1999; Gartner, 1999). Because of traditional masculine gender role prohibitions on acknowledging victimization, many men do not willingly reveal the extent of their abuse to others. Because males "have been socialized not to show weakness, they are less likely to come forward with an accusation even if they know that, as children, they were smaller and less powerful than their perpetrators" (Long, Burnett & Thomas, 2006, p. 262). Cultural factors may contribute to underreporting in some cases. For example, taboos about having open discussions about sexuality and an emphasis on emotional stoicism may deter disclosure among some Asian American populations, while the Latino cultural norm that children obey adults may lead Latino boys to "comply with adults' sexual advances and to maintain silence if any adult has forbidden disclosure" (Kenny & McEachern, 2000, p. 911).

Counselors can approach childhood abuse issues patiently and with empathy for the shame that many men feel in revealing these episodes in their lives. It is not unusual for a man to downplay the psychological damage done by childhood abuse and to not reveal the extent of the abuse until later in treatment. Even when abuse is disclosed, counselors must be sensitive and supportive to the sense of foreignness or strangeness that may be experienced in the revelation. In autobiographical interviews of male survivors of sexual abuse, researchers found consistent themes about anger, betrayal, fear, helplessness, isolation, loss, shame, humiliation, self-blame, guilt, questions about one's sexuality, questions about the legitimacy of one's abuse experience, negative interpersonal relationships, and negative schemas about oneself and others (Dhaliwal, Gauzas, Antonowicz, & Ross, 1996; Lisak, 1994).

Men and Depression

There has been increased attention on depression as a serious, yet often undiagnosed, condition in men (Cochran, 2001; Cochran & Rabinowitz, 2000; NIMH, 2003; Pollack, 1998; Real, 1997). Depression in men is likely to be underdiagnosed due to the expression of symptoms that differ from the *DSM-TR* criteria (Real, 1997). The term *masked depression* has been used to refer to male experience of depression. Cochran and Rabinowitz (2000) noted the influence of gender role socialization, which encourages stoicism and suppression of emotion, as one of the several factors that obscures the expression of depressed mood in many men. Hegemonic masculinity prohibitions placed on men against the experience of mood states of depression (e.g., sadness) and the behavioral expression of these mood states (e.g., crying) make clear and simple descriptions of male depression difficult (Cochran & Rabinowitz, 2000). Thus the true expression of depression for many men creates a conflict. Further, since depression often becomes "masked," it is difficult for primary care physicians and other health professionals to determine when men are actually experiencing depressive spectrum disorders (Cochran & Rabinowitz, 2000).

Many men, after experiencing interpersonal or traumatic loss, react by plunging into a depressive episode (Cochran & Rabinowitz, 1996). It is not uncommon for men to use alcohol or other mood-altering substances or activities to medicate depression (Hanna & Grant, 1997). At the extremes of depression lie difficulties associated with suicide and homicide. Men are more prone to an aggressive acting out of their depressed mood given their tendency toward action and externalization (Cochran & Rabinowitz, 2000). This tendency may lie, in part, at the root of findings indicating that suicide is a significant mortality risk for depressed men (Moscicki, 1997). Despite reporting half the depression than women report in epidemiological surveys, men commit suicide 3 to 4 times more frequently than women (Cochran & Rabinowitz, 2000). This risk rises even higher with increasing age (Kennedy, Metz, & Lowinger, 1995). In addition to suicide, homicide is associated more frequently with men (U.S. Department of Justice, 2003). This, too, often occurs in conjunction with a depressive episode. Careful assessment of the risk of both suicide and homicide is warranted when working with depression in men (Cochran & Rabinowitz, 2000).

Cochran (2001) suggested counselors assess depression from a masculine-sensitive approach. The traditional symptoms of depression such as dysphoria, thoughts of death, appetite change, sleep change, fatigue, diminished concentration, guilt, psychomotor changes, and loss of interest in previous activities should also be supplemented by other male-focused approaches. This includes looking at important comorbid conditions (e.g., alcohol abuse and dependence; substance abuse and dependence; and related antisocial, compulsive, and narcissistic personality features); masculinity-related symptom expression, such as somatic or physical complaints, increases in interpersonal conflict, work-related difficulties and conflict, and wounds to self-esteem (i.e., job loss or relationship loss); and an extensive suicide and homicide risk assessment. Cochran added an additional assessment in regard to culturally influenced manifestations of emotional distress, such as class and race considerations regarding emotional expressivity, level of awareness and acceptance of traditional male gender roles, and an understanding about family of origin role models and norms regarding emotional expressivity.

A PROACTIVE STANCE: MEN AND SOCIAL JUSTICE

This chapter has promoted the notion that understanding men and masculinity is a core component of multicultural competency. Counselors with knowledge and appreciation for diverse conceptions of masculinity who can assess masculinity-related concerns and conceptualize how masculinity influences clinical work will be able to promote male-friendly clinical settings. In many ways, broadening one's understanding of multicultural competency to include men and masculinity is the first and most important step toward providing effective services to their male clients. Since this book has a social justice focus, it seems appropriate to close this chapter by addressing concerns about social justice and men.

Some have discussed the role of engaging men as social justice allies in ending violence against women (Berkowitz, 2002; Fabiano, Perkins, Berkowitz, Linkenbach, & Stark, 2003) and in HIV prevention (Grieg, 2003). It is far less common, however, for attention to be given to many of the social justice issues that specifically concern men in which they are the victims or the injured party. One of the problems that clouds social justice issues and men is that many of the institutions that maintain inequities or carry out oppressive actions are dominated by men or male privilege. For the most part, many acts of aggression and domination have males as both the perpetrator and victim. The recent Catholic priest sexual abuse of boys scandal, acts of gang violence, and the majority of acts of murder and homicide are all examples of male-to-male aggression.

There are many explanations and ways to understand the enactment of male power and privilege that are beyond the scope of this chapter, yet it is worth noting that many of the problems that boys and men experience are firmly grounded in social policies, norms, and expectations.

Since men have historically and currently exercised considerable privilege across almost all domains in society, it may be easy to overlook, discredit, or not acknowledge the pain and injustice that many groups of boys and men experience. In that sense, counselors need to be reminded that even though men and male privilege are powerful, not *all* men are/feel privileged or experience power in the same manner.

In one of the few scholarly works on social justice counseling and men, Kiselica and Woodford (2007) outlined three ways that counselors can use a social justice approach. First, counselors can work to eradicate sexist attitudes that adversely affect male development. This involves eliminating sexism toward women and gaining an appreciation for how sexism toward women hurts females and males. Kiselica and Woodford noted that

> the detrimental effects of sexism on women and society—death, sexual harassment, assault, rape and domestic violence—do not fit the notion of healthy male development, specifically healthy interpersonal relationships between boys or men and women. If we look at the sexist notions of males needing to be dominant and aggressive over women to be "real men," then we can easily make a case for a correlation between sexist training and the maltreatment of women. (pp. 116–117)

Second, counselors can support the rights of boys and men who have been neglected and harmed by society. This can include working with male advocacy groups (i.e., mythopoetic men's movement, child custody and visitation, responsible fatherhood, etc.) that are genuinely concerned for populations of boys and men whose needs are not supported by society. Third, counselors can work within the mental health profession to eliminate harmful stereotypes and assumptions about men, such as the notion that males are hypoemotional and the equating of aggression with masculinity. These assumptions can adversely affect the counseling process and lead boys and men to being perceived as flawed or needing to be fixed.

Exploring the social justice issues of men requires counselors in many circumstances to examine the larger social issues of society; the social institutions that maintain them; and the health, educational, and social statistics pertaining to boys and men. For example, there is a tremendous opportunity for counselors to develop prevention programs against violence by boys and men. In the United States, men experience higher victimization rates than women for all types of violent crime except rape/sexual assault. Further, 77.7% of murder victims were male (U.S. Census Bureau, 2006). Further, one of the outcomes of crime is the incarceration of men. In 2005, almost 65% of the incarcerated populations at correctional facilities were male (U.S. Department of Justice, 2006).

Another area where social justice counseling can be effective has to be with promoting responsible fatherhood. Fathers historically have been greatly neglected in social policy and understudied in research (Rohner & Veneziano, 2001). Many behavioral scientists prior to the 1960s and 1970s assumed that fathers were relatively unimportant in the development of their children and in many ways science was reflecting society's standards about the role of fathers (Cabrera et al., 2000). The emergence of fatherhood studies has been an important step toward reflecting on the needs and experiences of fathers. Over the past several decades, many psychologists who study child development and family relations have shifted their perspectives on father–child relations in a positive direction. Hawkins and Dollahite (1996) and their associates have devoted considerable attention to the ways that fathers care for the next generation through positive father work, or generative fathering, which refers to the way a father responds readily and consistently to his child's developmental needs over time (Dollahite & Hawkins, 1998). Fathering thus becomes a way for men to provide and protect their children, but also a means to contribute to the development of a new generation of men. Being a "good" father becomes an important aspect of identity for many men and a way of contributing to social welfare. Counselors can work with fathers and organizations like the National Fatherhood Initiative and the National Center for Fathering to promote and support responsible fatherhood.

A final thought about social justice issues and men is that one of the main things counselors can do is begin to consider and appreciate the unique concerns, needs, and difficulties that men experience in life that are brought and reenacted in the counseling setting. When counselors are gender aware, supportive, and male affirming in their approach, men can have the opportunity to tell their story and make sense of what is chaotic, distilling, and conflicting. For many men, safe spaces such as this are rarely found. The hope and promise of effective counseling with men is that a male client can learn that asking for help will not kill nor weaken him, understand that his own history has impacted his current life situations, gain the ability to open up with others and not give up his power, learn to value the importance of relationships, experience that vulnerability is a form of strength, and, ultimately, gain awareness of how to get to know himself.

REFERENCES

Abreau, J. M., Ramirez, E., Kim, B. S. K., & Haddy, C. (2003). Automatic activation of yellow peril Asian American stereotypes: Effects on social impression formation. *The Journal of Social Psychology, 143*, 691–706.

Addis, M. E., & Cohane, G. H. (2005). Social scientific paradigms of masculinity and their implications for research and practice in men's mental health. *Journal of Clinical Psychology, 6*, 633–647.

Addis, M. E., & Mahalik, J. R. (2003). Men, masculinity, and the contexts of help-seeking. *American Psychologist, 58*, 5–14.

American Psychological Association. (2003). Guidelines on multicultural education, training, research, practice, and organizational change for psychologists. *American Psychologist, 58*, 377–402.

American Psychological Association. (2006). *Guidelines for psychological practice with girls and women.* Manuscript in preparation.

Anderson, R. N., Kochanek, K. D., & Murphy, S. L. (1997). Report of final mortality statistics, 1995. *Monthly Vital Statistics Report, 45/11*, suppl. 2. Hyattsville, MD: National Center for Health Statistics.

Arias, E., Anderson, R. N., Kung, H. C., Murphy, S. L., & Kochanek, K. D. (2003). *Deaths: Final data for 2001* (National vital statistics reports; vol. 52, no. 3). Hyattsville, MD: National Center for Health Statistics.

Arredondo, P., Toporek, R., Brown, S. P., Jones, J., Locke, D. C., Sanchez, J., & Stadler, H. (1996). Operationalisation of multicultural counselling competencies. *Journal of Multicultural Counselling & Development, 24*, 42–78.

Baker, D., & King, S. E. (2004). Child sexual abuse and incest. In R. T. Francoeur & R. J. Noonan (Eds.), *International encyclopedia of sexuality* (pp. 1233–1237). New York: Continuum.

Baruth, L. G., & Manning, M. L. (1999). *Multicultural counseling and psychotherapy: A lifespan perspective.* Upper Saddle River, NJ: Prentice Hall.

Berkowitz, A. D. (2002). Fostering men's responsibility for preventing sexual assault. In P. A. Schewe (Ed.), *Preventing intimate partner violence: Developmentally appropriate interventions across the life span* (pp. 163–196). Washington, DC: American Psychological Press.

Bernard, J. (1981). The good-provider role: Its rise and fall. *American Psychologist, 36*, 1–12.

Blazina, C. (1997). Mythos and men: Toward new paradigms of masculinity. *The Journal of Men's Studies, 5*, 285–294.

Bolton, R. G., Morris, L. A., & MacEachron, A. E. (1989). *Males at risk: The other side of child sexual abuse.* Thousand Oaks, CA: Sage.

Brannon, R. (1976). The male sex-role: Our culture's blueprint of manhood and what it's done for us lately. In D. S. Brannon & R. Brannon (Eds.), *The forty-nine percent majority* (pp. 1–45). Reading, MA: Addison-Wesley.

Brooks, G. (1998). *A new psychotherapy for traditional men.* San Francisco: Jossey-Bass.

Brooks, G. R., & Good, G. E. (Eds.). (2001). *The new handbook of psychotherapy & counseling with men: A comprehensive guide to settings, problems, & treatment approaches* (Vols. 1 and 2). San Francisco: Jossey-Bass.

Brown, L. S. (1986). Gender role analysis: A neglected component of psychological assessment. *Psychotherapy, 23,* 243–248.

Cabe, N. (1999). Abused boys and adolescents: Out of the shadows. In A. M. Horne & M. S. Kiselica (Eds.), *Handbook of counseling boys and adolescent males: A practitioner's guide* (pp. 199–218). Thousand Oaks, CA: Sage.

Cabrera, N. J., Tamis-LeMonda, C. S., Bradley, R. H., Hofferth, S., & Lamb, M. E. (2000). Fatherhood in the twenty-first century. *Child Development, 71*(1), 127–136.

Caldwell L. D., & White, J. L. (2001). African centered therapeutic and counseling interventions for African American males. In G. Brooks & G. Good (Eds.), *The handbook of counseling and psychotherapy approaches for men* (pp. 737–753). San Francisco: Jossey-Bass.

Casas, J. M., Wagenheim, B. R., Banchero, R., & Mendoza-Romero, J. (1994). Hispanic masculinity: Myth or psychological schema meriting clinical considerations. *Hispanic Journal of Behavioral Sciences, 16,* 315–331.

Chen, A. S. (1999). Lives at the center of the periphery, lives at the periphery of the center: Chinese American masculinities and bargaining with hegemony. *Gender and Society, 13,* 584–607.

Clare, A. (2000). *On men: Masculinity in crisis.* London: Chatto & Windus.

Cochran, S. V. (2001). Assessing and treating depression in men. In G. Brooks & G. Good (Eds.), *The new handbook of psychotherapy and counseling with men* (pp. 229–245). San Francisco: Jossey-Bass.

Cochran, S. V., & Rabinowitz, F. E. (1996). Men, loss and psychotherapy. *Psychotherapy, 33,* 593–600.

Cochran, S. V., & Rabinowitz, F. E. (2000). *Men and depression: Clinical and empirical perspectives.* San Diego: Academic Press.

Commonwealth Fund. (1998). *Women's and men's health survey 1998.* Washington, DC: Author.

Connell, R. W. (1990). An iron man: The body and some contradictions of hegemonic masculinity. In M. A. Messner & D. F. Sabo (Eds.), *Sport, men, and the gender order.* Champaign, IL: Human Kinetics Press.

Connell, R. W., & Messerschmidt, J. W. (2005). Hegemonic masculinity: Rethinking the concept. *Gender and Society, 19,* 829–859.

Courtenay, W. H. (1998). College men's health: An overview and a call to action. *Journal of American College Health, 46,* 279–290.

Courtenay, W. H. (2000). Engendering health: A social constructionist examination of men's health beliefs and behaviors. *Psychology of Men & Masculinity, 1*, 4–15.

D'Arcy, C., & Schmitz, J. A. (1979). Sex differences in the utilization of health services for psychiatric problems in Saskatchewan. *Canadian Journal of Psychiatry, 24*, 19–27.

Dhaliwal, G., Gauzas, L., Antonowicz, D., & Ross, R. (1996). Adult male survivors of childhood sexual abuse: Prevalence, sexual abuse characteristics, and long-term effects. *Clinical Psychology Review, 16*, 619–639.

Dollahite, D. C., & Hawkins, A. J. (1998). A conceptual ethic of generative fathering. *The Journal of Men's Studies, 7*, 109–132.

Doss, B. D., & Hopkins, J. R. (1998). The multicultural masculine ideology scale: Validation from three cultural perspectives. *Sex Roles, 38*, 719–741.

Doucet, A. (2004). "It's almost like I have a job, but I don't get paid": Fathers at home reconfiguring work, care, and masculinity. *Fathering, 2*, 277–302.

Englar-Carlson, M., & Stevens, M. A. (Eds.). (2006). *In the room with men: A casebook of therapeutic change.* Washington, DC: American Psychological Association.

Enns, C. Z. (1997). *Feminist theories and feminist psychotherapies: Origins, themes, and variations.* New York: The Harrington Park Press.

Fabiano, P., Perkins, H. W., Berkowitz, A., Linkenbach J., & Stark, C. (2003). Engaging men as social justice allies in ending violence against women: Evidence for a social norms approach. *Journal of American College Health, 52*, 105–111.

Franklin, A. J. (1998). Treating anger in African-American men. In W. Pollack & R. Levant (Eds.), *New psychotherapy for men* (pp. 239–258). New York: Wiley.

Franklin, A. J. (1999). Invisibility syndrome and racial identity development in psychotherapy and counseling African American men. *The Counseling Psychologist, 27*, 761–793.

Gartner, R. B. (1999). *Betrayed as boys: Psychodynamic treatment of sexually abused men.* New York: Guilford.

Gibbons, J. L., Hamby, B. A., & Dennis, W. D. (1997). Researching gender-role ideologies internationally and cross-culturally. *Psychology of Women Quarterly, 21*, 151–170.

Good, G. E., Dell, D. M., & Mintz, L. B. (1989). Male role and gender role conflict: Relations to help-seeking in men. *Journal of Counseling Psychology, 36*, 295–300.

Good, G. E., Gilbert, L. A., & Scher, M. (1990). Gender aware therapy: A synthesis of feminist therapy and knowledge about gender. *Journal of Counseling and Development, 68*, 376–380.

Good, G. E., & Sherrod, N. (2001). The psychology of men and masculinity: Research status and future directions. In R. Unger (Ed.), *Handbook of the psychology of women and gender,* (pp. 201–214). New York: Wiley.

Good, G. E., Thomson, D. A., & Brathwaite, A. (2005). Men and therapy: Critical concepts, theoretical frameworks, and research recommendations. *Journal of Clinical Psychology, 6,* 699–711.

Good, G. E., & Wood, P. K. (1995). Male gender role conflict, depression, and help-seeking: Do college men face double jeopardy? *Journal of Counseling and Development, 74,* 70–75.

Grieg, A. (2003). *HIV prevention with men: Towards gender equity and social justice.* Retrieved December 28, 2006, from http://www.un.org/women-watch/daw/ egm/ men-boys2003/ EP7-Greig.pdf

Guspers Van Wuk, C. M. T., Kolk, A. M., Van Den Bosch, W. J. H. M., & Van Den Hoogen, H. J. M. (1992). Male and female morbidity in general practice: The nature of sex differences. *Social Science Medicine, 35,* 665–678.

Haldeman, D. C. (2001). Psychotherapy with gay and bisexual men. In G. Brooks & G. Good (Eds.), *The handbook of counseling and psychotherapy approaches for men* (pp. 796–815). San Francisco: Jossey-Bass.

Haldeman, D. C. (2006). Queer eye on the straight guy: A case of gay male heterophobia. In M. Englar-Carlson & M. Stevens (Eds.), *In the room with men: A casebook of therapeutic change* (pp. 301–318). Washington, DC: American Psychological Association.

Hammond, W. P., & Mattis, J. S. (2005). Being a man about it: Manhood meaning among African American men. *Psychology of Men and Masculinity, 6,* 114–126.

Hanna, E., & Grant, B. (1997). Gender differences in DSM-IV alcohol use disorders and major depression as distributed in the general population: Clinical implications. *Comprehensive Psychiatry, 38,* 202–212.

Hawkins, A. J., & Dollahite, D. C. (Eds.). (1996). *Generative fathering: Beyond deficit perspectives.* Thousand Oaks, CA: Sage.

Hayes, J. A., & Gelso, C. J. (2001). Clinical implications of research on countertransference: Science informing practice. *In Session: Journal of Clinical Psychology, 57,* 1041–1051.

Heesacker, M., Wester, S. R., Vogel, D. L., Wentzel, J. T., Mejia-Millan, C. M., & Goodholm, C. R. (1999). Gender-based emotional stereotyping. *Journal of Counseling Psychology, 46,* 483–495.

Hodgetts, D., & Chamberlain, K. (2002). The problem with men: Working class men making sense of men's health on television. *Journal of Health Psychology, 7,* 269–284.

Holmes, W. C., & Slap, G. B. (1998). Sexual abuse of boys: Definition, prevalence, correlates, sequelae, and management. *JAMA, 280,* 1855–1862.

Hunter, A. G., & Davis, J. E. (1992). Constructing gender: An exploration of African American men's conceptualization of manhood. *Gender and Society, 6,* 464–479.

Hunter, A. G., & Davis, J. E. (1994). Hidden voices of Black men: The meaning, structure, and complexity of manhood. *Journal of Black Studies, 25,* 20–40.

Husaini B. A., Moore S. T., & Cain V. A. (1994). Psychiatric symptoms and help seeking behavior among the elderly: An analysis of racial and gender differences. *Journal of Gerontological Social Work, 21,* 177 –195.

Jansz, J. (2000). Masculine identity and restrictive emotionality. In A. H. Fischer (Ed.), *Gender and emotion: Social psychological perspectives* (pp. 166–186). New York: Cambridge University Press.

Johnson, P. D. (2006). Counseling African American men: A contextualized humanistic perspective. *Counseling and Values, 50,* 187–196.

Kennedy, G., Metz, H., & Lowinger, R. (1995). Epidemiology and inferences regarding the etiology of late life suicide. In G. Kennedy (Ed.), *Suicide and depression in late life* (pp. 3–22). New York: Wiley.

Kenny, M. C., & McEachern, A. G. (2000). Racial, ethnic, and cultural factors of childhood sexual abuse: A selected review of the literature. *Clinical Psychology Review, 7,* 905–922.

Kessler, R. C., McGonagle, K. A., Zhao, S., Nelson, C. B., Hughes, M., Eshelman, S., et al. (1994). Lifetime and 12-month prevalence of DSM–III–R psychiatric disorders in the United States: Results from the National Comorbidity Survey. *Archives of General Psychiatry, 51,* 8–19.

Kilmartin, C. T. (2007). *The masculine self* (3rd ed.). Cornwall-on-Hudson, NY: Sloan Publishing.

Kim, B. S. K., Atkinson, D. R., & Umemoto, D. (2001). Asian cultural values and counseling process: Current knowledge and directions for future research. *The Counseling Psychologist, 29,* 570–603.

Kim, B. S. K., Atkinson, D. R., & Yang, P. H. (1999). The Asian Values Scale: Development, factor analysis, validation, and reliability. *Journal of Counseling Psychology, 46,* 342–352.

Kimmel, M. (2005). *Manhood in American: A cultural history* (2nd ed.). New York: Free Press.

Kimmel, M., & Messner, M. (Eds.). (2004). *Men's lives* (6th ed.). New York: Macmillan.

Kiselica, M. S. (2006, August). Contributions and limitations of the deficit model of men. In M. S. Kiselica (Chair), *Toward a positive psychology of boys, men, and masculinity.* Symposium presented at the Annual Convention of the American Psychological Association, New Orleans, LA.

Kiselica, M. S., Englar-Carlson, M., & Fisher, M. (2006, August). A positive psychology framework for building upon male strengths. In M. S. Kiselica (Chair), *Toward a positive psychology of boys, men, and masculinity.* Symposium presented at the Annual Convention of the American Psychological Association, New Orleans, LA.

Kiselica, M. S., & Robinson, M. (2001). Bringing advocacy counseling to life: The history, issues, and human dramas of social justice work in counseling. *Journal of Counseling and Development, 70,* 387–397.

Kiselica, M. S., & Woodford, M. S. (2007). Promoting healthy male development: A social justice perspective. In C. Lee (Ed.), *Counseling for social justice* (pp. 111–135). Alexandria, VA: American Counseling Association.

Komiya, N., Good, G. E., & Sherrod, N. B. (2000). Emotional openness as predictor of college students' attitudes toward seeking psychological help. *Journal of Counseling Psychology, 33,* 148–154.

Kupers, T. A. (1993). *Revisioning men's lives: Gender, intimacy, and power.* New York: Guilford.

Levant, R. F. (1990). Introduction to special series on men's roles and psychotherapy. *Psychotherapy, 27,* 307–308.

Levant, R. F. (1995). Toward the reconstruction of masculinity. In R. Levant & W. Pollack (Eds.), *A new psychology of men* (pp. 229–251). New York: Basic.

Levant, R. F. (1997). The masculinity crisis. *Journal of Men's Studies, 5,* 221–231.

Levant, R. F., & Kopecky, G. (1996). *Masculinity reconstructed: Changing the rules of manhood.* New York: Dutton/Plume.

Levant, R., & Pollack, W. S. (Eds.). (1995). *The new psychology of men.* New York: Basic.

Levant, R. F., & Silverstein, L. S. (2005). Gender is neglected in both evidence based practices and "treatment as usual." In J. Norcross, L. E. Beutler, & R. F. Levant (Eds.), *Evidence based practice in mental health: Debate and dialogue on the fundamental questions* (pp. 338–345). Washington, DC: APA books.

Lisak, D. (1994). The psychological consequences of childhood abuse: Content analysis of interviews with male survivors. *Journal of Traumatic Stress, 7,* 525–548.

Lisak, D. (2001). Male survivors of trauma. In G. Brooks & G. Good (Eds.), *The new handbook of psychotherapy and counseling with men* (pp. 263–277). San Francisco: Jossey-Bass.

Liu, W. M. (2002a). Exploring the lives of Asian American men: Racial identity, male role norms, gender role conflict, and prejudicial attitudes. *Psychology of Men & Masculinity, 3,* 107–118.

Liu, W. M. (2002b). The social class-related experiences of men: Integrating theory and practice. *Professional Psychology, 33,* 355–360.

Liu, W. M. (2005). The study of men and masculinity as an important multicultural competency consideration. *Journal of Clinical Psychology, 6,* 685–697.

Liu, W. M., & Chang, T. (2007). Asian American masculinities. In F. T. L. Leong, A. Ebero, A. Kinoshita, A. G. Arpana, & L. H. Yang (Eds.), *Handbook of Asian American psychology* (2nd ed., pp. 197–211). Thousand Oaks, CA: Sage.

Liu, W. M., & Iwamoto, D. K. (2006). Asian American gender role conflict: The role of Asian values, self-esteem, and psychological distress. *Psychology of Men and Masculinity, 7,* 153–164.

Long, L. L., Burnett, J. A., & Thomas, V. (2006). *Sexuality counseling: An integrative approach.* Upper Saddle River, NJ: Pearson/Merrill/Prentice/Hall.

Majors, R. G., & Billson, J. M. (1992). *Cool pose: The dilemmas of Black manhood in America.* New York: Lexington.

Mahalik, J. R., Good, G. E., & Englar-Carlson, M. (2003). Masculinity scripts, presenting concerns and help-seeking: Implications for practice and training. *Professional Psychology: Research & Practice, 34,* 123–131.

Martin, S. B., Wrisberg, C. A., Beitel, P. A., & Lounsbury, J. (1997). NCAA Division I athletes' attitudes toward seeking sport psychology consultation: The development of an objective instrument. *Sport Counselor, 11,* 201–218.

Mays, V. M. (2000). A social justice agenda. *American Psychologist, 55,* 326–327.

Mellinger, T., & Liu, W. M. (2006). Men's issues in doctoral training: A Survey of counseling psychology programs. *Professional Psychology: Research and Practice, 37,* 196–204.

Möller-Leimkuehler, A. (2002). Barriers to help-seeking in men. A review of the socio-cultural and clinical literature with particular reference to depression. *Journal of Affective Disorders, 71,* 1–9.

Moore, R., & Gillette, D. (1991). *King, warrior, magician, lover: Rediscovering the archetypes of the mature masculine.* San Francisco: Harper.

Moscicki, E. (1997). Identification of suicide risk factors using epidemiological studies. *Psychiatric Clinics of North America, 20,* 499–517.

National Institute of Mental Health. (2003). *Real men. Real depression.* Retrieved December 21, 2006, from http://menanddepression.nimh.nih.gov

Neighbors, H., & Howard, C. (1987). Sex differences in professional help seeking among adult Black Americans. *American Journal of Community Psychology, 15,* 403–17.

Neighbors, H. W., Musick, M. A., & Williams, D. R. (1998). The African American minister as a source of help for serious personal crises: Bridge or barrier to mental health care. *Health Education & Behavior, 26,* 759–777.

O'Neil, J. M., & Egan, J. (1992). Men's gender role transitions over the lifespan: Transformations and fears of femininity. *Journal of Mental Health Counseling, 14,* 305–324.

Paniagua, F. A. (2005). *Assessing and treating culturally diverse clients: A practical guide* (2nd ed.). Thousand Oaks, CA: Sage.

Park, S. (2006). Facing fear without losing face: Working with Asian American men. In M. Englar-Carlson & M. A. Stevens (Eds.), *In the room with men: A casebook of therapeutic change* (pp. 151–173). Washington, DC: American Psychological Association.

Plante, T. G. (Ed.). (2004). *Sin against the innocents: Sexual abuse by priests and the role of the Catholic Church.* Westport, CT: Greenwood.

Pleck, J. H. (1997). Paternal involvement: Levels, sources, and consequences. In M. E. Lamb (Ed.), *The role of the father in child development* (3rd ed., pp. 61–103). New York: Wiley.

Pleck, J. H., Sonenstein, F. L., & Ku, L. C. (1993). Masculinity ideology and its correlates. In S. Oskamp & M. Costanzo (Eds.), *Gender issues in social psychology* (pp. 85–110). Newbury Park, CA: Sage.

Pollack, W. S., & Levant, R. F. (1998). *New psychotherapy for men.* New York: Wiley.

Rabinowitz, F. E., & Cochran, S. V. (2002). *Deepening psychotherapy with men.* Washington, DC: American Psychological Association.

Real, T. (1997). *I don't want to talk about it: Overcoming the secret legacy of male depression.* New York: Fireside.

Real, T. (2002). *How can I get through to you? Reconnecting men and women.* New York: Scribner.

Robertson, J., & Fitzgerald, L. F. (1990). The (mis)treatment of men: Effects of client gender role and life-style on diagnosis and attribution of pathology. *Journal of Counseling Psychology, 37*, 3–9.

Robertson, J., & Fitzgerald, L. F. (1992). Overcoming the masculine mystique: Preferences for alternative forms of assistance among men who avoid counseling. *Journal of Counseling Psychology, 39*, 240–246.

Rochlen, A. B., & O'Brien, K. M. (2002). The relation of male gender role conflict and attitudes toward career counseling to interest and preferences for different career counseling styles. *Psychology of Men and Masculinity, 3*, 9–21.

Rohner, R. P., & Veneziano, R. A. (2001). The importance of father love: History and contemporary evidence. *Review of General Psychology, 5*(4), 382–405.

Rosenbaum, A., & Leisring, P. A. (2003). Beyond power and control: Towards an understanding of partner abusive men. *Journal of Comparative Family Studies,34*, 7–22.

Sachs-Ericsson, N., & Ciarlo, J. A. (2000). Gender, social roles, and mental health: An epidemiological perspective. *Sex Roles, 43*, 605–628.

Sandman, D., Simantov, E., & An, C. (2000). *Out of touch: American men and the health care system.* New York: Commonwealth Fund.

Scher, M. (2001). Male therapist, male client: Reflections on critical dynamics. In G. Brooks & G. Good (Eds.), *The handbook of counseling and psychotherapy approaches for men* (pp. 719–733). San Francisco: Jossey-Bass.

Seligman, M., & Csikszentmihalyi, M. (2000). Positive psychology: An introduction. *American Psychologist, 55*, 5–14.

Shin, J. (2002). Help-seeking behaviors by Korean immigrants for depression. *Issues in Mental Health Nursing, 23*, 461–476.

Sloan, T. (2001). *Critical psychology: Voices for change.* New York: St. Martin's Press.

Smiler, A. P. (2004). Thirty years after the discovery of gender: Psychological concepts and measures of masculinity. *Sex Roles, 50,* 15–26.

Solberg, V. S., Ritsma, S., Davis, B. J., & Tata, S. P. (1994). Asian-American students' severity of problems and willingness to seek help from university counseling centers: Role of previous counseling experience, gender, and ethnicity. *Journal of Counseling Psychology, 41,* 275–279.

Stevens, M. A. (2006, August). Engaging men in psychotherapy: Respect and challenge. In M. S. Kiselica (Chair), *Toward a positive psychology of boys, men, and masculinity.* Symposium presented at the Annual Convention of the American Psychological Association, New Orleans, LA.

Sue, D. (2001). Asian American masculinity and therapy: The concept of masculinity in Asian American males. In G. R. Brooks & G. E. Good (Eds.), *The new handbook of psychotherapy and counseling with men: A comprehensive guide to settings, problems, and treatment approaches* (pp. 780–795). San Francisco: Jossey-Bass.

Sue, D. S., & Sue, D. (2007). *Counseling the culturally diverse: Theory and practice* (5th ed.). New York: Wiley.

Sue, D. W., Arredondo, P., & McDavis, R. (1992). Multicultural counseling competencies and standards: A call to the profession. *Journal of Counseling and Development, 70,* 477–484.

Timlin-Scalera, R. M., Ponterotto, J. G., Blumberg, F. C., & Jackson, M. A. (2003). A grounded theory study of help-seeking behaviors among White male high school students. *Journal of Counseling Psychology, 50,* 339–350.

U.S. Census Bureau. (2006). *The 2007 Statistical Abstract of the United States.* Retrieved December 28, 2006, from http://www.census.gov/compendia/statab/law_enforcement_courts_prisons/crimes_and_crime_rates/

U.S. Department of Justice. (2003). *Criminal victimization in the United States, 2002 statistical tables.* Retrieved December 28, 2006, from http://www.ojp.usdoj.gov/bjs/pub/pdf/cvus0202.pdf

U.S. Department of Justice. (2006). *Prison statistics.* Retrieved December 28, 2006, from http://www.ojp.usdoj.gov/bjs/prisons.htm

Vessey, J. T., & Howard, K. I. (1993). Who seeks psychotherapy. *Psychotherapy, 30,* 546–553.

Vogel, D. L., Epting, F., & Wester, S. R. (2003). Counselors' perceptions of female and male clients. *Journal of Counseling and Development, 81,* 131–141.

Vogel, D. L., Wade, N. G., & Haake, S. (2006). Measuring the self-stigma associated with seeking psychological help. *Journal of Counseling Psychology, 53,* 325–337.

Weeks, R. & Widom, C. S. (1998). Self-reports of early childhood victimization among incarcerated adult male felons. *Journal of Interpersonal Violence, 13,* 346–361.

Wester, S. R., Vogel, D. L., Pressly, P. K., & Heesacker, M. (2002). Sex differences in emotion: A critical review of the literature and implications for counseling psychology. *The Counseling Psychologist, 30,* 629–651.

Zane, N., & Yeh, M. (2002). The use of culturally-based variables in assessment: Studies on loss of face. In K. S. Kurasaki & S. Okazaki (Eds.), *Asian American mental health: Assessment theories and methods* (pp. 123–138). New York: Kluwer Academic/Plenum.

6

COUNSELING WITH AFRICAN AMERICANS

Marc A. Grimmett and Don C. Locke

The idea of a book chapter on counseling African Americans is inherent with fundamental challenges. After all, African Americans as a social demographic group are quite diverse and are not as easily categorized and described as racial descriptors suggest. Although often perceived and understood to be a distinct racial group in the United States, how individuals within this group define and ascribe meaning to being African American is not necessarily universal. At the same time, there are historical roots, cultural characteristics, and social experiences that do indeed connect the members of what will be broadly referred to in this chapter as the African American community.

DEMOGRAPHIC CHARACTERISTICS OF THE AFRICAN AMERICAN COMMUNITY

Over 36 million people, nearly 13% of the total U.S. population, identify their race as African American or Black (U.S. Census Bureau, 2000). Less than 1% of this group indicates they are African American or Black in combination with one or more races. The significance and meaning associated with racial identity is discussed in a section that appears later in this chapter. Most of the African American or Black population lives in the southern United States (58%), with 47% concentrated in 9 states: Texas, Florida, Georgia, North Carolina, Maryland, Louisiana, Virginia, South Carolina, and Alabama (McKinnon, 2001).

About 18% live in the Northeast, 18% in the Midwest, and about 9% live in the West.

When individuals who identified themselves as African American or Black were statistically analyzed as one population in the Census 2000 special report, *We the People: Blacks in the United States*, the following group characteristics emerged (McKinnon & Bennett, 2005). Compared to the total U.S. population median age of 35.4, the African American population is younger with a median age of 30.4. This is indicative of a shorter life span for African Americans, particularly African American males whose median age was 28.7. The proportion of African American females ages 30–44 is higher than that of women in the total U.S. population; while the proportion of African American males is lower, which has possible implications for adult male–female relationships, such as marriage.

Family Household

More African American males (42%), incidentally, were married than African American females (31%), who were more likely to be separated, widowed, or divorced; while 41% of the current African American population has never been married compared with 27% of the total U.S. population (McKinnon & Bennett, 2005). Married couples make up just over one third of African American households. This number is slightly more than households maintained by an African American woman with no spouse, which is nearly 3 times higher than the general population (31% compared to 12%).

The median income of married African American couples ($50,700) was greater than that of female-headed households ($20,600) and male-headed households ($29,000) with no spouse present. The total median income for all African American households combined (i.e., married and single-parent families) was $33,200, compared to the total population of $50,000. For the total population, the income of married couples was $57,300, $35,000 for males with no spouse present, and $25,500 for females with no spouse present. Finally, more African Americans rented (54%) and less owned (46%) their homes than people in the total population (34% rented and 66% owned).

Education

More African American women had earned a bachelor's degree (15%) than African American men (13%), yet both fall short of the total U.S. population (23% for women and 26% for men). Furthermore, just under 5% of African Americans had earned advanced degrees compared to 10% for White Americans, 17% for Asian Americans, and nearly 4%

for individuals who identify as Latino or Hispanic (Bauman & Graf, 2003). Educational attainment is strongly correlated with occupation and earnings as will be shown in the following sections.

Occupations

African American women and men had nearly equal rates of participation in the labor force at around 60%. The participation of African American women, however, exceeded that of women in the total population, whereas that of African American men was nearly 10 percentage points less than the total population of men. Similarly, the occupational profile of the African American community also demonstrated differences by sex. African American women held a greater proportion of management, professional, and related occupations than African American men (30% vs. 20%). A significant number of African American men work in the construction, extraction, and maintenance (13%) sectors, which is greater than the total population but less than the men in the total population (17%). African Americans as a whole are more likely to hold jobs in service and production, transportation, and material-moving occupations than the total population (22% vs. 15%).

Earnings

African Americans who worked full time, year round earned about $85 for every $100 earned by all U.S. workers. About the same difference is true for African American women when compared to African American men. The earnings of African American women, however, are almost equivalent to that of women in the total population. Women in the total population still only earn $73 for every $100 earned by men. The proportion of African Americans living in poverty is twice that of the total population, which disproportionately affects African American women.

High-Need Populations

African Americans as a group are overrepresented in several high-need populations that are vulnerable to mental health problems. These populations include individuals who are: (a) homeless (about 40% are African American); (b) incarcerated (nearly 50% of all prisoners in state and federal jurisdictions and almost 40% of juveniles in legal custody are African American); (c) exposed to violence (African Americans of all ages are more likely to be victims of serious violent crime than non-Hispanic Whites); and (d) children in the foster care and child welfare system (African American children constitute about 45% of children in public foster care and more than half of all children waiting to be adopted; U.S. Department of Health and Human Services, 2001).

Summary

What has just been presented is a broad demographic overview of the African American community. It is not comprehensive or complete. Rather, the purpose of the information provided is to give the reader general background information on African Americans as one racial or ethnic group in the United States. It should be noted again, however, that there is great variation and diversity within the African American community. Counselors working with clients who identify as African American, then, may use this information as a contextual beginning to understanding their African American client's worldview and social experience. At the same time, the counselor must remain open to the client providing unexpected details for their story or creating an original story from a context altogether different from the one that has been presented.

For the remainder of the chapter, the term *African American* will be primarily used. It is fair to write that there is not a general consensus among the group of individuals who identify as African American or Black regarding which term is most appropriate, suitable, or meaningful. Successive generations of African Americans, in response to various historical, social, cultural, and political events and conditions have accepted or embraced different racial identifiers that objectified, affirmed, or empowered them individually and collectively. The authors have chosen to use the term African American because of its relationship to ethnicity, defined by cultural traditions and nationality (though nationality is difficult to nearly impossible to specifically determine for most African Americans; Franklin & Moss, 2002).

HISTORICAL CONTEXT OF AFRICAN AMERICAN CULTURE

The historical context of the culture of African American people in the United States is one that often begins with the slavery portion of history. It must be noted that Africans had a thriving culture before being sold in slavery and transported to the Americas. For purposes of this chapter, the focus will be on the historical context of slavery in the United States, as that institution continues to influence the beliefs, values, attitudes, customs, and struggles in contemporary life.

Leary (2004) coined the phrase *post traumatic slave syndrome* to describe the continuing struggles of many contemporary African Americans. Post traumatic slave syndrome is defined as the "multigenerational trauma together with continued oppression and the absence of opportunity to access the benefits available in the society" (p. 125).

Several patterns of behavior develop from this syndrome, including vacant esteem, ever-present anger, and racist socialization.

Vacant esteem is described as the "state of believing oneself to have little or no worth, exacerbated by the group and societal pronouncement of inferiority" (Leary, 2004, p. 129). Some of the ways African American parents have socialized their children to submissive and docile behaviors are examples of parenting practices that contribute to vacant esteem. Communities demonstrate their esteem beliefs in standards and values regarding acceptable behavior, educational attainment, and professional possibilities. The laws, institutions, and policies communicate how the larger society views its members. Segregated and inferior educational institutions in low-income, largely people-of-color populated areas do little to enhance the esteem of children who attend those schools. These children see more poverty, violence, and degradation than any child should ever see. When we look at some of the demographic data on poverty we see some rather obvious reasons for the existence of vacant or low esteem in African Americans.

The poverty rate in 2000 for African Americans was at 22%, the lowest since 1959. The annual median income for householders who reported themselves as African Americans was $29,177. The poverty rate for African Americans is more than twice the rate for White Americans, which was 8%. Poverty among African American children is particularly pronounced: 31% of African American children lived in poverty in 2000. This percentage is higher than both the percentage of White children (9%) and the percentage of Latino children (28%) living below the poverty level. The percentage of African American female-headed households below the poverty level in 2000 was nearly 6 times higher than the percentage of African American married-couple households below the poverty level. Thirty-five percent of all African American female-headed households were below the poverty level in 2000 (U.S. Department of Commerce, 2001)

Many reasons have been given to explain this phenomenon. It seems that African Americans have a higher turnover rate in jobs and many of the jobs filled by African Americans are short-term to begin with. Level of education and issues of discrimination and racism also influence poverty. Billingsley (1968) concluded that even when the income levels are similar for African Americans and members of the dominant culture, the two groups are not comparable. This is so because the African American group must reflect its experience with job discrimination and racism, both of which set the conditions for growing up African American in the United States.

Young (1986) pointed out that African American poverty levels are, to some extent due to the following factors: "scarcity of jobs in central cities; (2) black women are younger and have younger children; (3) the gap between black and white unemployment rates appear to be widening; (4) racial discrimination; (5) enormous increase in white females in the labor force" (p. 63). These factors remain relevant even to this day and time. Billingsley (1968) suggested that even when the income levels are similar for African Americans and members of the dominant culture, the two groups are not comparable. This is so because the African American group must reflect its experience with job discrimination and racism, both of which set the conditions for growing up African American in the United States. Traditionally, African Americans experience higher rates of joblessness, underemployment, mortality, morbidity, family instability, poor housing, homicide, and institutionalization than their White counterparts. There is no greater issue facing African Americans than the economic one.

The "ever-present anger" expressed by Leary (2004) is a result of the frustration of blocked goals and the fear of failure. This was pointed out clearly by Gunnar Myrdal (1944) in *An American Dilemma* when he compared the emotions of African American anger when interacting with Whites with the White American feeling of fear when interacting with African Americans. This is the same phenomenon that Grier and Cobbs (1968) described in their book *Black Rage*. They described the "rage" as resulting from a history of slavery and the failure of U.S. society to successfully integrate its African American citizenry into the basic fabric of the culture while allowing them full, fair, and equal access.

Leary's (2004) concept of racist socialization is characterized by the adoption of the slave master's value system as one of the most insidious and pervasive symptoms of racist socialization. The adoption of White standards of beauty and material success, while simultaneously glamorizing thug life and lack of education, reflects a very destructive value system socialization. Understanding this socialization is the first step in resocializing African American children to a nontraumatic outcome.

LEGISLATION AND AFRICAN AMERICANS

The role of legislation in shaping the cultural context of African Americans can best be seen from an evaluation of the comprehensive set of laws that were enacted in the United States relating to African Americans. Before one can begin to understand the psychological status of contemporary African Americans in the United States, it is important that one understand the roots of racial oppression and the tractability of racial structures of domination. The present focus on race is not new; indeed it has a very long history. The roots of racial oppression are based in much of the legislation of this country. Terkel (1992) characterized race as "the American obsession." DuBois (1996) identified race as the "problem of the twentieth century." We find ourselves in the 21st century and race remains a significant variable in almost all of life.

The first slaves arrived in Virginia in 1619. Individual colonies, prior to 1787, managed all legislation regarding the Black Africans who had been brought to the Americas. In 1787 the United States of America made slavery illegal in the Northwest Territory and allowed states to continue importing slaves until 1808. The Constitution further stipulated that only three-fifths of the population of slaves would be counted for enumeration purposes for both the distribution of taxes and the determination of the members of the U.S. House of Representatives. In 1793 a federal fugitive slave law was enacted, providing for the return of slaves who had escaped and crossed state lines. The Missouri Compromise banned slavery north of the southern boundary of Missouri. Southerners defeated the Wilmot Proviso, introduced in Congress in 1846 to ban slavery in territory gained in the Mexican War. In the Compromise of 1850, California was admitted as a free state while ending the slave trade in Washington. It also established a much stricter fugitive slave law than the original.

The Supreme Court entered the slavery conversation when it held in 1857 that Congress does not have the right to ban slavery in states and extended the debate by declaring that slaves were not citizens. The debate continued into the Civil War where the Confederacy was founded when states in the Deep South seceded from the Union. President Abraham Lincoln issued the Emancipation Proclamation in 1863, declaring that all persons held as slaves in the Confederate states "are, and henceforward shall be free." When the Civil War ended in 1865, the U.S. Congress established the Freedmen's Bureau to protect the rights of the newly emancipated African Americans, while many Southern states passed Black Codes, drastically restricting the rights of the newly freed Americans. In the same year the 13th Amendment to the Constitution was ratified, prohibiting slavery. In 1867 a series of Reconstruction acts was passed, guaranteeing the civil rights of freedmen.

In 1868 the 14th Amendment was ratified, defining citizenship, and declaring that all individuals born or naturalized in the United States are American citizens, including those born as slaves. The 14th Amendment nullified the Dred Scott decision. In 1870 the 15th Amendment was ratified, giving African Americans the right to vote. Reconstruction officially ended in 1877 and federal attempts to provide basic civil rights for African Americans quickly eroded.

The next major national action was the Supreme Court decision in *Plessy v. Ferguson* in 1896, which held that racial segregation was constitutional. This case paved the way for the repressive Jim Crow laws in the South. Segregation was legal in the United States until the *Brown v. Board of Education of Topeka, Kansas* decision in 1954 that declared segregation in the schools as unconstitutional.

The Culture of Jim Crow

Wilson (1980) reported that African Americans made up nearly 40% of the southern population in the years following the Civil War; "they were central to the economy as cheap laborers; and they were highly visible in virtually every region of the South" (p. 137). It was the high number and their visibility that led to the establishment of the Jim Crow laws, many of which remained in effect until the 1950s. These practices included laws that discriminated against African Americans with concern to attendance in public schools and the use of facilities such as restaurants, theaters, hotels, cinemas, and public baths. Trains and buses were also segregated and in many states marriage between Whites and African American people was illegal. Williamson (1984) described African Americans as powerless in the South as a result of the Jim Crow laws and the 4,000 lynchings that took place between 1890 and 1920.

Jim Crow was not a person, yet affected the lives of millions of people. Named after a popular 19th-century minstrel song that stereotyped African Americans, "Jim Crow" came to personify the system of government-sanctioned racial oppression and segregation in the United States. Jim Crow was the name of the racial caste system that operated primarily but not exclusively in Southern and border states between 1877 and the mid-1960s. Jim Crow was more than a series of rigid anti-Black laws. It was a way of life. Under Jim Crow, African Americans were relegated to the status of second-class citizens. Jim Crow represented the legitimization of anti-Black racism. Many Christian ministers and theologians taught that Whites were the Chosen people, African Americans were cursed to be servants, and God supported racial segregation. Craniologists, eugenicists, phrenologists, and Social Darwinists, at every educational level, buttressed the belief that African Americans were innately intellectually and culturally inferior to Whites. Prosegregation politicians gave eloquent speeches on the great danger of integration: the mongrelization of the White race. Newspaper and magazine writers routinely referred to African Americans as niggers, coons, and darkies; and worse, their articles reinforced anti-Black stereotypes. Even children's games portrayed African Americans as inferior beings. All major societal institutions reflected and supported the oppression of African Americans.

The Jim Crow system was undergirded by the following beliefs or rationalizations: Whites were superior to African Americans in all important ways, including but not limited to intelligence, morality, and civilized behavior; sexual relations between African Americans and Whites would produce a mongrel race that would destroy America; treating African Americans as equals would encourage interracial sexual unions; any activity that suggested social equality encouraged interracial sexual relations; if necessary, violence must be used to keep African Americans at the bottom of the racial hierarchy.

Jim Crow etiquette operated in conjunction with Jim Crow laws (Black Codes). When most people think of Jim Crow they think of laws (not the Jim Crow etiquette), which excluded African Americans from public transport and facilities, juries, jobs, and neighborhoods. The passage of the 13th, 14th, and 15th Amendments to the Constitution granted African Americans the same legal protections as Whites. However, after 1877 and the election of Republican Rutherford B. Hayes as president, Southern and border states began restricting the liberties of African Americans. Unfortunately for African Americans, the Supreme Court helped undermine the Constitutional protections of African Americans with the infamous *Plessy v. Ferguson* (1896) case, which legitimized Jim Crow laws and the Jim Crow way of life.

In 1890, Louisiana passed the Separate Car Law, which purported to aid passenger comfort by creating "equal but separate" cars for African Americans and Whites. The Louisiana law made it illegal for African Americans to sit in coach seats reserved for Whites, and Whites could not sit in seats reserved for African Americans. In 1891, a group of African Americans decided to test the Jim Crow law. They had Homer A. Plessy, who was seven-eighths White and one-eighth Black (therefore, Black), sit in the White-only railroad coach. He was arrested. Plessy's lawyer argued that Louisiana did not have the right to label one citizen as White and another Black for the purposes of restricting their rights and privileges. In *Plessy*, the Supreme Court stated that so long as state governments provided legal process and legal freedoms for African Americans equal to those of Whites, they could maintain separate institutions to facilitate these rights. The Court, by a 7–2 vote, upheld the Louisiana law, declaring that racial separation did not necessarily mean an abrogation of equality. In practice, *Plessy* represented the legitimization of two societies: one White and advantaged; the other Black, disadvantaged, and despised.

African Americans were denied the right to vote by grandfather clauses (laws that restricted the right to vote to people whose ancestors had voted before the Civil War), poll taxes (fees charged to poor African Americans), White primaries (only Democrats could vote, only Whites could be Democrats), and literacy tests ("Name all the Vice Presidents and Supreme Court Justices throughout America's history"). *Plessy* sent this message to Southern and border states: Discrimination against African Americans is acceptable.

Jim Crow states passed statutes severely regulating social interactions between the races. Jim Crow signs were placed above water fountains, door entrances and exits, and in front of public facilities. There were separate hospitals for African Americans and Whites, separate prisons, separate public and private schools, separate churches, separate cemeteries, separate public restrooms, and separate public accommodations. In most instances, the Black facilities were grossly inferior—generally, older and less well kept. In other cases, there were no Black facilities—no Colored public restroom, no public beach, no place to sit or eat. *Plessy* gave Jim Crow states a legal way to ignore their constitutional obligations to their African American citizens.

The preceding discussion provides a basis for understanding the unique values that are held by many African Americans in the United States. The racial socialization of African Americans offers a clear picture of the struggles that have left their marks on the beliefs, attitudes, and values of a major segment of the U.S. population.

CULTURAL VALUES

The African American community in the United States constitutes a distinct cultural group connected by ancestry, historical experiences, shared values, or cultural tradition (Franklin & Moss, 2002). African American racial identification, then, is also indicative of cultural affiliation. Boyd-Franklin's (2003) description of the strengths of African American families summarizes cultural values characteristic to the African American community, which include: (a) strong kinship bonds and extended family relationships, (b) adaptability of family roles, (c) strong emphasis on work and ambition, (d) strong educational and achievement orientation, and (e) spirituality and religious orientation.

RACIAL IDENTITY DEVELOPMENT

Identity development encompasses many interrelated parts—gender, sexual, ethnic, racial, religious, and others—that shape experiences, worldview, and behavior. Although racial identity is the focus of this section, it is important to emphasize that this is a conceptual isolation for the purpose of analysis and understanding. In reality, each African American, like everyone else, has multiple dimensions to their identity that cumulatively form the self.

Children are formally introduced to the concept of race as early as preschool when their parents or caregivers complete requisite local, state, or federal documentation for student enrollment (Quintana et al., 2006; Tatum, 2003). The imposition of race into the educational system and process is one example of the many structural components of racial socialization in the United States. Prior to the beginning of school, however, children are able to make racial distinctions and form racial associations based on observations of their social environment and experiences (Tatum, 2003). A recent short documentary titled *A Girl Like Me* (2005), created by Kiri Davis, a 16-year-old, African American, female, high school student at the time, powerfully demonstrated how race impacts children. Although nonstandardized, she reconducted Clark & Clark's (1939, 1940) classic Black doll–White doll experiment. The original research findings that showed Black children preferred White dolls to Black dolls were reaffirmed in the Davis experiment. Racial identity, therefore, begins during the concrete experiences of early childhood in the United States and becomes a sophisticated and dynamic developmental process that evolves over the life span.

Unlike the neat, square check boxes designated for race on federal forms, racial identity has the potential and capacity to transform. Racial identity refers to the meaning and significance a person attributes to race, the relationship of race to personal identity, and the role of race in everyday life. Rather than a uniform, singular choice event, racial identity is dynamic, continuously shaped and defined by personal relationships, life experiences, social conditions, cognitive interpretations, and even existential or spiritual elements.

African American racial identity, therefore, is multidimensional and complex (Sellers, Smith, Shelton, Rowley, & Chavous, 1998). What being African American means to an African American client is related to their own developmental history, sociocultural context, and meaning derived from their experiences. Several models of African American racial identity have been created over the last 30 years. Two different racial identity development models will be covered in this section. The first model, developed by Cross (1995), describes the *process* of racial identity development in African Americans. Conversely, the second model, the Multidimensional Model of Racial Identity (MMRI), describes the racial identity of an African American person at a specific point in time in their lives (Sellers et al., 1998). These particular models were chosen, in part, because the Cross model was perhaps the first comprehensive model of Black racial identity development and the Sellers et al. model is a relatively more recent alternative racial identity conceptualization, derived at least in part from the Cross model.

Cross Model of Psychological Nigrescense

The stages of the Cross model can be compared figuratively to a walking trail (dynamic developmental process) that has at least five entry points (stages) with pathways that allow walkers a chance to come back (recycle) to particular locations in case they did not see or experience something that may have been important, or simply had the need or desire to revisit it. In terms of racial identity development, African Americans can start their walk at different points on the trail. An African American client named Stephanie, for example, who grew up on a U.S. military base in Germany, likely enters the trail at a different place than Marcos, an African American male client raised in a majority African American neighborhood in Birmingham, Alabama. If Stephanie is in the *pre-encounter* stage of the Cross model, or the earliest developmental entry point, she would emphasize the other parts of her identity such as being a writer or environmentalist, more than her racial identity. During this stage race is not considered to be an important aspect of her identity or a significant factor in daily life. Stephanie may even have negative associations with her racial group because of unexamined messages she has received. Marcos, on the other hand, may begin to wonder why there are only two African American students in his advanced placement courses when African Americans constitute almost 50% of his school population. His classroom experience is an example of the *encounter* stage where race becomes personally meaningful and is increasingly incorporated in how one views the world and interprets life events. Further down the trail, beyond pre-encounter and encounter, lies the *immersion–emersion* stage where Stephanie and Marcos feel compelled to embrace their African American heritage and to involve themselves in what they understand to be African American culture. At this point, their racial identity has not yet developed depth or dimensionality. Their initial efforts may be in reaction to perceived prejudice, such as being mistreated in a department store, or in response to a particularly inspiring experience involving other African Americans, such as watching "The State of Black America" on C-SPAN with Tavis Smiley. In either case, the significance and meaning of race in the lives of Stephanie and Marcos is altogether different from where either began. The *internalization* stage is reached when Stephanie and

Marcos begin again to acknowledge and value the other aspects of their identity, personal and social, in addition to their racial identity. At the last point on the trail, *internalization–commitment*, global changes in self-understanding and worldview become incorporated into the way Stephanie and Marcos exist in their respective worlds. They each will have formal and informal plans of actions that fit with who they are as human beings aware of the role race has and plays in their lives.

Multidimensional Model of Racial Identity

Sellers et al. (1998) offer an alternative model of racial identity, conceptually different than the developmental model presented by Cross. The Multidimensional Model of Racial Identity (MMRI), specifically, is not a process model; rather, it can be thought of as taking a picture of a person's racial identity at a particular point in time and space, then putting that picture into a theoretical frame to understand what it means. The framework of the MMRI includes four dimensions: (a) racial centrality and (b) racial salience, which assess the importance of race to the self-concept of an African American person; and (c) racial ideology and (d) racial regard, which assess what being African American means to the individual person. In summarizing research findings related to the MMRI, Marks, Settles, Cooke, Morgan, and Sellers (2004) concluded that "attitudes and beliefs regarding what it means to be Black are only predictive of important outcomes ... [when] ... race is a central identity in how they view themselves" (p. 399).

Based on the two models of racial identity presented, counselors working with African American clients should understand that the process of racial identity development and racial identity itself are not the same for all clients, though fundamental similarities do exist. In addition, there are individuals who may have been born or grew up on a Caribbean island, the African continent, or in Central and South America and now live in the United States, who also identify as Black, but not necessarily African American. Clients who identify as African American or Black, therefore, may make a distinction between their race (Black) and ethnicity (Puerto Rican).

With that in mind, it is important for counselors to assess the significance and meaning of racial identity from the perspective of their African American clients as it will help to foster the therapeutic alliance, contextualize presenting issues, and inform counseling strategies. Even before taking their clients racial identity into consideration, however, counselors must have an awareness of their own racial identity and how it impacts themselves, their worldview, and interactions with others

(Sue, Arredondo, & Roderick, 1992; Torres-Rivera, Phan, Maddux, Wilbur, & Garrett, 2001).

AFRICAN AMERICAN YOUTH

There are developmental and generational/contextual factors that need to be taken into consideration when counseling African American youth. This information helps counselors to better understand the experiences, perceptions, and worldviews of young African Americans, as well as to connect meaningfully with them to facilitate their growth, development, and success. For the purposes of this chapter, African American youth will be defined as elementary school-, middle school-, and high school-aged African American children and adolescents. Although adolescence, the developmental period that occurs between childhood and adulthood, can continue into the college or postsecondary years, individuals beyond the high school age group are considered adults (the primary focus of the other sections in this chapter). Distinctions are necessary for childhood, adolescence, and adulthood as the physical, cognitive, emotional, interpersonal, and identity development that occurs during each of these life stages has its own developmental challenges that can result in mental health concerns (Santrock, 2006). A 5-year-old African American boy, for example, may struggle with being separated from his parents or caregivers when he begins school; whereas a 16-year-old, African American, female, adolescent may argue with her parents about her curfew. Both examples involve challenges experienced by parents and children, however, they differ along developmental lines. A developmental approach, therefore, provides clues to the tasks and trials clients are experiencing at certain points in their lives. With this information, in addition to cultural knowledge, counselors are better able to determine if the behavior and emotional disposition of African American youth are developmentally appropriate or if there are potential underlying mental health issues.

The generational differences characteristic of the larger U.S. society also exist in the African American community. Technological advances in particular, including text messaging with cellular phones, electronic mailing with handheld computers, social networking (e.g., My Space, Facebook, Friendster, etc.) with the Internet, or all of the above using one device, have created a distinct generational culture in which youth are socialized. However, there are cultural–generational differences unique to African American youth. Such differences are often a source of friction and misunderstanding between the older *civil rights* generation and the younger *hip-hop* generation, which includes parents and children, teachers and students, older adult counselors and young adult clients, and adult counselors and adolescent or child clients. African American youth, particularly rap artists, hip-hop celebrities, professional athletes, and even alleged criminals on local news broadcasts, receive unprecedented exposure in popular media (e.g., television, radio, magazines, Internet, etc.), which serves to influence the identity and values of other African American youth (Kitwana, 2002). This type of cultural socialization contrasts with previous generations of African Americans whose parents, caregivers, and surrounding community were the primary source of their identity and values (Franklin & Moss, 2002). Having to contend with capitalistic powers of around-the-clock marketing targeting African American youth poses a great challenge to present-day parents and caregivers who seek to instill and pass on their own values (Kitwana, 2002).

Other significant generational characteristics that distinguish African American youth are their experiences with the U.S. educational and criminal justice systems. Educational issues such as underachievement, dropout rates, underenrollment in advanced placement courses, and the so-called acting White phenomenon (i.e., negative characterization of African American youth perceived to excel in school or who associate with White students made by other African American youth) represent generational barriers and are in contrast to the high value placed on educational achievement evident throughout the history of African American culture (Perry, Steele, & Hillard, 2003). While education remains a primary value in the African American community, structural barriers continue to exist in the education system that serve as impediments to the success of all African American children, including educational tracking of students, inequitable property tax funding of schools, and high-stakes educational testing (Darling-Hammond, 2001; Fine & Weis, 2003; Gordon, Della Piana, & Keleher, 2000; Kozol, 1991; McNeil, 2000).

The number of African American males ages 18–19 in state and federal prisons is almost double the number of White males and Hispanic males in the same age group. Many African American youth are cognizant and conversant about this reality, especially when they are aware of relatives, peers, or others in their community who have gone to court, jail, or prison. It is reasonable, then, that African American youth may have concerns about the possibility of being associated with or suspected of criminal involvement, due to racial profiling or other factors outside of their control, even when they are not involved in criminality.

One final generational consideration pertains to suicidal behaviors. The Centers for Disease Control and Prevention (1998) reported that between 1980 and 1995, the suicide rate among African Americans ages 10 to 14 increased 233%, while the suicide rates for comparable Whites increased 120%. Such an increase warrants the attention of mental health professionals working with African American youth exhibiting symptoms of depression, and necessitates use of suicide assessments and personal safety plans (Spann, Molock, Barksdale, Matlin, & Puri, 2006).

These are just a few of the reasons that young African American clients act within their phenomenological world—or the world as they see, experience, and interpret it—much differently than may be predicted by their adult parents, teachers, counselors or elders in general, without seriously taking generational differences into account. Counselors have to vigilantly guard against imposing their generational perspective onto their young African American clients experience. Awareness of inherent generational differences, then, opens an avenue for effective communication and understanding that would otherwise be inhibited or derailed completely.

COUNSELING STRATEGIES

In the introduction for this chapter, the diversity that exists within the African American community is given as the preliminary context from which the counseling strategies for African American clients will be introduced. It should be clear at this point in the chapter that there is no prototypical African American individual; therefore, neither could there be such an African American client. African Americans differ with respect to age, socioeconomic status, level of education, family structure, occupation, family history of mental illness, and so on. To link the words *individual* and *African American* together is interesting and noteworthy to begin the following discussion on counseling strategies. Every human being is indeed an individual, while at the same time she or he is born into a social and cultural system that even before birth there are preassigned and even predetermined groups to which that individual already belongs (e.g., race, ethnicity, gender, social class, family net worth, etc.). Specific aspects of an individual's experience related to African American group membership will guide the following discussion on counseling strategies with African American clients.

There are several approaches that can be taken when counseling an African American client. It is unlikely that a generic approach to counseling African American clients would be appropriate for each individual and their presenting issue(s). A counselor that recognizes the diversity that exists in the African American population could take the position that an individualized approach is the best that one can offer. This section, however, will emphasize the importance of using cultural and environmental information in case conceptualization and in the counseling process; as well as the importance of counselor authenticity, regardless of the specific counseling theory, method, or intervention used. The acronym *BE TRUE* is a cognitive reference point that can be used when working with African American clients. BE references the application of information related to *Black or African American culture* and *environmental factors* to the process of case conceptualization (i.e., the process of developing a theoretical explanation of the client's presenting issues). TRUE references the interpersonal dimension of counseling where the counselor of an African American client needs to establish that they are *trustworthy, real, understanding, and effective.* Each aspect of the BE TRUE approach will be discussed in the following sections on case conceptualization and the counseling relationship. In the concluding section, a case example will be provided to illustrate this approach.

Case Conceptualization (Black Culture, Environmental Factors)

A counselor that is informed with an understanding of particular aspects of African American culture (i.e., Black culture) will likely find that such information is facilitative of the therapeutic relationship and helps to put the client's presenting issues into a perspective that more closely approximates the client's actual experience (Harper & McFadden, 2003). The cultural backgrounds of the counselor and client affect how they interact with and understand each other. Language, points of reference, nonverbal behaviors, and shared and nonshared experiences all moderate the effectiveness of their communication. Counselors of the same race are not immune to cultural barriers, but may have more bridges than interracial counselor–client pairs (C. E. Thompson, Worthington, & Atkinson, 1994; V. L. S. Thompson & Alexander, 2006). When trying to develop an understanding of a client's situation, it is important to ask "What are the relevant cultural factors (see previous section on cultural factors) that need to be considered when working with an African American client having this presenting issue?"

Environmental factors include all external elements, aspects of the client's life not directly within their control, which may have an impact on their presenting issue (Harrell, 2000). For an African American client, environmental issues include social issues, such as racism, sexism, classism, and heterosexism, as well as unequal pay, hostile work settings, or access to and provision of quality health care services (Thompson &

Neville, 1999). These environmental factors and others affect the health and wellness of African American clients. An African American, gay, male client, for example, may experience frustration while being followed in a department store (racial profiling) and depression related to being ostracized in his religious community (discrimination; Greene, 2000; Loiacano, 1989; Savage & Harley, 2005). Therefore, it is critical to ask "What are the relevant environmental factors (see section titled "Demographic Characteristics of the African American Community") that need to be considered when working with an African American client having this presenting issue?"

The Counseling Relationship

It is often written that an effective counseling relationship is built on trust (Fong & Cox, 1983; Teyber, 2005). Trust is understandably earned as the counseling relationship develops. With African American clients, however, trust may not be as easily established as with White American clients (Ward, 2005). Many, if not most, African Americans have developed what is often termed a *healthy mistrust* of social institutions, which includes professional counseling (Boyd-Franklin, 2003). This healthy mistrust has grown out of an enduring legacy of abuse, exploitation, and maltreatment of African Americans in the United States by federal, state, and local agencies, as well as commercial and small businesses (Franklin & Moss, 2002). Given this historical and contemporary context, the initial task of counselors working with African American clients is to establish that they are trustworthy. In other counseling situations, this may be a passive, expected development that will happen over time; however, with African American clients, trust is not necessarily granted because of the services provided, the passage of time, or an established relationship. Rather, a counselor's trustworthiness is merited through an awareness of their client's sociocultural experiences and worldview, and thoughtful, intentional, ongoing efforts by the counselor to overcome the underlying mistrust likely to exist.

Authenticity, or being real, tends to be highly valued in the African American community (Ward, 2005). At the same time that trust is being established in the counseling relationship, clients that are members of historically oppressed groups also need to know that their counselor is sincerely invested in their health and well-being. Traditional counseling models that emphasize objectivity or strictly maintaining professional distance are often contrary to African American cultural norms of demonstrating care and concern (Boyd-Franklin, 2003; Franklin & Moss, 2002). African American clients may then perceive their counselor not to be truly committed, therefore, not worthy of their trust and ultimately not suitable to help them with their needs.

The second area of multicultural counseling competency is to develop an understanding of the client's worldview, experiences, and sociocultural and historical background (Sue et al., 1992). A client and their presenting issues cannot be truly understood from the perspective of the counselor. Rather, the task of the counselor is to understand the client's perspective. The same is true for clients who are African American, regardless of the race or ethnicity of their counselor. While African American counselors may share common historical, social, and cultural backgrounds and experiences with their African American client that can be helpful to the counseling process, they too must be careful not to overidentify with the client. Overidentification can cause counselors to miss important information or otherwise interfere with the helping process. The projection of the counselor's personal experiences onto the client's presenting issues, for example, "you know that *exact* same thing happened to me and here is how I handled it," illustrates how overidentification is potentially problematic.

Counselors who are not African American have several points of connection with their African American clients as well given the multidimensionality of individual identity. A Latino counselor, for example, may find that they have ancestry in common with their African American client and that their Latin heritage is very important to them both. Again, understanding African American clients is an active process and not a passive given. It is not to be assumed that worldviews and interpretation of life events are the same as from the counselor's perspective. Even if what you are hearing from your client seems fairly straightforward and easily understood, it is helpful to ask clarifying questions and to provide summary statements that reflect the meaning of the clients experience for verification, for example, "What I am hearing you say is there are times when you find it difficult and stressful to be the only woman and African American at your engineering firm, is that accurate?" Incorporating questioning and summarizing into the counseling process is highly valuable in establishing meaningful, productive, trustworthy, counseling relationships with African American clients.

Finally, the counseling process needs to be effective for an African American client to be engaged, committed, and return for additional sessions (Ward, 2005). Effectiveness in counseling can be difficult to define, assess, and measure (Leiburt, 2006). When clients understand the purpose of counseling and have a sense that counseling is personally valuable and beneficial to them, they are more likely to judge it as effective and continue. The responsibility of counselors, then, is to mutually define what effectiveness means with their African American client, which includes a collaborative understanding of the counseling process, goals, interventions, and method of evaluation. Concrete indicators of success, decided by the counselor and the client, enable both to have confidence that the process is working well and alerts them when a different direction is needed. A structured dialogue regarding the desired outcomes of counseling serves as a guide that can be adapted as life changes or goal achievement warrants. The counselor and client need to continually assess if together they are achieving the goals set for counseling and to have clearly defined terms for making this judgment. If the goal is to become more physically active, for example, effectiveness could be determined by creating and evaluating an exercise log. Ultimately, discussing what effectiveness means empowers African American clients, actively engages them in the therapeutic process, and makes them informed consumers and active investors in their personal counseling.

In summary, from intake to termination, keep BE TRUE in mind when working with an African American client. African American culture (i.e., Black culture) and environmental factors that impact the health and wellness of African Americans provide the context necessary to understand the problems experienced by African American clients (BE). As such, this information needs to be incorporated into the conceptualization of the client's presenting issues. Finally, it is important that counselors establish trustworthiness, exhibit realness (authenticity), convey understanding, and communicate about effectiveness throughout the counseling process (TRUE). An application of the BE TRUE approach is presented in the following section.

COUNSELING IMPLICATIONS

The need for counseling and the counseling process are often stigmatized in society and perhaps even more in communities of color (U.S. Department of Health and Human Services, 2001). Counseling is increasingly regarded as necessary and acceptable if needed, however, with (a) increased visibility (e.g., TV commercials) and availability (e.g., schools, Internet) and of counseling information and services, (b) the apparent need for mental health services (e.g., having friends or family members who have needed and directly benefited from mental health services), and (c) higher educational attainment in the African American community (i.e., people are more likely to value counseling once educated about mental health issues).

Case Example: Victoria

Victoria is a 25-year-old, African American, heterosexual, female engineer who is good friends with a licensed professional counselor named Sandra. Before Victoria met Sandra, she thought counseling was either for "crazy" people or for people who did not have high self-esteem or good coping skills. Although Victoria's favorite aunt Janice had worked with a counselor after her uncle Clive died unexpectedly, counseling was not something she thought of for herself because she always handled things effectively. As Victoria and Sandra became better friends, they often talked about their jobs and Victoria learned that people seek counseling for a variety of reasons and she actually had a lot in common with many of them. When Victoria's boyfriend, Andrew, decided he was no longer interested in a relationship with her after being together for a year, the life she was planning for herself suddenly changed. After 6 months had passed since her breakup, Victoria still could not make sense of it and it was interfering with her life. Reluctantly, she asked Sandra to refer her to a counselor. What follows illustrates how the BE TRUE approach can be used to understand Victoria and her presenting issue, as well as to form a working therapeutic alliance with her.

African American (Black) Culture Victoria was raised by her two African American parents who have been married for 34 years. She grew up going to Faith African Methodist Episcopal Zion church every Sunday with her family, including her older sister Jasmine (age 28), who has been married to James for 3 years. Family has always been a source of happiness for Victoria as she grew up near many of her cousins and enjoyed their family reunions every summer. The importance of education was emphasized throughout Victoria's upbringing because her parents strongly believed that education provided more opportunities for success, especially for people of color. Victoria also learned that marriage was to be valued, husbands and wives complement each other, and that children were a great source of joy and pride for their parents. Another clear message Victoria received from both of her parents and her African American teachers throughout the years was that she was special and needed to do well, represent a positive image of African Americans, and give back to her community.

Environmental Factors As the only woman and only African American in her engineering position, Victoria often feels isolated and closely scrutinized, both professionally and personally. She is also the youngest member of her team and has to deal with colleagues, who indirectly or directly question her competence. Although Victoria has served as the leader on several successful projects, she often feels as if she is being tested and has something to prove to her peers. Her work experience, though stressful and exhausting, is familiar and predictable. She usually talks about her work environment and coworkers with her friend Sandra, who understands as she has similar experiences of her own. She and Sandra also talk about being in their mid-20s, single, heterosexual, professional, African American women who hope to be married someday and have children, though neither is currently dating. Victoria often doubts that that she will meet other men like her former boyfriend Andrew, also a successful, African American engineer, or like her father, who is a licensed pharmacist. She even recently read an article in *Black Enterprise* that indicated African American women are earning college and graduate degrees at a higher rate than African American men.

Establishing the Counseling Relationship   Sandra referred Victoria to a licensed professional counselor named Zuri, who identifies as African American and Korean, although she selected Black as her race before other multiracial categories were an option. When Victoria made an appointment with Zuri, she informed her that Sandra had recommended her and that this was her first time in counseling. Zuri was welcoming to Victoria over the phone and expressed that "beginning counseling for the first time can often cause people to feel anxious because they are not quite sure what to expect." Victoria acknowledged that she did "feel a bit uneasy about calling," but trusted her friend Sandra and decided to take her advice. Zuri validated Victoria's feelings and shared that she would "honor the trust Sandra had placed in her as well by recommending her counseling services." Zuri informed Victoria that they would talk in detail about the counseling process during their first session together and address any concerns that she had. The conversation ended with Zuri saying to Victoria, "I celebrate your courage and look forward to walking with you along this part of your personal journey." With just this phone conversation, Zuri has begun to establish herself as trustworthy, authentic, and understanding. She has also provided an opportunity to demonstrate that she can be effective by outlining a few goals for the first session that she is confident they will be able to accomplish together: (a) explaining the counseling process and (b) answering her questions.

Summary   A counseling relationship, or working therapeutic alliance, is not established with a brief phone call between a counselor and an African American client. The initial contact that an African American client makes with a counseling service provider is, however, important as this task can be stressful, given the client's previous experiences, reasons for making contact, or present emotional state. Knowledge of African American culture and environmental factors that may have an impact on Victoria's presenting issue (i.e., difficulty coping with the end of her relationship to Andrew) provides contextual information. This specific information helps to illustrate that Victoria's situation is more complex and multidimensional than it would appear if culture and environment were not taken into consideration (e.g., Is Victoria feeling pressure from her family to get married? Is she envious of her sister? Is her work life interfering with her ability to form new relationships?). Without such information, Victoria's counselor would be limited in understanding her experiences, which could hinder the counseling process.

What Other Issues May Have an Impact on Victoria's Presenting Problem?

At a minimum, counselors should try to be familiar with group demographic information for African American people in the communities they serve and to have an awareness of typical characteristics of African American culture (e.g., importance of education, family, religious involvement). More specific information on racial identity, African American culture, and environmental context, however, is valuable to meaningfully connect with African American clients, to understand the significant nuances of presenting issues, and to collaboratively develop an effective method of working together. Finally, *be courageous* enough to ask your African American clients questions that make you uncomfortable because you are not sure how they might respond; *be open* to their feedback. It will help you to become a better counselor and person; and *BE TRUE*, authenticity can be respected even when there are different points of view.

QUESTIONS TO CONSIDER BEFORE WORKING WITH AN AFRICAN AMERICAN CLIENT

1. What are traditional values within African American culture?
2. What environmental factors constitute the social reality of African Americans in the United States? (How are the social experiences of African Americans in the United States unique?)
3. What can I do to show my African American clients that I am trustworthy?
4. How can I exhibit authenticity?

5. How do I convey understanding?
6. How will I gauge the effectiveness of my work?

REFERENCES

Bauman, K. J., & Graf. K. L. (2003). *Educational attainment: 2000. Census 2000 Brief.* Washington, DC: U.S. Census Bureau.

Billingsley, A. (1968). *Black families in White America.* Englewood Cliffs, NJ: Prentice-Hall.

Boyd-Franklin, L. (2003*). Black families in therapy: Understanding the African American experience* (2nd ed.). New York: Guilford Press.

Clark, K. B., & Clark, M. K. (1939). Segregation as a factor in the racial identification of negro pre-school children: A preliminary report. *Journal of Experimental Education, 8,* 161–163.

Clark, K. B., & Clark, M. K. (1940). Skin color as a factor in racial identification of negro preschool children. *The Journal of Social Psychology, 11,* 159–169.

Cross, W. E., Jr. (1995). The psychology of nigrescence: Revising the Cross model. In J. G. Ponterotto, J. M. Casas, L. A. Suzuki, & C. M. Alexander (Eds.), *Handbook of multicultural counseling* (pp. 93–122). Thousand Oaks, CA: Sage.

Darling-Hammond, L. (2001). The challenge of staffing our schools. *Educational Leadership, 58*(8), 12–17.

Davis, K. (Director). (2005). *A girl like me* [Reel Works Teen Film Making]. Retrieved on March 11, 2007, from http://video.google.com/videoplay?docid=1091431409617440489

DuBois, W. E. B. (1996). *The souls of Black folk.* New York: Penguin Books.

Fine, M., & Weis, L. (2003). *Silenced voices and extraordinary conversations.* New York, NY: Teachers College Press.

Fong, M. L., & Cox, B. G., (1983). Trust as an underlying dynamic in the counseling process: How clients test trust. *Personnel and Guidance Journal, 62*(3), 163–166.

Franklin, J. H., & Moss, A. A., Jr. (2002). *From slavery to freedom: A history of African Americans* (8th ed.). New York: Alfred A. Knopf.

Gordon, R., Della Piana, L., & Keleher, T. (2000). *Facing the consequences: An examination of racial discrimination in U.S. public schools.* Oakland, CA: Applied Research Center.

Greene, B. (2000). African American lesbian and bisexual women. *Journal of Social Issues, 56*(2), 239–249.

Grier, W. H., & Cobbs, P. M. (1968). *Black rage.* New York: Basic Books.

Harper, F. D., & McFadden, J. (Eds.). (2003). *Culture and counseling: New approaches.* Needham Heights, MA: Allyn & Bacon.

Harrell, S. (2000). A multidimensional conceptualization in racism-related stress: Implications for the well-being of people of color. *American Journal of Orthopsychiatry, 70,* 42–57.

Kitwana, B. (2002). The hip-hop generation: Young Blacks and the crisis in African American culture. New York: Basic Civitas.

Kozol, J. (1991). *Savage inequalities: Children in America's schools.* New York: Crown.

Leary, J. D. (2004). *Post traumatic slave syndrome: America's legacy of enduring injury and healing.* Milwaukie, OR: Uptone Press.

Leiburt, T. (2006). Making change visible: The possibility of assessing mental health outcomes. *Journal of Counseling and Development, 84*(1), 108–113.

Loiacano, D. K. (1989). Gay identity issues among Black Americans: Racism, homophobia, and the need for validation. *Journal of Counseling and Development, 68,* 21–25.

Marks, B., Settles, I. H., Cooke, D. Y., Morgan, L., & Sellers, R. M. (2004). African American racial identity: A review of contemporary models and measures. In R. L. Jones (Ed.), *Black psychology* (4th ed., pp. 383–404). Hampton, VA: Cobb and Henry.

McKinnon, J. (2001). *The Black population: 2000. Census 2000 Brief.* Retrieved March 24, 2007, from U.S. Census Bureau, http://www.census.gov/prod/2001pubs/c2kbr01-5.pdf

McKinnon, J. D., & Bennett, C. E. (2005). *We the people: Blacks in the United States.* Retrieved on March 19, 2007 from U.S. Census Bureau, http://www.census.gov/prod/2005pubs/censr-25.pdf

McNeil, L. (2000). Creating new inequalities: Contradictions of reform. *Phi Delta Kappan, 81*(10), 728–734.

Myrdal, G. (1944). *An American dilemma: the Negro problem and modern democracy.* New York: Harper & Brothers.

Perry, T., Steele, C., & Hillard, A. (2003). *Young, gifted, and Black: Promoting high achievement among African-American students.* Boston: Beacon Press.

Quintana, S. M., Aboud, F. E., Chao, R. K., Contreras-Grau, J., Cross, W. E., Jr., Hudley, C., et al. (2006). Race, ethnicity, and culture in child development: Contemporary research and future directions. *Child Development, 77*(5), 1129–1141.

Santrock, J. W. (2006). *Life-span development* (10th ed.). Boston: McGraw-Hill.

Savage, T. A., & Harley, D. A. (2005). African American lesbian, gay, and bisexual persons. In D. A. Harley and J. M. Milton (Eds.). *Contemporary mental health issues among African Americans* (pp. 91–105). Alexandria, VA: American Counseling Association.

Sellers, R. M., Smith, M. A., Shelton, J. N., Rowley, S. A. J., & Chavous, T. M. (1998). Multidimensional model of racial identity: A reconceptualization of African American racial identity. *Personality and Social Psychology Review, 2*(1), 18–39.

Sue, D. W., Arredondo, P. M., & Roderick, J. (1992). Multicultural counseling competencies and standards: A call to the profession. *Journal of Multicultural Counseling and Development, 20*(2), 64–88.

Tatum, B. D. (2003). *"Why are all the Black kids sitting together in the cafeteria?" and other conversations about race.* New York: Basic Books.

Terkel, S. (1992). *Race: How Blacks and Whites feel about the American obsession.* New York: New Press.

Teyber, E. (2005). *Interpersonal process in therapy: An integrative model.* Pacific Grove, CA: Brooks/Cole.

Thompson, C. E., Worthington, R., & Atkinson, D. R. (1994). Counselor content orientation, counselor race, and Black women's cultural mistrust and self-disclosures. *Journal of Counseling Psychology, 41*(2), 155–161.

Thompson, V. L. S., & Alexander, H. (2006). Therapists' race and African American clients' reaction to therapy. *Psychotherapy: Theory, Research, Practice, Training, 43*(1), 99–110.

Torres-Rivera, E., Phan, L. T., Maddux, C., Wilbur, M. P., & Garrett, M. T. (2001). Process versus content: Integrating personal awareness and counseling skills to meet the multicultural challenge of the twenty-first century. *Counselor Education and Supervision, 41*(1), 28–40.

U.S. Department of Commerce, Bureau of the Census. (2001). *Poverty in the United States: 2000* (Current Population Reports, Series P60–214). Washington, DC: U.S. Government Printing Office.

U.S. Department of Health and Human Services. (2001). *Mental health: Culture, race, and ethnicity—A supplement to mental health: A report of the surgeon general.* Rockville, MD: Author.

U.S. Census Bureau. (2000). *Statistical abstract of the United States: 2000* (120th ed.). Springfield, MA: National Technical Information Service.

Ward, E. C. (2005). Keeping it real: A grounded theory study of African American clients engaging in counseling at a community mental health agency. *Journal of Counseling Psychology, 52*(4), 471–481.

Williamson, J. (1984). *The crucible of race: Black-white relations in the American South.* New York: Oxford University Press.

Wilson, W. J. (1980). *The declining significance of race.* Chicago: University of Chicago.

Young, C. (1986). Afro-American family: Contemporary issues and implications for social policy. In D. Pilgrim (Ed.), *On being Black: An in-group analysis* (pp. 58–75). Bristol, IN: Wyndham Hall Press.

7

COUNSELING WITH ASIAN AMERICANS

Anneliese A. Singh

"Growing up in predominantly white schools in Texas, where Asian Americans were marginalized as model minorities and undesirable people, my sister dealt with body image problems," Noh said. "She hated looking Asian American."

(Amusa, 2006)

I experienced a lot of racism, and I just remember being just always kind of wanting, craving this other world where I was powerful. Those memories of wanting to be accepted as a South Asian are strong for me, and that was kind of juxtaposed against a lot of ostracism, and otherness, so it was just bad all around. It was pretty scary too. The racism meant I didn't have a lot of ways to cope with stress, so I acted out a lot.

(Singh, Hays, Watson, & Chung, 2006)

I'm not going to die because I failed as someone else. I am going to succeed as myself.

—Margaret Cho, Korean American comedian

Taking a social justice approach to counseling with Asian Americans encourages counselors to examine the social context in which they counsel, as well as how relevant counseling theories and interventions are for this population. This chapter will challenge counselors to consider how history and other sociopolitical factors have shaped the experience of Asian Americans and their mental health. In this challenge, the myth of the "model minority" will be deconstructed so that counselors may view Asian Americans through a lens that is more representative of their lived experience in America. As this chapter examines the nature of Asian Americans in America particular attention is given to the importance of culturally appropriate interventions that will assist counselors in supporting the coping mechanisms and resilience of the Asian American clients with whom they will work.

HISTORICAL AND SOCIOPOLITICAL CONTEXT OF ASIAN AMERICANS

It is important to define exactly who Asian Americans are, yet in many ways their definition defies any one category (Ho, 1998). A basic definition might include Asian Americans as those individuals of Asian heritage living in the United States (Cao & Novas, 1996). This definition is immediately challenging though, as the countries represented by the Asian continent (i.e., China, Japan, Thailand), the Asian subcontinent (i.e., India, Bhutan, Pakistan), and Asian diaspora (i.e., Nigeria, United Kingdom) are incredibly diverse in terms of cultural values, history, and language. Keeping in mind the politics of language, counselors should be aware that *Asian American* emerged as a term of empowerment by Asian American activists who wanted to refer to all Americans of Asian descent (Hong & Domokos-Chen Ham, 2001). The use of this term was an astute political move and an act of resistance against previous terms, such as *Oriental*, which labeled Asian Americans as foreigners in addition to grouping them with those living in Asian countries (Cao & Novas, 1996).

In the United States, the numbers of Asian Americans continue to increase. A large increase of Asian Americans occurred between 1981 and 1983 (2.3 million), reaching a total population of 10 million in 1995 and estimated to be over 17 million by 2000 and at 38 million in 2010 (U.S. Census Bureau, 1990, 1995). A large part of providing a social justice approach to counseling with Asian American clients is simply recognizing the incredible diversity that exists within the words *Asian American*. In fact, there are 43 ethnic groups that fall under the umbrella of Asian American, including Pacific Islander groups (for purposes of this chapter, Asian American will be used to include Pacific Islanders and the Asian diaspora). Therefore, there is not just one culturally specific way to provide culturally relevant interventions to Asian Americans, but in fact there are several approaches that can be understood and used by counselors. Therefore, it is critical for counselors to possess knowledge of general Asian American history and their cultural practices while guarding against the assumption that all Asian Americans share one common value set. Although a thorough discussion of the immigration patterns of each of the subgroups within Asian Americans is beyond the scope of this chapter, it is important that counselors be aware of historical and legislative events that have shaped the lives of Asian Americans.

ROLE OF LEGISLATION IN ASIAN AMERICAN IMMIGRATION

Viewing the Asian immigration to the United States through a social justice lens, the racism embedded in U.S. legislation with regard to Asian Americans becomes immediately evident. Hong and Domokos-Chen Ham (2001) identify two pivotal times during Asian immigration: pre-Word War II and post-World War II. During the pre-World War II period, the initial majority of Asian immigrants came to the United States from China as laborers to work on the transcontinental railroad or to work in the California gold mines. The next wave of immigration comprised Japanese, Koreans, and Filipinos who arrived in Hawaii to work on the sugarcane plantations. Asian Indian farmers entered the United States in the early 1900s after they were denied immigration by Canada's racist immigration policies. As the number of Asian immigrants rose, prejudice and discrimination increased toward them as well. Two U.S. laws that were explicitly discriminatory toward Asian immigrants stand out during the pre-World War II immigration period: (a) the Chinese Exclusion Act of 1882 (Congressional legislation that denied Chinese immigrants citizenship) and (b) the antimiscegenation laws (state legislation that denied intermarriage between Whites and Chinese immigrants; Cao & Novas, 1996).

The post-World War II Asian immigration period saw a different pattern of entry of Asians into the United States. Many of the discriminatory laws were repealed, while simultaneously the Immigration and Naturalization Act of 1965 was passed. This legislation prioritized the entry of individuals who held professional and technical degrees, unlike the pre-World War II period where Asian immigrants were primarily laborers without access to gaining an education.

Impact of the Migration Story

When working with Asian American clients, having knowledge of the role that legislation has played in shaping the cultural context of their lives becomes significant because of the impact on the migration story of the family. In understanding the migration story, one must have a thorough grasp of the concepts of acculturation, assimilation, and generational status. Acculturation is the process that Asian Americans experience as their Asian cultural worldview comes into contact with the dominant culture of the United States (Uba, 1994), whereas assimilation is the actual specific behaviors and situations that Asian Americans encounter in the United States that move them from being more Asian identified to more Western identified. Stressors of acculturation and assimilation (i.e., racism, self and collective identity, familial values, kinship networks, education) are important to understand because they define the migration stories of Asian Americans. It is also important to underscore that these migration stories are not homogeneous for Asian Americans, and when faced the stressors of acculturation and assimilation for Asian American subgroups may look very different (Iwamasa, 1996).

Counselors must keep in mind the importance of generational status in relation to the migration stories of Asian Americans with whom they work. Generational status refers to the number of generations that a client's family has been in the United States. A first-generation immigrant is someone who was born outside of the United States, whereas a second-generation individual is someone with one or both of their parents born outside of the United States. A third-generation individual is someone with both parents born in the United States. Generational status is an important factor to consider with clients, as the mental health stressors facing an individual and their family may vary according to their length of stay in the United States (Inman, Chang, & Singh, 2006).

DECONSTRUCTING THE MYTH OF THE MODEL MINORITY

In order to provide culturally responsive treatment with Asian Americans, counselors must understand the sociopolitical roots of the origin of the myth of the model minority (Sue & Sue, 2003). This myth holds that Asian Americans strive for and achieve the "American dream" at higher rates and more quickly than other ethnic minority groups in the

United States. In a classic case of the "personal is political"; when one unearths the reality behind the myth, there are significant counseling implications for Asian Americans and opportunities for counselors to engage in advocacy and social justice work within this realm.

As one of the most oppressive stereotypes that Asian Americans labor under, the myth posits that Asian Americans are the model minority because they embody the American dream determination and perseverance that result in success (Peterson, 1966). In reality, the myth serves to make the very real challenges that face Asian Americans invisible. For instance, B. C. Kim (1973) pointed out that the myth that Asian Americans are the model minority makes it difficult to both acknowledge and demand attention to issues of health, education, housing, employment, social services, and other issues that they face. From a social justice perspective, this denial of challenges is additionally problematic because it serves to deny the existence of racism, classism, and other oppressions for Asians in the United States.

The first unveiling of the myth occurs when one remembers that Asian Americans who had research and technical skills were recruited to come to the United States on a voluntary basis in the '50s and '60s. Therefore, Asian immigrants landing on U.S. soil were not only brought to the country without forced immigration, but they also tended to hail from families with academic and class privilege. This combination of privilege allowed Asian Americans to have a drastically different beginning in the United States than other ethnic minority groups. Therefore, it was relatively easy for the capital-owning and political classes in the United States to tag Asian Americans' unique recipe of unearned privilege and status as earned class mobility due to the apparent Asian American success to the outside world.

Like any stereotype, there is a double-edged sword to the myth of the model minority. On the one hand, Asian Americans may have benefited from aspects of the myth, as they may be viewed as hard working, passive, and determined to achieve success. On the other hand, this myth serves to separate the issues that Asian Americans as a group face from other ethnic minorities in the United States. D. W. Sue and D. Sue (2003) underscore this point by acknowledging that the myth may push Asian Americans to not critically examine racism and other oppressions they experience, while simultaneously making any within-group differences in Asian culture invisible in order to create the illusion that Asian American culture is homogeneous.

ASIAN WORLDVIEW: COLLECTIVISM
AND THE FAMILIAL SELF

The Asian culture tends to be collectivistic and family oriented, which gives the family or group identity primacy over individual identity (Uba, 1994). When healthy and in balance, a collectivistic orientation demands that Asian individuals rely on the family system for support of basic needs, daily functioning, and decision making. Therefore, it is important for counselors to remember that when Asian American clients present for counseling that it may be more effective to visualize the client's family with them in the counseling room. Whether their experience with their families is positive, negative, or neutral, it is likely that Asian American clients' experiences in their families have left an indelible mark on their values, interpersonal style, and belief systems. Children of Asian Americans are expected to succeed individually in the United States with the expectation that their success will be shared with and reflected by the family unit (D. W. Sue & D. Sue, 2003).

This brings tension to the lives of Asian American individuals who may feel constantly pulled between feeling pressure to seek individual success, while simultaneously finding ways to be relationally connected to the family. For instance, filial piety is defined as the practice and value of obedience and respect of children to parents (Yeh & Hwang, 2000). This practice may be in direct opposition to values of individuation that are emphasized outside of the family, therefore causing issues of stress within a more traditional family system if a child is learning and following more Western and individualistic values. Further, in the academic or work setting, Asian Americans may be viewed from a Western lens as being "not assertive enough" or "enmeshed with the family."

SPIRITUALITY AND WORLDVIEW

In addition to considering the resilience and coping skills of Asian American clients, counselors should have knowledge of non-Western religions and spiritual beliefs. Some Asian countries are dominated by certain organized religions such as Buddhism (Thailand), Hinduism (India), Christianity (Korea), and Islam (Indonesia), whereas in other countries, people's belief systems and worldviews are often influenced by traditional philosophies (e.g., China). In general, even if Asian American clients do not actively define themselves as religious or spiritual, there can be a belief in a mind–body connection (Das & Kemp, 1997; D. W. Sue & D. Sue, 2003). Therefore, counselors may not only honor and acknowledge this worldview, but also invite Asian American clients to share other modalities (e.g., acupuncture, praying, chanting, scripture, meditation) that they have experienced as healing. In bringing attention to the Asian holistic view of health, counselors may simultaneously strengthen the therapeutic relationship and empower Asian American clients to reclaim modalities of healing that they may have been disconnected from as a result of the acculturation process.

In addition to being aware of the Eastern religious and spiritual view of the mind–body connection, counselors should also be aware of the importance of the ideas of being "feminine" or "masculine." For example, Hinduism has similar views as Taoism, such as recognizing the importance of balance between female (*shakti*) and male (*shiva*) qualities in the world. Traditional Asian philosophical teachings (e.g., Confucian and Taoism) additionally emphasize straight adherence to prescribed gender roles and male–female relationships in hierarchical social structures. These teachings also include complementarity between yin (female, darkness, softness, etc.) and yang (male, light, strength, etc.), as well as continuation and expansion of the family through reproduction.

ASIAN AMERICANS AND COUNSELING

Asian Americans have been shown to underutilize counseling, and there is limited research on their counseling outcome modalities (Leong, 1986). Questions remain as to whether this underutilization is due to a lack of culturally relevant treatment, a cultural stigma about counseling, or acculturative stressors (D. W. Sue & D. Sue, 2003; Yeh & Hwang, 2000). Asian Americans have been shown to have high dropout rates and underutilization of mental health services (Atkinson, Lowe, & Matthews, 1995; Bui & Takeuchi, 1992), and there is limited information about their participation in or success with group counseling (Leong, Wagner, & Kim, 1995). Many scholars attribute the Asian absence from counseling to the emphasis on family honor and privacy (Atkinson et al., 1995). Additionally, research has shown that the individualistic perspective of Western counseling approaches often conflict with the collectivistic coping style of Asian culture whose perspective emerges from using social support systems (i.e., kinship networks; Solsberg, Choi, Ritsma, & Jolly, 1994; Yeh & Hwang, 2000). From a social justice perspective, it is important for counselors to question how the major counseling frameworks (i.e., psychodynamic, cognitive-behavioral, person centered) attempt to explain coping skills and mental health, as well as to explicitly explore with clients how these approaches might go directly against their cultural values of wellness. In order to understand Asian cultural ideas of wellness, counselors must first have knowledge of how Asian mental health is shaped by their racial and ethnic identity development.

RACIAL AND ETHNIC IDENTITY DEVELOPMENT: ACCULTURATION AND RACISM

Keeping in mind the large diversity that exists within the Asian American population, one can imagine that understanding the racial and ethnic identity development of Asian Americans in general, in addition to the various subgroups, is very challenging. There are several models of racial and ethnic identity development that exist for Asian Americans, with the first model based on Chinese Americans (S. Sue & D. W. Sue, 1971). There are also Asian American identity development models based on Japanese American identity development (J. Kim, 1981; Kitano, 1982). One of the most widely used models is the Suinn-Lew Asian Self-Identity Acculturation Scale (Suinn, Ahuna, & Khoo, 1992), which measures levels of acculturation for Asian Americans. In general, these models tend to classify Asian Americans based on their values and behaviors. For example, "traditional" Asian Americans are individuals who ascribe more to Asian values, "assimilationist" Asian Americans are those who adopt more Western values, and "bicultural" Asian Americans hold both Asian and Western values.

One can see that the challenges in using the Asian American racial and ethnic identity development models is that they are normed on specific subgroups of Asian Americans (J. Kim, 1981; Kitano, 1982; Sue & Sue, 2003), but they are generalized to all Asian Americans (Suinn, Ahuna, & Khoo, 1992) without attention to the diversity between ethnicities in the Asian American population. A social justice critique of these models has been that the models do not account for the reality that Asian Americans experience prejudice and discrimination due to racism in the United States and how this shapes their ethnic identity (Uba, 1994).

For this reason, the minority development model (Table 7.1) has been applied to Asian Americans as a way to acknowledge the fluidity of ethnic identity in relation to stressors of acculturation and racism. The first stage is the conformity stage, where Asian Americans are moving toward Western values in the assimilation process and ascribing less to the more traditional Asian values. For example, an Asian American female client may compare herself to Western standards of beauty, resulting in lower self-esteem and dissatisfaction with her Asian

Table 7.1 Minority Development Model as Applied to Asian Americans

Stage One: Conformity	Moving toward Western values
Stage Two: Dissonance	Experience of racism and questioning of Western values
Stage Three: Resistance and Immersion	Return to Asian values and social support
Stage Four: Introspection	Increased sense of self and security in one's Asian American identity
Stage Five: Synergetic Articulation and Awareness	Ascribing to Asian or Western values based on individual choices and recognition of negative and positive aspects of both worldviews

Source: Mintz & Kashubeck, 1999.

physical features (Mintz & Kashubeck, 1999). In the second stage, the dissonance stage, Asian Americans have an experience with racism or face acculturative stressors that cause them to question their valuation of Western values. At this stage, the same female Asian American client may describe feeling confused about beauty standards and experience immense tension between Asian and Western values, situations, and behaviors. She may also begin to notice how other people of color experience similar tensions and confusion and begin to feel connected with their struggle as well.

Whereas in the third stage, the resistance and immersion stage, Asian Americans consciously return to their Asian values and social support systems, while rejecting a Western worldview and feeling less comfortable in Western spaces. In our example, the Asian American woman may describe in counseling her anger at feeling ashamed of her Asian features and intentionally remove herself from Western media and social groups, while seeking a like-minded Asian-identified community. This client may deem Asian physical features as more beautiful than Western physical features. She may also begin to identify further with the ways that other people of color experience oppressive Western beauty standards.

The introspection state is the fourth stage, where Asian Americans feel more secure in their ethnic identity and are able to question the "either–or" thinking concerning Asian versus Western community and values characterized by the previous stage. The Asian American female client may feel more comfortable with her own standard of beauty, and then is able to question some of her previously held beliefs as she identifies positive aspects of both Asian and Western concepts of beauty. Finally, in the fifth stage, synergetic articulation and awareness, Asian Americans ascribe to Asian or Western values based on their individual preferences and valuing of their own individuality and worth, while realizing that both worldviews have positive aspects.

It is important for counselors to keep in mind that Asian American racial and ethnic identities cannot be thought of as one homogeneous identity, but rather should be carefully assessed and understood collaboratively with the client. Despite the challenges that the models of Asian American racial and ethnic identity development bring, they may be helpful tools to begin a dialogue and strengthen conceptualization of clients' presenting issues. Because of the history of racism, which has saddled Asian Americans with unequal treatment and discriminatory practices in the United States, any exploration of an Asian American's racial and ethnic identity should include attention to the impact of racial oppression. As racial oppression is a component of the Asian American's experience, counselors need to recognize how Asian Americans attempt to work through oppressive conditions.

RESILIENCE AND COPING STRATEGIES

Counselors may most effectively work with Asian American clients when they remember to explore the degree of resilience and coping that they have in response to acculturative stressors. Resilience is defined as the capacity to manage adversity successfully, especially in terms of developmental outcomes (Luthar, Cicchetti, & Becker, 2000). The collectivistic orientation of Asian Americans can be a protective factor against this undervaluation of their values in the United States (Singh, Hays, Watson, & Chung, 2006), as they may seek social support from their intimate networks in response to experiences of oppression. However, this resilience seems to also be shaped by the ethnic identity development of Asian Americans and the intensity of the discrimination that the individual faces. For example, Lee (2005) found in a study of perceived discrimination and resilience for Korean Americans that pride in one's ethnic identity served as a protective factor against discrimination. However, ethnic pride provided less positive results and protection as the level of discrimination increased.

Although there is a need for further research on resilience and coping strategies of Asian Americans, it becomes clear from a social justice perspective that it is important for counselors to collaboratively find ways to identify and actively support the development of their resilience through recognizing Asian Americans' degree of acculturation and assimilation.

COUNSELING ISSUES FOR ASIAN AMERICANS

This section gives an overview of some of the common presenting issues that Asian Americans may bring into the counseling office, as well as guidelines for culturally relevant treatment from a social justice perspective, which counselors may use to increase effectiveness of treatment. The section begins with reference to the myth of the model minority and its impact on Asian American mental health, and then moves into an introduction of more "taboo" issues (e.g., family stressors, intimate partner violence, substance abuse) that counselors may see Asian Americans present with in their offices.

Mental Health Impact of the Myth of the Model Minority

Once counselors have a good understanding as to how and why the model minority myth exists, they may assess the degree to which this myth is masking or amplifying the client's distress. Because the myth can make challenges that Asian Americans face difficult to identify, counselors may explicitly and collaboratively explore the impact the myth may have had on the client's life. This exploration is most effectively done after a solid therapeutic relationship has been established between the counselor and client. Within this relationship, counselors may introduce the idea of the model minority as a way to check if the clients have awareness and knowledge of the myth. Counselors will also want to pay close attention to the client's racial and ethnic identity development, as the degree to which they ascribe to Asian and/or Western values will shape this exploration.

Somatization of Stress

Asian American clients may discuss the impact of stress in their life through somatic complaints (Uba, 1994). These somatic complaints may be described as headaches, stomachaches, muscle aches, and general feelings of tension in the body. It is important to acknowledge the value of this cultural way of expressing distress without shaming, questioning, or pathologizing the client from a Western perspective. Counselors can validate the distress of these somatic symptoms and use them as symbols or metaphors for how the client may decrease stress in their life. For instance, a South Asian female survivor of intimate partner violence may describe her "head being in pain." Empathizing with her physical pain and assessing the frequency and duration of her symptoms is an important way to increase the client's sense that the counselor understands her stress, while assessing the extent to which the somatic complaints are being treated medically or with other modalities.

Family Concerns

Asian American clients may enter counseling once they have exhausted the use of their kinship networks and other support systems (e.g., religious/spiritual, meditation, friendships, family). Asian clients may feel additionally anxious about being in counseling due to fear of bringing shame to the family by disclosing private matters outside of the home. Normalizing this anxiety is a critical way to build trust within the therapeutic relationship. Counselors may also explicitly explore the needs of Asian American clients in order to help the clients feel more comfortable and clear about their goals for counseling. For example, clients may express discomfort or that it "feels strange to just talk about their problems with a stranger."

It is also possible that Asian American clients may request that family members or other people in their kinship networks attend therapy with them. Carefully exploring how these individuals may or may not help the client achieve his or her desired counseling goal is important in these situations. It is also critical to understand that families in Asian American culture tend to be hierarchical (Das & Kemp, 1997). If this is afforded to Asian American clients, you may find that Asian American clients may defer to their elders for guidance in decision making and other matters of distress. Counselors may find this helpful if it can be used to work on the behalf of the client.

Academic and Career Concerns

Many Asian American clients will often present for counseling with concerns about their academic or career goals. This is largely for two reasons: (a) the cultural stigma against discussing personal problems and (b) the pressure to be successful in academic and career pursuits. Because of the Asian values of family piety and withholding of emotionality, it may be difficulty for Asian American clients to present for counseling for a mental health issue. Therefore, it is important for counselors to conduct a thorough assessment (e.g., family, social support systems, mental health history, substance abuse, trauma) when academic or career concerns are reported. Additionally, as discussed earlier in the chapter, the pressures of the model minority myth combined with family and cultural expectations to succeed may translate into emotional distress for a client. For instance, a Vietnamese family may expect their son to attend pharmacy school, which they have deemed a stable and profitable profession that will bring financial independence to the family, as well as public esteem. In his quest to succeed in his studies, this client may forego the social outlets that college students typically engage in, which causes him to feel isolated and distant from his peers. This same student may also be not performing at the level expected by his parents, and he may be experiencing shame about his abilities to succeed as a student and to be a reliable member of the family. Identifying the cultural values and pressures that the student is experiencing, in addition to helping the student set goals for counseling that are culturally congruent to him, is critical.

Substance Abuse

Substance abuse is rarely discussed within Asian American families, and there is scarce attention to this issue in research as well. This is not only a critical area to assess with every Asian American client within a thorough intake, but it is also a form of stress that may be underreported by clients in counseling. When an Asian American client's substance abuse issues require specialized treatment, counselors may serve as advocates for their clients to help ensure that they receive culturally relevant substance abuse counseling. Because support groups (e.g., Alcoholics Anonymous) use a Western framework of recovery and sobriety, counselors may also serve as advocates by helping clients clarify how their cultural values (e.g., religion/spirituality) may or may not be reflected in their treatment and how they might incorporate their cultural worldview into treatment goals.

Intimate-Partner Violence and Child Sexual Abuse

Violence may be a taboo topic for Asian Americans and may be especially difficult to explore due to shame and feelings of betrayal of family members. Research is lacking on the numbers of Asian Americans who experience violence within their families, however intimate-partner violence and child sexual abuse are issues that Asian American clients may struggle with in their lives. Counseling may be the only place where clients feel safe to discuss the impact of violence on their emotional well-being (Abueg & Chun, 1996). Because the client may have internalized shame or guilt about the violence within their family, it is important for counselors to assist them in externalizing these feelings and identifying coping strategies that are healing for them. In a study of South Asian women who had survived child sexual abuse, resilience strategies of the individuals in the study were shown to be having a sense of hope about the future, self-care, connection with social support, and reconnection with a South Asian community (Singh et al., 2006). Counselors may want to explore similar coping strategies for Asian Americans who present with issues of trauma.

DSM–IV–TR Disorders

Asian American youth have been shown to have high rates of youth depression and suicide rates, with suicide being the second leading cause of youth deaths among Asian Americans in the United States after unintentional injuries (Centers for Disease Control and Prevention [CDC], 2000). Yet, counselors may miss the signs of depression, suicidality, and other *Diagnostic and Statistical Manual of Mental Health Disorders* (American Psychiatric Association, 2000, 4th ed., text revision; [*DSM–IV–TR*]) due to expectations that clients self-disclose symptoms, in addition to a lack of culturally sensitive diagnosis. An additional challenge exists in that Asian American clients may feel distrustful about psychiatric treatment due to discriminatory experiences with health care and lack of attention to cultural concerns. Therefore, it is important that counselors remember to assess other healing modalities that the client may use or have access to from their culture. Counselors should also keep in mind that Asian Americans may be particularly sensitive to certain psychiatric medications (Abueg & Chung, 1996) and that the diagnostic criteria used within the *DSM–IV–TR* are not based on Asian cultural norms of development (Eriksen & Kress, 2005).

Gender Concerns

Although an exhaustive exploration of gender with Asian Americans is beyond the scope of this chapter, it is important for counselors to be aware that gender concerns may be a critical aspect of mental health challenges that Asian Americans face. Clients may describe acculturative stressors that shift family dynamics and power, and they may experience similar shifts in gender roles depending on how narrowly these roles are defined within their culture (Das & Kemp, 1997). Asian American women and men both experience being stereotyped based on their gender, so it is important that counselors withhold assumptions about how Asian American clients feel about their gender. An accurate assessment of their acculturation process, generational status, and values should yield information that is helpful for counselors to understand how Asian American clients see their gender role within the family and in other settings (e.g., work, school, social support groups).

Intersecting Identities

Because the racial and ethnic identity of Asian Americans may be only one of several salient parts of their identities that factor into their mental health and coping, the following section will explore how intersecting identities may shape mental health of this population. Due to the limits of space, this section will explore how intersecting identities impact Asian American sexual minorities.

Sexual Orientation   Asian Americans who are LGBTQQ (lesbian, gay, bisexual, transgender, queer, questioning) have an intersection of identities that can serve as particularly oppressive. Because of the predominantly White and Western culture that is the LGBTQQ community in the United States, Asian American LGBTQQ individuals can experience being stereotyped not only for their race, but also for their gender. For instance, Asian American gay men may be perceived to be nonsexual or sexually unattractive, whereas Asian American lesbian women may be eroticized. Also, the coming out process can look very different for Asian American LGBTQQ people. They may experience homophobia within the Asian community, while also experiencing racism within the predominantly white LGBTQQ community (Chan, 1989). The end result can be a marginalization from both communities, which can create more acculturative stress for Asian American LGBTQQ people (Chung & Syzmanski, 2007; Singh, Chung, & Dean, 2007).

When assessing for this acculturative stress with LGBTQQ individuals, it is important that counselors draw upon their knowledge of both Asian American issues and LGBT issues and their intersection. Research has been limited with this population, although there have been studies examining the intersection of internalized homophobia and their sexual and ethnic identity development (Chung & Szymanski, 2007; Singh et al., 2007). These studies have found that higher rates of internalized homophobia are associated with higher levels of acculturation, demonstrating that Asian American LGBTQQ individuals may dissociate their ethnic and sexual identities from one another to maintain their connections with both communities. Therefore, it is important that counselors tailor their interventions with this population to consider the client's level of acculturation *and* their sexual identity development.

Asian American LGBTQQ people may also experience significant resilience as a result of their unique coming out process, depending on the extent to which they have internalized negative stereotypes of their identity. When working with this population, counselors may use their awareness, knowledge, and skills concerning the intersection of racism, sexism, and heterosexism for Asian American LGBTQQ individuals to support their resilience and coping and to validate their experiences. Bringing this type of cultural sensitivity to work with this population, counselors may help clients identify coping resources, supportive communities, and specific ways to manage feelings of tension between their sexual and ethnic identity.

This chapter has highlighted several multicultural issues in counseling work with Asian Americans from a social justice perspective. In general, Asian Americans have lived with prejudicial and discriminatory practices within Asian and Western contexts, and it is important for counselors to be aware of this history of oppression and its impact on Asian Americans' mental health. In order to understand how these stressors have affected their coping and to provide culturally relevant treatment, guidelines for clinical work are included in Table 7.2. In this table, the reader will find that establishing a counseling office with resources and symbols relevant to Asian Americans are important ways of creating a welcoming and inclusive environment for Asian Americans who may hold negative stigmas about seeking counseling. As one reviews these guidelines for practice and utilizes them in tandem with more traditional counseling theories, counselors should consistently recognize that Asian Americans are not a homogeneous, monolithic group.

CASE STUDY

Satyam is a 21-year-old of South Asian heritage presenting at the college counseling center. She checks the following issues on the intake form: mood disorders, eating concerns, career concerns, and multicultural issues. When asked about precipitants to seeking counseling, Satyam shares that she is "feeling stressed out and having headaches a lot." She shares that she recently changed majors from biomedical engineering to sociology and that she has not told her parents about her desire to become a social worker. Satyam reports that she lives in the dorm during the week and goes home on the weekends to help her parents take care of legal difficulties they have been having with their business. She shares that she translates important legal documents for her parents, as they have difficulty understanding some of the terminology.

Satyam's parents have had financial challenges recently, and she reports that she herself is struggling financially without their support. She expresses concern that her parents are getting older and wonders how she will be able to take care of them if she follows her dream to be a helping professional. Satyam reports that she has had difficulty sleeping and reports a low appetite over the past 4 weeks since she changed her major. She shares that she has been unable to maintain her daily meditation practice and fears that she is "losing her mind because of the headaches." Satyam also reports missing her younger sister who

Table 7.2 Guidelines for Culturally Relevant Practice with Asian American Clients

1. Avoid stereotyping of Asian Americans' cultural beliefs and worldview.
2. Carefully assess for adherence to gender roles.
3. Consider how the myth of the model minority may have impacted your client. Always assess for current history of trauma, substance abuse, self-other harm or injurious behavior, and abuse.
4. Use caution when assessing for adherence to Asian or Western cultural values using the model minority development model.
5. Ask about how the family may view the presenting issue that concerns the client in order to acknowledge possible collectivistic orientation and/or view of current and past stressors.
6. Assess and explore how the migration story of the family impacts how the client views coping strategies and problem solving.
7. Be aware that due to concerns of family privacy, shame, and cultural stigma about counseling that clients may present with career or other adjustment issues rather than describing the extent of their distress.
8. Collaboratively explore and understand the client's racial/ethnic identity and what stage they may be in with regard to dealing with the stressors of acculturation and racism.
9. Seek to understand how clients' various identities (i.e., race/ethnicity, gender, sexual orientation, age, disability, socioeconomic status, generational status) intersect and create sources of challenge and/or resilience.
10. When assessing the client's presenting issue and throughout treatment, specifically ask and explore the extent of somatic symptoms that the client may be having in response to stressors (i.e., tension, headaches, stomachaches).
11. Gather and display resources (i.e., books, magazines, Web sites, brochures) on issues impacting Asian American mental health (i.e., acculturation, racism, cultural stigma about counseling, resilience, and coping strategies).
12. Take an inventory of your counseling office and organization from the perspective of an Asian American client who is entering this space for the first time. What do you see that would increase or decrease their discomfort with the space? What could you change to make the environment more welcoming to Asian American clients?
13. List the ways that you may be an advocate for the Asian American client you are working with, keeping in mind the challenges they may face in addition to their resilience to adversity.

recently moved across the country to attend college. She believes that she could relate most to her sister, since her parents have "spent all of their time in the Indian community since they came to the U.S." Satyam says that she would like you to help her solve her problems and make her parents understand her academic and career choices. She also asks you about legal and financial resources for her parents.

Discussion Questions

As Satyam's counselor, answer the following questions:

1. What are the presenting issues and how might the myth of the model minority impact Satyam's stressors and/or coping resources. How would you explore the myth of the model minority with Satyam?
2. Where do you assess Satyam to be in terms of her racial/ethnic identity development? How might you further explore her racial/ethnic identity with her in counseling? How would you assess acculturation and generational status issues with Satyam?
3. What is the role of family, gender, spirituality, and other intersecting identities in Satyam's life? What other information would you need to gather to assess and understand these roles?
4. How might you work with and understand Satyam's somatic complaints?
5. What resources would you like to have gathered previous to working with Satyam? What individual and/or community resources (e.g., books, magazines, Web sites, community organizations) would be important to collect during your work together?
6. What are the social justice issues present in Satyam's presenting concerns? How might you explore these issues with her?

CONCLUSION

This chapter has used a social justice lens to explore how counselors may work with Asian Americans in a culturally competent manner that acknowledges their experiences of privilege and oppression in the United States. Although the numbers of Asian Americans continue to increase rapidly, the counseling profession has a limited understanding of the mental health needs of this population. Counselors must recognize the immense diversity that exists within and between subgroups of the total population that comprises Asian Americans. Recognizing that each Asian American group has distinct traditions, customs, relations, and language, and unique life circumstances resulting from the immigration process is a critical way for counselors to understand the social advocacy needs of this group.

ADDITIONAL RESOURCES

Books

Garcia, K. (2001). *Yell-oh girls: Emerging voices explore culture, identity, and growing up Asian American.* New York: Harper Collins.

Leong, R. (1996). *Asian American sexualities: Dimensions of the gay and lesbian experience.* New York: Routledge.

Prashad, V. (2000). *The Karma of brown folk.* Minneapolis: University of Minnesota Press.

Zia, H. (2000). *Asian American dreams: An emergence of an American people.* New York: Farrar, Straus, and Giroux.

Magazines

Hyphen, Asian American culture and politics

Generation Rice, essays and reviews by Asian Americans

Web Sites

www.asianamericans.com, trends for Asian Americans in fashion, food, and culture

www.asian-nation.org, resources debunking the myth of the model minority

www.exoticizemyfist.com, challenging sexualization of Asian American women

www.sfaws.org, resources for survivors of intimate-partner violence

www.trikone.org, South Asian LGBTQQ resources

REFERENCES

Abueg, F. R., & Chun, K. M. (1996). Traumatization stress among Asians and Asian Americans. In A. J. Marsella, M. J. Friedman, E. T. Gerrity, & R. M. Scurfield (Eds.), *Ethnocultural aspects of posttraumatic stress disorder: Issues, research, and clinical applications.* Washington, DC: American Psychological Association.

American Psychiatric Association. (2000). *Diagnostic and statistical manual of mental health disorders* (4th ed., text revision). Washington, DC: Author.

Atkinson, D. R., Lowe, S., & Matthews, L. (1995). Asian American acculturation, gender, and willingness to seek counseling. *Journal of Multicultural Counseling and Development, 23,* 130–138.

Bui, H. T., & Takeuchi, D. T. (1992). Ethnic minority adolescents and the issue of community mental health services. *American Journal of Community Psychology, 20,* 430–417.

Cao, L., & Novas, H. (1996). *Everything you need to know about Asian American history.* New York: Plume Books.

Chan, C. S. (1989). Issues of identity development among Asian-American lesbians and gay men. *Journal of Counseling and Development, 68,* 16–20.

Chung, Y. B., & Szymanski, D. M. (2007). Racial and sexual identities of Asian American gay men. *Journal of LGBT Issues in Counseling, 1*(2), 67–93.

Das, A. K., & Kemp, S. F. (1997). Between two worlds: Counseling South Asian Americans. *Journal of Counseling and Development, 25,* 23–34.

Eriksen, K., & Kress, V. E. (2005). *Beyond the DSM story: Ethical quandaries, challenges, and best practices.* Thousand Oaks, CA: Sage.

Ho, D. Y. (1998). Indigenous psychologies: Asian perspectives. *Journal of Cross-Cultural Psychology, 29,* 88–103.

Hong, G. K., & Domokos-Cheng Ham, M. (2001). *Psychotherapy and counseling with Asian American clients.* Thousand Oaks, CA: Sage.

Inman, A., Chang, C. Y., & Singh, A. A. (April, 2006). *Competencies for working with Asian American/Pacific Islander (AAPI) clients.* Paper presented at the World Conference of the American Counseling Association. Montreal, Canada.

Iwamasa, G. Y. (1996). Acculturation of Asian American university students. *Assessment, 3,* 99–102.

Kim, B. C. (1973). Asian Americans: No model minority. *Social Work, 18*(3), 44–53.

Kim, J. (1981). The process of Asian American identity development: A study of Japanese American women's perception of their struggle to achieve personal identities as Americans of Asia ancestry. *Dissertation Abstracts International, 42,* 1551A.

Kitano, H. H. L. (1982). Mental health in the Japanese American community. In E. E. Jones & S. H. Korchin (Eds.), *Minority mental health* (pp. 149–164). New York: Praeger.

Lee, R. (2005). Resilience against discrimination: Ethnic identity and other-group orientation as protective factors for Korean Americans. *Journal of Counseling Psychology, 52,* 1–14.

Leong, F. T. L. (1986). Counseling and psychotherapy with Asian Americans: Review of literature. *Journal of Counseling Psychology, 33,* 196–206.

Leong, F. T. L., Wagner, N. S., & Kim, H. H. (1995). Group counseling expectations among Asian American students: The role of culture-specific factors. *Journal of Counseling Psychology, 42,* 217–222.

Luthar, S. S., Cicchetti, D., & Becker, B. (2000). Research on resilience: Response to commentaries. *Child Development, 71,* 573–575.

Mintz, L. B., & Kashubeck, S. (1999). Body image and disordered eating among Asian American and Caucasian college students: An examination of race and gender differences. *Psychology of Women Quarterly, 23,* 781–796.

Peterson, W. (1966). Success story, Japanese American style. *New York Times Magazine, 33,* 20–21.

Singh, A., Chung, Y. B., & Dean, J. K. (2007). Acculturation level and internalized homophobia of Asian American lesbian and bisexual women: An exploratory analysis. *Journal of GLBT Issues in Counseling, 1*(2), 3–19.

Singh, A. A., Hays, D. G., Watson, L., & Chung, Y. B. (2006). The resilience strategies of South Asian women who have survived child sexual abuse. *Dissertation Abstracts International.*

Solsberg, S., Choi, K. H., Ritsma, S., & Jolly, A. (1994). Asian American college students: It's time to reach out. *Journal of College Student Personnel, 35,* 296–301.

Sue, D. W., & Sue, D. (2003). *Counseling the culturally diverse: Theory and practice.* New York: John Wiley & Sons.

Sue, S., & Sue, D. W. (1971). Chinese American personality and mental health. *Ameriasian Journal, 1,* 36–49.

Suinn, R. M., Ahuna, C., & Khoo, G. (1992). The Suinn-Lew Asian Self-Identity Acculturation Scale: Concurrent and factorial validation. *Educational and Psychological Measurement, 52,* 1041–1046.

Uba, L. (1994). *Asian Americans: Personality patterns, identity, and mental health.* New York: The Guilford Press.

U.S. Census Bureau. (1990). *Statistical yearbooks of the immigration and naturalization service (1981–1988).* Washington, DC: U.S. Government Printing Office.

U.S. Census Bureau. (1995). *Census data* (P25-1111). Washington, DC: U.S. Government Printing Office.

Yeh, C., & Hwang, M. (2000). Interdependence in ethnic identity and self: Implications for theory and practice. *Journal of Counseling and Development, 78,* 420–429.

8

COUNSELING WITH SPANISH-SPEAKING CLIENTS

Robert L. Smith and R. Esteban Montilla

According to the U.S. Census Bureau (2003), the Latino population represents 42.7 million of the total population. Most recent estimates by the Pew Hispanic Center (2006) indicate that 44.7 million of the 300 million people living in the United States of America are of Hispanic origin. Close to 40% of the Latino population are largely Spanish speakers (Pew Hispanic Center/Kaiser Family Foundation, 2002). Another number of bilingual Hispanics prefer to address emotional and family issues in the Spanish language. There is a plethora of literature regarding counseling English-speaking Latinos and Latinas, but information about working with Spanish-speaking Hispanic clients is rare (Acosta, Evans, Hurwicz, & Yamamoto, 1987; Comas-Diaz, 1997; Delgado-Romero, 2001; La Roche, 2002; Lopez, 1997; Ruiz & Padilla, 1977; Torres-Rivera, Wilbur, Phan, Maddux, & Roberts-Wilbur, 2004). Subsequently there is a need not just for competent multicultural clinicians but also for multilingual service providers in all areas of life, including physical and mental health.

CULTURAL FACTORS IMPEDING MENTAL HEALTH SERVICES

The Hispanic population in general is underutilizing mental health services, which raises questions about how such services are perceived by Latinos and Latinas and the quality of the mental services being offered. There are many reasons for this situation including lack of health insurance, language–communication barriers, and racial discrimination issues (Bernal & Saenz-Santiago, 2006; Pew Hispanic Center/Kaiser Family Foundation, 2002).

As mentioned, the main three reasons impeding mental health care for Hispanics are a lack of health insurance, language–communication barriers, and individual and institutional discrimination as well as immigration status. About 37% of Latinos and Latinas do not have health coverage and Medicaid and other public health coverage reaches only 18% of Hispanics (U.S. Department of Health and Human Services, 1999). The health coverage situation is worse for noncitizen Hispanics, of whom about 58% lack health insurance (Schur & Feldman, 2001).

The second factor impeding mental health coverage is related to the language–communication barrier. There are about 40% of Spanish-speaking-only Latinos and Latinas and another number of bilingual Hispanics who prefer to receive their mental help in the Spanish language. They feel more comfortable expressing their concerns and dialoguing about their emotional issues in Spanish. The inaccessibility to mental health care increases because there are about only 20 Hispanic mental health providers for every 100,000 Latinos and Latinas living in the United States of America. This group of Latinas and Latinos is vastly diverse with regard to age, country of origin, socioeducation level, and length of time in the United States.

A third factor affecting Hispanic accessibility to mental health care has to do with individual and institutional discrimination. Eighty-two percent of Hispanics report experiencing discrimination and say that it is present at the workplace and school. Another 52% believe discrimination is a major problem (Pew Hispanic Center, 2006; Pew Hispanic Center/Kaiser Family Foundation, 2002). The research shows that self-reported discrimination is associated with poor mental health (Gee, Ryan, Laflamme, & Holt, 2006). Discrimination is not a stranger in the mental health field, as many founders of this discipline held the view that people of color were anatomically, physiologically, neurologically, and psychologically inferior. For instance, Carl Jung (1875–1961) thought that White Americans needed to be aware that their association with lower races such as Negroes would pull them down (as cited in Thomas & Sillen, 1972). Terman, a Stanford University professor, in 1916 wrote in his book *The Measurement of Intelligence* that Spanish-Indians, Mexicans, and Negroes were genetically abnormal and that no amount of schooling could equip them to be capable citizens. Today, this paradigm of discrimination is shown in many different ways, including denying mental health services, misdiagnosing, receiving poor treatment, and being prescribed less effective medication (Gee et al., 2006).

Although the need of mental health care for Hispanics is high, there are many impeding factors for these services to be provided. It is not a surprise, then, that less than 1% of Hispanics suffering a mental disorder seek treatment from mental health providers. Additionally only 24% of Latinos and Latinas with mood and anxiety disorders receive appropriate care (U.S. Department of Health and Human Services, 1999).

Bernal and Saenz-Santiago (2006) grouped the factors that impede access to mental health services in three categories: client variables (demographic characteristics, cultural and individual factors); client–therapist variables (confidentiality concerns and socialization with clients); and organizational and structural variables (location of mental health services, the cost of services, and availability of bilingual counselors). They suggest increasing the number of multilingual and culturally sensitive clinicians who are competent to evaluate, diagnose, and treat Hispanic patients or consultees.

Atkinson, Casas, and Abreu (1992) offered these additional reasons for the underutilization of mental health services by Spanish-speaking clients: (a) Hispanics may prefer ethnically similar counselors, of which there is a current lack, supported by García and Zea (1997); (b) mainstream counseling and psychotherapy values held by White therapists may conflict with those of many Mexican Americans; and (c) Mexican Americans believe counselors and family therapists will not provide them with culturally sensitive treatment.

Matching counselor–client characteristics by ethnicity has been previously suggested (Malgady & Constantino, 1998; Ponce & Atkinson, 1989; Sanchez & Atkinson, 1983; Santiago-Rivera, Arredondo & Gallardo-Cooper, 2002). Counselor–client matching, however, is complex when one considers the diversity within cultures, including race, language preference, subcultures, and country of origin (Santiago-Rivera et al., 2002; Smith & Montilla, 2006). The proportion of Latino professionals in mental health agencies in the United States is less than the proportion of Latinos in the general population, (Smith & Montilla, 2006). Ruiz (1971) reviewed the rosters of professional organizations. During that time in history, less than 2% of APA members had Latino surnames. Hess and Street (1991) also found that Hispanics were not well represented in counselor education programs with only 3.4% of the student body and 2.1% of the faculty. These figures have not changed drastically over recent years.

Through working with Spanish-speaking clients, some Latino and Latina clients prefer to work with a Hispanic counselor, whereas others may not. Some studies have suggested that ethnic matching of client and counselor has no influence on clients' perceptions of counselor credibility (Kouyoumdjian, Zamboanga, & Hansen, 2003). D. W. Sue (1988) stated that psychotherapeutic services provided by culturally similar and dissimilar therapists resulted in the same outcome. Due to the spurious findings, research on counselor ethnicity and counselor–client match must be reviewed and interpreted with caution (Smith & Montilla, 2006). It is believed that Latino perceptions of mental health providers do play a major role in whether these services are utilized. Many Latinos and Latinas may feel that non-Hispanic therapists are not cognizant or sensitive to their cultural understanding and needs.

Despite a lack of clinical support on the efficacy of cross-cultural counseling and family therapy practice, it is nevertheless safe to believe that multicultural sensitive practitioners need to provide services in a manner congruent with the culture of the client (Smith & Montilla, 2006). Barona and Santos de Barona (2003) indicate the need to increase the number of bilingual and bicultural mental health providers who are competent in evaluating, diagnosing, and treating Hispanic clients, and the need to develop effective and affordable models of mental health services for Latinas and Latinos.

CHARACTERISTICS OF THE LATINO POPULATION

The Hispanic population is a multiethnic, multicolored, and multicultural people that defy any simplistic grouping. There are Black Hispanics, White Hispanics, Asian Hispanics, Amerindians Hispanics, and Mestizo Hispanics. Most Latinos and Latinas see no need to disregard, diminish, and much less eliminate the cultures they encounter in their pilgrimage. There appears to be openness on their part to embrace aspects and dimensions of other cultures, as it is believed that diverse people that live together enrich and strengthen one anothers' lives.

Living together with diverse people begins at home where family is seen as including grandparents, parents, siblings, children, uncles, distant relatives, very close friends, and godparents. This understanding of expanded family is what has helped the Latino people survive the most difficult adversities and use their resiliencies and power to thrive and flourish. The Hispanic family is very complex and dynamic, and there is not a single way of being a family. They are so diverse that it is difficult to speak of a typical Latino family. Each family exists with its idiosyncrasies, distinctiveness, and decision- and solution-making methodologies, which members recognize and embrace as helpful.

The expanded family with its complexities represents the corner-stone and the building block of the Hispanic community, society, and culture. Latinos and Latinas tend to see the family as the place to seek refuge, draw strength, celebrate achievements, lament losses, perpetuate values, learn and maintain motivations, and experience the wholeness of life. The expanded family is charged with the process of encultura-tion as older members transmit the cultural knowledge, awareness, and skills into the next generations (Casas & Pytluck, 1995).

The understanding of family among Latinos and Latinas has been shaped by Iberian, African, and Amerindian views of family relations. In theory, the patriarchal model of family imposed by the Roman Catholic and Islam religions prevailed. However, in practice, this idea of the father as the head of the house with the authority to make all decisions regarding the future of the family is absent in most Hispanic families. Perhaps, inherited from Amerindians, the mother keeps the family together and promotes patterns of interdependency and living and working together toward sustaining the community. The elders of the family are trusted with passing the wisdom, culture, values, reli-gion, art, music, and principles from one generation to the next. They use storytelling as the main median to pass that heritage.

The African influence with the mother, father, grandparents, sib-lings, relatives, close friends, and neighbors coming together in soli-darity to face life challenges and to raise the children can be seen as well in most Hispanic families. *Familismo*, or the sense of loyalty, solidarity, cooperation, and interdependence, seems to be the cornerstone of most Latino families (Falicov, 1998). The idea that problems and conflicts belong and stay within the family is very much part of the Latino fami-lies' belief system.

ACCULTURATION OF HISPANICS

Many Latinos and Latinas understand acculturation as the process of enriching one's culture and roots by incorporating other worldviews found within the culture encountered in a life journey. Hispanics seem reluctant to use the word *acculturation* in the traditional sense of the word as it generally implies a discard of one's cultural roots in order to embrace the dominant culture.

Acculturation, according to Berry (1997), refers to *integration*. Some Hispanic families going through this phase may experience emotions and behaviors that range from a sense of alienation, psychosomatic symptoms, parenting confusion, identity issues, and interpersonal marital conflicts. However, most Hispanic families, perhaps for their indigenous heritage concerning hospitality and openness to embrace other cultures, show no signs of distress in incorporating values, customs, and religious practices from other cultures (Moyerman & Forman, 1992).

The four modes of acculturation suggested by Berry (1997)—assimilation, separation, marginalization, and integration—are examples of the difficulty in applying this social construct with Hispanics. Assimilation implies that the person has to abandon, disengage, and mutilate their native cultures and values to adapt to those found in the dominant cultures. Separation means people retaining their cultural heritages and backgrounds but rejecting those of the majority culture (Berry, 1997). The marginalization mode implies rejection of both the "mother" and dominant culture. The last stage, according to Berry, is integration, suggesting that people retain their ethnic culture but embrace many of the dominant culture features.

ETHNIC IDENTITY

Ethnic identity refers to the process of becoming aware of the impact of one's cultural roots (languages, beliefs, customs, nationality, gender, sexual orientation, age, religions, and socioeconomic status) on the total person. The traditional racial divisions such as Caucasian, Negroid, and Mongoloid are social and political constructs that have been used to perpetuate discrimination and to promote competence and divisions among different groups. Most Hispanics prefer to use an ethnic cultural identity that recognizes personal and group differences but calls to cultural cooperation and interdependence.

This process of ethnic identity takes a lifetime to develop, spanning from conception to death. The way Hispanics ethnically perceive themselves varies from person to person and from family to family. Ethnic identity as a life span experience cannot be reduced to a stage–hierarchical model because ethnicity for Hispanics is fluid, contextual, permeable, and based more on social and cultural factors than on physical characteristics.

SPIRITUALITY, RELIGION, AND HISPANICS

Most Hispanics consider spirituality and religion important factors that are used to when dealing with issues related to life, education, health, economic, politics, family, and personal challenges. The policulture nature of Hispanics is also seen in their diverse expressions of faith and spirituality. A syncretic religious practice that combines Amerindian, Christian, Islamic, Jewish, and African religion features is most common. Even the dominant denomination in Latin America, Roman Catholic, has embraced many religious and syncretic rituals. A large number of Hispanics see themselves as spiritual people but maintain a healthy suspicion of traditional Christian movements, such as Roman Catholicism and Evangelicalism. Many Hispanics find and make meaning out of their existence through many different religious avenues. A considerable number of Latinos and Latinas express their faith and religious practices by embracing faiths, such Spiritualism, Islam, Jewish, and Eastern religions.

This shows that although spirituality, religion, and faith are central to Hispanics, the way these resources are used to survive, thrive, and flourish vary from person to person and from to family to family. Faith and religion are connected to the context of community and call for respect and reverence for the transcendent, universe, nature, and neighbors. Spirituality and religion are intimately connected and are better understood when seen as an undivided whole. In other words, spirituality is revealed in the ways a person relates to others, nature, the universe, and the eternal. The idea of expressing respect and love to God but hating and disrespecting your neighbors is an oxymoron. Spirituality is about relationships and intimacy with the transcendent, self, and others. The person as a social and holistic being with a body, mind, and spirit that is indissolubly connected, achieves wholeness when able to relate with others, nature, and the eternal in a healthy way.

COMMUNITY AND COLLECTIVISM

Collectivism refers to a way of being in the world where connection to a group or community constitutes the most prevalent feature. Many Latino cultures ascribe to this existential paradigm that emphasizes that keeping and nurturing healthy relationships is the main duty of human beings. Under this worldview, people's measures of success and excellence are weighed by the quality of the relationships they maintain with their family, community, and society. Life satisfaction and realization comes from successfully connecting with others by keeping the social rules, meeting collective expectations, and fulfilling its obligations (Kim, Triandis, Kagitcibasi, Choi, & Yoon, 1994). Principles such as respect, solidarity, mutuality, freedom, harmony, benevolence, communication, and familism serve as the guarantors of the person and collective well-being, as well as people's relationships (Schwartz, 1992; Schwartz & Bilsky, 1987).

In collective societies, people's identities are connected, influenced, and shaped by members of the family, group, and cultural context, as well as by the social rules and norms established by the collective (Greenfield, 1994; Raeff, 1997; Triandis, 1994). Thus, a person's way of thinking, expressing emotions, acting, and relating could be fully understood when the collective as a whole is considered and studied.

The idea of intersustenance and interdependency is all encompassing; although each person is and respected as an indissoluble and indivisible unit, it is very difficult to speak of a self or selves capable of existing away from the collective (Markus & Kitayama, 1991; Tajfel, 1982; Triandis, 1989). This could explain why collective societies have difficulty finding a word in their language equivalent to *self*. The collective worldview starts out from the premise that life and being are not possible in disconnection from others, nature, and cosmos (Jordan, 2000; Leong, 1993; Markus & Kitayama, 1991).

The idea of belonging and affiliation is central to collectivists who consider that isolation from the group implies infirmity, shame, and anxiety (Triandis, 1995). The group serves for members of the collective as the source of support, social status, and protection. The commitment and loyalty to the in-group is reciprocal as the care is mutually provided and exercised. The dignity and value of the person is related to the dignity and reputation of the group (Triandis, McCusker, & Hui, 1990). This could explain the many social restrictions concerning thought, behavior, style of relating, and affective demonstrations when interacting with people of authority and out-groups.

However, these interconnections and relationships do not invalidate the uniqueness and freedom proper of each human being. On the contrary, autodetermination and individual responsibility is encouraged as it is believed that the collective is enhanced and respected when members courageously value who they are and seek excellence in all their transactions and activities. This kind of personal confidence is seen as a relational quality where people trust their capacities and resources, while knowing that their communities are supportive and behind their efforts (Jordan, 2000).

Collective societies capitalize on the reciprocal connection between the individual and community in which principles of equality, justice, and freedom are mutually respected. In these societies, a person's uniqueness is highly esteemed and valued but always in relation to the social responsibility to work together for the common good and well-being. People excel and enhance who they are and do by working together, harmoniously and collectively, to better the well-being of the group (Montilla & Medina, 2006; Smith & Montilla, 2006).

In this context, when collective interests conflict with individual interests, the decision is made based on the well-being of the group.

People from collective societies have their own goals and values but these are part of a bigger and shared scenario. Members of the collective tend to be willing to subordinate their personal gains and personal interests to the group welfare and group interests, as they know that their progress and livelihood is connected to the well-being of the group. They are very protective of the harmonious social relationships choosing this even at the cost of sacrificing personal achievements (Kim et al., 1994).

Collective societies are committed to making those existential gains a reality and they establish norms and rules with the intention to secure a healthy relational environment where people can thrive (Morris & Peng, 1994). The breaking of these agreed regulations could result in discipline and reprimand. In rare cases of extreme abuse of the sacredness of relationship, people could be outcast from the group and be considered an outsider and traitor. This result could be the most painful relational movement, but even in these cases people are moving from social relationship to self-relationship. This retirement or wilderness experience could help the person to develop a higher appreciation for empathy, community, and human connections (Montilla & Medina, 2006).

MULTICULTURAL AND MULTILINGUAL CLINICAL INTERVENTIONS

In today's world, culturally sensitive interventions are not a commodity but an ethical responsibility. Most mental health professional associations require of their affiliates to respect and embrace a multicultural and multidimensional perspective to helping people. The U.S. Department of Health and Human Services (1999) clearly points out that responsible clinicians understand the importance of culture and dimensions in the development and treatment of mental illnesses.

Bernal, Bonilla, and Bellido (1995), as well as Bernal and Saenz-Santiago (2006), suggest an eight-element framework for culturally sensitive interventions with Hispanics. This model comprises language, persons, metaphors, content, concepts, goals, methods, and context.

Language is the primary avenue to express the culture. Language is a universal phenomenon that human beings of all cultures use to communicate their ideas, complex reasoning, affections, dreams, and hopes. Hispanics, because of their high-context cultural variable, tend to rely on nonverbal contextual language, which is assumed to be understood by the in-group. Members are expected to "read" the hidden language present in the immediate context, and petitions and requisitions might not be stated overtly but they are implicit nonetheless. The deciphering tools used to understand the high-context symbols are deeply imbedded in the in-group and collective. It is assumed that listeners will receive the message and respond with the expected behavior without being told directly. For the Latino community, language is more than sounds, morphemes, and grammar. It is about many levels and generations of embedded nuances used to participate in transformative and creative experiences. Culturally sensitive clinicians working with Spanish-speaking clients would need not only to understand the language but the embedded cultural nuances.

The *person* refers to the clinician and the quality of the therapeutic relationship. People as social beings need relationships to survive, grow, and flourish. Hispanics make relationships the center of life and energy. For them, everything evolves around connections and relatedness. Relationship implies empowerment and mutuality, which Jordan (2000) understands as openness to mutual influence, emotional availability, and a cognitive commitment marked by loyalty. Miller (1986) proposes that relationships give people five main existential gains: (a) a space to increase vitality, aliveness, and energy; (b) a place to be empowered; (c) an ideal atmosphere to grow in knowledge about self and others; (d) an inviting and accepting world conducive to reaffirming a sense of worth; and (e) a place for fuller connections and enriching interchanges where collaboration, cooperation, trust, and respect reign.

The person of the clinician and the quality of the therapeutic relationship seem to be the most important factors in working with Hispanics. No single counseling approach or therapeutic model has been proven most successful with the Latino culture. It is argued that core conditions, such as empathic listening and a strong therapeutic alliance, transcend the cultural identities of the counselor and client in delivering effective treatment (Smith & Montilla, 2006).

The third element to consider when working with Hispanics is the use of *metaphors* and *cuentos* to illustrate the situation in question. The next element is the *content*, which refers to cultural values and worldviews embraced by Hispanics. Multicultural counseling researchers and professionals stress the assessment of worldview as a necessary step in understanding the client's frame of reference at the beginning of the therapeutic process (Ibrahim, Roysircar-Sodowsky, & Ohnishi, 2001; S. Sue & Zane, 1987). Worldview will not only provide information on the subjective realities of both counselor and client, but will also help expand the knowledge base of the professional in general (Ibrahim et al., 2001). A shared frame of reference between the therapist and client will also lead to enhanced effectiveness and successful engagement in therapy (Ibrahim et al., 2001). Clinicians need to be aware of the values and principles guiding the person's behavior and patterns of relationships.

Concepts refer to the theoretical stance used in the counseling intervention. Passive and introspective approaches with limited intervention by the clinician could hinder the therapeutic relationship, as an issue of credibility and authority may negatively affect the intervention. A client's expectations of counseling, as well as the particular issues that he or she wishes to address in session, merit special attention, as successful cross-cultural counseling implies both the counselor and client setting the clinical agenda (Tat Tsang, Bogo, & George, 2003).

Goals imply the establishment of an agreement between the therapist and client in relation to the objectives of the therapeutic intervention. The goals need to be a mutual enterprise established within the cultural values of the person. Therapists may want to discuss their designed interventions with the patient/client. The intent is to ensure that people are comfortable with the process and that therapeutic goals are appropriate for the situation and culture (Altarriba & Bauer, 1998). Understanding what the person wishes to gain from the therapeutic experience is a major challenge in developing an effective treatment plan (Santiago-Rivera et al., 2002).

Methods have to do with the procedures to follow for the achievement of the mutually agreed and culturally sensitive goals. The *context* element refers to the importance of taking into consideration the ecological, social, economic, and political contexts of the client, such as immigration status, social network, and length of time in the United States, as well as work conditions.

CONCLUSIONS

This chapter reviewed the background concerning Latinos and their interests/preferences as related to counseling and family therapy. With a dramatic increase in the Latino population and with the need for sensitive and quality physical and mental health services for Latino families, it becomes the ethical responsibility of counselors and family therapists to expand their level of awareness and multicultural competencies.

Helping professionals should possess certain personal characteristics deemed important by their clients (Satir, 1987). It is believed that effective relationship skills transcend culture when working with Latino families. This concept, a belief in transcultural universality, is viewed as having merit by the authors. However, counselors should continue to listen and seek direction from Latino family members concerning their preferences in potential helping professionals.

REFERENCES

Acosta, F. X., Evans, L. A., Hurwicz, M., & Yamamoto, J. (1987). Preparing Hispanic patients for psychotherapy. In M. S. Gaviria & J. D. Arama (Eds.), *Health and behavior: Research agenda for Hispanics* (pp. 257–266). Chicago: University of Illinois.

Altarriba, J., & Bauer, L. M. (1998). Counseling the Hispanic client: Cuban Americans, Mexican Americans, and Puerto Ricans. *Journal of Counseling and Development, 76*, 389–396.

Atkinson, D. R., Casas, A., & Abreu, J. (1992). Mexican-American acculturation, counselor ethnicity and cultural sensitivity, and perceived counselor competence. *Journal of Counseling Psychology, 39*, 515–520.

Barona, A., & Santos de Barona, M. (2003). Recommendations for the psychological treatment of Latino/Hispanics populations. In Council of National Psychological Associations for the Culturally Centered Psychosocial Interventions Advancement of Ethnic Minority Interests (Ed.), *Psychological treatment of ethnic minority populations* (pp. 19–23). Washington, DC: Association of Black Psychologists.

Bernal, G., Bonilla, J., & Bellido, C. (1995). Ecological validity and cultural sensitivity for outcome research: Issues for the cultural adaptation and development of psychosocial treatments with Hispanics. *Journal of Abnormal Child Psychology, 23*, 67–82.

Bernal, G., & Saenz-Santiago, E. (2006). Culturally centered psychosocial interventions. *Journal of Community Psychology, 34*(2), 121–132.

Berry, J. W. (1997). Immigration, acculturation and adaptation. *Applied Psychology, 46*, 5–68.

Casas, J. & Pytluk, S. (1995). Hispanic identity development: Implications for research and practice. In J. Ponterretto, J. Casa, L. Suzuki, and C. Alexander (eds), *Handbook of Multicultural Counseling* (pp. 155–180). Thousand Oaks, CA: Sage Publications.

Comas-Diaz, L. (1997). Mental health needs of Latinos with professional status. In J. G. Garcia & M. C. Zea (Eds.), *Psychological interventions and research with Latino populations* (pp. 142–165). Boston: Allyn & Bacon.

Delgado-Romero, E. A. (2001). Counseling a Hispanic/Latino client—Mr. X. *Journal of Mental Health Counseling, 231*(3), 207–221.

Falicov, C. J. (1998). *Latino families: A guide to multicultural practice.* New York: Guilford.

García, J. G., & Zea, M. C. (Eds.). (1997). *Psychological interventions and research with Latino populations.* Needham Heights, MA: Allyn & Bacon.

Gee, G. C., Ryan, A. M., Laflamme, D. J., & Holt, J. (2006). The association between self-reported discrimination and mental health among African descendents, Mexican Americans and other Latinos in the New Hampshire REACH Study: The added dimension of immigration status. *American Journal of Public Health, 96*(10), 1821–1828.

Greenfield, P. M. (1994). Independence and interdependence as developmental constructs: Implications for theory, research, and practice. *Cross Cultural Roots of Minority Child Development*, 1–40.

Hess, R. S., & Street, E. M. (1991). The effect of acculturation on the relationship of counselor ethnicity and client ratings. *Journal of Counseling Psychology, 38,* 71–75.

Ibrahim, F. A., Roysircar-Sodowsky, G., & Ohnishi, H. (2001). Worldview: Recent developments and needed directions. In J. Ponterotto, J. M. Casas, L. Suzuki, and C. Alexander (Eds.), *The handbook of multicultural counseling* (2nd ed., pp. 425–456). Thousand Oaks, CA: Sage.

Jordan, J. V. (2000). A model of connection for a disconnected world. In J. Shay & J. Wheelis (Eds.), *Odysseys in psychotherapy.* New York: Ardent Media.

Kim, U., Triandis, H. C., Kagitcibasi, C., Choi, S., & Yoon, G. (Eds.). (1994). *Individualism and collectivism: Theory, method, and applications.* Newbury Park, CA: Sage.

Kouyoumdjian, H., Zamboanga, B. L., & Hansen, D. J. (2003). Barriers to community mental health services for Latinos: Treatment considerations. *Clinical Psychology: Science and Practice, 10,* 394–422.

La Roche, M. J. (2002). Psychotherapeutic considerations in treating Latinos. *Harvard Review of Psychiatry, 10,* 115–122.

Leong, F. T. (1993). The career counseling process with racial-ethnic minorities: The case of Asian Americans. *The Career Development Quarterly, 42,* 26–40.

Lopez, S. R. (1997). Cultural competence in psychotherapy: A guide for clinicians and their supervisors. In C. E. Watkins, Jr., (Ed.), *Handbook of psychotherapy supervision* (pp. 570–588). New York: Wiley.

Malgady, R. G., & Constantino, G. (1998). Symptom severity in bilingual Hispanics as a function of clinician and language of interview. *Psychological Assessment, 10,* 120–127.

Markus, H. R., & Kitayama, S. (1991). Culture and the self: Implications for cognition, emotion and motivation. *Psychological Review, 98,* 224–253.

Miller, J. B. (1986). Women's psychological development: Theory and application. National Institute of Mental Health. *Occasional Paper Series on Women's Mental Health,* Washington, D.C.

Montilla, R. E., & Medina, F. (2006). *Pastoral care and counseling with Latino/as.* Minneapolis, MN: Fortress Press.

Morris, M. W., & Peng, K. (1994). Culture and cause: American and Chinese attributions for social and physical events. *Journal of Personality and Social Psychology, 67,* 949–971.

Moyerman, D. R., & Forman, B. D. (1992). Acculturation and adjustment: A meta-analytic study. *Hispanic Journal of Behavioral Sciences, 14*(2), 163–200.

Pew Hispanic Center. (2006). *2006 national survey of Latinos.* Washington, DC: Author.

Pew Hispanic Center/Kaiser Family Foundation. (2002). *2002 national survey of Latinos*. Washington, DC: Author.

Ponce, F. Q., & Atkinson, D. R. (1989). Mexican-American acculturation, counselor ethnicity, counselor style, and perceived counselor credibility. *Journal of Counseling Psychology, 36,* 203–208.

Ponterotto, J. G., Rieger, B. P., Barrett, A., & Sparks, R. (1994). Assessing multicultural counseling competence: A review of instrumentation. *Journal of Counseling and Development, 71,* 316–322.

Raeff, C. (1997). Maintaining cultural coherence in the midst of cultural diversity: Reply to "Cultural, self, and development: Are cultural templates useful or stereotypic?" *Developmental Review, 17*(3), 250–261.

Ruiz, R. A. (1971). Relative frequency of Americans with Spanish surnames in associations of psychology, psychiatry, and sociology. *American Psychologist, 26,* 1022–1024.

Ruiz, R. A., & Padilla, A. M. (1977). Counseling Latinos. *Personnel & Guidance Journal, 55,* 401–408.

Sanchez, A. R., & Atkinson, D. R. (1983). Mexican-American cultural commitment, preference for counselor ethnicity, and willingness to use counseling. *Journal of Counseling Psychology, 30,* 215–220.

Santiago-Rivera, A. L., Arredondo, P., & Gallardo-Cooper, M. (2002). *Counseling Latinos and la familia: A practical guide*. Thousand Oaks, CA: Sage.

Satir, V. (1987). The therapist story. In M. Baldwin & V. Satir (Eds.), *The use of self* (pp. 17–25). New York: Haworth.

Schwartz, S. M. (1992). Universals in the content and structure of values: Theoretical advances and empirical tests in 20 countries. In M. P. Zannes (Ed.), *Advances in experimental social psychology* (Vol. 25). San Diego, CA: Academic Press.

Schwartz, S. M., & Bilsky, W. (1987). Toward a universal psychological structure of human values. *Journal of Personality and Social Psychology, 13,* 550–562.

Schur, C. L., & Feldman, J. (2001). *Running in place: How job characteristics, immigrant status, and family structure keep Hispanics uninsured*. New York: The Commonwealth Fund.

Smith, R. L., & Montilla, R. E. (2006). *Family counseling and therapy with Latinos and Latinas: Strategies that work*. New York: Routledge.

Sue, D. W. (1988). Psychotherapeutic services for ethnic minorities: Two decades of research findings. *American Psychologist, 43,* 301–308.

Sue, S., & Zane, N. (1987). The role of culture and cultural techniques in psychotherapy: A critique and reformulation. *American Psychologist, 42,* 37–45.

Tajfel, H. (1982). *Social identity and intergroup relations*. Cambridge, UK: Cambridge University Press

Tat Tsang, A., Bogo, M., & George, U. (2003). Critical issues in cross-cultural counseling research: Case example of an ongoing project. *Journal of Multicultural Counseling and Development, 31,* 63–78.

Thomas, T., & Sillen, S. (1972). *Racism and psychiatry.* New York: Brunner/Mazel.

Torres-Rivera, E., Wilbur, W. P., Phan, L. T., Maddux, C. D., & Roberts-Wilbur, J. (2004). Counseling Latinos with substance abuse problems. *Journal of Addictions & Offender Counseling, 25,* 27–42.

Triandis, H. C. (1989). The self and social behavior in differing cultural contexts. *Psychological Review, 96*(3), 506–520.

Triandis, H. C. (1994). *Culture and social Behavior.* New York: McGraw-Hill.

Triandis, H. C. (1995). *Individualism and collectivism.* Boulder, CO: Westview Press.

Triandis, H., McCusker, C., & Hui, C. (1990). Multimethod probes of individualism and collectivism. *Journal of Personality and Social Psychology, 59*(5), 1006–1020.

U.S. Census Bureau. (2003). *General demographic characteristics: 2003 American community survey summary tables.* Retrieved March 24, 2005, from http://factfinder.census.gov/servlet/

U.S. Department of Health and Human Services. (1999). *Mental health: A report of the surgeon general.* Rockville, MD: Author.

9

COUNSELING WITH NORTH AMERICA'S INDIGENOUS PEOPLE

Sherri L. Turner and Mark Pope

When we view our counseling relationship through the lens of multiculturalism, we see ourselves and our clients in an environmental context. This awareness of context enables us to make an important transition in our thinking from assuming that our clients' problems are caused solely by intrapsychic or intrafamilial factors to recognizing that political, social, and economic explanations are often more accurate. (Lewis & Arnold, 1998, p. 52)

In this chapter, we will explore counseling with North America's indigenous people in the context of social justice. Social justice is defined as a societal state in which all members of a society have the same basic rights, security, opportunities, obligations, and social benefits (Department of Welfare, Republic of South Africa, 1997). Among American Indians, social justice has been an illusory concept, as time after time their status as full human beings has not been recognized, nor have they been granted full rights as national citizens. Social justice has been at the center of Indian–White relationships since expansionism and domination of the Indian began with the first genocidal war waged against the Pequot Indians in 1637 (in which women and children were burned to death in retaliation over trade disagreements).

Within the context of social justice, we will examine cultural differences as they help us understand the counseling needs of North America's indigenous people. We will discuss (a) the role of legislation

185

in shaping the cultural context of indigenous people, (b) issues of acculturation and racial identity development, (c) the devastating effects of alcoholism, (d) Native American family values, (e) cultures of Native American indigenous people, (f) Native American spirituality, and (g) suggestions for effective counseling strategies and the implications of providing counseling to Native American people. We write this chapter in hope that the issues raised will help mental health workers continue to provide more effective counseling services for Native American people.

THE ROLE OF LEGISLATION IN SHAPING THE CULTURAL CONTEXT OF INDIGENOUS PEOPLE

North America's indigenous peoples consist of 560 federally recognized tribes and over 250 state-recognized tribes in the United States, and 630 federally recognized First Nations bands in Canada. In addition, in both Canada and the United States, there are many people who are not officially affiliated with Native communities, but who have a Native American heritage that significantly influences their lives. The legislative history of the two countries is somewhat different; however, in both countries, legislation has supported maltreatment of the indigenous people.

Native Americans and mixed-blood Natives are the only racial/ethnic groups whose actual identities have been legislated by their governments. In order to participate in the benefits of tribal treaties (such as land usage, education benefits, health benefits, and proceeds from tribal casinos), they must meet specific criteria. Examples of these criteria include proving blood quantum ratios (e.g., 25% of one's "blood" must be from a Native American ancestor), and having parents who were enrolled Indians (in the United States) or status Indians (in Canada). In both the United States and Canada, in order to receive tribal protection rights (such as protection through Indian courts, or hunting and fishing subsistence rights), Native Americans must live on reservations or in tribal communities, and must practice indigenous religions or engage in recognized Native American cultural practices.

Treaties were those documents that defined relations between European governments (and later the United States and Canadian governments) and the individual Native Nations whose people inhabited the Americas before European immigration. As early as the 1400s, treaties between Native Americans and newly arrived European Americans defined Native American access to lands, food, lifestyles, and life space.

Each tribe has its own history of treaty making and treaty breaking. However, in general:

- Treaties were enacted between the corresponding governments and local tribal leaders.
- Treaties were typically forced, as Native Americans continued to lose the power to defend themselves against what they considered European American aggressors.
- Beginning in 1786 in the United States, and 1813 in Canada, treaties typically separated Natives from their White neighbors by removing them from their traditional lands and relocating them to reservations. Removals to reservations were typically forced by armed U.S. soldiers or Canadian Mounties, and were often done in the middle of winter.
- Treaties typically included payment to Native Americans for the lands they were leaving by granting them provisions of gold, educational facilities, food, and supplies to be received at their new reservation homes; however, policies were often implemented that distributed these rights and payments to "friendlies" only (DeMallie, 2001).
- Treaties did not grant Native Americans citizenship in either the United States or Canada.
- Treaties typically included phrases such as "in perpetuity" or "until the sun does not set." However, these treaties were typically broken within a 10- to 50-year period, when new treaties with fewer benefits for the Native Americans were enacted. For example, in the Treaty of 1868 between the Lakota and the U.S. federal government, the Lakota were promised the Black Hills (a sacred site for the Lakota Indians) in perpetuity. The promise of in perpetuity only lasted until gold was found in the hills in the 1870s. The federal government then forced the Lakota to relinquish the Black Hills portion of their reservation (DeMallie, 2001).

Reservation lands at times resembled prisoner of war camps. Starvation and disease, such as smallpox and tuberculosis, were rampant. Enforcement of governmental policies was provided by agents from the Bureau of Indian Affairs in the United States and the Department of Indian Affairs in Canada, who regulated Native lands, resources, and destinies. Native Americans were exploited by the agents who provided them with inferior, worm-infested food, while selling the better food to White settlers who had encroached on reservation land. Complaints about embezzlement and fraud quickly arose against the agents, although little was done about it. Between 1851 and 1951, Congressional appropriations based on treaty rights decreased by 80%, while Indian agents often retired with great wealth that they had gained from managing Indian money (Cohen, 1953).

In the 1860s, with the gaining popularity of Social Darwinism, new policies of assimilation were implemented. Social Darwinism posits that different races evolve at different rates in world history, and therefore, there are the more superior races and cultures (typically applied to the Caucasian race and White European culture) and inferior races (typically applied to all but the Caucasian race and White European culture). Drawing on this theory, European Americans decided that they would help Native Americans by assimilating them into the superior American Western European civilization. Assimilationism policies drove the legislative and social decisions regarding Native Americans for at least the next 150 years causing tremendous anxiety and despair among the indigenous people who struggled to keep their own ancient cultures and traditions alive.

Using Social Darwinism to undergird the social construction of the 1800s, governments and religious organizations began to build boarding schools to further civilize Native Americans. By the early 1900s, 80% of all Native American children across the United States were being removed, often forcibly from their family homes, to attend boarding schools. In these schools, school administrators and teachers cut children's hair, which was against Native spiritual traditions, and forced them to dress in European American clothing. They changed the children's names to American Christian names, forced them to speak English instead of their Native languages, suppressed their cultural practices, and subjected them to harsh, demeaning, and often cruel discipline. Children in the boarding schools were instructed in European American domestic arts, manual labor, and agricultural skills, instead of the skills of their forefathers. Thus during the boarding school era, the majority of the Native American languages and a great deal of Native American culture were lost. For many Native American children, the boarding school experience led to confusion, cultural and self-alienation, homesickness, and resentment. Boarding schools were prolific until the 1940s, although some existed through the 1970s, when the majority were closed or turned over to the tribes to run (Adams, 1995; Mankiller & Wallis, 1994).

In the late 1800s, the United States and Canada continued their policies of assimilation toward Native Americans through land allotment and distribution laws. In 1887, the U.S. Congress passed the Dawes General Allotment Act, which dissolved 90% of all reservations. Native

Americans who could prove their ancestry received family allotments of 80 to 160 acres. The rest of the reservation land (over 60 million acres) was opened to White settlement with proceeds from these sales going to the U.S. government. The stated purpose of the Dawes Act was to teach Native Americans to become "civilized" by wearing "civilized clothes," living in houses, riding in Studebaker wagons, sending children to school, drinking whiskey, and owning property.

In Canada, the Act for Gradual Civilization (1857), the British North America Act (1867), and the Indian Act (1876) also were designed to civilize Native Canadians, but to do so by teaching them European Canadian ways while keeping them on reservations. Thus, land was distributed to Native American men who could read, write, and speak English, while reservations were otherwise kept intact. In addition, the Indian Act caused Native Canadian women who married White men to lose their Indian status; and the British North America Act of Canada brought "Indians, and Lands reserved for the Indians" under the direct control of the Canadian government.

The allotment acts of both countries proved disastrous for Native American tribes, and changed Native lifeways permanently. Under the allotment acts of Canada, the Canadian Parliament quickly passed a system of laws that replaced politically powerful Aboriginal governments with politically weak band councils. The Canadian government took control of Canadian Natives' financial reserves, and outlawed their traditional marriage and parenting practices. In both the United States and Canada, Native religions were outlawed. Traditional matricentral practices (where women had owned houses and children, and were responsible for agriculture, and where men were responsible for hunting and fishing) were replaced with Western European patriarchal practices. Hunting lands were closed, Native men were forced into the fields, and Native women were domesticated, becoming economically and emotionally dependent on their husbands. Native men were declared head of household for the purposes of property rights, and Native women lost their coequal social and political status with men. Thus, European American values congruent with Western European American religious ideals, nuclear families, individual wealth accumulation, and individual land ownership were imposed on Native American society. Native identity was weakened and Native communal life was compromised (Portman & Garrett, 2005).

Under the Dawes Commission, which implemented the Dawes Act in the United States, corruption marred the distribution of land. Because many Native Americans who lived on reservations could not prove their Native American ancestry by producing the required documents, they were de-enrolled from their tribes and removed from their reservations without any compensation at all. An estimated 75% of all Native American people were officially removed from the American Indian census roles, while European Americans who had had no previous connection to the tribes were declared full-blood Natives.

For those Native Americans who did receive land distributions, few attained the economic self-sufficiency envisioned by humanitarian groups. Desperate Natives sold their land allotments to buy food and provisions. Greedy speculators and politicians swindled unsuspecting Indians out of their property. Within 20 years, much allotment property was lost. For example, by the early 1920s, 80% of all Indian lands in Oklahoma (which had previously been Indian territory and totally owned by Native Americans) were in White hands (Debo, 1984). In both the United States and Canada, previous and subsequent to the allotment acts, Native Americans had been and did remain the most economically deprived, worst educated, and least physically healthy of any American ethnic group.

In 1926 there was growing national concerns about the plight of Native Americans. Although U.S. Native Americans had been offered United States citizenship in 1924, the Meriam Report (Meriam et al., 1928), commissioned by the U.S. Secretary of the Interior, documented that assimilation in general had been a dismal failure. The report stated that the destruction of the Indian way of life had not been successfully replaced by European American culture or values. The report stated that "an overwhelming majority of the Indians are poor, even extremely poor; and they are not adjusted to the economic and social systems of the dominant white civilization." It was apparent that effective, immediate action needed to be taken to reverse the terrible circumstances of the Native American people. Thus in 1934, the U.S. Indian Reorganization Act was passed.

The U.S. Indian Reorganization Act stopped the sale of allotments, provided funding mechanisms for tribal economic development, sought to decrease enrollments in boarding schools, and sought to strengthen tribal governments and assist Native American tribes in regaining their cultures and religions. However, implementation of the act was poorly managed, and the benefits of the act were short lived. The Bureau of Indian Affairs still maintained custodial rights over "Indian" money, and Native American people still suffered from racism and discrimination in ways that kept them economically oppressed. Opponents of the act, principally people who were more politically and conservatively religious, resented the new toleration of Native American religions.

They stated that the Reorganization Act promoted "degrading tribalism" and even promoted communism (Debo, 1984).

Subsequent to the Indian Reorganization Act, the United States government again reversed its stance toward Native American assimilation and made another policy decision to speed up the assimilation of Natives within its borders. Officials within the Bureau of Indian Affairs and Congress deemed the process of Indian assimilation too costly and inefficient. As a result, the federal government began to look for ways to end the trustee relationship it had with certain tribes, using the rationale that these tribes had been sufficiently assimilated. Moreover, European American corporate leaders suggested that they could more efficiently exploit the vast natural resources on those Indian reservations that remained. Consequently, in 1953, United States House Resolution 103 was implemented. This was a resolution that terminated tribal entities, tribal government, and tribal status for over 100 tribes and over 10,000 Native American people. In conjunction with the resolution, a relocation program was instituted, which strongly encouraged Native Americans from many tribes to move off reservations and into areas that were more economically viable. In order to reward participation, Native Americans who relocated were promised one-month's wages, and help in finding jobs and housing. Thus, from 1952 to 1962 there was a mass migration of Native Americans from reservations to designated cities around the nation (including Chicago, Cleveland, Dallas, Denver, Los Angeles, Oklahoma City, Tulsa, St. Louis, and San Francisco) and a quick and continuous reduction in tribal rights and tribal government.

Today in the United States, almost half of all Native Americans live in metropolitan areas, have received public education in English-speaking schools, and have been exposed to urban life (Nagel, 1995). In these cities, Native Americans typically live in ethnically stratified, inner-city neighborhoods characterized by high concentrations of poverty (greater than 40%), and high rates of crime, teenage pregnancy, and school dropout rates that are at least 34% above the national mean (National Research Council, 1993). Native Americans living in these poverty-stricken areas often have only minimal education and poor employment prospects. The reversals in Native American circumstances that were expected through first stopping the process of forced assimilation through the Indian Reorganization Act, and then speeding up assimilation through Resolution 103 did not materialize, but instead increased the suffering of the Indian people (Hirschfelder, 1986).

There was no legislative parallel to the Indian Reorganization Act in Canada. However, the Canadian federal government implemented a relocation policy that had widespread effects in the 1950s. This program moved bands of Indians from one place to another at the will of the government in order to help them find more plentiful game, training that would lead them into a wage economy, better health and sanitary services, and more accessible housing. Relocations in Canada also were used to remove Natives from lands that were designated for agricultural or other types of expansion projects. If Indian lands contained unexploited natural resources, Indians could be removed in the "national interest." However, as benevolent as some of the Native removals seemed, these removals appeared to be motivated by paternalism. Relocation decisions were made with little consultation from the individuals or bands involved. In addition, the loss of livelihood associated with the relocations severely hampered Canadian Indian's abilities to be economically self-sufficient, and the relocation process itself appeared to lead to symptoms of bereavement and traumatic stress (Dussault et al., 1996).

Policy reversals against assimilationism began in 1968 in the United States. A number of federal acts were passed to strengthen tribal sovereignty, provide educational assistance to Native American young people, enforce Native American civil rights, and allow Native Americans once again to recover their culture and customs. The Indian Civil Rights Act of 1968 allowed tribal governments to formulate autonomous administrations. The Indian Self-Determination and Educational Act of 1975 allowed tribal governments to manage their own housing, education, health care, social services, forestry, and law enforcement programs. The Tribally Controlled Community College Assistance Act of 1978 provided assistance for tribal governments to establish their own tribal colleges. The Indian Child Welfare Act of 1978 placed Native American families under the jurisdiction of tribal courts with respect to out-of-home placements, such as boarding school placement, foster home placement, or transracial adoption. The American Indian Religious Freedom Act of 1978 provided for the reestablishment and protection of Native American religious freedoms. The Indian Gaming Regulatory Act of 1988 allowed tribal sovereignty over gaming conducted on tribal lands. The Native American Graves Protection and Repatriation Act of 1990 caused the return of Native American human remains, funerary objects, sacred objects, objects of cultural patrimony, and cultural items, thus providing the opportunity for Native Americans to reinforce and strengthen their own traditional customs and cultures.

Today, there are some successes with the Indian policies of the last 50 years. There are more tribally owned businesses, such as gaming parlors, tobacco shops, convenience stores, and oil and gas companies that are bringing much needed capital into U.S. Indian tribes and nations. These business entities are making Native American tribal groups more self-sufficient than ever before and providing local employment opportunities. Indian Health Care was remanded to the control of the tribes, with hospitals and clinics that were at one time administered by Bureau of Indian Affairs personnel, now being managed and staffed by the designees of local tribal governments. There are more Native American attorneys, more Native American politicians, and more Native American PhD-level psychologists than ever before. However, legislative changes have not necessarily changed society's attitudes about the "Indian problem." Native American people still have the lowest family incomes, the least education, and the poorest physical and psychological health of any other American ethnic group. There is much more to be done.

In Canada, major legislation providing relief for centuries of abuse is still being debated. So far, Natives are relying on the implementation of a few minor laws. For example, the British Columbia Indian Cut-off Lands Settlement Act (1984), provides for the settlement of claims by Indian bands in British Columbia relating to certain lands cut off from their reserves. In 1985, the Indian Act of Canada was changed to reverse the loss of Indian status for women who marry White men. In addition, through case law and the courts, millions of acres of Indian land have been returned to Canadian bands, along with millions of dollars in compensation for lands and natural resources that cannot be returned.

Whatever the gains in Native American law and policy, or culture and customs, there is still an overarching social justice issue that has not been addressed or resolved. Today both Native Americans and Canadian Aborigines are classified as dependents of their respective federal governments, just as they were in the 1830s when Chief Justice Marshall declared that the relationship of the Indian to the federal government resembled that of a ward to a guardian. The tribes and their members have the inherent right to occupy their lands, until the federal government chooses to evict them. Both the Department of Indian Affairs in Canada and the Bureau of Indian Affairs in the United States collects and controls rents, leases, and other monies owed to Native American individuals and tribes. This ward status has not changed. Thus, as wards of the United States, Native Americans are the only human beings in either country who do not have full constitutional and status rights (Canby, 1998).

ISSUES OF ACCULTURATION AND RACIAL
IDENTITY DEVELOPMENT

The recruiter for a large university in a state inhabited by many Native Americans was bemoaning the turnout he had had at an "Indian" recruiting fair. "It just wasn't much good," he said. "What happened?" asked his friend. "Oh, we got a number of applications for the fair from students who look like they will actually come to the university, but, 'I wish we had had more Indian-looking people.'"

Racial identity refers to a person's identifying or not identifying with his or her racial group, and the quality or manner of this identification (Helms, 1990). Acculturation, for ethnic minorities, is the process of identification with the values and customs of the dominant culture. Some researchers believe that racial identity development is antithetical to acculturation (Andujo, 1988), although others suggest that bicultural people can be both acculturated, at least somewhat, to the dominant society and have strong identification with their own racial/cultural group (Jones, 1991; Kim, Lujan, & Dixon, 1998). In either case, researchers suggest that racial/ethnic minorities need to have a strong identification with their own racial/ethnic group in order to maintain emotional and psychological health (Gonzales & Cauce, 1995).

Racial identity is developed, just as are other identities, in a young person's life. Just as a young person learns what it is to be a man or a woman, to be gifted in music or sports, to be a son or a daughter, a friend or a foe, a spiritual/existential being, or the many other identities that we develop as human beings, so does the young person learn what it is to be a person of his or her race or ethnicity. Developing a healthy racial identity is very much a part of developing a healthy sense of self-identity, self-esteem, and self-confidence.

As with other minority groups in the United States, Native American racial identity development can be problematic (Trimble, 2000). Embracing one's own racial identity as a Native American can mean facing racism and oppression; claiming a family heritage that may include alcoholism, poverty, and violence; and living a less privileged life than one's European American contemporaries. Overt racism can be especially devastating for Native American people. Accepting one's own racial and ethnic identity in the midst of such circumstances can indeed be a difficult experience for Native Americans.

Further, racial identity can be impeded by stereotyping (e.g., tribal people are descended from several ancient races, and thus have phenotypical expressions that do not match the stereotypical image of the stoic, long-haired, and dark Native; Novick et al., 1998; Schurr et al.,

1990; Tokunaga, Ohashi, Bannai, & Juji, 2001), multiracial heritage (52% of all Native Americans marry outside of their race; Spickard, 1989), racial denial among one's ancestors (Davidson, 2006), and the lack of social and cultural support for being a Native American minority person. Racial denial in particular has had wide-ranging effects on Native American families, as generations have denied their Native American heritage to avoid detection and destruction under the doctrines of colonialization, expansionism, and assimilation. Frightening expressions of overt hatred, such as "civilization or death" (popularized in the 1770s; Pearce, 1967) and "the only good Indian is a dead Indian" (popularized in the 1880s) are stark warnings for those who would admit that they are Indians. Little wonder that Native Americans at times struggle with their racial identities.

Research also has suggested that racial identity development is affected by the internalization of both stereotyping and racism (Sue & Sue, 2003). Stereotyping and racism are based on two concepts. The first is that inherited physical attributes of particular minority groups influence their psychological and intellectual characteristics and social behavior. The second is that some racial groups, such as White European Americans, are inherently genetically superior, whereas others, such as Native Americans, are inherently genetically inferior (Bowker, 1993). Stereotyping and racism are ingrained in the social fabric of the United States and Canada, and are perpetuated through a system of unequal power relationships in public and private institutions. As Native young people develop, they unconsciously accept the stereotypical traits that are ascribed to them, such as untrustworthiness, dishonesty, laziness, indolence, inferiority, and the drunken Indian (Oswalt, 2001).

Bray (2006) developed a five-stage model that illustrates the identity development of Native American young people living in communities bordering nonreservation lands. In Bray's model, Native American children first pass through the innocence stage (preschool to 3rd grade), in which they become friends and play with Anglo children. In the disillusionment stage (4th to 6th grade), all relationships between Native American and Anglo children are terminated, as Anglo children become acculturated into racist practices. In the segregation stage (middle school to junior high school), segregation and racial violence between Anglo and Native American children become "the norm." During this stage, many Native American children are tracked into special or vocational education. In the push-out, drop-out, or wise-up stage (high school), Native American young people either are pushed out of school, drop out of school, or develop a tolerance for the disparaging racial attitudes displayed toward them. In this stage, it has become apparent to them that they are in positions of lower power, prestige, and privilege (Huff, 1996). Some young people who develop tolerance pursue advanced education, some leave the community and never come back, and some take low-paying jobs in the community. Young people who do not develop tolerance for racism and stereotyping may live lives marred by alcohol, drugs, unemployment, and misery.

ALCOHOLISM AND THE RESERVATION

Proportionately more Native Americans die in automobile and other fatal accidents, are imprisoned, and commit suicide than people from any other ethnic group in the United States or Canada. In many of these cases, alcohol and drug abuse are primary co-occurrents. Though it is impossible using the current numbers to clearly define the overall role alcohol plays in Native American injury and death, it is currently estimated that 75% of all Native American deaths are related to alcohol. Suicides among U.S. Native Americans is 1.5 times higher than the national average in the United States, with greater than 70% of completed suicide victims having detectable levels of blood alcohol (LaFromboise & Howard-Pitney, 1995; Trujillo, 2000; U.S. Bureau of Justice Statistics, 1991). In Canada, the suicide rate, which is also connected to alcohol abuse, is at least 6 times higher among Native Canadians than the national average. In fact, the Aboriginal community in Canada has the worst suicide problem of any group in the world (Kirmayer, 1994).

Alcohol abuse/dependence also contributes to high rates of school dropouts. For example, American Indians have higher K–12 school dropout rates, about 30% nationwide, than any other United States ethnic group (Reyhner, 1994; National Center for Education Statistics, 1997). Alcohol abuse/dependence contributes to high rates of unemployment. For example, less than 10% of all adult Native American males are consistently employed, and 80% to 90% of the Native peoples on some reservations are continually unemployed (Tropman, 1986). In addition, alcohol abuse/dependence contributes to high rates of incarceration. Moreover, alcohol abuse/dependence contributes to high rates of cirrhosis and diabetes (the overall rates for diagnosed diabetes among Native Americans is 12.2% for those over 19 years of age, 25% among the Oklahoma tribes, and 50% among members of the Pima Tribe, which is the highest rate of diabetes in the world; National Institute of Health, 2006). Finally, alcohol abuse/dependence contributes to high rates of depression, criminal felonies including homicide, and domestic abuse (Centers for Disease Control and Prevention, 1992, 1994).

The most devastating effects of alcohol abuse may be found in the children of Native American people. Fetal alcohol syndrome (FAS), which is cause by the mother's drinking during pregnancy, is found 30 times more often among Native American children than among White children. FAS causes behavioral dysfunctions, intellectual impairment, and deficits in learning. Alcohol abuse can totally disrupt families and cause harmful effects to children that can last throughout life (Parsons, 2003).

Since alcohol was first introduced to Native Americans by European American settlers, it has been a constant source of sorrow and destruction (Turner, in press). Among many Native Americans, the pattern of alcohol abuse is to drink in order to become inebriated rather than engaging in social drinking. Moreover, many Natives become dependent on alcohol at the same time they become users.

Theories about the reasons that alcohol abuse/dependence is so prevalent in the Native community include genetic predisposition, enculturation pressures, social prohibition, and integration theories. Genetic predisposition theorists cite the lack of genetic capability among Native Americans to metabolize alcohol in the same way other races of people can (e.g., Caucasian race). This genetic variability is shared with the people of Japan and China, and is thought to be related to common ancestry with Native Americans. Among Natives, Japanese, and Chinese people, alcohol consumption is marked by a distinctive facial reddening, accelerated heartbeat, increased blood pressure, and a lack of acetaldehyde, which is the chemical that metabolizes alcohol in the liver. However, in comparison to Native Americans, Chinese and Japanese Americans have the lowest alcoholism rates of all American racial groups, whereas American Indians have the highest such rates (Ebberhart, Luczak, Avanecy, & Wall, 2003; Substance Abuse and Mental Health Services, 2006). Thus, genetic prohibition cannot account fully for the high rates of alcoholism found among American Indian people.

Enculturation theories of alcohol abuse propose that the conflict between indigenous values and those of the broader American culture leads to alcoholism among Natives. These theories posit that the desperate economic and social conditions of many Native Americans lead to internalized oppression and despair. Mass grieving over the loss of culture and the traditional way of life, boredom, stoicism, intense pride, and the lack of cultural models for seeking help lead to alcohol abuse as a self-medication.

Prohibition theories suggest that Native Americans learned to binge drink from frontiersmen with whom they had initial contact. According to these theories, Native Americans believe that alcohol has tremendous power and that they cannot control its effects. In contrast,

Chinese and Japanese Americans believe that alcoholism is a weakness and that people can and should control their drinking. Thus, they are less likely to drink to the point that intoxication radically influences their behavior.

Finally, integration theorists combine components of the genetic, enculturation, and social prohibition theories. These theorists emphasize that alcoholism is a symptom of the complex problems plaguing Native communities, and that alcoholism is itself a distinct problem that breeds an abundance of negative outcomes (Turner, in press). These theorists remind us that regardless of the origins of alcoholism in the Native community, the mental health challenges of alcohol abuse and dependence must be successfully treated if there is to be a livable future for Native American people.

In this chapter, we have thus far examined the legislative history of Native Americans as it has affected their quality of life. We have discussed the challenges presented by acculturation pressures and racial identity development, and one of the most devastating results of these pressures, which is alcohol abuse. In the next sections of this chapter, we will discuss Native American families, Native American spirituality, Native American culture, and finally, strategies for and implications of counseling with Native American people.

FAMILY VALUES

Traditional Native American families tend to be based on an extended family structure rather than the nuclear family structure that is found among European Caucasian Americans. This is true for many reasons, including the care of and respect for elders, and the extended family involvement in the raising and care of children (Garrett & Garrett, 2002).

Among Native American families, children are seen as a gift from the Creator. Children are taught by means of role modeling and storytelling. These activities are essential to carrying on traditions from generation to generation as most Native American culture and beliefs are not written. Most Native American children are expected to know their family lineage and to be able to recite this lineage upon meeting people they have not known before.

However, there has been great social and cultural disruption among Native American families and children. Today, single mothers head approximately twice as many Native families as European American families. Before 1978, an estimated 25% to 35% of all Native American children were taken from their homes to foster care homes, with 90% of these children being placed in White foster families. It was argued by Native Americans that officials and social workers from both public and private agencies, who claimed that removal of Native American children from their families were in the children's best interests, failed to understand traditional Native American child-rearing practices. Native American children were sometimes taken through fraudulent means, and parents were often misled or relinquished their children under duress. In 1978, the U.S. Indian Child Welfare Act was passed in response to these concerns, with the goal of preventing adoptions of Native American children without judicial oversight from the tribes. The act, although amended several times and still highly contested, has sharply reduced the permanent removal of Native American children from their families and changed the way that Native American children are adopted (Hollinger, 1993). As of 1997, only 30% of Native American children who are adopted are adopted transracially, with the majority being adopted by a member of the child's extended family, other members of the child's tribe, or other Native American families (Gummerson & Rausch, 2006).

CULTURE OF INDIGENOUS PEOPLE

In order to provide more effective counseling services for Native American people, counselors must understand worldview differences that impact mental health care. There are many customs among Native American tribes. However, there are some common cultural assumptions that can be used to understand how Native American people as a whole may approach their lives. One primary cultural value is Native Americans' understanding of the nature of human beings, and the nature of relationships (Garrett & Garrett, 1996). Native Americans typically believe that the good of the tribe, group, or family unit supercedes the good of the individual. This worldview is primarily circular, meaning that Native Americans believe that the good they do toward others will return to them, and the evil they do toward others will likewise return to them. Shared values, shared power, shared sustenance, and cooperation are primary ways to relate. Patience is important as decisions are made by consensus. Speech is indirect and humor is dry, relying on shared contexts and meanings. Respect is based on acknowledging the equality of all beings and of allowing others to make choices for themselves.

In contrast, European Americans believe that the world, including the world of nature, should be conquered and ruled. Underlying these values is a sense that the values, powers, and rights of European Americans are God given, and that European Americans are responsible to rescue others from their heathenism and teach them the ways of right living. European Americans believe in the good of the individual as a means to promote the ultimate good of the group. In the European American social structure, deserving people rise to the top, and less deserving people learn to obey and cooperate with their betters. The worldview is primarily in a pyramid shape, with fewer people in rulership positions and more people who are ruled. European Americans believe that domination will ensure that they will receive good things. The emphasis is more on acquiring and less on sharing, with status gained through individual wealth and surplus. Community or group values are based on the decisions of those in power. Power is shared only with those who are also superior, either by race, gender, political acumen, or individual differences. Speech is direct and humor needs to be intentionally contextualized to be understood. Respect is based on allowing others to compete and to win in fair competitions. All beings are not held as equals, and those individuals in lesser positions of power and control are allowed to make fewer decisions for themselves.

Native American culture is expressed in a variety of ways. Most tribes have traditional clothes that are worn at ceremonial times. The majority of Native American tribes celebrate their tribal traditions by dancing. Dances, especially performed by Native American young people, honor young people and their potential to contribute to the community. Dances are often a major source of socialization in the Native American community. Culture is also expressed in community meals. During these meals, each family brings special dishes to share. Different tribes have different traditions. For example, among the Creek people in Oklahoma, traditional brown beans, cornbread, wild onions, and sophke (flat bread with honey) are served. Among the Lakota in the north, buffalo and fry bread are served. Cultural expressions among Native American people also include stories that are based on oral traditions. These stories can be told at certain times of the year to honor the spring, the harvest, or the snow.

SPIRITUALITY

Before contact with European Americans, Native American religious traditions were essentially animistic (i.e., the belief that all things have spirit). Many tribes also had the concept of a supreme being that ruled over all (in some tribes, this deity was known as grandfather), and that there was a lesser deity as well, known as a hero or trickster. These deities were responsible for teaching moral behavior to the people. Most tribes had beliefs that included creation (although creation stories differed from tribe to tribe), had sacred texts that included oral and sometimes written traditions, had a theory of the afterlife that could include translation to another plane of existence or reincarnation, had religious leaders (sometimes known as Shamans or Medicine People), had a vision quest (where young people separate themselves from the tribe for a prescribed period of time in order to identify their own paths), had purification ceremonies (e.g., sweat lodges or smudging), had renewal ceremonies (e.g., the Lakota Sundance or the Cherokee Green Corn Dance), and had prophets (who spoke the will of the Creator to the people). Because of the wide range of habitats in North America, these religions evolved to meet the needs and lifestyles of their adherents.

Upon contact, European Americans judged that Native American religions were heathen, worthless, and evil (Mankiller & Wallis, 1994). Many Native American people were forcibly converted to Christianity. For example, Southwestern Native Americans were baptized into Christianity upon threat of death. Native American children in boarding schools were punished for not practicing Christianity. Native American religions were outlawed. Native American spiritual leaders were jailed.

Whether Christian or traditional in religious beliefs and practices, the most important aspect of Native American spirituality is the all-encompassing way it is practiced (Garrett & Garrett, 1996). Native Americans tend to bring spirituality into everyday life. All things are seen as connected, and the spiritual dimensions of life are honored throughout the day. Thanks are given to God and creatures for sustenance, to God for providing sustenance, and to both animate and inanimate creatures for giving their lives that people may be fed, clothed, and sheltered. Asking the Creator for help in both important and mundane things is seen as honorable and important. Spiritual connections are seen as both vertical, with the Great Spirit, and horizontal, with the creation.

COUNSELING STRATEGIES AND IMPLICATIONS

In order to treat Native American clients more effectively, it is important to understand their history, as well as their political and social realities. Ever-present feelings of betrayal, together with real loss and devastation have led to strong grief reactions and what some researchers call postcolonial or transgenerational trauma (Brave Heart & DeBruyn, 1998; Walters & Simoni, 1999).

Many, but certainly not all, Native Americans lack mental and emotional well-being. Disharmony disrupts Native American lives. Domestic violence, childhood abuse and neglect, homicide, and suicide are scourges on Native American people and their communities. Poor physical health, including diabetes, cirrhosis, and unusually high infant mortality, attack Native people, reducing their quality of life. Generations of Native Americans have lived under the control of others. Thus many struggle with having a sense of who they are as tribal members or even as worthy members of the human race.

However, Native Americans may look with suspicion on counseling. Some researchers suggest that Native people believe that mental health treatment is a potential form of social control (Whaley, 1998). Others have suggested that the construct of mental illness was imposed on Native American people (Walker & Ladue, 1986) in order to deny them the human right to be different. Further, psychological challenges and mental illness can be seen as stigmatizing, shaming, disgracing, and further dishonoring Native American people (Thompson, Walker, & Silk-Walker, 1993). In particular, some tribal groups attach great stigma to most alcohol and substance abuse problems (Grandbois, 2005). These beliefs about mental health and the treatment of mental illness tend to increase the challenge of conducting interracial counseling with Native Americans successfully.

To offer effective counseling services, researchers have suggested that helping Native Americans come to terms with transgenerational traumatic experiences is a first step in bringing closure. Just as with other trauma survivors, assisting Native Americans to encounter their past, talk about their feelings, make sense of their experiences, grieve their losses, and set their faces toward new futures can diminish the effects of past events and help them reestablish their lives. For Native Americans that are more traditional, and less acculturated to the majority culture, the most powerful strategies could include traditional ceremonies (e.g., sweat lodges or smudging), traditional prayers, and counseling services provided by professional helpers who themselves are Native American (Pope, 2002). Some Native American people use Western interventions to get relief of acute medical symptoms, but prefer traditional healing practices to restore their sense of balance, harmony, and unity after an acute or traumatic event (Buchwald, Beals, & Manson, 2000; Garrett & Garrett, 1996). For Native Americans that are struggling with their own racial/ethnic/cultural identities, helping them explore their own history and backgrounds can give them the courage to claim those parts of themselves they have previously rejected. Helping Native people establish a new sense of racial and cultural identity, and a sense of cultural pride can assist them in setting goals that are important to them, rather than goals that are important to others.

There is little research to support the effectiveness of treatment for alcoholism and other chemical abuse and dependency issues among Native Americans. However, grassroots efforts that include family support, tribal support, and community education could have positive effects in helping Native Americans manage sobriety. We suggest providing counseling services (a) in which cultural symbols, pictures, signs, and stories are used, (b) that address the impact of intergenerational trauma and chemical abuse on both families and communities, (c) that use Native languages where appropriate, (d) that use Native art forms, (e) that employ traditional interpersonal techniques, such as talking circles, and (f) that employ tribal elders as both consultants and mental health service providers, as ways to help Native American clients find their own healing, peace, and balance as they struggle to gain or maintain mental health.

Finally, counseling professionals and other mental health workers need to practice competently when providing services to diverse clients. Competent counseling includes not only demonstrated competencies at the individual and professional levels, but also demonstrated competencies at organizational and societal levels (Sue, 2001). Multicultural competencies include "promoting societal understanding, affirmation, and appreciation of multiculturalism against the damaging effects of individual, institutional, and societal racism, prejudice, and all forms of oppression based on stereotyping and discrimination" (American Psychological Association, 2002, p. 15). Comas-Díaz (2000) asserts that psychologists are uniquely able to promote a wealth of initiatives based on racial equity and social justice. This is aided by an exploration of their own personal values regarding minority clients, as well as awareness of their impact on others and the influence of their personal and professional roles in society. Professionals in other mental health professions, such as orthopsychiatry, social work, school counseling, career development counseling, public health, and community health education, have called for similar professional reflection and action in promoting equity, inclusion, and empowerment for diverse peoples, and social change in our pluralistic society (Arthur, 2005; Falk-Rafael, Fox, & Bewick, 2005; Howard & Solberg, 2006; McNicoll, 2005; Pope, 2002; Regidor et al., 2006; Russo, 2006; Winder, 2004).

In this chapter, we have explored how legislation in the United States and Canada has shaped the cultural context of Native Americans. We examined how issues of acculturation and racial identity development can contribute either positively or negatively to the mental health and wellness of Native American people. We discussed the possible etiologies and devastating effects of alcoholism, and suggested that providing treatment for alcoholism in the Native community could be one of the most important services we can offer to our Native clients. We then discussed Native family values, cultures, and spirituality, as a way to consider how each of these life areas could contribute to mental health treatment issues among Native Americans. Finally, we offered suggestions for effective counseling strategies and counseling implications with Native American people.

The implications of providing counseling services for Native American people could have great and lasting benefits for people who have been oppressed and disposed for hundreds of years. Several challenges exist that can hamper efforts to provide counseling services. There is a lack of trained Native American mental health professionals. In addition, there is a lack of understanding of the historical nature of the mental health challenges that Native American people face. Moreover, although this chapter offered broad interpretations of Native American culture, there are many intertribal differences of which mental health workers should be aware. We suggest that mental health professionals become familiar with the traditions and customs that are specific to their clientelle. Finally, there is little outcome research on the effectiveness of treating mental health issues among Native American people. We hope that the mental health profession will continue to explore ways to successfully provide counseling services to a very important segment of North American societies, Native Americans.

REFERENCES

Adams, D. W. (1995). Education for extinction: American Indians and the boarding school experience, 1875–1928. Lawrence: University Press of Kansas.

American Psychological Association. (2002). *Guidelines on multicultural education, training, research, practice, and organizational change for psychologists*. Retrieved May 31, 2006, from http://www.apa.org/pi/multiculturalguidelines.pdf

Andujo, E. (1988). Ethnic identity of transethnically adopted Hispanic adolescents. *Social Work, 33,* 531–535.

Arthur, N. (2005). Building from diversity to social justice competencies in international standards for career development practitioners. *International Journal for Educational and Vocational Guidance, 5*(2), 137–148.

Bowker, A. (1993). *Sisters in the blood: The education of women in Native America.* Newton, MA: WEEA Publishing Center.

Brave Heart, M. Y. H., & DeBruyn, L. M. (1998). The American Indian holocaust: Healing historical unresolved grief. *American Indian & Alaska Native Mental Health Research, 8*(2), 60–82.

Bray, S. W. (2006). *The Native American border community: Racial Identity Development (RID) model.* Retrieved April 4, 2006, from http://www. nisj.org/Racism_charts/Bray%20RID%20Model.pdf

Buchwald, D. S., Beals, J., & Manson, S. M. (2000). Use of traditional healing among Native Americans in a primary care setting. *Medical Care, 38*(12), 1191–1199.

Canby, W. C., Jr. (1998). *American Indian law in a nutshell* (3rd ed.). St. Paul, MN: West Group.

Centers for Disease Control and Prevention. (1992, October 16). Alcohol-related hospitalizations—Indian health service and tribal hospitals, United States, May 1992. *Morbidity and Mortality Weekly Report, 41*(41), 757–760.

Centers for Disease Control and Prevention. (1994, January 14). Prevalence and characteristic of alcohol consumption and fetal alcohol awareness—Alaska, 1991 and 1993. *Morbidity and Mortality Weekly Report, 43*(1), 3–6.

Cohen, F. S. (1953). The erosion of Indian rights, 1950–1953: A case study in bureaucracy. *Yale Law Journal, 62,* 348–290.

Comas-Díaz, L. (2000). An ethnopolitical approach to working with people of color. *American Psychologist, 55,* 1319–1325.

Davidson, T. G. (2006). *Spiritual and cultural genocide.* Retrieved March 24, 2006, from http://www.nemasys.com/ghostwolf/Native/genocide.shtml

Debo, A. (1984). *A history of the Indians of the United States.* Norman: University of Oklahoma Press.

DeMallie, R. J. (2001). Teton. In R. J. DeMallie (Ed.) & W. C. Sturtevant (Gen. Ed.), *Handbook of North American Indians: Plains* (Vol. 13, Pt. 2, pp. 794–820). Washington, DC: Smithsonian Institution.

Department of Welfare, Republic of South Africa (1997). *White paper for social welfare.* Retrieved July 2, 2006, from http://www.welfare.gov. za/Documents/1997/wp.htm

Dussault, R., Erasmus, G., Chartrand, P. L. A. H., Meekison, J. P., Robinson, V., & Sillett, M. (1996). *Report of the Royal Commission on Aboriginal peoples.* Ottawa, ON: Canada Communication Group.

Ebberhart, N. C., Luczak, S. E., Avanecy, N., & Wall, T. L. (2003). Family history of alcohol dependence in Asian Americans. *Journal of Psychoactive Drugs, 35*(3), 375–377.

Falk-Rafael, A., Fox, J., & Bewick, D. (2005). Health care reforms in Ontario, Canada: Moving toward or away from primary health care? Report of a 1999 survey of public health nurses in Ontario, Canada. *Primary Health Care Research and Development, 6*(2), 172–183.

Garrett, J. T., & Garrett, M. T. (1996). *Medicine of the Cherokee: The way of right relationship.* Rochester, VT: Bear & Company.

Garrett, J. T., & Garrett, M. T. (2002). *The Cherokee Full Circle: A practical guide to ceremonies and traditions.* Rochester, VT: Bear & Company.

Gonzales, N. A., & Cauce, A. M. (1995). Ethnic identity and multicultural competence: Dilemmas and challenges for minority youth. In W. D. Hawley & A. W. Jackson, (Eds.), *Toward a common destiny: Improving race and ethnic relations in America* (pp. 131–162). San Francisco: Jossey-Bass.

Grandbois, D. (2005). Stigma of mental illness among American Indian and Alaska Native nations: Historical and contemporary perspectives. *Issues in Mental Health Nursing, 26*(10), 1001–1024.

Gummerson, R. M., & Rausch, T. E (2006). *Preferences created by the Indian Child Welfare Act.* Retrieved May 27, 2006, from http://www.gummersonrausch.com/article.jsp?practArea=29&articleIndex=2

Helms, J. E. (1990). *Black and White racial identity: Theory, research, and practice.* New York: Greenwood Press.

Hirschfelder, A. (1986). *Happily may I walk: American Indians and Alaska Natives today.* New York: Charles Scribner's Sons.

Hollinger, J. H. (1993). Adoption law. *The Future of Children, 3*(1), 44–63. Retrieved May 27, 2006, from http://www.futureofchildren.org/pubs-info2825/pubs-info_show.htm?doc_id=77427

Howard, K. A. S., & Solberg, V. S. H. (2006). School-based social justice: The achieving success identity pathways program. *Professional School Counseling, 9*(4), 278–287.

Huff, D. J. (1996). *Institutional racism and American Indian education.* Albany: State University of New York Press.

Jones, J. (1991). Piercing the veil: Bi-cultural strategies for coping with prejudice and racism. In H. J. Knopke, R. J. Norrell, & R. W. Rogers (Eds.), *Opening doors: Perspectives on race relations in contemporary America* (pp. 179–197). Tuscaloosa: The University of Alabama Press.

Kirmayer, L. J. (1994). Suicide attempts Canadian Aboriginal peoples. *Transcultural Psychiatric Review, 31*, 3–45.

Kim, Y. Y., Lujan, P., & Dixon, L. D. (1998). "I can walk both ways": Identity integration of American Indians in Oklahoma. *Human Communication Research, 25*(2), 252–274.

LaFromboise, T. D., & Howard-Pitney, B. (1995). *Suicidal behavior in American Indian female adolescents.* New York: Springer.

Lewis, J. A., & Arnold, M. S. (1998). From multiculturalism to social action. In C. C. Lee, G. R. Walz, & G. Richard (Eds.), *Social action: A mandate for counselors* (pp. 51–65). Alexandria, VA: American Counseling Association.

Mankiller, W., & Wallis, M. (1994). *Mankiller: A chief and her people.* New York: St. Martin's Press.

McNicoll, P. (2005). Against common sense: Teaching and learning toward social justice. *Social Work with Groups, 28*(2), 102–105.

Meriam, L. M., Brown, R. A., Cloud, H. R., Dale, E. E., Duke, E., Edwards, H. R., et al. (1928). *The problem of Indian administration: Report of a survey made at the request of Honorable Hubert Work, Secretary of the Interior, and submitted to him, February 21, 1928.* Baltimore: Johns Hopkins Press/The Lord Baltimore Press.

Nagel, J. U. (1995). American Indian ethnic renewal: Politics and the resurgence of identity. *American Sociological Review, 60*(6), 947–965.

National Center for Education Statistics. (1997). *Characteristics of American Indian and Alaska Native education* (U.S. Department of Education, Office of Educational Research and Improvement, Publication No. NCES 97-451). Washington, DC: U.S. Government Printing Office.

National Institutes of Health. (2006). *The Pima Indians: Pathfinders for health.* Retrieved June 1, 2006, from http://diabetes.niddk.nih.gov/dm/pubs/pima/index.htm.

National Research Council, Commission on Behavioral and Social Sciences and Education, Panel on High-Risk Youth. (1993). *Losing generations: Adolescents in high-risk settings.* Washington, DC: National Academy Press.

Novick, G. E., Novick, C. C., Yunis, J., Yunis, E., Antunez De Mayolo, P., Scheer, W. D., et al. (1998). Polymorphic Alu insertions and the Asian origin of Native American populations. *Human Biology, 70,* 23–39.

Oswalt, W. H. (2001). *This land was theirs: A study of Native Americans* (7th ed.). New York: Oxford University Press.

Parsons, T. (2003, December 14). Alcoholism and its effect on the family. *AllPsych Journal.* Retrieved June 8, 2006, from http://allpsych.com/journal/alcoholism.html

Pearce, R. H. (1967). *Savagism and civilization: A study of the Indian and the American mind.* Baltimore: Johns Hopkins University Press.

Pindus, N. (2004). *Overcoming challenges to business and economic development in Indian country.* Washington, DC: Department of Health and Human Services.

Pope, M. (2002, January). Traditional Cherokee ways of healing. *Counseling Today,* 26–28.

Portman, T. A. A., & Garrett, M. T. (2005). Beloved women: Nurturing the sacred fire of leadership from an American Indian perspective. *Journal of Counseling & Development, 83,* 284–291.

Regidor, E., Ronda, E., Pascual, C., Martinez, D., Calle, M. E., & Dominguez, V. (2006). Decreasing socioeconomic inequalities and increasing health inequalities in Spain: A case study. *American Journal of Public Health, 96*(1), 102–108.

Reyhner, J. A. (1994). *American Indian/Alaska Native education.* Bloomington, IN: Phi Delta Kappa.

Russo, N. F. (2006). Orthopsychiatry in the 21st century. *American Journal of Orthopsychiatry, 76*(2), 151–153.

Schurr, T. G., Ballinger, S. W., Gan, Y. Y., Hodge, J. A., Merriwether, D. A., Lawrence, D. N., et al. (1990). Amerindian mitochondrial DNAs have rare Asian mutations at high frequencies, suggesting they derived from four primary maternal lineages. *American Journal of Human Genetics, 46*, 613–623.

Spickard, P. R. (1989). *Mixed blood: Intermarriage and ethnic identity in twentieth-century America*. Madison: University of Wisconsin Press.

Substance Abuse and Mental Health Service. (2006). *Results from the 2004 National Survey on Drug Use and Health*. Retrieved May 31, 2006, from http://oas.samhsa.gov/nsduh/2k4nsduh/2k4results/2k4results.htm

Sue, D. W. (2001). Multidimensional facets of cultural competence. *The Counseling Psychologist, 29*, 790–821.

Sue, D. W., & Sue, D. (2003). *Counseling the culturally diverse: Theory and practice* (4th ed.). Hoboken, NJ: John Wiley & Sons.

Thompson, J. W., Walker, R. D., & Silk-Walker, P. (1993). Psychiatric care of American Indians and Alaska Natives. In A. C. Gaw (Ed.), *Culture, ethnicity, and mental illness* (pp. 189–243). Washington, DC: American Psychiatric Press.

Tokunaga, K., Ohashi J., Bannai M., & Juji T. (2001). Genetic link between Asians and Native Americans: Evidence from HLA genes and haplotypes. *Human Immunology, 62*, 1001–1008.

Trimble, J. E. (2000). Social psychological perspectives on changing self-identification among American Indians and Alaskan Natives. In R. H. Dana (Ed.), *Handbook of cross-cultural and multicultural personality assessment* (pp. 197–222). Mahwah, NJ: Erlbaum.

Tropman, J. E. (1986). *Conflict in culture: Permission versus controls and alcohol use in American society*. Lanham: University of Michigan.

Trujillo, M. H. (2000). *Facts on Indian Health disparities*. Washington, DC: Indian Health Service.

Turner, S. L. (in press). Alaskan Natives. *Encyclopedia of Counseling* (Vol. 4). Thousand Oaks, CA: Sage.

U.S. Bureau of Justice Statistics. (1991). *Correctional populations in the United States*. Government Documents: J29.17991, p. 58.

Walker, R. D., & Ladue, R. A. (1986). An integrative approach to American Indian mental health. In C. B. Wilkinson (Ed.), *Ethnic psychiatry* (pp. 146–194). New York: Plenum.

Walters, K. L., & Simoni, J. M. (1999). Trauma, substance use, and HIV risk among urban American Indian women. *Cultural Diversity & Ethnic Minority Psychology, 5*(3), 236–248.

Whaley, A. L. (1998). Racism in the provision of mental health services: A social cognitive analysis. *American Journal of Orthopsychiatry, 68*(1), 47–57.

Winder, A. E. (2004). Caring for the vulnerable. *International Quarterly of Community Health Education, 23*(4), 387–389.

10

COUNSELING WITH GAY, LESBIAN, BISEXUAL, AND TRANSGENDER PEOPLE

Toni R. Tollerud and Linda S. Slabon

This is first and foremost a chapter about people—their yearnings, fears, loves, hopes, disappointments, losses, and all else that encompasses their life journeys. Those trained as counselors have an ethical obligation to understand the complexity of oppressions, both internalized and external, that queer folk face. Like the word *fag*, the word *queer* is often used as an abusive and scornful epithet by those who hate or fear anyone outside the heterosexual experience. But words once used as slurs are being taken back by queer-identified people as a sign of pride and affirmation for the right to be different (Feinberg, 1996; Spargo, 1999). Sex matters, yet the sex act is only a small portion of what makes a person identify him- or herself as a sexual minority. Queer folk are those who identify as BGLT (bisexual, gay, lesbian, or transgender), that is, a person of a sexual minority within a predominately heterosexual society. We, the authors, begin this chapter by asking you to ponder some challenging questions:

- In what ways do you regard yourself as unique?
- What roles do biology, parenting, social convention, social control, politics, religion, and popular culture play in determining acceptable norms and mores for human relationships?
- What shapes your desires? How do you know that they are "normal"?
- What makes one erotic activity good and another bad?

The growing number of books, articles, workshops, online resources, and educational materials on gay, lesbian, bisexual, and transgender issues suggest that BGLT concerns have come out of the closet and into the light of day. Over the past 50 years there have been significant changes in society as BGLT people have claimed identity, legitimacy, and personal power. These developments fueled movements for political inclusion, and civil and legal rights. Although serious obstacles such as verbal abuse, suicide, substance abuse, reparative therapy, condemnation and rejection by religious bodies, hate crimes, discrimination, and violence still plague this community, more and more of these ills are seen as the result of the systems and structures of society's intolerance and are not to be blamed on the oppressed population (Jennings, 1994; Lee, 2007; Ryan & Futterman, 2001). It is clear that BGLT people will no longer be silenced and that issues are being raised in the arenas of education, media, relationships, and politics. These realities point to the heightened ethical and legal obligation of professional counselors to support, advocate for, and work with this population.

This chapter introduces counselors to what they need to know about counseling people who identify as gay, lesbian, bisexual, or transgender. It can also help address the needs of people who are in a state of confusion and who are questioning their sexual orientation. Key components will include selected issues in BGLT history and culture in the United States; the development of queer identity; the coming out process for youth, adults, and family dynamics; contemporary issues; counseling strategies; and implications for the counselor who advocates for justice and equity.

BGLT HISTORY BASICS

Each June in cities across the United States—from San Francisco to Chicago to New York—millions have gathered to celebrate in gay-pride parades and to commemorate what is regarded as the marker of the contemporary gay rights movement, the Stonewall riots. The Stonewall riots occurred on the heels of the civil rights movement, the Vietnam War, the women's movement, and the assassinations of John F. and Robert Kennedy and Martin Luther King, Jr. Respect, freedom, and a demand for acceptance became the community's cry for justice.

On June 27, 1969, at the Stonewall Inn, a predominantly gay male club in Greenwich Village, the police continued their established practice of coming to the club to provoke the club's patrons. Those with no ID or who were wearing clothes of the opposite sex were to be taken away to lockup. All others were released to go home, but on this night people congregated outside the bar. The mood was light until three drag queens and a cross-dressed lesbian were loaded into the wagon. Historian Martin Duberman chronicles, "Craig Rodwell's view probably comes as close as we are likely to get to the truth: 'A number of incidents were happening simultaneously. There was not one thing that happened or one person, there was just … a flash of group—of mass—anger'" (Jennings, 1994, p. 203). The police turned a fire hose on the crowd and the crowd retaliated throwing bricks and bottles, and set fires in trash cans. Thirteen were arrested.

The second night of the riots took on a definitively political tone. Graffiti added to the walls announced "They Invaded Our Rights; Legalize Gay Bars; Support Gay Power" (Miller, 1995, p. 366). By the third night the riot had quelled, but the gay community had experienced a fundamental internal shift. No more hiding in darkness and cowering in shame. Within one month after Stonewall, the Gay Liberation Front was organized. It is estimated that 300 to 400 BGLT people marched to the original site of the riot singing "We Shall Overcome" and chanting "Gay power!" (Miller, 1995, p. 368).

Although the Stonewall riots lay claim to a legendary status, it is simply incorrect, and it ignores history, to name the riots as the beginning of the gay movement. One hundred years before Stonewall, Karl Heinrich Ulrichs (1825–1895) was delivering speeches in Germany about gay rights. Sigmund Freud (1856–1939) argued that all human beings were innately bisexual and refused to categorize homosexuality as an illness. Although Freud was convinced that it was a sign of "arrested development," he doubted that a homosexual could be transformed into a heterosexual and he would not agree to treat someone merely because they presented as homosexual (Miller, 1995). But Freud's views did not hold sway.

By the 1950s the views of Sandor Rado (1890–1972) became dominant. Rado, of Columbia University's Psychoanalytic Clinic, rejected Freud's theories believing that homosexuality was caused by fear of the opposite sex, and that the only sexual orientation was heterosexual. A psychiatrist at New York Medical College, Irving Bieber (1908–1991) took the next step toward pathologizing homosexuality. Bieber argued that most male homosexuals came from families where there is a "detached, hostile father and a close-binding, intimate, seductive mother" (Miller, 1995, p. 247). Bieber was convinced that through psychoanalysis, clients would change from the pathology of homosexuality to heterosexuality. Charles Socarides (1922–2005), also of the Columbia University psychoanalysts, argued that homosexuality was sick; with over half who engaged in homosexual practice likely to suffer from mental illness such as schizophrenia, paranoia, or manic-depression, and with the other half likely to be obsessive, phobic, or addicted to their need for masculinity.

In the early 1950s, while the causes of homosexuality remained shrouded in mystery, the authors of the American Psychiatric Association's *Diagnostic and Statistical Manual of Mental Disorders* (1994, 1st ed.; *[DSM–I]*) were able to reach a near consensus on this point: Homosexuality was pathology and was listed among the sociopathic personality disorders. In 1968 for *DSM–II*, it was moved to "other non-psychotic mental disorders" (Miller, 1995, p. 249).

Not until after Stonewall, after the emergence of the gay liberation movement and after concerted gay actions for social justice, did the American Psychiatric Association in 1973 remove homosexuality from its list of disorders. Over 30 years have passed, yet "sexual minorities continue to experience discrimination when they seek mental health services ... Fassinger (1991) identified studies revealing that mental health professionals are uninformed, work from heterosexist perspectives, and hold on to societal stereotypes about gay and lesbian people" (Lassiter & Barret, 2007, p. 35). Many counselors remain untrained and uncomfortable with sexual minority clients, but there is much we can do to improve the situation. We begin with the commitment to heighten our awareness of heterosexual privilege and of our own biases and prejudgments, and to listen and learn from the lives of others.

THE LANGUAGE OF BGLT CULTURE

To understand the basics of bisexual, gay, lesbian, and transgender culture, a professional counselor must be familiar with common terms and what they mean. The set of initials BGLT is often used as a shortcut reference for this population. The term *gay* is sometimes used to describe both male and female homosexuals. When people referring to gay culture seek to use more specific language, the term *gay* is used to describe men who are attracted to other men physically, sexually, spiritually, and emotionally. The term *lesbian* is the counterpart for women who are physically, sexually, spiritually, and emotionally attracted to other women. The origin of the word *lesbian* comes out of Greek mythology. Born in the 7th century BCE, Sappho, a noted poet, is the only ancient female author whose work about lovemaking between women exists to the present day (Jennings, 1994; Miller, 1995). Sappho lived on the island of Lesbos, which is how the word *lesbian* became synonymous with homosexual women.

Words to describe homosexuals have often derived from religious, legal or clinical origins, and due to the discrimination, ignorance, prejudice, and the cultural norms at the time, these words conveyed negative connotations. Examples include *sodomite, deviant, pervert, faggot,* and *dyke.* The word *gay* was in common usage within the homosexual community by the late 1920s. *Gay* was sufficiently ambiguous and nonderogatory to the insider population, such that it gained popular usage. Over time negative stereotypes became associated with gay men who were said to act effeminate, and with gay women who were castigated as man-haters or as women who act like or want to be men, but gay men and lesbians are as diverse as heterosexuals. They may wear leather or cotton, ride motorcycles or SUVs, use makeup or not, be CEOs of large corporations or factory workers or medical professionals, be parents, play professional sports or be a professional musician. Most lesbians and gay men take on a variety of roles in their relationships that oppose gender stereotyping. Combating stereotypes is an important advocacy role for counselors in supporting gay and lesbian people and their families.

BISEXUALITY

A bisexual person is someone who is attracted sexually, physically, emotionally, and spiritually to both men and women. Many issues may affect a person's identity as bisexual. Huegel (2003) suggests that people who are questioning their identity may call themselves bisexual while they work to determine their true identity. Others may identify as bisexual because of their struggle with cultural norms around traditional marriage and having children, or to maintain an image that allows them to pass in the culture as straight when necessary. A person may hold onto their bisexual identity in order to preserve religious values, family connections, or from a need to safeguard their job or professional position. It must also be noted, however, that as society's sexual constraints loosen, more and more people, aware of sexual options, are more freely identifying themselves as bisexual.

Dworkin (2000) suggests that people who identify as bisexual are faced with additional challenges from people who identify as gay or lesbian. Because bisexuals may pass in mainstream culture, gays have seen this behavior as a political ploy to maintain heterosexual privilege while still claiming sexual minority status. Bisexual people exist in the middle and therefore often find that they are rejected from both the heterosexual and the homosexual communities.

As with gays and lesbians, misinformation and stereotypes about bisexuals are rampant. Here are some observations to set the record straight:

Not all bisexuals are in a phase or denying their homosexuality; they are bisexual.

Bisexuals do not have to date or have lovers of both sexes to claim a bisexual identity; identity and behavior are not identical.

Bisexuals are as capable of monogamy as are heterosexuals or homosexuals.

Monogamy is a choice.

Not all bisexuals appear androgynous. Manly men, such as Cary Grant and James Dean, and womanly women, such as Marlene Dietrich, Billie Holiday, and Sandra Bernhard, have had sex and relationships with both men and women.

Some bisexual people feel they have a preference for one gender over another, but many argue that their attractions are most powerfully based on the qualities of an individual. John Leland in a 1995 cover article for *Newsweek*, wrote:

Bisexuality is less a root than a construction—different in each individual—of passions and actions we are accustomed to calling heterosexual or homosexual. In its ambiguities, it calls into question the certainties of both gay and straight identities. Pushed far enough it absorbs both ... This is the new bisexual moment in a nutshell: hard fought, hard thought, and distinctly individual. It is a thorny narrative, fraught with questions of identity and belonging. (p. 50)

THE TRANSGENDER COMMUNITY

A common question asked of parents following the birth of a child is "Is it a boy or a girl?" In American culture, gender socialization begins at birth with pink hats and frilly dresses for little girls, while little boys had best be seen in clothing with clean lines and in soft shades of blue. "Sissy" boys, who cross their legs or throw like a girl, or "tomboy" girls, who hate wearing dresses or playing with dolls, are quickly coaxed, urged, or pushed to conform to socially prescribed, acceptable behaviors by their parents who are fearful of the ostracism, discrimination, or violence that their child will likely face. Mallon (1999) notes that while gender nonconforming behaviors alone do not constitute a transgender child, "children who question their birth assignment are pathologized and labeled 'gender-dysphoric'" (p. 52). Our Western culture has promoted, with vehemence, the belief that sex and gender are binary systems. With sex, the options are heterosexual or homosexual; with gender, the options are male or female. Medical and mental health professionals have pathologized transgender people, seeking to cure them, and at the same time have served as gatekeepers to hormonal therapy and sex reassignment surgeries. Religious organizations and political structures have either ignored or demonized these people.

But with the rise of political activism on the part of the transgender community, and with the analyses of power and sexuality by queer theorists such as Michael Foucault (*The History of Sexuality*, Vol.1, 1980), Judith Butler (*Gender Trouble: Feminism and the Subversion of Identity*, 1990), and Leslie Feinberg (*Trans liberation: Beyond Pink or Blue*, 1998), the door has opened to a deeper and more complex understanding of sex and gender identity development. As Feinberg (1996) observes:

> The more I studied, the more I believed that the assumption that every society, in every corner of the world, in every period of human history, recognized only men and women as two immutable social categories is a modern Western conclusion. ... There are societies all over the world that allowed for more than two sexes, as well as respecting the right of individuals to reassign their sex. And transsexuality, transgender, intersexuality, and bigender appear as themes in creation stories, legends, parables, and oral history. (p. 43)

Changes in traditional binary thinking about sex and gender have enormous implications for counselors. The focus of treatment is no longer solely the gender dysphoria of the transgender person, but includes the awareness that a culture sickened by ignorance, rigid social conformity, prejudice, and fear or hatred of difference must also be treated. Carroll, Gilroy, and Ryan (2002) stress that "clinicians need to rethink their assumptions about gender, sexuality, and sexual orientation and to adopt a 'trans-positive' or 'trans-affirmative' disposition to counseling" (p. 133). Such an approach requires more than the alleviation of distress a transgender person may experience. Trans-positive counseling will include education and advocacy on behalf of this sexual minority.

The transgender community is unlike gay men, lesbians, or bisexuals in a strikingly significant way: transgender has to do with gender identity, not sexual orientation. Transgender people begin, not with questions of sexual attraction or desire, but with questions about gender identification, that is, their internal sense of being male, female, or intersexual. Many transgender people have described a feeling of being trapped in the wrong body. The word *transgender*, or *trans*, is an umbrella term that includes people who challenge the boundaries of sex and gender. Trans people see and experience gender fluidly, as on a continuum. For many, the terminology, variety, and fluidity within

Table 10.1 Transgender Identities

Cross-dressers or transvestites (less favorable term)	Those who take on the mannerisms and dress, partially or completely, in the clothing of the societal norm for the "opposite" gender. Most are heterosexual and cross-dress occasionally for a variety of reasons.
Drag queens or drag kings (female or male impersonators)	Gay or lesbian people who cross-dress for public entertainment purposes.
Transgenderists	Disidentify with their assigned birth sex and live full time within the norms and dress of their gender identity. They may seek hormone therapy, but typically do not pursue sex reassignment surgery.
Transsexuals	Strongly disidentify with the body of their birth sex. They seek to align their bodies with the psychological, emotional, and spiritual expression of their internal gender identity and will use hormones and sex reassignment surgery to that end. Male-to-female (MTF) are born in the body of a male and believe self to be female. Female-to-male (FTM) are born in the body of a female and believe self to be male.
Intersexuals or hermaphrodites (less favorable term)	Those whose bodies deviate from absolute sexual dimorphism and are born with ambiguous genitalia. Typically surgery is done soon after birth to "correct" the "problem." "The Intersex movement seeks to halt pediatric surgery and hormone treatments that attempt to normalize infants into the dominant 'male' and 'female' roles" (Carroll, Gilroy & Ryan, 2002, p. 139).
Androgynes, two-spirit people, gender benders, gender blenders, and shape shifters	Others who self-identify within the trans community.

the transgender community can be quite confusing. Table 10.1 displays various transgender identities.

Eyler and Wright (1997) developed a clinical tool, a framework that assists us in thinking about gender identity along a 9-point continuum (see Table 10.2).

Attempts to estimate the prevalence of transgender people in our society is fraught with difficulties but we are confident that counselors will encounter transgender clients over the course of their career. Certainly counselors who intend to work with transgender people must be knowledgeable and familiarize themselves with standard diagnosis of

Table 10.2 Individually Based Gender Continuum

Female	I have always considered myself to be a woman (or girl).
Female with	I currently consider myself to be a woman, but at times I have thought of myself as really more of a man (or boy).
Gender blended	I consider myself predominantly (in some significant way) to be both a woman and a man, but I am somehow more of a woman.
Other gendered	I am neither a woman or a man, but a member of some other gender.
Ungendered	I am neither a woman, a man, or a member of some other gender.
Bigendered	Sometimes I feel or act more like a woman and other times more like a man, or sometimes like both a woman and a man.
Gender blended	I consider myself predominantly (in some significant way) to be both a man and a woman, but I am somehow more of a man.
Male with	I currently consider myself to be a man, but at times I have thought of myself as really more of a woman (or girl).
Male	I have always considered myself to be a man (or boy).

Source: Eyler & Wright, 1997, pp. 6–7.

gender identity disorder. As Grossman, D'Augelli, Salter, and Hubbard (2005) state, "Counselors are called on not only to assist gender non-conforming youth in their psychological and developmental processes, but also to engage the transgender youth and their families to adapt to the changes that gender nonconforming children bring into family interactions" (p. 56). In addition, we believe that counselors are called upon to support values of openness, diversity, and individual freedom and choice, that is, to engage the changes that transgender people bring to American culture as a whole.

Q

Another term used in referencing BGLT issues is a Q. Q can symbolize the reclamation of the word *queer* used by the BGLT community as a verb, noun, or adjective. Queers are celebrating queer films, music, a queer literary explosion, and expansive online and Web resources. Queer theory and history can now be studied in courses at various universities. And while sexuality remains a focal point in our lives, most queer folk do not seek to be defined solely by their sexuality. As Spargo observes, "[Queer analysis] is increasingly being examined in relation to other categories of knowledge involved in the maintenance of unequal power relations: race, religion, nationality, age, and class" (1999, pp. 68–69).

We, the authors, have seen Q used to refer to the word *questioning*, by youth centers in our geographic region. For youth, a BGLTQ center allows the option to work through periods of uncertainty. Questioning can be important for adolescents as they experience the wide variety of changes in their bodies and emotions.

Professional counselors must become comfortable in both using these terms and saying them during the course of counseling. A therapist's ability to communicate on issues of sex and gender convey sensitivity, openness, and safety helping the BGLT client feel accepted and supported in their concerns.

HISTORICAL OVERVIEW OF RESEARCH CONCERNING BGLT

Rothblum (2000) provides a detailed overview of the psychological research that has influenced BGLT development and suggests that it is only in the past 30 years that any focus has been given to this population. The first noted study of gay men was recorded in 1953 by a researcher named Evelyn Hooker who did a comparison study of normal gay men and heterosexual men who were not psychiatric patients or prisoners. Hooker's study was funded by a grant from the National Institute of Mental Health and revealed that the gay men were as psychologically well adjusted as were the heterosexual men. These findings were presented at an American Psychological Association conference in 1956 and made a significant impact on the future of homosexuality, opening the door for many more studies focused on this population (Rothblum, 2000).

Additionally, as Coleman (1987) argues, the labels and words used to describe homosexual, bisexual, and heterosexual seem meaningless and limiting due to the complexity of variations in sex role and orientation identity. Theorists and researchers such as Alfred Kinsey (as cited in Rothblum, 2000; Coleman, 1987) and Fritz Klein (Klein, Sepekoff, & Wolf, 1985) played an important role by expanding the understanding of sexual orientation to extend beyond the dichotomous choice of gay or straight, and by presenting sexual orientation as neither fixed in time nor grounded in permanent biological determinism (Coleman, 1987).

Kinsey's Continuum and Klein's Sexual Orientation Grid

In the 1940s, a scientist by the name of Alfred Kinsey made a controversial claim based on his research that people were not completely straight (heterosexual) or completely gay/lesbian (homosexual). Kinsey and his colleagues developed a 7-point scale on a continuum from 0 (exclusively heterosexual) to 6 (exclusively homosexual). He also considered two parameters that measured *overt sexual experience* and *psychosexual reactions* (Kinsey, Pomeroy, & Martin, 1948, p. 647). Kinsey's data supported Evelyn Hooker's efforts, demonstrating that the sexual behaviors of homosexual people spanned across a continuum, and that these people did not fit into a single, separate, sick category.

In the 1980s, a scholar by the name of Fritz Klein took homosexual identity one step further adding depth, dimension, and clarity to the complexity of sexual orientation. Klein investigated sexual orientation beyond the sex act (behaviors) and attraction by consideration of additional components that comprise a person's self concept. Klein, Sepekoff, and Wolf (1985) suggested there are several variables that can be ascribed to Kinsey's 7-point scale besides sexual behavior and psychosexual reactions. Sexual orientation concepts could include a person's fantasies, emotional preference, social preference, self identification, and choice to live a heterosexual or homosexual lifestyle. The Klein Sexual Orientation Grid (KSOG) demonstrates that a person may feel same-sex attraction, prefer same-sex relationships, and have homosexual fantasies, yet can be living a heterosexual lifestyle; or how a person may engage in same-sex behaviors and yet may vehemently and clearly *not* identify himself or herself as gay, lesbian, or bisexual. In Table 10.3,

Table 10.3 The Klein Sexual Orientation Grid (1985)

1	2	3	4	5	6	7
Hetero-sexual only	Hetero-sexual mostly	Hetero-sexual somewhat	Equal or bisexual	Homo-sexual somewhat	Homo-sexual mostly	Homo-sexual
My sexual attraction is to			Present____ Past _____ Ideal _____			
My sexual behaviors is with			Present____ Past _____ Ideal _____			
My sexual fantasies involve			Present____ Past _____ Ideal _____			
My emotional preference is for			Present____ Past _____ Ideal _____			
My social preference is for			Present____ Past _____ Ideal _____			
My self-identification is with			Present____ Past _____ Ideal _____			
My lifestyle involves			Present____ Past _____ Ideal _____			

Klein et al. (1985) present the characteristics to be ranked from 1 to 7 as experienced in a person's present, past, or ideal state.

We, the authors, have seen firsthand how tools such as Kinsey's continuum and Klein's Sexual Orientation Grid can be used therapeutically to help clients conceptualize how they might name themselves in relation to others as they develop their sexual identity. This, in turn, assists and prepares them to begin the coming out process.

THE COMING OUT PROCESS

One of the most difficult aspects about being BGLT is the need to identify oneself as different from the main social constructs of sex and gender within our society. The process called *coming out* occurs when a person acknowledges their BGLT identity and decides to make known their identity. It is imperative to note that the coming out process is just that, a process that the BGLT person engages in over and over and over and over again, always needing to assess the safety of the situation and what impact the decision to come out will have. Often a BGLT person who comes out must navigate the treacherous waters of stigma, stereotyping, anxiety, and even violence. Generally the coming out process occurs on two levels; first in coming out to oneself, and second, coming out to others both in the queer community and to nongay people.

As a result of this revelatory process, a person experiences complex changes around their feelings, thoughts, and behaviors that result in the development of a BGLT identity (Reynolds & Hanjorgiris, 2000). This "restructuring" includes changes in a person's sense of self as well as how they see themselves in relation to others in society. Most literature identifies stages as a way to signify a person's movement from assuming they are heterosexual to the discovery and acceptance of their queer identity. Tables 10.4 and 10.5 illustrate different aspects of the coming out process and how a person may work through these stages.

In 1979, Cass presented a six-stage model (Table 10.4) of homosexual identity formation. Reynolds and Hanjorgiris (2000) highlighted the importance of Cass's model, which provided a way to "explain a common gay and lesbian experience" (p. 38). As you review Cass' model and the characteristics associated with each stage, contemplate how you might advocate for a client who is working through these stages during counseling.

For youth, the recognition that there may be an attraction to a person of the same sex often occurs around the age of 10 (McClintock & Herdt, 1996). As this occurs, the fear, doubts, and awareness of being stigmatized and marginalized can be devastating to the young person.

Table 10.4 Cass Model of Identity Formation (1979)

Stage	Description of the Client at This Stage
One: Identity Confusion	The client may experience confusion, cognitive dissonance, depression, anxiety, and dismissal of erotic or emotional feelings or thoughts, yet private recognition that he or she might be queer. Some are in such denial that they act out in ways such as drug or alcohol use or abuse.
Two: Identity Comparison	The client begins to struggle with the question "Am I a homosexual?" Strong feelings of difference, not fitting into society's traditional norms, and alienation from family and friends. Client needs to acknowledge grief and loss issues or else may withdraw, become isolated, and resort to at-risk behaviors. Increased inner conflict over community values and/or religious traditions may result in internalized shame, blame, sinfulness, condemnation, or sickness.
Three: Identity Tolerance	The client begins to replace denial and confusion with exploration of what it may mean to be BG or L, and how to deal with sexual, emotional, and spiritual needs. Social isolation is replaced with a desire to find community, leading to discovery of role models, support, companionship, and a positive environment.
Four: Identity Acceptance	The client moves from tolerance to acceptance and therefore becomes more involved in the BGL community. The client tends to renounce all forms of homophobia in society including their own.
Five: Identity Pride	The client, faced with homophobic individuals and a culture of nonacceptance, experiences the emergence of pride and anger, the ability to critique injustice, and speak out against those who are fearful of diversity. The client is willing to reveal his or her sexual orientation and raise issues around oppression, discrimination, and stigma in a public manner.
Six: Identity Synthesis	The client moves beyond an "us and them" mentality in the bifurcated homosexual/heterosexual world, recognizing there are those who are supportive and willing to work for a better society. The client sees his or her oppression in a larger context of oppressions (i.e. race, class, etc.).

Troiden (1989) proposed a coming out model composed of four stages adapted specifically for gay and lesbian youth (Table 10.5). In Troiden's model for adolescence, as with Cass' model, it is important to remember

Table 10.5 Troiden Model for Gay and Lesbian Youth (1989)

Stage	Description of Youth
One: Sensitization	Often occurs in early adolescence. The adolescent acknowledges feeling "different" from peers before the age of twelve. The focus is not necessarily about sexual attraction.
Two: Confusion	Occurs during middle and/or early high school years. The adolescent feels increased tension, confounded by the onset of puberty. Social mores and rules carry a strong impact such that youth often hide or discount their feelings. Students may hate school, struggle academically as well as socially, experience isolation, and be at risk for depression, alcohol or drug abuse, and suicide.
Three: Identity Assumption	Youth begin to admit their gay or lesbian identity, dating people of the same gender. Potentially a volatile phase, youth may alienate friends and family, risking rejection or being thrown out of his or her home. Ryan and Futterman (1998) suggest that it is critical to help youth find safe community resources and support.
Four: Commitment	The youth moves from acceptance of their gay or lesbian identity to a sense of pride. Youth may form intimate relations with a same-sex partner, may become politically active, and/or become a role model and advocate for other BGLTQ youth. These youth may become watchdogs against hate and oppression in their school and ultimately confront issues that threaten youth in their community.

that stages are not fixed and that individuals may vary considerably in the manner in which they progress in coming out.

Coming out for students who are still in school is an extremely risky activity. School counselors are in a strategic position to help youth who struggle with sexual orientation questions or who are engaged in the coming out process. Although some school counselors have done an outstanding job in this area, all too often the literature suggests that school counselors are not prepared to handle these issues with their students.

In a seminal study completed in 2001 called *Hatred in the Hallways* (Human Rights Watch), researchers reported that there are "attacks on the human rights of lesbian, gay, bisexual, and transgender youth who are subjected to abuse on a daily basis by their peers and in some cases by teachers and school administrators" (p. 3). Interviews with BGLT youth across the nation do yield some positive accounts of help, but the Human Rights Watch reported negative feedback on counselors' responses. The report results indicated that school counselors were misinformed and held strong negative attitudes about BGLT youth. In addition, students felt that counselors needed specific training on BGLT issues, especially in the following areas: use of correct language when working with BGLT youth, how to raise the topic sensitively with clients and appropriately in school settings, knowledge of the coming out process, and understanding the feelings of depression or isolation that BGLT youth experience (Human Rights Watch, 2001).

Finally, it is imperative that school counselors understand the importance of maintaining the confidentiality of their student clients. Shockingly, BGLT students report that their counselors did not go over confidentiality concerns with them, and even more unethical, some counselors outed students to parents or to administrators. Students report that this is one of the major reasons why they are cautious and hesitant to talk to the school counselor, and trust is increasingly difficult for those students who have been survivors of assault, sexual abuse, or hate crimes in their school or community (Human Rights Watch, 2001). If counselors want to be trusted by BGLT youth, they will have to prove themselves to be ethical and trustworthy.

All people who work through the coming out process experience the impact of stigma. Ryan and Futterman (1998) make several recommendations for counselors working with GLB individuals. They observe that people who are involved in the coming out process often become hypervigilant, try to hide their identity, and take precautions to be seen as a heterosexual. This is referred to as *passing*. Some GLB people may even resort to anonymous sex to protect their privacy and keep from disclosing their identity. Although this isolation may protect the GLB person from discrimination or abuse, it cuts them off from community support, positive role models, and even mental health services.

It is important to be aware of how the coming out process intersects with other aspects of life including career, family issues, circle of friends, and religion. For example, Gelberg and Chojnacki (1996) discuss the strong relationship between identity and work, and note that coming out can have a negative impact on accomplishing a meaningful career. Often there is a tremendous amount of stress associated with all the stages of the coming out process (Dworkin, 2000). Counselors must understand that the client's gender, culture, class, and ethnicity intersect with the process, and so therapists are wise to pay attention to the ego strength of their clients. Sometimes other mental health problems such as depression, chronic stress and anxiety, eating disorders, substance abuse, and even suicide ideation may be present and negatively intervene with the coming out process. If a client is mentally ill, the illness may be exacerbated by the additional anxiety of coming out. Professional counselors must regard the whole client and pay attention to a wide array of concerns if they are to be effective in treatment.

WORKING WITH THE BGLT CLIENT IN TREATMENT

The BGLT client comes to counseling for a plethora of issues. All too often, however, the inexperienced counselor may assume that the BGLT client's presenting problem leads directly back to difficulties with gender identity or sexual orientation. Gender identity or sexual orientation issues may indeed become relevant, but the counselor must take care not to impose his or her agenda upon the client. As with any client, the first concern in therapy is the safety and welfare of the client. If a crisis exists, counselors should handle it first before exploring any gender identity issues. After a client stabilizes, then the counselor may query about additional concerns and explore unique aspects of the client's story.

Sometimes as a result of their own discomfort, counselors may too quickly focus therapeutic goals on helping the client adjust to inequities or to develop coping strategies to get along in mainstream culture. "Adjustment" that perpetuates injustice, however, is not an appropriate goal, particularly when inequality and discrimination are social norms.

Healthier options that the counselor might endorse include aiding the client to explore appropriate emotions, especially fear or anger at injustice; providing community contacts and online resources; or participating in groups that contribute to social change. Gutierrez (2004) cautions that "to continue addressing only the psychological maladjustment is like treating the symptom rather than the cause" (p. 331). A society that is hostile toward BGLT people perpetuates extreme anxiety and sanctions barriers to healthy living. Hershberger and D'Augelli (2000) state, "Most contemporary counselors and mental health workers now acknowledge that in providing mental health services to LGB people, it is not sexual orientation that needs to be repaired but the hostility expressed against it" (p. 241).

Those therapists who are committed to transforming the homosexual rather than transforming societal views may turn to reparative therapy. The counselor who believes that homosexuality is a sin against God may see reparative therapy, otherwise known as transformational ministry, as an option for treatment. This will be a serious conflict of authorities for the counselor. It is important to note that this particular perspective is in direct opposition to the *American Counseling*

Association Code of Ethics (2005), as well as to other competencies that inform the profession.

Counselors must address the issue of conflicting authorities and how this may impact their career and ability to serve clients. Hermann and Herlihy (2006) describe the United States Court of Appeals ruling in 2001 that "an employer's statutory obligation to make reasonable accommodations for employees' religious beliefs does not include accommodating a counselor's request to be excused from counseling homosexual clients on relationship issues" (p. 414). The counselor, Bruff, had refused to counsel a client on how to improve her lesbian relationship because homosexuality conflicted with Bruff's religious beliefs. Bruff requested to her employer, the North Mississippi Medical Center, to be excused from actively helping homosexuals improve their relationships with their partners. When the management placed Bruff on leave without pay, she appealed the decision to the vice president of the medical center. Bruff ultimately informed the vice president that she would "not be willing to counsel anyone on any subject that went against her religion" (*Bruff v. North Mississippi Health Services, Inc.*, 2001, p. 498). Although the jury found in her favor, the U.S. Court of Appeals overturned this ruling, determining that accommodation to Bruff's religious beliefs would put an undue, illegal, and discriminatory effect on her colleagues. The possible negative impact on clients was also considered by the court, including the fact that homosexual employees might be prevented from getting the assistance to which they were entitled through their employee assistance program.

Hermann and Herlihy (2006) observe that while standards for professional practice may seem clear, difficulties arise in actual practice. They ask, "How do counselors determine that they are unable to be of professional assistance? How do counselors decide their boundaries of competence? How should the ethical standards related to competence and referral be interpreted?" (p. 417). Violating the moral principles of justice, doing good, imparting no harm to clients, and respect for clients' autonomy can have serious consequences for the counselor and his or her client. The client, feeling betrayed and judged by the person who was to support her, could have filed a complaint with the State Board of Examiners for Licensed Professional Counselors. The board could have leveled sanctions, or suspended or revoked the counselor's license. "Counselors need to remain cognizant that they are ethically obligated to seek the knowledge, skills, and sensitivity required to effectively counsel a diverse client population" (Hermann and Herlihy, 2006, p. 418).

The authorities of religious convictions, spiritual beliefs, and professional ethics clearly need to be explored by counselors so that conflicts may be identified and options considered. It is the counselor who bears the responsibility to inform a potential client, at the intake session, of the values or beliefs that may limit a therapeutic relationship. The counselor can then offer options for referral so that the client does not experience betrayal, judgment, or additional discrimination at the hands of the very person in whom they had hoped to find support, safety, and healing.

Counselors must be aware of the homoprejudice that resides within the people and structures of this society. Lassiter and Barret (2007) argue that despite the fact that the *DSM* has removed the classification of homosexuality as a sickness, there are three myths that help to perpetuate oppression and injustice against BGLT people. First is the myth of equal rights, that heterosexual and BGLT people are treated equally. The fact is that BGLT people are only assured of equal access if they hide or deny their orientation or gender identity. Rights denied may include access to health benefits for a partner, the legal benefits of marriage, decision-making power for a partner who is hospitalized, and inheritance. The second myth suggested by Lassiter and Barrett is that gays recruit and molest children. Despite strong evidence that 90% of the crimes committed that involve sexual abuse of a child were perpetrated by heterosexuals, this highly erroneous myth creates a fear mentality that exacerbates unjust discrimination and can lead to violence against BGLT people. It has led to the dismissal of teachers and public officials from their jobs simply based on their sexual orientation. The final myth identified by Lassiter and Barrett concerns the argument over choice: Are BGLT people born that way or is it a choice they make? We argue that be it biology or choice, a counselor's professional obligations remain firm. In light of the *ACA Code of Ethics* and professional commitments, counselors should regularly assess their own biases and work on personal prejudices. These are crucial steps to becoming informed, positive advocates for BGLT clients.

Rare is the client who comes to counseling with a single concern. Issues tend toward complexity and counselors need to prepare themselves for problems as varied and layered as are the clients who bring them. Social locations intersect across sexual orientation, culture, race, gender, and disability, to name a few. Existential issues such as loss and grief, life's meaning or purpose, and spiritual uncertainty may cause anxiety or depression. Drug or substance abuse, eating or sleep disorders, trauma, sexual problems, loneliness, isolation, family fighting and dysfunction, or work-related difficulties may also drive a person to seek out professional treatment. Some BGLT clients will also exhibit psychopathology or mental illness.

Counselors best serve their clients by completing a thorough intake assessment that includes the presenting problem as described by the client, and by recommending secondary goals based on the client's history and need. For example, mental illness may be exacerbated by, or be the result of, the long-term pain, discrimination, and, in some cases, physical abuse that BGLT people face when dealing with a homoprejudiced society and a negative coming out experience. Dworkin (2000) suggests that the counselor should pay attention to three areas: (1) exploration of the client's internalized philosophy of being BGLT and the homophobia associated with this; (2) the coming out process and where the client is at in the process; and (3) sexual fantasies and behaviors the client may experience. Focus on these areas allows time for the counselor to demonstrate trustworthiness as the client tells his or her story.

Having built a therapeutic bond, and with sufficient information, the counselor is capable of creating a treatment plan that better serves the issues a BGLT client brings to the counseling setting. The treatment plan may then include helping a client explore the stages and options they face in coming out, strengthening relationships and connections to the larger BGLT community, and providing resources to build self-esteem and clarify sexual identity.

CONTEMPORARY ISSUES FOR BGLT PEOPLE

Race and Ethnicity

For people who belong to ethnic minority groups, race and ethnicity are a critical part of their identity. They must already negotiate their racial and ethnic identity development in White, mainstream American culture. Having to negotiate one more issue that stigmatizes and oppresses their identity can result in excessive stress and difficulty. Dworkin (2000) writes:

> Coming out may cause more emotional distress for people already experiencing prejudice and discrimination, because different denigrated aspects of the client's identity may be more salient at different times. For example, members of racial or ethnic minority groups often feel the need to choose between their minority community and the LGB community for support. (p. 166)

Religious values and family mores may impact the questioning person's identity development and may even cause the person to deny deeply held feelings and thoughts in order to cope with their social reality. Minority people who struggle in a racist culture with a visible stigma learn skills, often from family and from their culture, to respond to the discrimination and prejudice experienced in an inequitable society. BGLT minority people face additional stressors and challenges as they learn to consider not only their racial and ethnic identities, but their sexual orientation and gender identity as well. Ethnic minority BGLT people become a minority group within a minority group through the devaluation and discrimination based on their ethnic and sexual identities.

The emphasis and meanings given to sexuality and BGLT identity vary based on different cultural and ethnic traditions. Greene (1994) suggests that it is influenced by such factors as attitudes, values and beliefs, stereotypes, gender roles, religious values, cultural assimilation, and the level of support within the community. The role of the family and expectations regarding family connection versus individuation is an essential consideration for ethnic groups. When a minority person comes out as BGLT to their family it may be perceived as a rejection of the cultural heritage of the family. Fear, ignorance, and the perpetuation of negative stereotypes, which may be reinforced within a particular culture or ethnic group, often leads to ostracism and isolation of the BGLT person from their cultural community. The results of these actions can be devastating. The minority BGLT person now faces the emotional fallout and physical realities of oppression and discrimination by mainstream society, as well as from their own ethnic group. In addition, they are all too likely to experience racism within the BGLT community. For example, Logan (2006) points out that "women of color who do risk coming out are faced with discrimination from within the gay and lesbian community. They, in turn, feel marginalized by both communities, never truly part of any group, alone and isolated" (p. 294).

Because of the many levels of rejection BGLT minority people face, many hide their sexual orientation or gender identity. Ryan and Futterman (1998) report that BGLT people who are minorities are less visible than BGLT people who are White. In one example, Greene (1994) reported Latino men who have sexual relations with men hide these relationships and will not identify as gay. There is a strong cultural bias against being openly gay or lesbian in this culture. Latino men often marry and raise a family, leading a bisexual lifestyle but hiding their gay identity. Many do not practice safe sex and consequently have a much higher rate of AIDS. The secretiveness of the gay sex and the stigma of gay relationships may contribute to this behavior. Educating Latino men about prevention strategies is more difficult than it might be in White culture because they do not affiliate with the BGLT community and so are unaware of the risk behaviors they practice or of the myths that may guide their choices (Tews, 2006).

Focusing on BGLT people of color, Fukuyama and Ferguson (2000) highlight four ethnic groups: Native Americans, African Americans, Latin Americans, and Asian Americans. Fukuyama and Ferguson caution professionals from making any broad generalizations about clients from specific cultures, and they raise deep concerns about counselors' need for better education. Therapists are "taught to be sensitive to clients' needs and issues but are not taught how to be sensitive to issues of oppression, discrimination, and prejudice" (p. 97). The worldview of minority clients is shaped by the inequities they face, therefore counselors must work carefully to address the complexity of problems experienced by minority BGLT people.

Sexism and Family Choice

Women who identify as lesbian or bisexual often digress from traditional societal roles (Dworkin, 2000). These women, who struggle with the tension between being different and the desire to blend into society, may ultimately face nontraditional choices in the areas of careers, bearing children, child custody (for those who come out after being in a heterosexual relationship), and response to prior sexual abuse. Brown (1995) disputed the idea that sexual abuse is a cause for a woman to become a lesbian, but did report that there is a high probability that at least one partner in a lesbian couple will have some experience with sexual abuse. As lesbian couples seek to build healthy family relationships, a woman may bring children from a prior relationship into the family or they may seek to bear a child together. Logan (2006) observed that more lesbians are selecting to have children, and they are using alternative means to accomplish this.

The explosion in reproductive technologies has dismantled the separation of parenting and family formation and it has fueled the debate on "natural" family processes. Surrogate motherhood, open adoptions, abortion rights, blended families and stepfamilies, and the escalating number of single parents all led to a broader discourse on the family, challenging traditional nuclear family assumptions. One of the most significant contributors to the phenomena of lesbian families was artificial or alternative insemination, the "technique most closely associated with the lesbian baby boom" (Weston, 1991, p. 168). The lesbian baby boom (Murphy, 1987; Weston, 1991) arose with the pronatalism of the 1970s and 1980s. Many of the lesbian baby boom women were those who had come of age at the height of the women's and gay liberation movements. Choosing children reaffirmed the centrality of choice as the organizing principle for families. Reflecting on the conceptual shift from "no family" to "chosen family," BGLT people have explored their desire to procreate and their motives for parenting. Pies (1989) argues that lesbians choose to parent for some of the same reasons as heterosexual women: personal and psychological fulfillment. Clausen (1987) echoes, "Having kids, being with kids, looking toward a new generation, is part of being human, and in one sense I think the current public and publicized interest in having babies is another way the lesbian-feminist community has of stretching into a new-found sense of its rights to the full range of human and female experience" (p. 339).

Inequities of Ability and Age

BGLT people face other problems raised by issues of diversity including ageism and ableism, that is, the discrimination endured by people with a disability. Little has been written about BGLT people who have a physical disability. Coming out for these people is exacerbated by the dependency needs on other able-bodied people for help and survival. A physically disabled person may feel they are defective and, as a result, may experience low self-concept and shame. Those BGLT people with a disability who take the risk to come out may find the ableism of the BGLT community to be extremely unwelcoming. Like racial and ethnic groups, these people are a minority within a minority and will benefit greatly from the support of a counselor advocate as they address the layers of oppression they face.

Our society's adoration of youth is flagrantly evident. Surgical procedures to smooth wrinkles, tuck sagging skin, and turn back time are more and more common. This emphasis on youth impacts us all and yet, there are some unique challenges to BGLT people. Because of the secrecy that many BGLT people still endure, they face increasing isolation as the bloom of youth fades. Issues around hospitalization, health care, insurance, legal rights, and dying are often left unexamined until a crisis is imminent. If the biological family has disowned or rejected the BGLT person, often a "selected" family or "family of choice" has taken their place. These people, however, do not have legal rights nor will they have access or status in many health care settings unless the BGLT person has taken specific legal action to insure their rights.

By assessing and understanding how the complexity of layered oppression, societal norms, and family expectations impact the BGLT person, a counselor has a clearer starting point from which to offer their compassion, knowledge, and professional support.

Religion, Spirituality, and Gay Marriage

The 1969 Stonewall riots and the American Psychiatric Association's removal of homosexuality from its list of disorders in 1973 stand as markers for pride and health of BGLT people. The Judeo-Christian tradition, however, has been a source of alienation, shame, guilt, and repression. Through biblical texts, church doctrines, historical traditions, sermons, and religious custom, gays have been denounced as sinful, contaminated, and an abomination to the extreme of justifying hatred and cruelty against them (Boswell, 1980; Helminiak, 1995). Conflict continues in religious traditions worldwide over acceptance and provision of a religious home for BGLT people.

One example of such conflict is the threat of schism before the Episcopal Church in the United States. Researchers estimate that since the 2003 consecration of V. Gene Robinson, an openly gay bishop, roughly 38,300 people left the denomination over a 2-year period because of conflicts over Robinson (Barakat, 2006). It is appalling to think that the binding factor for people of faith is their hostility toward homosexuals. As Robinson observed, "The damage done to gay and lesbian people by organized religion—Christianity, Judaism, Islam—is so deep and so violent that it's overwhelming … God didn't get it wrong, the church got it wrong. Of course, we had it wrong before about slavery, and about women. So the huge debate now is about getting it right about gays and lesbians" (Sahagun, 2006). It is no wonder that BGLT people have kept their distance from traditional organized religion, and yet today, many seek spiritual depth and a religious community that will honor the inherent worth and sacredness of BGLT people, as well as bless their relationships and families.

It is a fascinating tribute to the diversity of American culture that the rise of the gay rights movement parallels the rise of evangelical Christians as a political force. Over the course of three decades—1970s, 1980s, and 1990s—conservative Christian organizations, such as Jerry Falwell's Moral Majority and Pat Robertson's Christian Coalition, gained political power and influence. The Religious Right movement has grown from thousands of people to millions, with approximately 30 million Christians represented by the National Association of Evangelicals, a lobbying group. One of the primary issues for concern among members in this movement was, and continues to be, same-sex unions or same-sex marriage. These unions are regarded as sinful and morally repugnant by most within the Religious Right. One who regards gay sex as sinful is evangelical radio therapist Dr. James Dobson. Dobson warned the 220 million listeners who hear his "Focus on the Family"

radio broadcasts, to get out and vote in order to protect traditional heterosexual marriage. With same-sex marriage initiatives on the ballot in
eight states, Dobson, "evoked what he hoped would be dark and scary
visions for his fellow evangelical Christians: a nation filled with married gay couples" (Miller, 2006, p. 32).

Why does this matter to counselors? Because we have BGLT clients
who are angered, frightened, or devastated by the teachings of religious
leaders, and who come to us to regain a sense of self-regard, spiritual
integrity, and communal support. Because we ourselves may have a
faith identity or be part of a religious community that regards homosexuality as sinful and same-sex unions as immoral. Because we live in
a cultural and political climate of change with regard to our ideas about
sex, marriage, and the family. Because eight couples exchanged vows
of love and commitment and were married in a legal ceremony at the
American Counseling Association National Convention in Montreal,
Canada, on April 1, 2006 "in front of five past presidents of ACA" (Dew,
2006, p. 3) and before about 350 colleagues and supporters. Because
personal sexual, emotional, and spiritual choice is an issue that counselors must face here and now.

How we as a society have defined marriage has shifted enormously
over the centuries. Go back to the 19th century, roughly 200 years,
and you will find that African Americans could not legally marry. Go
back a mere 50 to 100 years and you will find arguments that proclaim
contraception as the evil that will undermine marriage, the state, and
civilization, as well as strict prohibitions against allowing people of different races to marry. Each change in our understanding of marriage
has been hit with similar charges: destructive to the moral fiber of society, not God-ordained, not biblical, promoting lust and sin, degrading
the sanctity of marriage, and harmful to children. Conservative faith
traditions have certainly had an impact on U.S. social policy.

And yet, BGLT people seek validation and legal recognition for their
relationships. In May of 2004, over 600 gay couples applied for marriage licenses in Massachusetts, while in San Francisco, the California
Supreme Court invalidated the licenses of over 4,000 couples married
there in February. In 2006, the Federal Marriage Amendment endorsed
by President George W. Bush was defeated. Many conservative voices,
from Vice President Dick Cheney to syndicated columnist George Will,
spoke against a federal policy that would write legal discrimination into
the Constitution. At the state level, votes by state legislatures, lawsuits,
and appeals to the courts go on.

In *What Is Marriage For? The Strange Social History of Our Most
Intimate Institution*, E. J. Graff (1999) concludes:

Define marriage as a lifetime commitment, and divorce flouts its very definition. Define marriage as a vehicle for legitimate procreation, and contraception violates that definition ... Define marriage as a bond between one man and one woman, and same-sex marriage is absurd. But define marriage as a commitment to live up to the rigorous demands of love, to care for each other as best as you humanly can, then all these possibilities—divorce, contraception, feminism, marriage between two women or two men—are necessary to respect the human spirit ... Putting same-sex couples into marriage law will endorse the changes in marriage that have been growing since 1800 ... it will insist on something that is quite unnerving to acknowledge: that we must each pay rigorous attention to—and believe in—each individual spirit. (pp. 252–253)

While some faith traditions maintain that marriage between same-sex people is immoral, other faith traditions do not. What each of us believes about the individual spirit and authority—moral, spiritual, and/or religious—will shape our approach to BGLT clients.

HOW COUNSELOR ETHICS MANDATE SOCIAL ACTION

Professional counselors can draw from three resources that guide their ethical and professional behavior: the *ACA Code of Ethics* (2005); the Multicultural Competencies (Sue, Arredondo, & McDavis, 1992), which were developed for the ACA by the Association for Multicultural Counseling and Development in 1992; and the Advocacy Competencies (Lewis, Arnold, House & Toporek, 2003), also developed for the ACA by the Counselors for Social Justice. There are sections of the *ACA Code of Ethics* that specifically direct the counselor to not discriminate when working with BGLT clients (see C.5 in the following list) and to guard against having any negative impact on clients. In addition, the *ACA Code* focuses on the relationship and the obligation professional counselors have in working with all populations justly and competently, including BGLT people. The welfare of BGLT clients, as elucidated by the *ACA Code*, include behaviors of "respect," "examination of potential barriers and obstacles," maintaining confidentiality (that is, not outing a client), and promotion of the client's dignity.

- A.1.a. "The primary responsibility of counselors is to respect the dignity and to promote the welfare of clients."
- A.6.a. "When appropriate, counselors advocate at individual, group, institutional, and societal levels to examine potential

barriers and obstacles that inhibit access and/or the growth and development of clients."

- B.1.c. "Counselors do not share confidential information without client consent or without sound legal or ethical justification."
- C.5. "Counselors do not condone or engage in discrimination based on age, culture, disability, ethnicity, race, religion/spirituality, gender, gender identity, sexual orientation, martial status/partnership, language preference, socioeconomic status, or any basis proscribed by law. Counselors do not discriminate against clients, students, employees, supervisee, or research participants in a manner that has a negative impact on these people."

The Multicultural Competencies (Sue, Arredondo & McDavis, 1992) are divided into three areas that facilitate effective work with populations that are regarded as different from the mainstream culture. The three areas that professional counselors are urged to develop are self and other awareness, knowledge, and appropriate cultural skills. Competence begins with an honest and hard look inward. The fact is that we all bring our own biases and values into the counseling office. Counselors, however, are called upon to acknowledge their biases and values so as to limit the ways they might harm or influence a client. It is our hope that the questions we posed for your consideration at the start of this chapter will help you to scrutinize your personal feelings around issues of sexuality and gender identity.

Reflection on oppression and discrimination is crucial for the professional counselor. Schiffman, DeLucia-Waack, and Gerrity (2005) conducted a study to see if antihomosexual behavior is really a "phobia" or if it is more a "prejudice." Their results indicate that while society has long used the term *homophobia*, antihomosexual responses resemble a prejudice more than a phobia. There is power in language. As counselors, in the roles we hold as leaders, teachers, and change agents, we can use that power effectively to educate and transform. It serves us and our clients well to use language that more honestly reflects the changes in society that need to be addressed. We can use the more appropriate term *homoprejudice*, a word that points to the cultural bias and judgment, in lieu of the word *homophobia*, that points to a fear of people who are different. As Schiffman et al. state, "By reframing anti-homosexual responses as prejudice rather than phobia, mental health professionals are thrust into a position to work against the detrimental nature of homoprejudice, just as they would any other form of prejudice" (p. 91). It becomes a call for advocacy on the part of the counselor.

Table 10.6 Six Domains of the Advocacy Competencies

Domain	Description
Client/Student Empowerment	Help clients identify strengths and resources as well as social, political, economic and cultural factors that are barriers. Help clients develop a plan of action and assist them to operationalize it.
Client/Student Advocacy	Help clients get the services needed to move beyond the barriers. When needed, negotiate for these services on behalf of clients.
Community Collaboration	Help clients identify environmental factors that restrict their development and work to build alliances and groups that will facilitate change in the community. Use counseling skills to build collaboration and to network.
Systems Advocacy	In collaboration with others, develop a vision for change and work to implement these strategies into the community. Consider ways to handle resistance.
Public Information	Help clients communicate intolerance of oppression and discrimination when it is present in the community. Support those who promote health for your clients.
Social/Political Advocacy	Identify issues that require social or political action and provide support through activities such as contacting policy makers, joining ally groups, and making your own voice known as an ally for your clients.

In 2003, the Advocacy Competencies (Lewis, Arnold, House, & Toporek, 2003) that target best practices were introduced to the field. Holcomb-McCoy and Mitchell (2007) "define advocacy as action a counselor takes to facilitate the removal of external and institutional barriers to clients' well being" (p. 147). The Advocacy Competencies provide counselors with direction in how to address internal and external barriers that impede a client's growth and development. Table 10.6 briefly describes these domains.

CLOSING THOUGHTS

It was the intent of this chapter to introduce the reader to the complex culture of queer folk. It is a culture that yearns to be accepted and yet fears the loss of uniqueness. Some desire inclusion to the extent of blending with the mainstream, whereas others celebrate with great joy the flaming flavors of gay pride—from butches to queens to fairies to leather lovers. BGLT people love as deeply as heterosexual people love. Some will commit to long-lasting monogamous relationships, some will experience serial monogamy, and some will explore other realms of sexual expression.

It is a culture that hopes for legal, political, and spiritual inclusion, and knows bitter disappointment when prejudice and hate are demonstrated yet again. It is a culture that has known the loss of civil rights, family, and of loved ones to AIDS, as well as other diseases. It is a culture that like the mythical phoenix, rises again and again when hate crimes kill or when hate speech aims to kill relationships.

Authoring this chapter reminds us that this work is, first and foremost, about people. This chapter focused on BGLT people, but also focuses on you, the reader, with respect to:

- How you see yourself as unique
- How well you grasp that societal structures, historical and religious traditions, social conventions, biology, and personal beliefs have shaped you as a person and, utilizing self-awareness, knowledge, and insight, you must determine how you will administer care as a professional counselor
- How well you balance the truth that sex matters, yet the sex act is only a small portion of who we are; that your desires may change as you change
- How well you will integrate your morals, values, and spiritual or philosophical perspective with your professional ethics and responsibilities as a counselor
- If you can see your fellow human beings as having worth, dignity, and possessing within that which is inherently sacred about life, and if you will choose to support, stand with, and advocate for justice

RESOURCES

American Counseling Association (ACA), www.counseling.org
Association of Gay and Lesbian Psychiatrists (AGLP), www.aglp.org
Gay, Lesbian and Straight Education Network (GLSEN), www.glsen.org
Human Rights Campaign (HRC), www.hrc.org
Intersex Society of North America, The (ISNA), www.isna.org
Lambda Legal, www.lambdalegal.org
National Association of Social Workers (NASW), www.social-workers.org
National Gay and Lesbian Task Force (NGLTF), www.ngltf.org
National Transgender Advocacy Coalition (NTAC), www.ntac.org

National Youth Advocacy Coalition (NYAC), www.nyacyouth.org

OutProud: The National Coalition for GLBT Youth, www.outproud.org

Parents, Families, and Friends of Lesbians and Gays (PFLAG), www.pflag.org

Soulforce, www.soulforce.org

Southern Poverty Law Center (SPLC), www.splcenter.org

Teaching Tolerance, www.teachingtolerance.org

REFERENCES

American Counseling Association. (2005). *ACA code of ethics.* Alexandria, VA: Author.

American Psychiatric Association. (1994). *Diagnostic and statistical manual of mental disorders* (4th ed.). Washington, DC: Author.

Barakat, M. (2006, December 17). Two parishes bolt from Episcopal Church. More may follow in fight over gay relationships [Electronic version]. *The Associated Press.* Retrieved December 17, 2006, from http://news.aol.com/.../a/two-parishes-bolt-from-episcopal-church/2006121715260999001?ncid=NWS00010000000001

Boswell, J. (1980). *Christianity, social tolerance and homosexuality: Gay people in Western Europe from the beginning of the Christian era to the fourteenth century.* Chicago: University of Chicago Press.

Brown, L. S. (1995). Lesbian identities: Concepts and issues. In A. R. D'Augelli & C. J. Patterson (Eds.), *Lesbian, gay, and bisexual identities over the lifespan: Psychological perspectives* (pp. 3–23). New York: Oxford University Press.

Bruff v. North Mississippi Health Services, Inc., 244 F. 3d495 (5th Cir. 2001).

Butler, J. (1990). *Gender trouble: Feminism and the subversion of identity.* New York: Routledge.

Carroll, L., Gilroy, P. J., & Ryan, J. (2002). Counseling transgendered, transsexual, and gender-variant clients. *Journal of Counseling & Development, 80,* 131–139.

Cass, V. C. (1979). Homosexual identity formation: A theoretical model. *Journal of Homosexuality, 4*(3), 219–235.

Clausen, J. (1987). To live outside the law you must be honest: A flommy looks at lesbian parenting. In S. Pollack & J. Vaughn (Eds.), *Politics of the heart* (pp. 333–342). Ithaca, NY: Firebrand Books.

Coleman, E. (1987). Identity formation: Assessment of sexual orientation. *Journal of Homosexuality, 14,* 9–24.

Dew, B. (2006, Summer). From our president. *AGLBIC (Association for Gay, Lesbian and Bisexual Issues in Counseling) News, 26*(2), 1–3.

Dworkin, S. H. (2000). Individual therapy with lesbian, gay and bisexual clients. In R. M. Perez, K. A. DeBord, & K. J. Bieschke (Eds.), *Handbook of counseling and psychotherapy with lesbian, gay, and bisexual clients* (pp. 157–181). Washington, DC: American Psychological Association.

Eyler, A. E., & Wright, K. (1997, July–September). Gender identification and sexual orientation among genetic females with gender-blended self-perception in childhood and adolescence [Electronic version]. *The International Journal of Transgenderism, 1*(1). Retrieved October 2006 from http://www.symposion.com/ijt/ijtc0102.htm

Fassinger, R. E. (1991). The hidden minority: Issues and challenges in working with lesbian women and gay men. *The Counseling Psychologist, 19,* 151–176.

Feinberg, L. (1996). *Transgender warriors: Making history from Joan of Arc to Dennis Rodman.* Boston: Beacon Press.

Feinberg, L. (1998). *Trans liberation: Beyond pink or blue.* Boston: Beacon Press.

Foucault, M. (1980). *The history of sexuality: Vol. 1. An Introduction.* New York: Vintage.

Fukuyama, M. A., & Ferguson, A. D. (2000). Lesbian, gay, and bisexual people of color: Understanding cultural complexity and managing multiple oppressions. In R. M. Perez, K. A. DeBord, & K. J. Bieschke (Eds.), *Handbook of counseling and psychotherapy with lesbian, gay, and bisexual clients* (pp. 81–105). Washington, DC: American Psychological Association.

Gelberg, S., & Chojnacki, J. T. (1996). *Career and life planning with gay, lesbian, and bisexual persons.* Alexandria, VA: American Counseling Association.

Graff, E. J. (1999). *What is marriage for? The strange social history of our most intimate institution.* Boston: Beacon Press.

Greene, B. (1994). Mental health concerns of lesbians of color. In L. Comas-Diaz & B. Greene (Eds.), *Women of color and mental health* (pp. 389–427). New York: Guilford Press.

Grossman, A. H., D'Augelli, A. R., Salter, N. P., & Hubbard, S. M. (2005). Comparing gender expression, gender nonconformity, and parents' responses of female-to-male and male-to-female transgender youth: Implications for counseling. *Journal of LGBT Issues in Counseling, 1*(1), 41–59.

Gutierrez, F. J. (2004). Counseling queer youth: Preventing another Matthew Shepard story. In D. Capuzzi & D. R. Gross (Eds.), *Youth at risk: A prevention resource for counselors, teachers, and parents* (pp. 331–352). Alexandria, VA: American Counseling Association.

Hershberger, S. L., & D'Augelli, A. R. (2000). Issues in counseling lesbian, gay, and bisexual adolescents. In R. M. Perez, K. A. DeBord, & K. J. Bieschke (Eds.), *Handbook of counseling and psychotherapy with lesbian, gay, and bisexual clients* (pp. 225–247). Washington, DC: American Psychological Association.

Helminiak, D. A. (1995). *What the Bible really says about homosexuality.* San Francisco: Alamo Square Press.

Hermann, M. A., & Herlihy, B. R. (2006). Legal and ethical implications of refusing to counsel homosexual clients. *Journal of Counseling & Development, 84*(4), 414–418.

Holcomb-McCoy, C., & Mitchell, N. A. (2007). Promoting ethnic/racial equality through empowerment-based counseling. In C. C. Lee (Ed.), *Counseling for social justice 2nd edition* (pp. 137–157). Alexandria, VA: American Counseling Association.

Huegel, K. (2003). *GLBTQ: The survival guide for queer & questioning teens.* Minneapolis, MN: Free Spirit Publishing.

Human Rights Watch. (2001). *Hatred in the hallways: Violence and discrimination against lesbian, gay, bisexual, and transgender students in U.S. schools.* New York: Author.

Jennings, K. (Ed.). (1994). *Becoming visible: A reader in gay and lesbian history for high school and college students.* Los Angeles: Alyson Publications.

Just the Facts Coalition. (1999). *Just the facts about sexual orientation & youth: A primer for principals, educators & school personnel.* Washington, DC: American Psychological Association.

Kinsey, A. C., Pomeroy, W. B., & Martin, C. E. (1948). *Sexual behavior in the human male.* Philadelphia: W. B. Saunders.

Klein, F., Sepekoff, B., & Wolf, T. J. (1985). Sexual orientation: A multi-variable dynamic process. *Journal of Homosexuality, 11*, 35–49.

Lassiter, P. S., & Barret, B. (2007). Gay and lesbian social justice: Strategies for social advocacy. In C. C. Lee (Ed.), *Counseling for social justice* (2nd ed., pp. 31–50). Alexandria, VA: American Counseling Association.

Lee, C. (Ed.). (2007). *Counseling for social justice* (2nd ed.). Alexandria, VA: American Counseling Association.

Leland, J. (1995, July 17). Bisexuality emerges as a new sexual identity. *Newsweek Magazine,* 44–50.

Lewis, J., Arnold, M. S., House, R., & Toporek, R. (2003). *Advocacy competencies.* Retrieved November 8, 2006, from http://www.counselorsforsocialjustice.org/advocacycompetencies.html

Logan, C. (2006). Counseling lesbian clients. In C. C. Lee (Ed.), *Multicultural issues in counseling: New approaches to diversity* (3rd ed., pp. 291–301). Alexandria, VA: American Counseling Association.

Mallon, G. P. (1999). Practice with transgendered children. *Journal of Gay & Lesbian Social Services, 10*(3/4), 49–64.

McClintock, M., & Herdt, G. (1996). Rethinking puberty: The development of sexual attraction. *Current Directions in Psychological Science, 5*, 178–183.

Miller, L. (2006, November 13). Evangelicals at the crossroads. *Newsweek,* 30–37.

Miller, N. (1995). *Out of the past: Gay and lesbian history from 1869 to the present.* New York: Vintage Books.

Murphy, M. (1987). And baby makes two. In S. Pollack & J. Vaughn (Eds.), *Politics of the heart* (pp. 125–130). Ithaca, NY: Firebrand Books.

Pies, C. (1989). Lesbians and the choice to parent. *Marriage and Family Review, 14*(3-4), 137–154.

Reynolds, A. L., & Hanjorgiris, W. F. (2000). Coming out: Lesbian, gay, and bisexual identity development. In R. M. Perez, K. A. DeBord, & K. J. Bieschke (Eds.), *Handbook of counseling and psychotherapy with lesbian, gay, and bisexual clients* (pp. 35–55). Washington, DC: American Psychological Association.

Rothblum, E. D. (2000). "Somewhere in Des Moines or San Antonio": Historical perspectives on lesbian, gay, and bisexual mental health. In R. M. Perez, K. A. DeBord, & K. J. Bieschke (Eds.), *Handbook of counseling and psychotherapy with lesbian, gay, and bisexual clients* (pp. 57–89). Washington, DC: American Psychological Association.

Ryan, C., & Futterman, D. (1998). *Lesbian and gay youth care and counseling: The first comprehensive guide to health and mental health care.* New York: Columbia University Press.

Ryan, C., & Futterman, D. (2001). Experiences, vulnerabilities and risks of lesbian and gay students. *The Prevention Researcher, 8*(1), 6–8.

Sahagun, L. (2006, November 2). Gay Episcopal bishop says communities of faith may be at crossroads [Electronic version]. *Los Angeles Times.* Retrieved December 18, 2006, from http://www.hrc.org/PrinterTemplate.cfm?Section=Religion4&CONTENTID=34453&TEMPLATE=ContentDisplay.cfm

Schiffman, J. B., DeLucia-Waack, J. L., & Gerrity, D. A. (2005). An examination of the construct of homophobia: Prejudice or phobia? *Journal of LGBT Issues in Counseling, 1*(1) 75–93.

Spargo, T. (1999). *Foucault and queer theory.* New York: Totem Books.

Sue, D. W., Arredondo, P., & McDavis, S. (1992). Multicultural counseling competencies and standards: A call to the profession. *Journal of Counseling and Development, 70,* 477–486.

Tews, D. (2006). *Factors influencing condom use among Latino men who have sex with men (MSM).* Unpublished doctoral dissertation, Northern Illinois University, DeKalb.

Troiden, R. R. (1989). The formation of homosexual identities. *Journal of Homosexuality, 17*(1-2), 43–73.

Weston, K. (1991). *Families we choose: Lesbians gays kinship.* New York: Columbia University Press.

11

COUNSELING WITH NEW CITIZENS

Adam Zagelbaum

The importance of understanding how to work with immigrant clients within a counseling context cannot be overemphasized, especially in the United States. Our country is currently embroiled in significant debate over immigration reform that will continue to concern all individuals for years to come. Many individuals come to this country because of perceived opportunities that cannot be readily obtained within native countries. The lure of financial prosperity, political freedom, and availability of resources are usually driving forces behind the decision to immigrate. However, once within the United States, immigrants are often faced with many unexpected realities that create many forms of dissonance and self-doubt with significant emotional consequences for themselves and their families (Van Ecke, 2005).

Some immigrants are forced to leave their country of origin due to political oppression and duress, whereas others make voluntary choices in order to provide better resources for significant others who stay behind (Mitrani, Santisteban, & Muir, 2004). No matter what the specific reasons are, the realities of establishing oneself within U.S. culture and gaining access to enough physical, emotional, and financial resources takes time. Often, this time is quite longer than what many immigrants originally anticipated before leaving their native lands (Van Ecke, 2005). The longer the time away from their native culture(s) and family members, the greater the likelihood of developing significant issues of depression, anxiety, and paranoia due to separation issues (Van Ecke, 2005). In many cases, such individuals may not recognize that these conditions are treatable because they are viewed as work-related stressors, which do not imply a sense of personal control. Thus, seeking mental health services does not appear to be a viable option (Hovey & Magana, 2002). For others, mental health services appear to be foreign concepts in the first place due to cultural factors and variables that carry negative implications for those who would seek such services (Yakushko & Chronister, 2005). Therefore, it is necessary that when immigrant clients do seek mental health services that counselors are prepared to address specific factors and issues that may significantly influence the services provided and the benefits expected.

This chapter provides overviews about the many different ways in which counseling services are perceived by different immigrant clients. It also contains specific ideas and guidelines that can be useful to counselors who wish to provide services to these various individuals. General statistics and background details of immigrant clients are provided as frameworks for understanding what issues such clients bring to the counseling office, before intake assessments or screening interviews are performed. It is the author's intent to speak of counseling techniques and processes in order to assist mental health care workers, rather than speak of technicalities regarding language barriers and immigration status. Certainly, these matters are of tremendous concern and should be handled in accordance with codes of ethics and standards of practices germane to the counseling profession. However, the intended goal of this chapter is to develop an understanding of how to provide appropriate services that effectively address the presenting concerns of immigrant clients. As this chapter is attempting to address a great deal of diversity from a variety of angles, there are some limitations with regard to the depth of this chapter to generalize to all groups. All counselor educators need to recognize that knowing one member of one group does not mean you know them all. Although we have some credible information on these groups, counselors need to allow for individual differences.

ACCULTURATION

The concept of acculturation is commonly discussed when dealing with immigrant populations because it refers to problems associated with adjusting to another culture (American Psychiatric Association, 1994) and incorporates issues that may result due to socialization problems regarding language, gender, biracial/multicultural heritage, spiritual/religious orientations, sexual/affectional orientation, age, special needs, historical life experiences, and socioeconomic status (American

Psychological Association, 2003). The use of the term *acculturation*, however, does not necessarily refer to symptoms or patterns of behavior that may result due to the acculturation process. The adjustments that immigrants make to the dominant culture can often result in stress, depression, anxiety, and various other forms of socioemotional reactions that may or may not be diagnosable according to official criteria, such as those found in the *Diagnostic and Statistical Manual of Mental Disorders* or the *International Classification of Diseases*.

Studies have suggested that immigrants' acculturation to the host culture is strongly related to the reference group they form while establishing themselves. Immigrants who form social reference groups with coethnics such as themselves are more likely to adhere to their culture of origin, whereas those who form social reference groups with a majority of individuals from the host country are less likely to adhere to their culture of origin (Kosic, Kruglanski, Pierro, & Mannetti, 2004). Furthermore, age differences may compound these effects, especially within immigrant families because younger children who do not have as much exposure to their native country as their parents may encounter cultural conflicts that manifest themselves within their home and social environments (Foster, 2001; Klassen, 2004; Mitrani et al., 2004; Rothbaum, Morelli, Pott, & Liu-Constant, 2000). These matters can often exacerbate stressors that may already exist within the parent–child relationship (Smith, Lalonde, & Johnson, 2004), which may or may not serve as motivation to seek help from a professional.

Matters of trust are often complicated for immigrant clients due to language barriers, race/ethnicity of a counselor, and sheer unfamiliarity with the host culture. In cases of immigrants exposed to war-related trauma, these matters may prevent them from seeking services altogether (Asner-Self & Marotta, 2005). The unpredictability and uncontrolled nature of war-based and politically charged events are often so shocking and salient to one's memory that it is no surprise that many of these immigrant clients experience mental disorders such as posttraumatic stress disorder, depression, and anxiety. However, the nature of these conditions naturally impairs the individual's ability to accurately assess his or her level of functioning. This decreases the likelihood that these immigrant clients will seek counseling services in the host country. This is especially true when counseling professionals of the same or similar cultural origin are not available. However, it is important to note that counselors and psychologists are encouraged to apply culturally appropriate skills in clinical and other applied psychological practices (American Counseling Association, 2006; American Psychological Association, 2003). It is important for a counselor to recognize that roles of advocacy, consultation, and assessment are also part of the counseling process. To assume that counseling involves only the clinical elements of therapy is erroneous. This type of restrictive thinking minimizes the effectiveness of the counselor. Also, counseling professionals make erroneous assumptions about immigrant clients. These erroneous assumptions can limit the range of therapeutic activity that counselors and clients can potentially perform over the course of treatment.

ERRONEOUS ASSUMPTIONS

Many individuals who are not familiar with immigrants are apt to carry negative biases or beliefs about these groups because of media portrayal, interpersonal influences, and sheer ignorance about the subject. Many assume that immigrants are intellectually impaired because of their inexperience in matters related to the dominant culture or their inability to speak nonnative languages fluently (Van de Vijver & Willemse, 1991). However, research suggests that some testing instruments that measure intelligence and aptitude of both immigrant and nonimmigrant samples do not appear to be invalid or inappropriate methods (Nijenhuis, Tolboom, Resing, & Bleichrodt, 2004). There is research that indicates that many immigrant children and adolescents, especially those from subgroups such as the Caribbean (Mitchell, 2005) and Dutch countries (Nijenhuis et al., 2004; Van Ecke, 2005) are prone to difficulties with academic performance and may be at risk for dropping out of school. It can be reasoned, though, that some of these results are due to the fact that immigrants are able to understand and comprehend the material enough to obtain appropriate scores on such tests, even though these tests are not written in their native language(s) and/or are not normed on their culture(s). Indeed, the fact that some immigrants are able to come to the United States and obtain basic needs and social connections suggests that they possess adequate levels of intelligence. Understanding this information is important for counselors because assuming a lack of intelligence can set up an uncomfortable power dynamic within the therapeutic relationship, which can undermine the effectiveness of therapy.

Another mistaken belief held by some counselors is that immigrants do not have an understanding of what the counseling process entails. It appears more valid to assume that immigrants have some understanding of the profession, but attitudes toward the counseling process may shed a negative or positive light on the subject (Panganamala & Plummer, 1998). Biases do not imply lack of knowledge. In fact, understanding how immigrants understand the counseling process and expectations of what a counselor's services are can actually open a dialogue between the counselor and client. The need to identify goals and label client needs is essential to the counseling process and by the counselor's willingness to gain this level of understanding about an immigrant client, the relationship is likely to start out with positive expectations of how to work together (Amir, 1992). Fortunately, there is information available to counselors about how such services are provided around the world and recent surveys of counselors and clients provide much in-depth information about the counseling process in different countries.

COUNSELING WITHIN DIFFERENT CULTURES

A recent survey of counselors around the world was published in *Counseling Today* (Rollins, 2006) highlighting the various ways in which services are provided in different countries. Understanding various cultural perceptions and definitions of counseling is important, especially since there is such a large, diverse immigrant population in the United States. Schmidley (2001) estimated that approximately 28 million individuals are immigrants according to U.S. Census Bureau data, which represents 10.4% of the U.S. population. There is no exact way to know what these estimates would look like if illegal immigrants were taken into account, but it is clear that a significant amount of the people living in the United States come from other countries. Counselors must be aware of how other countries conceptualize the idea of counseling and the roles counselors are expected to perform if they are to effectively communicate their ideas to immigrant clients.

England

According to the British Association for Counseling and Psychotherapy, which is the professional organization similar to the American Psychological Association (APA) and American Counseling Association (ACA), England's definition of counseling is very similar to the one used within the United States. The profession requires similar training and regulations that follow guidelines related to the ACA's Codes of Ethics and Standards of Practice. However, there are different divisions within the profession: Counseling at Work, Pastoral and Spiritual Care and Counseling, University and College Counseling, Independent Practitioners, and the Faculty of Health for Counselors and Psychotherapists, Ltd. Services are provided in individual, couples, and group-based fashions, which provides several options for clients within different settings. This is highly similar to the United State's approach to counseling, but this is about the only society surveyed by *Counseling Today* that can be considered this similar (Rollins, 2005).

Like many American clients, younger English clients are being diagnosed with mental health problems and psychiatric disorders (Connell, Barkham, & Mellor-Clark, 2007). Depression, anxiety, and trauma-based issues are the most common presenting problems. Children and adolescents often become exposed to counseling for the first time through their school counselor (Fox & Butler, 2007) or when first engaging in career education and exploration (McCash, 2006). There are fair amounts of young adults who often seek personal counseling within university counseling centers (Jenkins & Potter, 2007). Most clients, regardless of age and gender, expect some form of assessment to be included in the counseling process (Malde, 2006). Thus, it is not surprising to note that English clients respond well to cognitive-behavioral approaches because of the operational definitions involved with defining and assessing goals and progress. Though family and couples counseling are popular approaches, individual counseling appears to be the most preferred form of treatment. Though English immigrants are not duplicates of American clients, it is important to focus on the parallels that exist between these two groups when trying to establish rapport and defining the purpose of the counseling relationship.

Latin America and Portugal

Within Latin American culture, counseling is primarily based on the notion of family and systemic strengths due to strong beliefs in family identity that abound in society. Because of European influence, however, people prefer the practice of psychology over counseling. Thus, if individuals from such a culture should seek counseling, it would take place within a professional, psychoanalytic environment. This means that the process of counseling is expected to take fair amounts of time, as opposed to brief therapy sessions. It is even less likely that clients from Portugal will seek counseling services because of the fact that counseling is practically nonexistent.

Professional counseling services are not available in Portugal. This type of work is equated with spiritual and moral issues and is called *consellerio*. It is more important to address personal matters through religious and spiritual guidance, as opposed to a licensed professional (Rollins, 2005). Clients from Portugal who immigrate, however, do turn to mental health and welfare professionals in order to facilitate action plans that can help them acculturate into the host culture. The focus of counseling is more community based, and is considered to be action focused (Bloemraad, 2006). Also, community-based institutions such as schools, government agencies, and religious organizations provide counseling services because of the communal norms of the culture (Rollins, 2005).

When most youths seek counseling services, it is largely for vocational guidance purposes. Furthermore, the Spanish verb for counseling, *aconsejar*, translates into the English phrase "to tell someone what to do" (Espin & Renner, 1974). Even within recent years, research studies have shown that Latin American immigrant clients often seek counseling services that are used to facilitate social connections with members of the community (Yeh & Inose, 2003). In other words, counseling is designed to create action plans. It is not necessarily designed to uncover deep rooted psychological issues that may impact clients on a subconscious or unconscious level. The same principle applies to adult clients.

Although many Latin American clients migrate due to political pressure or socioeconomic stress that do not provide enough support for their families, narrative approaches used to uncover emotional trauma are not the dominant treatment modalities that are used throughout the counseling process (Hernandez, 2002). The focus on taking action allows for clients to appropriately address issues of trauma without dwelling on negatives to the point by which fear- and anger-based emotions do not overpower the positive momentum of counseling. It is important for counselors who are to work with Latin American immigrant clients recognize the importance of emphasizing thoughts and behaviors.

Botswana

"Street children" are present within Botswana. Most people in this culture believe they can handle issues on their own. There are significant fears related to confidentiality issues due to the tight-knit structures of most villages and communities where people reside. Thus, when counseling services are sought, they are due to extreme circumstances such as pre-/post-HIV/AIDS treatment, violence within relationships, and desperate situations related to unemployment. Adolescents dealing with alcoholism, teen pregnancy, and school dropout issues also comprise much of the clientele (Rollins, 2005). Because there are many clients who may not be able to visit counseling centers on their own, home-based care programs are often used where counselors and healers visit the clients (Jacques & Stegling, 2004). Also, missions are popular places for clients to seek services.

In many parts of East Africa, as well as other areas throughout the continent, missionaries provide significant counseling services (Rosik, Richards, & Fannon, 2005). Pastoral care is usually given in conjunction with professional counseling, trauma debriefing, and spiritual guidance. These procedures are often provided for the missionaries as well as the clients because of the communal relationships that are significant to African culture. No member of the community is considered to be insignificant to the healing process, and the whole village works together to monitor the progress that clients, missionaries, and counselors make when services are provided (Rosik et al., 2005). It is important for counselors to incorporate the concept of spirituality into therapeutic work because of the heavy influence that religion has always played within African culture. The importance of religion can never be understated, regardless of a client's age, personal history, or presenting problem.

Kenya

The AIDS pandemic has largely contributed to the need for counseling services in Kenya (Grinstead, Van Der Straten, & the Voluntary HIV-1 Counseling and Testing Efficacy Study Group, 2000). Though people turn to counselors for social and emotional support, they are not likely to admit to others that they are utilizing such services. For young girls, counseling issues are related to their concerns about arranged marriages, domestic violence, rape, and depression. Other individuals seek help for issues of alcoholism, which has recently been on the rise in Kenya. Many counselors provide group therapy because of the preferred nature of group support within Kenyan culture, and these groups are commonly held in churches. The importance of groups cannot be understated within this culture due to the communal identities citizens hold (Rollins, 2005). The communal identity concept is also a critical element to address when working with Kenyan clients.

Recent reports have also stated that humanistic approaches are gaining significant momentum within Kenyan culture (McGuiness, Alred, Cohen, Hunt, & Robson, 2001). Especially considering the emotional and social tolls that AIDS and HIV have placed on clients who seek counseling, counseling that emphasizes personal worth and individualism has become essential. Family planning consultations are also important reasons as to why Kenyan clients seek counseling (Kim, Odallo, Thuo, & Kols, 1999).

Nigeria

Street children dealing with drug and alcohol abuse are also present in Nigeria, and they are the targeted population for social services provided by counselors. However, it is interesting to note that although counseling is a social service, most Nigerians choose to pay counselors as a courtesy whenever it is possible. Counselors are held in high regard in many parts of the country, with special attention paid to their work with marital and couples issues (Rollins, 2005).

Similar to the people of Kenya, AIDS poses a significant threat to Nigerians (Olley, 2006). Many of these patients experience significant levels of stress, anxiety, and depression not only because of the debilitating effects of the disease, but also because of the psychosocial stigma associated with having such a disease. Counselors have begun to use more objective assessments such as the Beck Depression Inventory to screen individuals for suicidality, and psychoeducational approaches are often incorporated into the counseling relationship to teach clients how to develop coping skills when dealing with the effects of their illness (Olley, 2006). Issues of grief are also likely to surface when dealing with these clients, as well as their family members.

Nigerian schoolchildren and university students recently listed time management as their greatest personal need (Aluede, Imhonde, & Eguavoen, 2006). Other significant issues, listed in order of importance, included drug concerns, family problems, career needs, relationship problems, financial issues, sexual harassment, academic performance, personality matters, anxiety/depression, differential treatment, and self-criticism. It is interesting to note that Nigerian students appear to have numerous concerns that are similar to various clients from numerous cultures. However, it is clear that cultural differences make the approaches to counseling somewhat different for Nigerian clients.

Because of the Nigerian culture, holistic approaches to counseling and psychotherapy are normally used (Awanbor, 1982). The holistic approach involves spiritual, physical, emotional, and cognitive healing methods. Symbolism and tribal customs are also huge parts of the therapeutic process because they are highly reliant on generational themes and patterns that are part of the client's culture and community. Thus, counselors need to exercise extensive action when gathering the client's background information. Treatment for Nigerian clients must be sensitive to the region, community, and area where they were born and raised. Different tribal customs and values exist from region to region and the effective counselor takes these matters into full account (Awanbor, 1982).

Ireland

The profession of counseling within Irish culture is similar to other European countries in that it deals with family, couples, and individual clients. However, most counselors in Ireland serve as secondary supports for people dealing with issues of substance abuse and physical violence. Perhaps some of the issues are attributed to the political climate within the culture, but these are the issues with which most clients seeking services present (Rollins, 2005).

One study that compared Irish clients to American clients found that Irish immigrants who engaged in therapy evaluated the concepts of anger and guilt more positively than Americans (Page & O'Leary, 1997). Furthermore, Irish clients appeared more comfortable in exploring their anger and guilt within counseling sessions than American counterparts. Irish clients have also viewed counseling as a more potent process when compared to American clients (O'Leary, Page, & Kaczmarek, 2000). These findings are believed to be due to the fact that Irish clients are highly invested in the Catholic Church and view counseling as a profession that serves as an extension of this spiritual outlet. A high amount of person-centered techniques and approaches are often used when Irish clients engage in counseling (O'Leary et al., 2000). Even though Irish culture is often characterized as conflict-laden because of struggles that exist between socioeconomic classes and English descendants who are believed to be nonrightful citizens within the country, research shows that many Irish clients appear to approach counseling relationships in a very open and appreciative manner (Gavin, 2001). Many clients struggle with issues of cultural identity because of the torrid nature of the sociopolitical environment of Ireland that has divided many communities for numerous generations. Other clients struggle with issues related to sex and sexuality. These issues have recently surfaced within counseling literature because of perceived inadequacy regarding formal sex education programs within Ireland (Rolston, Schubotz, & Simpson, 2005). Regardless, it appears clear that social issues largely relate to the counseling issues that clients from Ireland are likely to present when seeking therapy. The astute counselor is wise to use both person-centered and interpersonally focused techniques when approaching such clients.

Russia and Latvia

Russia, due to its historical influence of communism, did not traditionally provide counseling services to individuals for many years. The notion of psychology and counseling was mainly an academic pursuit and not an applied science. Political and economic conditions in the contemporary culture do not allow for clinical work to be conducted, though issues of alcoholism and spousal abuse are common issues for which individuals often seek assistance. The role of the counselor is believed to be more of a diplomat as opposed to an analyst, which carries with it expectations that a counselor is to provide facilitative and encouraging services as opposed to direct questioning and intervention (Rollins, 2005).

Currently, clients are seeking therapeutic service within Russia for treatment of substance abuse, psychological distress, and severe anger management (Janey, Janey, Goncherova, & Savchenko, 2006). The severity of certain psychological issues is evident from the fact that the amount of homicidal deaths are 20 times greater in Russia than in Western European nations (McKee & Shkolnikov, 2001). Many of the clients who seek service are men (Janey et al., 2006). Karavaeva (2006) reported that the most frequently used treatment method is rational therapy. The belief as to why clients and counselors prefer this method most is because of its active and explanatory nature. It appears that Russian clients prefer didactic approaches, especially during the initial stages of therapy, in order to better understand why counseling services can help them. Other psychotherapeutic methods are used, and, in order of preference, they are personality-oriented (reconstructive) psychotherapy, relaxation training, classical hypnosis, cognitive psychotherapy, Gestalt therapy, solution-focused therapy, Ericksonian hypnosis, psychoanalytic therapy, body-oriented psychotherapy, and neurolinguistic programming. It is also important to recognize that most clients seek counseling services from medical professionals within Russian culture because of the field's emergence as an independent medical discipline during the second half of the 20th century (Vasilyeva, 2006). Thus, a counselor who works with Russian immigrants may be expected to provide very specific services to these clients because of their expectations of expertise and training.

Within Latvia, however, there is mostly a psychoanalytic focus used within counseling services (Rollins, 2005). Dream work and dream analysis are preferred methods of treatment, even for similar presenting problems that Russian clients experience (Letunovsky, 2004a). Also, existential therapy that emphasizes the mind–body connection is considered to be quite popular (Letunovsky, 2004b). Citizens of Latvia consider themselves in many cases to be bi- or tricultural because of generational roots shared with the former Soviet Union. It is believed that Latvian counseling is more focused on Christian and spiritual matters, whereas the Soviet emphasis is more focused on mental illness treatment. In any case, the concept of counseling is relatively new within this culture as well because of political and economic matters entrenched in the country's history (Rollins, 2005).

Vietnam

Much like Latin American culture, Vietnamese culture focuses on the family. However, the notion of family often extends beyond several generations and members all live together within the same space. The culture is just now gaining interest in psychotherapy, and specifically believes in team theory and group approaches to maintain its collectivistic integrity. Major contemporary issues for the Vietnamese people involve high prevalence rates of schizophrenia and depression among the adult population, coupled with issues of violence against women and children within family systems. Divorce rates have been on the increase, and many teenagers within Vietnamese culture are dealing with issues of suicide and drug abuse. Some counselors believe that the latter issues are related to Western influences that have permeated the culture since the 1960s. This may create negative biases if Vietnamese immigrants seek counseling services within the United States (Rollins, 2005).

Recent research and literature have called specific attention to the experiences of Vietnamese refugees (Nghe, Mahalik, & Lowe, 2003; Phan, Rivera, & Roberts-Wilbur, 2005). Both men and women struggle with acculturative stress, especially considering the accommodations provided to them upon arrival within the host country are often deplorable. The pressure to find financial and emotional stability while providing for the family creates significant stress and conflict among family members. The paternalistic norm of Vietnamese culture may also explain why domestic violence is a common occurrence. Suffice it to say that counselors who work with Vietnamese immigrants must pay attention to these matters, but also speak to clients about how adjusting to the new culture has impacted family and gender roles. Women are not always accustomed to providing financially for the benefit of the family (Phan et al., 2005), and men are not accustomed to having their masculine roles challenged (Nghe et al., 2003). Counselors are also encouraged to explore reactions to racism, which are likely to occur when Vietnamese clients settle in many Western cultures. This obviously does not apply to all Western countries, but many Asian clients because of their Eastern upbringings are often perceived as radically different within Western societies. Being able to openly address these differences is important.

United Arab Emirates

Unlike the collectivistic nature of Vietnamese culture, the United Arab Emirates family system believes in keeping family issues within the family. If family problems are shared with individuals in the community, family reputation and identity are damaged. Much of the counseling performed within the culture takes place in schools and mostly focuses on academic- and career-based issues. Approaches are expected to be brief and solution focused because of the norm of keeping private matters private. However, recent economic developments have provided many residents with options to seek personal counseling that were not previously allowed. Also, many people are living in nuclear families as opposed to joint families, which may also indicate that family matters are becoming more privatized within the culture (Rollins, 2005).

The primary expectation that clients and family members of these clients have when seeking psychological treatment is that pharmaco-therapy will be the primary form of treatment (Sayed, 2003a). Also, the doctor is seen as an omnipotent agent whose expertise and recommendations are held to the highest power possible. Much of these expectations appear to relate to the fact that most Arab clients view any form of disease, be it related to physical or mental status, as a foreign threat to the body that must be treated by outside agents. The concept of the self, or self-control, is not the significant vehicle by which social and emotional issues are treated. Thus, the counselor is expected to have full understanding and control of what the client needs to do to manage his or her presenting problem. There is a significant need for a counselor to assess and diagnose as opposed to interview and empathize. Within other Arab countries, counseling and psychotherapy are not even viewed as necessary services for people to seek. It is a cultural difference that can be quite disruptive to the therapeutic process if a counselor is not aware of the position of power he or she is considered to have.

Saudi Arabia

Saudi Arabian culture views counseling as a luxury and not a necessity for individuals to have. Similar to the United Arab Emirates, issues are expected to be kept within family and social networks. The notion of seeing a counselor implies that the interaction will be brief, but weaknesses are analyzed more than strengths. About 10 years ago, it was still unlikely that Saudi women would seek such services due to the paternalistic values of the host culture (Sayed, 2003a). Currently, men seek these services more than women, though more women are independently able to participate in the counseling process. It is ultimately the client who is responsible for solving problems or resolving issues, and it is not the counselor's main job to identify such solutions (Rollins, 2005).

Recent trends, however, show that many of these Arab clients are seeking more Western-based treatments for psychological matters

(Sayed, 2003b). Many of these clients will travel to other countries to obtain such treatment because of the empirically validated studies that speak of the relative speediness and efficiency that Western treatments often provide. It is important for counselors who are not from the Saudi Arabian culture to recognize that Saudi Arabian clients do not view psychological problems as something that the mind has complete control over. In other words, many of these clients are not seeking a collaborative therapeutic relationship, but rather a specific and directive relationship that places the practitioner in almost complete control of the curative process. Thus, concepts such as empathy may not be effectively translated from the Western counselor to an Arab client. This is not to say that therapy can never be conducted in such a manner whereby corrective emotional experiences can occur, but counselors who are to work with these types of immigrant clients are more likely to be analyzing and diagnosing problems as opposed to engaging in narrative dialogues where a mutual understanding of counseling issues can be reached (Sayed, 2003b).

Turkey

Turkey also holds to the notion of keeping family concerns within the family, and counseling mainly targets the youth population. Most of the counseling provided with Turkish culture takes place in schools, and deals with issues of school violence, communication skills, and developmental needs of adolescents. The role of the counselor is mostly educational, though there are some elements of social work included since social workers are not present in Turkish schools (Rollins, 2005). Though counseling services have largely focused on academic needs of children and some career-related concerns of adults (McWhirter, 1983; O'Neil, 1966), crises and traumatic events have caused many Turkish citizens to vacate certain parts of the country. Therefore, counselors are likely to provide information about social agencies and governmental programs as well.

One of the more prominent issues that has impacted Turkey in recent years involved dealing with the shock and aftermath of two massive earthquakes that killed over 25,000 people in 1999 (Munir, Ergene, Tunaligil, & Erol, 2004). The trauma and emotional toll that many Turkish citizens experienced as a result of these disasters exposed what many believed to be major flaws within the Turkish mental health services system. At the time of the earthquakes, one third of the population was 15 years of age and under, and there were not enough mental health professionals who could effectively address this population. Elders are largely respected by youths within Turkish culture, and a significant portion of elders was lost during these disasters. Now that many of these individuals have been displaced, the shock of the events and the readjustment issues they are experiencing are of primary concern. Greater emphasis has now been placed on providing psychosocial services within Turkish schools (Munir et al., 2004). It is clear that younger clients are benefiting from psychoeducational approaches, but many clients are still in need of services that will allow for debriefings about the traumatic events to take place.

Turkish families are also starting to seek services within community mental health centers and school systems (McWhirter, 1983; Munir et al., 2004). Some of the economic and social pressures that were created by the earthquakes, coupled with the grief certain individuals experienced by losing family members, have resulted in a greater need for family units to seek counseling services together. Many family members were only seeking medical treatment at the time of the disasters, but recently have come to recognize the issues regarding their mental health as a result. The needs of the family unit are often shared by its members, so counselors are advised to engage the collective unit in the counseling process so as to encourage healing and forward progress. Current movements within Turkey have also commissioned the use of collaborative intervention teams to deliver services to clients. Medical practitioners, counselors, social workers and nonprofit agents such as UNICEF have been coordinating their efforts to deal with such clients; thus, it is recommended that counselors who work with Turkish immigrants also coordinate their efforts with similar professionals if they have been displaced by these events. However, it is important to recognize that regardless of whether clients are seeking service due to earthquake-related trauma, the use of social skills training and behavioral techniques appear to be important to many Turkish clients (McWhirter, 1983).

India

The notion of counseling remains a foreign concept in India. People do not generally believe in seeking help from professionals who are not connected in some personal way to them (Rollins, 2005). However, some universities in India are starting to offer specialization of this practice for interested students. Perhaps the foreign concept will start to change eventually. Recent literature points to the use of social skill development programs for socially withdrawn children who attend school within Indian culture (Prakash & Coplan, 1999). Socially withdrawn boys and girls appear to express feelings of depression and loneliness, and respond to treatment in similar ways. It is important for counselors to bear this in mind because Indian immigrants often struggle with the acculturation process (Zagelbaum & Carlson, 2008). Acculturative stress can often cause individuals to become more socially withdrawn, even from their own family members (Krishnan, 2005). Within certain parts of India, it also results in domestic violence, which will often bring some clients into therapy (Martin, Tsui, Maitra, & Marinshaw, 1999).

Pakistan

The profession of counseling is not licensed in Pakistan. Though people seek services, it is most focused on career guidance and development (Rollins, 2005). There have been therapeutic movements within the country. Third force therapy was a form of counseling that was used along with medical treatment for clients who exhibited symptoms such as manic-depressive psychosis, depression, and panic anxiety attacks (Jahangir, 1995). The approach involves restoring the connection between man and God, which is largely believed to contribute to most psychological issues. Interpersonal problems are not considered to be significant matters for counseling. This religious and spiritual focus appears to have major importance for Pakistani clients.

Cyprus

For many years, the counseling profession was viewed as controversial in Cyprus because of the heavy reliance on priests to deal with personal matters. Counselors were clashing with religious influences, which gave the profession a significant negative stigma among citizens. Also, people equated the use of counseling with the notion of having mental illnesses. However, contemporary society does not appear to hold this negative stigma to the same degree as in the past. Nevertheless, counseling services are not always viewed by citizens as completely positive influences (Rollins, 2005).

Some of the mixed reactions to counseling appear to relate to the tensions and conflicts that exist among the country's population of Greek Cypriots, Turkish Cypriots, and Turkish immigrants (Danielidou & Horvath, 2006). Communities remain segregated and cohabitation among these groups appears unlikely. People appear to keep to themselves and do not seek counseling services out of a need to remain private. Cases of mental illness largely compose clientele, but matters of depression and anxiety are also common referral and presenting problems. It is important to recognize the lack of communal integration that appears to shelter many people from Cyprus, which may contribute to some resistance factors on the part of clients who seek counseling services.

Australia

Australia's counseling profession is supported more by clients than other professionals in the mental health field. Specifically, psychologists are usually opposed to the use of such services based on the notion that effective change cannot occur within brief sessions. Many clients are referred to counseling by medical practitioners, or seek counseling because they believe that they are not able to employ effective coping skills when stressors arise (Manthei, 2006). Because of the counseling profession's use of brief therapy, sometimes within one or two sessions, Australians synonymously used the term *shrink* for many years to apply to all individuals who practiced psychology. Only within the last few years has the counseling profession taken on a divergent view from psychology among the Australian public and social science field (Rollins, 2005). Because of the dramatic increase in the elderly population over the past few years, many counselors and psychologists are working with clients who suffer from dementia (Lister & Benson, 2006). This matter also places significant stress on family members who are attempting to care for said individuals. Furthermore, immigrant clients who live within Australia are less likely to seek hospital treatment for related issues. There appears to be a preference for home-based services (Lister & Benson, 2006). These matters suggest that counseling services are best provided within private locations and for somewhat lengthy periods of time as opposed to the Western medically based approaches that are often used in our society.

Israel

Israeli culture does not specifically use counseling professionals, as understood by U.S. culture, to carry out the duties of the profession. Though social workers are present in Israel and are the dominant social service, they do not provide counseling service. Rabbis are usually seen for interpersonal issues and guidance. This is mostly because of the religious influence and historic base of the country (Rollins, 2005).

School counselors are present within the system, and they primarily take a wellness perspective when working with clients (Cinamon & Hellman, 2006). This means that counseling relationships are focused on dealing with personal strengths and positive assets that people possess. There is no significant emphasis on pathology or diagnostic material. Most counselors, especially those within school-based areas, are focused on dealing with developmental difficulties that children experience as a result of social issues and academic concerns. However, with increased levels of terrorism and security threats that have become present within

Israel, crisis counseling has become significantly important (Cinamon & Hellman, 2006). Within recent years, counselors have been trained to deal with concerns related to posttraumatic stress disorder (PTSD), as well as stress and depression. There have been significant shifts toward emotional well-being as opposed to exclusive academic progress. It has also been discovered in related studies that novice counselors, even in crisis situations, rely more on written techniques when dealing with clients. Veteran counselors use more processing techniques along with debriefing exercises. Although both approaches are seen as valuable approaches to counseling, it is important to note that Israeli clients are quite focused on social environments and respond well to treatments that involve collaborative relationships with others within their school and home environments (Cinamon & Hellman, 2006).

Though many clients throughout the world are dealing with war-based and terrorism-related trauma, Israeli clients deal with these factors on what appears to be an almost consistent basis (Cinamon & Hellman, 2006). Many clients from Israel who may require counseling services are likely to present with highly emotional material that can impact counselors as well. Professionals who work with such clients are recommended to find supervisory relationships that allow for personal debriefings to take place. Emotionally charged material such as the relaying of posttraumatic events within therapy can sometimes cause counselors to experience feelings of pain, self-doubt, and burnout (Cinamon & Hellman, 2006). Israeli clients are likely to present this material and often benefit from focusing on issues that tap into their resiliency.

Both Arab and Israeli clients, especially adolescents, appear to respond well to group counseling because of their social and interpersonal needs (Shechtman & Halevi, 2006). Though Arab clients appear to provide more self-disclosure within group settings than their Israeli counterparts, social dynamics and systemic issues are usually related to the clients' presenting problems and are frequently used as part of therapeutic treatment. In other words, clients perceive their presenting problems through interpersonal definitions and appear to benefit from therapeutic approaches that also emphasize the strengths of personal relationships.

Italy and France

The Italian and French view of counseling is quite negative as compared to the United States' perception. It is believed that the counseling process is associated with people who cannot think for themselves and are unable to work their way through issues. In other words, counseling is for the mentally ill. Though some services are provided for adult couples who are dealing with divorce and separation issues, there is no formal, legal definition that applies to the counseling profession (Rollins, 2005).

Treatment modalities often involve exclusive work with children (Muratori et al., 2004) or with children and their parents (Piovano, 2004). Many referrals are made by school counselors who are concerned about student dropouts or when at-risk labels are given to struggling students (Adamo, 2004; Simonetta, Serpieri, Giusti, Contarini, & Valerio, 2005; Soresi, Nota, & Ferrari, 2005). Counseling often involves assessment and diagnosis, followed by a combination of cognitive-behavioral interventions (Piovano, 2004). However, in cases of separation anxiety, psychodynamic approaches are often used (Muratori et al., 2004). Medication is often supplied with treatment as well. Thus, it is fair to say that many of these clients are somewhat resistant to counseling and psychotherapy at first because of the largely negative stigma that such services entail within their native countries. It is important for counselors to recognize these values and to reassure clients about the fact that counseling is not considered to be an exclusively negative form of treatment in their host culture.

Barbados

Barbados does not appear to have a negative view of counseling and counseling services. Many residents seek advice and guidance from others in an open and public fashion. However, there is no legal or professional regulation as to who can provide these services (Rollins, 2005). So, the notion of seeing a counselor in Barbados does not equate to a specific type of individual who adheres to specific roles and guidelines.

Much attention is given to patients who suffer from AIDS and the social stigmas that are often associated with this disease (Rutledge & Abell, 2005). Significant tension exists within society about how infected individuals are perceived as threats due to the threat of spreading the disease. This not only creates stress and insecurity for the clients, but also the counselors who treat them. There are tremendous strides being taken toward training professionals and paraprofessionals to deal with these social stigmas, and various modeling approaches are used to empower counselors to become advocates and support systems for such clients. Some of the models follow Buddhist principles of mindfulness, which emphasize heightened levels of consciousness and self-awareness. Thus, it appears that the counseling profession is open to Eastern and Western treatment modalities when treating medical and mental illness (Rutledge & Abell, 2005).

Perhaps another reason as to why counseling services are so open to the public within Barbados is because of the open concerns people express about Black family breakdown (Barrow, 2001). This concept refers to the dissipation of the traditional extended family (parents, children, grandparents, and other relatives) in favor of the nuclear family (parents and children only) within society. Political and sociopolitical constituents have made statements suggesting that this phenomenon has been linked to increases in teenage pregnancy, child abuse, adolescent sexuality, teenage pregnancy, divorce, and poor care of the elderly. Counselors are viewed as significant agents for helping address these matters, and recent reviews of statistics suggest that many of these trends are reversing at the present time. The use of counseling services in Barbados appears to address many of the same issues that American families contend with on a regular basis.

Jamaica (and the West Indies)

Within Jamaican culture, women seek more counseling services than men. Most of the presenting concerns appear to focus on grief, death, and issues of dying. There is an expectation that a counselor will be able to listen and support clients during times of stress, and the services are mostly provided to adults. There is a push to get counseling services to occur within schools at the present time, but this process may take some time before results are clear and noticeable (Rollins, 2005).

It appears extremely important to provide more counseling services within Jamaica for adolescents and young adults because of issues related to domestic violence and sexual abuse (Geary, Wedderburn, McCarraher, Cuthbertson, & Pottinger, 2006). Issues of violence and aggression significantly impact children and their families. Psycho-educational approaches appear to be significantly missing. Therefore, counselors must be prepared for the fact that many Jamaican immigrants may not view their presenting problems in systemic fashion. The use of person-centered approaches may yield a decent rapport, but it is important to help individuals focus on how their thoughts, feelings, attitudes, and beliefs impact those around them as well.

The Netherlands

The Netherlands did not formally recognize the counseling profession until recently. Currently, the person-centered approach is preferred (Rollins, 2005). Thus, open-ended tasks are usually the norm and counselors are expected to use this approach. Recent research and literature has focused primarily on clients who struggle with career competence (Kuijpers, Schyns, & Scheerens, 2006) and burnout (Mommersteeg, Keijsers, Heijnen, Verbraak, & Van Dooernen, 2006). It is because of career-related struggles that many citizens of the Netherlands migrate.

Thus, counselors must recognize the importance of addressing career-related issues when working with many of these clients. Constructivism and narrative techniques are often preferred and well-received by such clients. These clients are also used to working with pharmacological treatments, especially since research within the Netherlands has managed to link cortisol levels within the hypothalamus with stress-related reactions (Mommersteeg et al., 2006). Thus, it can be said that clients from the Netherlands are somewhat similar to North American clients. Dream work and analysis has also become more popular within recent years (Reeskamp, 2006). However, without enough formal counseling research studies available at the time of this writing, it is difficult to say that no differences exist between these groups.

Japan, China, and the Northern Mariana Islands

In Japan, counseling is primarily viewed by citizens as synonymous with testing and analysis. This usually carries with it a negative social stigma for those who seek services. However, the profession is recognized through specialization of service providers. This is a shift from earlier centuries when Buddhist priests were the primary providers of counseling services. The main concern that counseling professionals have is that psychologists and psychiatrists tend to speak in jargon that does not allow for effective communication about clients. Even counselors do not like the idea of being equated with testing and analysis in Japan (Rollins, 2005).

Much of the Taiwanese definition of counseling appears to be focused on advocacy for minority groups within the culture. However, collectivism is the cultural norm. Hence, there is a strong need for family privacy. Thus, most people within the culture do not formally and consciously seek the services of counselors. Doing so could be considered a source of shame (Rollins, 2005).

Citizens of the Northern Mariana Islands do not have a specific understanding of counseling as a service that deals with mental illness and personal issues. The concept of counseling is more of an information-sharing role that is expected to aid people's decisions regarding career and professional development. This does not mean that personal matters are not shared with counselors, but mental health does not appear to be a conscious goal of those who seek such services. Because of the paucity of research and literature that exists about this culture's view of counseling, readers are encouraged to read more of Rollins's (2005) work.

Recent research has suggested a high prevalence of mood disorders that exist among Japanese clients and some natives of the Pacific Islands

(Hirano et al., 2007). Similar issues exist within Chinese culture, but often manifest themselves in the form of youth violence and rebelling from the family (Spencer & Le, 2006). The current way by which these matters are treated are through pharmacological methods. This is not to say that counseling techniques are completely ignored, but cultural norms often dictate that mental health issues are to be treated as medical illnesses. Issues of child abuse, sexual abuse, and incest are also becoming more prevalent (Adams, 2007). For many years, Japanese law did not formally recognize most forms of incest and sexual abuse unless rape or indecent assault had occurred and the victim was prepared to press charges. This rigidity was in place as recently at the early 2000s (Adams, 2007). Now that society has begun to formally address these matters, these topics are no longer considered as taboo to approach.

Counselors must be aware of the fact that they are likely to use many structured interviews and assessment-based techniques when working with many Japanese and Chinese clients.

TECHNIQUES

The techniques that are used for different immigrant clients are as varied as the countries they come from (Foster, 2001). Although this section is not meant to be an exhaustive list that completely encapsulates every technique that must be used to produce effective therapeutic outcomes, it is intended to persuade counselors to consider the tangible aspects of therapeutic approaches that can be incorporated into sessions. Recent research and documented accounts of these techniques, when taken into consideration with the assumptions and biases immigrant clients have of the counseling process and role of the counselor, provide strong evidence to support the following ideas.

Working with the Family

The concept of family is significant within every culture, but takes on primary significance in most Eastern, African, Latin American, and Asian cultures. This is due to the notions of collectivism and shared responsibility, which are attributed to issues within these societies. It is particularly distressing for immigrant families within these cultures to deal with issues of separation, either with family members who are left behind in their country of origin as a result of the transition or with family members who make the transition and deal with different levels of acculturation issues while doing so (Mitrani et al., 2004). It is because of these specific separations that many counselors and researchers familiar with such cases recommend family systems approaches and attachment theory perspectives (Mitrani et al., 2004).

General approaches that counselors are normally recommended to take upon meeting with these families during the initial stages of therapy are centered on the idea of looking for patterns that exist within the family system before and after the immigration process occurred. Mitrani and colleagues (2004) noted such patterns as:

1. Disruptions in parental functioning. Children who are left behind by parents or who are not given as much attention by parents when the acculturation process is occurring may be at risk for behavioral problems due to escalating levels of family resentment, lack of exposure to parental leadership and/or discord among the parents, which further lead to conflicts within the system. In other words, the family becomes divided due to feelings of uncertainty and/or frustrations that may make them resent their immigration.

2. Inexperienced parenting. Parents, especially mothers, may not be used to setting limits for their children that are common to the dominant culture to which they have immigrated. This lack of experience, coupled with guilt and feelings of frustration due to the transitions that acculturation necessitate, may further exacerbate feelings of learned helplessness within the parental parts of the family system, and resentment issues among the children.

3. Problems in parental alliances. This matter does not only refer to families that immigrate, but also to families that blend families once within their host country. New marriages and relationships are not uncommon to many immigrated family members who are leaving behind abusive or desperate situations in their countries of origin (Mitrani et al., 2004; Coatsworth, Maldonado-Molina, Pantin, & Szapocznik, 2005). Unfortunately, sometimes parents covertly violate the other adult's disciplinary rules or parenting style, which not only sends mixed messages to the children, but also creates further disconnects between family members. Again, these factors can lead to increased resentment within the family and places further stress on the parent–adolescent relationship.

Once these patterns are identified, there are several strategies that can be implemented. Some strategies have been researched more extensively on certain immigrant clients than others, but this does not necessarily mean that these tools are confined to one particular set of clients. It is the counselor's role to be informed about the techniques that are available and use cross-cultural data as effectively as possible in order to ensure the best treatment possible.

Cognitive (Re)framing Strategies

Many immigrant families come to therapy with the understanding that their issues and problems primarily lie on the shoulders of one particular member, usually an adolescent child (Mitrani et al., 2004). Under circumstances where immigration was more of a conscious choice, as opposed to a forced political threat, adult family members are less likely to accept responsibilities for such issues because they view themselves as hard-working, well-intentioned individuals who made significant sacrifices for the greater good of the family. This is where the notion of the collectivistic society can often aid the counselor and client(s) in reframing their issues in a way that is more conducive to making improvements within the family system.

One characteristic feature of collectivistic and family-focused cultures is the expectation that problems are shared among family members. Hence, it is important to re-emphasize this theme throughout the course of therapy. This method not only calls attention to the fact that the clients are undergoing an adjustment challenge underscored by acculturative stress, but also calls attention to the fact that the family has traditionally had the ability to come together as a collective unit in the past to effectively address many issues (Mitrani et al., 2004). However, it is important to note that if reframing strategies involve shifting focus away from an identified client, such as an adolescent, and more toward acculturative stress, that the possibility of a reshifting of blame can occur (Mitrani et al., 2004; Smith et al., 2004; Xiong, Eliason, Detzner, & Cleveland, 2005). An alert counselor should be able to notice these matters and re-emphasize the theme of collectivism frequently, so as to keep the system focused on making improvements. There are specific methods of doing this that have been researched on particular immigrant clients.

Latino Clients   Within the Latino family, Mitrani and colleagues (2004) propose specific questions to be asked to particular family members. Many of their experiences with clients often involve single-parent families, usually single mothers, who have separated from their children in order to establish a better financial and emotional space within the United States. Parents are often asked to describe the reasons they came to the United States, along with the particular hopes they had for their family. Also included in this questioning are details about how difficult it was to make the decision to immigrate, find a job, and settle into the host culture. Additionally, engaging in a narrative about the most difficult aspects of relocating to a new country, in many cases by oneself, also helps to enrich the therapeutic discourse among family members.

Child and adolescent clients are often asked to speak about the people with whom they were left with back home after their parent came to the United States, the quality of the relationship with these people at the time of the separation, the explanation they received as to why the separation occurred, what they were told about their parent, the image they had of the parent during the period of separation, and reactions to the level and type of contact they had with one another during the years of separation (Mitrani et al., 2004). This dialogue engages the parent and child in a fundamental understanding of emotional concerns, as well as issues of perception versus reality during the transitional period.

When the parent and child have been reunited and have revealed their feelings and beliefs about their individual experiences, there are questions posed to the family. These questions consist of: How was the reunion different from what you expected it to be? How is life here different from your country? What do you like and dislike about living here? How would you like your family to be now? What can we [including the therapist] work toward? (Mitrani et al., 2004). The family is reunited literally in the sense that the therapeutic discourse focuses on all members as a collective unit, but also figuratively in the sense that everyone has had a chance to hear and expound on one another's ideas during the therapeutic process. Within many Latin American families, this process is a template for what ideal family patterns of communications should look like. Therefore, counselors are advised to approach these types of clients in this way because of how these systemic interventions tap into the collective strengths of the family unit.

Asian Clients   Within Asian immigrant populations, it is important to remember that many of these individuals will not seek counseling regarding emotional issues. Most are willing to seek counseling services about academic or career and financial concerns (Gim, Atkinson, & Whitely, 1990). However, many Asian clients, such as those from Vietnamese, Lao, and Cambodian groups, equate academic-related attributes to good parenting styles and proper behavior of their children (Xiong et al., 2005). Other primary concerns include communication-related attributes, such as talking nicely and not yelling or hitting someone, and protection-related attributes, such as monitoring friends of children and observing children's behavior. Although there are different levels of significance that Asian adults and children place on these concerns, it is fair to state that discussions that are emotion focused will not be the immediate conscious goals that these clients will likely seek when coming for service.

Counselors are encouraged to start with a more assessment-oriented approach when first working with Asian immigrant families. Instruments such as the Parent Success Indicator (Strom & Strom, 1998) and the Suinn-Lew Self-Identity Acculturation Scale (Suinn, Ahuna, & Khoo, 1992) are some effective tools that may be chosen. This is mostly because of research suggesting that knowledge of customs and recognition of identity are more likely to be perceived as positive qualities within the family system (Buki, Ma, Strom, & Strom, 2003). Much of what Chinese and Korean family members communicate to one another within their family systems is focused on how much knowledge one has of their culture and work-related successes (Buki et al., 2003; Yeh et al., 2005). By providing an assessment-based dialogue, clients are able to provide factual information that can help operationalize basic concerns that exist within the family without necessarily intruding upon deep-rooted socioemotional concerns that are not considered proper matters to discuss with someone who is not part of the family system. It is after this point, when tangible goals are identified with the use of data-based analyses, that more open dialogues about personal feelings and affective components can be addressed.

Issues of identity are of frequent concern to Asian immigrant clients, especially when they are adolescents (Yeh et al., 2005). The acculturation process does not occur at the same rate for every individual, and within a multigenerational family system such as that of an Asian family, this process can create multiple levels of conflict. One of the best predictors of ability to deal with acculturative stress within Asian families appears to be level of education (Buki et al., 2003). Highly educated mothers, for example, appear to have more accurate perceptions of their own acculturation levels and how their acculturation levels impact their relationships with their children. It is this correlation that suggests that the most effective role the counselor can initially play in the counseling process is to gain cognitive understandings of what the family members perceive of their acculturation levels, and then draw parallels between family members' experiences. These parallels, which highlight the family system's experiences with both Asian and American cultures, compose the technique known as *frame switching* (Yeh et al., 2005).

Though frame switching is an effective tool to use during the process of counseling, it is still important to note that the collectivistic nature of Asian culture may not encourage such clients to actively seek counseling services. Thus, in order to extend services to Asian immigrants, outreach activities are often preferred methods by which to engage such clients in the process. Within schools, for example, counselors are encouraged to emphasize the notion of peer support groups because of the collectivistic notion of youth cohorts (Yeh et al., 2005). Further suggestions are to engage clients in family get-togethers at school or in local community groups. These extra efforts align with Asian culture and can help establish trust and credibility within the counseling relationship. It also shows that the professional is not trying to take control of the family system in order to make changes, but rather is using the collectivistic identity of the system to bring out its natural strengths. Such actions are often appreciated by Asian immigrant clients (Dinh, Sarason, & Sarason, 1994).

African Clients   African clients are also heavily focused on family issues. Mental health professionals have not always paid attention to certain immigrant subgroups. West Indian culture and Afro-Caribbean individuals are one such group (Smith et al., 2004). There has been considerable attention paid to the fact that instruments used to assess personality characteristics and psychopathology are not usually normed on African American clients (Foster, 2001). All clinicians need to realize that instrumentation has its limits and that no one group is homogeneous. It is because of this notion that assessment instruments should be carefully selected for working with this immigrant population. Especially in cases where bilingual staff is available, it is important for counselors to utilize these resources because it can help many clients understand the process better, as well as reduce anxieties that may result from perceived differences between cultures (Foster, 2001). This information is important for all immigrant clients, but is more relevant for African immigrants.

One of the main issues that African immigrants experience when acculturating to the United States is the fact that they have a dual issue of contending with the issues of being Black within America and also being an African immigrant within America. Within-group ethnic diversity can often be a source of stress and struggle for such clients (Kibour, 2001). Many Ethiopians choose Europeans as their reference group within their host country, especially when struggling with racial identity issues. This results in cognitive shifts that distance family members from one another because they deny identification with their racial group, and place greater endorsement on their mainstream culture (Kibour, 2001). For older clients, such as 40- and 50-year-olds, the wisdom and life experience they possess helps buffer much of these stressful adjustments. Young adults and teenage clients often struggle more with this matter, which manifests in the form of low achievement scores and school dropout (Mitchell, 2005). Working Afro-Caribbean and African clients also must contend with financial stressors that are the result of poor job security, low-income tiered positions, and perceptions of lower status positions within American society (Mitchell, 2005). It is important, however, to note that despite these factors and statistics, which indicate that such clients are likely to experience frustrations and depression-inducing experiences centered on race and class issues within the host culture, African and Afro-Caribbean immigrant clients have fairly decent views of their self-concepts (Kibour, 2001; Mitchell, 2005).

It is because of the resilient self-concepts that these clients have the ability to rely on one another for support. Caribbean American immigrant students and African immigrant students represent one of the largest subgroups in the U.S. Black population (Kibour, 2001; Mitchell, 2005). One of the main issues that results from this fact is that counselors may tend to generalize similarities that may not be accurate for each individual client. School counseling literature has indicated that Black children's aspirations are at least at the same level of White children's (Nieto, 2000). However, many studies have indicated that school counselors do not advocate for immigrant students due to assumptions that are often made about parents' ability to pay for college and student socioeconomic status (Mitchell, 2005).

Techniques that center on group activities and family constellations are strongly recommended when working with such clients. School counselors are encouraged to provide culture awareness events that seek to change school climate when it comes to matters of dealing with negative biases that majority cultures may harbor toward minority cultures (Mitchell, 2005). Family work must include direct education of parents when it comes to exploring issues of academic success and career options for their children. Often, many African and Afro-Caribbean immigrants do not understand the differences between U.S. educational approaches and European educational approaches. Therefore, it is the counselor's job to provide families with realistic orientations to the host culture, while calling attention to the strengths and individual interests of the clients (Mitchell, 2005). Visual displays of family constellations (Coatsworth et al., 2005) and career constellations (Zagelbaum as cited in Hecker & Sori, 2006) can also provide visual aid to such clients. The point is that the African and Afro-Caribbean family is considered to be highly integrated and communal. When counselors are able to engage the family system, similar in many ways to which

Latino family systems are engaged in the process of counseling, anxieties are likely to decrease and proactive work is likely to occur because clients can see that there are connected patterns and support networks that exist within the host culture. A counselor from the host culture serves as an ambassador to said culture. By encouraging and reinforcing the principles of the family system, the counselor is able to provide an important piece of encouragement and support to the immigrant family, which allow them to be themselves within the counseling environment. By not compromising the family's identity and simultaneously representing the host culture, the counselor can model for these clients the fact that the family can feel relatively safe within the environment of a host culture. In other words, if the family system can present its cultural values in a therapeutic environment with a counselor from the host culture that does not judge or dismiss such values, the system feels more able to function within the host culture. Ideally, all counselors should be able to engage in these processes when working with all clients, but specific attention should be paid to immigrant clients who come from communal and collectivistic cultures.

Working with Immigrant Clients Individually

Essentially, many of the same principles of working with families may be applied to working with immigrant clients who seek individual counseling services. The notion of the family system does not fade when dealing with clients from collectivistic cultures who wish to engage in the counseling process on their own. However, there are some immigrant clients who are likely to see counseling services through an individualistic cultural lens and counselors are advised to note the importance of working with such clients. Clients who struggle with war-based trauma, hail from societies where individualism is the norm, or are elders are likely to seek such individual counseling services.

Two of the most significant immigrant subgroups who deal with war-based trauma and refugee status within the United States are Bosnian and Central American clients (Asner-Self & Marotta, 2005; Miller, Worthington, Muzurovic, Tipping, & Goldman, 2002). Common themes that have been found in research among such clients consist of PTSD, depression, anxiety, and somatic distress. These mental health issues are relevant to all immigrants who seek exile, regardless of age and gender (Miller et al., 2002). Much of this is due to the stressful process of exile itself, but the added stressors of assimilating into the host country can often exacerbate the symptoms.

Studies of the narrative of Bosnian refugees reveal themes of social isolation and the loss of community, the loss of life projects, a lack of environmental mastery, loss of social roles and meaningful activities, depletion of resources such as housing and income, and physical ailments (Miller et al., 2002). Essentially, exiled individuals do not perceive a sense of community when first acculturating to America because there is not likely to be an established exile community present (Weine et al., 2006). These immigrants do not perceive themselves in many cases to be like other immigrant groups because they believe they lack personal control, coupled with the fact that there are many individuals in the United States who are not as connected with the war-based issues that placed these individuals into exile. In other words, most individuals within the host culture do not have a fundamental understanding of wars that do not have direct impact on their culture.

It is through the same narrative process by which problems are expressed that counselors can aid such clients in the counseling process. Though appropriate screening tools must be used to ensure that there are no disconnects from reality, having clients retell their war-based stories can be very helpful (Miller et al., 2002). It provides clients a way of establishing social rapport and validating their sense of who they are because they know someone is concerned about their mental health and well-being. Also, with appropriate reframing techniques, such clients can tell that there are positive aspects to their acculturative process and place within the host country. The point of this is to validate the client's experiences and to show that there are qualities of their present situation that are more advantageous than may have been the case in their native land.

Central American immigrants are quite similar to Bosnian refugees in many ways, but also appear to exhibit high levels of mistrust toward others within the host culture (Asner-Self & Marotta, 2005). There is a memory of their country and community letting them down, and it is very difficult not to generalize these negative feelings and perceptions toward others. This sense of mistrust and confusion can often manifest as paranoid ideation, depression, and social withdrawal. Most Central American immigrants maintain their identity by comparing themselves to others within their culture that stayed behind. It is ultimately the goal to have these clients identify themselves in comparison and relation to the dominant U.S. culture and minority groups within this acculturated environment (Asner-Self & Marotta, 2005). It is advantageous for the counselor to know that these individuals also have a fairly open sense of seeking therapy and engaging in individual work. Garcia and Marotta (1998) liken this to a sense of identity development that can be used to establish an effective working alliance within a counseling relationship; Latino individuals want to tell their stories and reconnect parts of their selves that may have been left behind as they fled their native country. They suggest a three-stage regenerative process.

The first stage is to establish rapport and provide clear messages to the client that the counseling environment is a safe place where difficult matters may be discussed. Many times, counselors will investigate the trauma before getting a sense of the client's current level of comfort within the counseling dyad. To ignore issues of rapport and trust at this stage can further isolate the client from engaging in candid discussion. Safety and stability are the themes of Central American immigrant issues when dealing with war-based trauma. Therefore, this matter needs to be of primary concern (Asner-Self & Marotta, 2002).

The second stage is to address the trauma. However, it is important to note that although Latin American clients can be very open and expressive about their feelings, issues of trauma are not necessarily easy to disclose. There may be several sessions before a client feels comfortable to do so. It is recommended that counselors use non-value-laden terms and describe behavioral concepts whenever possible to help normalize experiences and place as little bias as possible onto the narrative descriptions given by clients at this stage (Asner-Self & Marotta, 2005).

The third stage involves getting the client to assess meanings and attributions about dealing with the trauma and adjusting to the host culture. Although this stage may appear like a natural extension of the previous stages, it is important to note that the counseling model is regenerative, meaning that it is more of a circular than linear process. Clients may need further encouragement and trust building throughout the time they are working with a counselor. New traumatic issues may surface along the way. It is the counselor's responsibility to routinely screen for any issues that may impact the client's general well-being and sense of self. Suicidal ideation is not an uncommon factor to address with clients who are struggling with traumatic issues (Hovey, 2000). Whether done by assessment tools or through direct interviewing, it is important that the client maintains a sense of trust and safety as the counseling process unfolds (Asner-Self & Marotta, 2005). This routine check also helps maintain a sense of stability within the counseling relationship, which can be generalized to the client's social environment.

It is not unusual for Central American immigrants and Mexican immigrants to be living with unrelated people as they settle within the United States (Asner-Self & Marotta, 2005; Hovey & Magna, 2002). This serves as a social support system and underscores the importance of collectivistic culture. Therefore, counseling services not only benefit the individual client, but also the network of people with whom he or she associates. This is not the case for the more individualistic-based cultures.

Asian Indians who immigrated to the United States before age 10, for example, may have more positive views of counseling and psychotherapy than those who have immigrated at older points in their lives (Panganamala & Plummer, 1998). It is not culturally acceptable for such individuals to seek help outside of their family because of extreme needs for privacy. Because Indian immigrants usually come to the United States with college educations and compose a significant portion of urban, middle-class professionals, there is usually a sense of independence and competency that does not heavily motivate these clients to seek counseling services (Panganamala & Plummer, 1998). This is not to say that these individuals will never seek the aid of a counselor, but counselors are advised to note that issues of deep emotional concern are not likely to be the main focal points of discussion. Many of these clients will seek aid for depression and anxiety through clinical physicians. However, a counselor may be consulted in such cases.

Also, it is important to recognize that many Asian Indian immigrants struggle with career-related concerns because of trouble with having their licenses and certification status transferred to America (Zagelbaum & Carlson, 2008). Thus, counselors working with these clients are encouraged to provide resources for career support and governmental advocates. Clients may not so much be looking for emotional support as they are trying to facilitate problem-solving processes. However, when working with elderly clients, this delineation of service requests is not as clear.

Approximately 10% to 15% of elderly citizens living in America suffer from clinical depression (Lai, 2004). Although it is not completely known how much of this population is comprised of immigrants, it is clear that elderly immigrants are also at risk for depression and other related mental illnesses. A fair amount of elderly citizens are also women who have trouble establishing support networks due to age and cultural differences (Yakushko & Chronister, 2005). The counselor should be aware of these facts, especially when working with elderly Asian and Latino immigrants.

Counselors working with such clients are encouraged to address issues of communication within family and social support networks. Often Asian and Latino clients are usually cared for within a system of some kind (Weisman et al., 2005). The purpose of counseling is not to change the patterns of the caregiver, but rather to allow for better communication to occur within the system that can often neglect and dismiss much of what the elder is stating. This is especially true for clients who may be experiencing dementia (Weisman et al., 2005).

The system of human services needs to recognize that depression and dementia are common signs of old age and that they are natural phenomena. Such symptoms are not necessarily due to the particular actions of an individual or decision made by the family system. Informing the system of basic facts, such as the concept of dementia being a gradual process by which more recent memories decline first, and, over a relatively long period, slowly starts to cognitively impact established recollections of the elderly individual (Weisman et al., 2005). Though the process is not curable, using trigger words and cues such as the client's native language may help to make the process less stressful and negative for the individual and his or her system (Weisman et al., 2005). Also, since it is not unusual for declining individuals to want to pull away from others as they recognize their situation is not improving, counselors are encouraged to engage these clients in group therapy. This approach not only provides novel stimuli for elderly clients that focus on their personal experiences and communication patterns, but also keeps the integrity of their cultural values regarding extended networks and collectivism intact. Elderly immigrants often experience a loss of identity, for example, that of a wise or powerful person who may have played a highly salient role in the native country. The counselor who asks these clients about losses of these roles, as well as tangible resources, is likely to build greater rapport and a sense of trust with such clients (Weisman et al., 2005). Also, if indigenous methods are to be incorporated into treatment in some way, counselors are advised that Latino and Asian elderly clients respond well to meditation, which also carries with it a spiritual and religious component that validates the client's cultural identity.

CONCLUSION

Through an examination of cultural practices and definitions of counseling around the world, we have come to understand the complexity and practicality of working with immigrant clients. There will always be the need for counselors to pay particularly close attention to cross-cultural data that affects work with diverse individuals. However, working with immigrants provides more challenge and diversity of counseling roles. In addition to being a therapist, one must also be an advocate, mediator, educator, group facilitator, consultant, and family/couples therapist in many cases if truly comprehensive work is to be successfully performed. It is a lot of work, but also one of the most important challenges a counseling professional can take on because of the contemporary climate regarding immigration in the United States. If the counseling profession is to remain true to its goals of helping clients deal with academic, personal/social, career, family, couples and group concerns, working with immigrants needs to be integrated into the counselor's repertoire as a viable and important function.

REFERENCES

Adamo, S. (2004). An adolescent and his imaginary companions: From quasi-delusional constructs to creative imagination. *Journal of Child Psychotherapy, 30,* 275–295.

Adams, K. (2007). The sexual abuse of children in contemporary Japanese families. *Journal of Psychohistory, 34,* 178–207.

Aluede, O., Imhonde, H., & Eguavoen, A. (2006). Academic, career and personal needs of Nigerian university students. *Journal of Instructional Psychology, 33,* 50–57.

American Counseling Association. (2006). *Multicultural Counseling Competencies.* Alexandria, VA: Author.

American Psychiatric Association. (1994). *Diagnostic and statistical manual of mental disorders* (4th ed.). Washington, DC: Author.

American Psychological Association. (2003). Guidelines on multicultural education, training, research, practice, and organizational change for psychologists. *American Psychologist, 58,* 377–402.

Amir, Y. (1992). Social assimilation or cultural mosaic. In J. Lynch, C. Modgil, & S. Moddgil (Eds.) *Cultural diversity and the schools* (Vol. 1). Washington D.C.: Falmer.

Asner-Self, K., & Marotta, S. (2005). Developmental indices among Central American immigrants exposed to war-related trauma: Clinical implications for counselors. *Journal of Counseling and Development, 83,* 162–171.

Awanbor, D. (1982). The healing process in African psychotherapy. *American Journal of Psychotherapy, 36,* 206–213.

Barrow, C. (2001). Contesting the rhetoric of 'Black Family Breakdown' from Barbados. *Journal of Comparative Family Studies, 32,* 419–441.

Bloemraad, I. (2006). *Becoming a citizen: Incorporating immigrants and refugees in the United States and Canada.* Berkley: University of California Press.

Buki, L., Ma, T., Strom, R., & Strom, S. (2003). Chinese immigrant mothers of adolescents: Self-perceptions of acculturation effects on parenting. *Cultural Diversity and Ethnic Minority Psychology, 9,* 127–140.

Cinamon, R., & Hellman, S. (2006). Israeli counselors facing terrorism: Coping and professional development. *British Journal of Guidance and Counseling, 43,* 209–229.

Coatsworth, J., Maldonado-Molina, M., Pantin, H., & Szapocznik, J. (2005). A person-centered and ecological investigation of acculturation strategies in Hispanic immigrant youth. *Journal of Community Psychology, 33,* 157–174.

Connell, J., Barkham, M., & Mellor-Clark, J. (2007). CORE-OM mental health norms of students attending university counseling services benchmarked against an age-matched primary care sample. *British Journal of Guidance and Counseling, 35,* 41–57.

Danielidou, L., & Horvath, P. (2006). Greek Cypriot attitudes toward Turkish Cypriots and Turkish immigrants. *Journal of Social Psychology, 146,* 405–421.

Dinh, K., Sarason, B., & Sarason, I. (1994). Parent-child relationships in Vietnamese immigrant families. *Journal of Family Psychology, 8,* 471–488.

Espin, O., & Renner, R. (1974). Counseling: A new priority in Latin America. *Personnel and Guidance Journal, 52,* 297–301.

Foster, R. P. (2001). When immigration is trauma: Guidelines for the individual and family clinician. *American Journal of Orthopsychiatry, 71,* 153–170.

Fox, C., & Butler, I. (2007). 'If you don't want to tell anyone else you can tell her': Young people's views on school counseling. *British Journal of Guidance and Counseling, 35,* 97–114.

Garcia, J., & Marotta, S. (1998). Counseling Latino clients: Cultural considerations for counselors. *Directions in Rehabilitation Counseling, 9,* 1–11.

Gavin, B. (2001). A sense of Irishness. *Psychodynamic Counseling, 7,* 83–102.

Geary, C., Wedderburn, M., McCarraher, D., Cuthbertson, C., & Pottinger, A. (2006). Sexual violence and reproductive health among young people in three communities in Jamaica. *Journal of Interpersonal Violence, 21,* 1512–1533.

Gim, R., Atkinson, D., & Whitely, S. (1990). Asian-American acculturation, severity of concerns, and willingness to see a counselor. *Journal of Counseling Psychology, 37,* 281–285.

Grinstead, O., Van Der Straten, A., & the Voluntary HIV-1 Counseling and Testing Efficacy Study Group. (2000). Counselor's perspectives on the experience of providing HIV counseling in Kenya and Tanzania: The Voluntary HIV-1 Counseling and Testing Efficacy Study. *AIDS CARE, 12,* 625–642.

Hecker, L., & Sori, C. (2007). *The therapists' notebook: Volume II: More homework, handouts, and activities for use in psychotherapy.* New York: Haworth Press.

Hernandez, P. (2002). Trauma in war and political persecution: Expanding the concept. *American Journal of Orthopsychiatry, 72,* 16–25.

Hirano, S., Onitsuka, T., Kuroki, T., Yokota, K., Higuchi, T., Wantanabe, K., et al. (2007). Attitudes of patients with mood disorder toward clinical trials in Japan. *Journal of Clinical Psychopharmacology, 27,* 93–94.

Hovey, J. (2000). Acculturative stress, depression, and suicidal ideation in Mexican immigrants. *Cultural Diversity and Ethnic Minority Psychology, 6*, 134–151.

Hovey, J., & Magana, C. (2002). Psychosocial predictors of anxiety among immigrant Mexican migrant farm workers: Implications for prevention and treatment. *Cultural Diversity and Ethnic Minority Psychology, 8*, 274–289.

Jacques, G., & Stegling, C. (2004). HIV/AIDS and home based care in Botswana: Panacea or perfidy? *Social Work in Mental Health, 2*, 175–193.

Jahangir, S. (1995). Third force therapy and its impact on treatment outcome. *International Journal for the Psychology of Religion, 5*, 125–129.

Janey, B., Janey, N., Goncherova, N., & Savchenko, V. (2006). Masculinity ideology in Russian society: Factor structure and validity of the Multicultural Masculinity Ideology Scale. *Journal of Men's Studies, 14*, 93–108.

Jenkins, P., & Potter, S. (2007). No more 'personal notes'? Data protection policy and practice in higher education counseling services in the UK. *British Journal of Guidance and Counseling, 35*, 131–146.

Karavaeva, T. (2006). The main tendencies of psychotherapy development in modern Russia. *International Journal of Mental Health, 34*, 53–56.

Kibour, Y. (2001). Ethiopian immigrants' racial identity attitudes and depression symptomatology: An exploratory study. *Cultural Diversity and Ethnic Minority Psychology, 7*, 47–58.

Kim, Y., Odallo, D., Thuo, M., & Kols, A. (1999). Client participation and provider communication in family planning counseling: Transcript analysis in Kenya. *Health Communication, 11*, 1–19.

Klassen, R. (2004). A cross-cultural investigation of the efficacy benefits of South Asian immigrant and Anglo Canadian nonimmigrant early adolescents. *Journal of Educational Psychology, 96*, 731–742.

Kosic, A., Kruglanski, A., Pierro, A., & Mannetti, L. (2004). The social cognition of immigrants' acculturation: Effects of the need for closure and the reference group at entry. *Journal of Personality and Social Psychology, 86*, 796–813.

Krishnan, S. (2005). Gender, caste, and economic inequalities and marital violence in rural south India. *Health Care for Women International, 26*, 87–98.

Kuijpers, M., Schyns, B., & Scheerens, J. (2006). Career competencies for career success. *Career Development Quarterly, 55*, 168–178.

Lai, D. (2004). Impact of culture on depressive symptoms of elderly Chinese immigrants. *Canadian Journal of Psychiatry, 49*, 820–827.

Letunovsky, V. (2004a). Analysis of the basic moods in dreaming and further work with them. *Existential Analysis, 15*, 298–306.

Letunovsky, V. (2004b). Existential therapy in working with the body. *Existential Analysis, 15*, 307–332.

Lister, S., & Benson, C. (2006). Comparative analysis of dementia and ethnicity in the New South Wales Aged Care Assessment Program: 1996 and 2001. *Australasian Journal on Ageing, 25,* 24–30.

Malde, B. (2006). Do assessment centres really care about the candidate? *British Journal of Guidance and Counseling, 34,* 539–549.

Manthei, R. (2006). Clients talk about their experience of seeking counseling. *British Journal of Guidance and Counseling, 34,* 519–538.

Martin, S., Tsui, A., Maitra, K., & Marinshaw, R. (1999). Domestic violence in northern India. *American Journal of Epidemiology, 150,* 417–426.

McCash, P. (2006). We're all career researchers now: Breaking open career education and DOTS. *British Journal of Guidance and Counseling, 34,* 429–449.

McGuiness, J., Alred, G., Cohen, N., Hunt, K., & Robson, M. (2001). Globalising counseling: Humanistic counseling in Kenya. *British Journal of Guidance and Counseling, 29,* 293–300.

McKee, M., & Shkolnikov, V. (2001). Understanding the toll of premature death among men in Eastern Europe. *British Medical Journal, 323,* 1051–1056.

McWhirter, J. (1983). Cultural factors in guidance and counseling in Turkey: The experience of a Fulbright family. *Personnel and Guidance Journal,* 504–507.

Miller, K., Worthington, G., Muzurovic, J., Tipping, S., & Goldman, A. (2002). Bosnian refugees and the stressors of exile: A narrative study. *American Journal of Orthopsychiatry, 72,* 341–354.

Mitchell, N. (2005). Academic achievement among Caribbean immigrant adolescents: The impact of generational status on academic self-concept. *Professional School Counseling, 8,* 209–224.

Mitrani, V., Santisteban, D., & Muir, J. (2004). Addressing immigration-related separations in Hispanic families with a behavior-problem adolescent. *American Journal of Orthopsychiatry, 74,* 219–229.

Mommersteeg, P., Keijsers, G., Heijnen, C., Verbraak, M., & Van Dooernen, L. (2006). Cortisol deviations in people with burnout before and after psychotherapy: A pilot study. *Health Psychology, 25,* 243–248.

Munir, K., Ergene, T., Tunaligil, V., & Erol, N. (2004). A window of opportunity for the transformation of national mental health policy in Turkey following two major earthquakes. *Harvard Review of Psychiatry, 12,* 238–251.

Muratori, F., Picchi, L., Apicella, F., Salvadori, F., Espasa, F., Ferretti, D., & Bruni, G. (2004). Psychodynamic psychotherapy for separation anxiety disorders in children. *InterScience, 21,* 45–26.

Nghe, L., Mahalik, J., & Lowe, S. (2003). Influences on Vietnamese men: Examining traditional gender roles, the refugee experience, acculturation, and racism in the United States. *Multicultural Counseling and Development, 31,* 245–261.

Nieto, S. (2000). *Affirming diversity: The sociopolitical context of multicultural education* (3rd ed.). New York: Longman.

Nijenhuis, J., Tolboom, E., Resing, W., & Bleichrodt, N. (2004). Does cultural background influence the intellectual performance of children from immigrant groups?: The RAKIT Intelligence Test for Immigrant Children. *European Journal of Psychological Assessment, 20*(1), 10–26.

O'Leary, E., Page, R., & Kaczmarek, C. (2000). A comparison of perceptions of counseling in Ireland and the United States. *Counseling Psychology Quarterly, 13,* 391–397.

Olley, B. (2006). Improving well-being through psycho-education among voluntary counseling and testing seekers in Nigeria: A controlled outcome study. *AIDS CARE, 18,* 1025–1031.

O'Neil, R. (1966). Attitudes and experiences of high school students living in Turkey. *Personnel and Guidance Journal,* 43–46.

Page, R., & O'Leary, E. (1997). A comparison of perceptions of love, guilt, and anger in Ireland and the United States: Implications for counseling. *Counseling and Values, 41,* 267–278.

Panganamala, N., & Plummer, D. (1998). Attitudes toward counseling among Asian Indians in the United States. *Cultural Diversity and Mental Health, 4,* 55–63.

Phan, L., Rivera, E., & Roberts-Wilbur, J. (2005). Understanding Vietnamese refugee women's identity development from a sociopolitical and historical perspective. *Journal of Counseling and Development, 83,* 305–312.

Piovano, B. (2004). Parenthood and parental functions as a result of the experience of parallel psychotherapy with children and parents. *International Forum Psychoanalysis, 13,* 187–200.

Prakash, K., & Coplan, R. (1999). Socioemotional characteristics and school adjustment of socially withdrawn children in India. *International Journal of Behavioral Development, 31,* 123–132.

Reeskamp, H. (2006). Working with dreams in a clinical setting. *American Journal of Psychotherapy, 60,* 23–36.

Rollins, J. (2006). Getting a global perspective: A glimpse of the counseling profession in 27 countries. *Counseling Today, 1,* 1–34.

Rolston, B., Schubotz, D., & Simpson, A. (2005). Sex education in Northern Ireland schools: A critical evaluation. *Sex Education, 5,* 217–234.

Rosik, C., Richards, A., & Fannon, T. (2005). Member care experiences and needs: Findings from a study of East African missionaries. *Journal of Psychology and Christianity, 24,* 36–45.

Rothbaum, F., Morelli, G., Pott, M., & Liu-Constant, Y. (2000). Immigrant-Chinese and Euro-American parents' physical closeness with young children: Themes of family relatedness. *Journal of Family Psychology, 14,* 334–348.

Rutledge, S., & Abell, N. (2005). Awareness, acceptance, and action: An emerging framework for understanding AIDS stigmatizing attitudes among community leaders in Barbados. *AIDS Patient Care and STDs, 19,* 186–199.

Sayed, M. (2003a). Conceptualization of mental illness within Arab cultures: Meeting challenges in cross-cultural settings. *Social Behavior and Personality, 31,* 333–342.

Sayed, M. (2003b). Psychotherapy of Arab patients in the west: Uniqueness, empathy and "otherness." *American Journal of Psychotherapy, 57,* 445–459.

Schmidley, D. (2001). Profile of the foreign-born population in the United States: 2000. In *Current population reports, P23-206,* (pp. 1–70). Washington, DC: U.S. Census Bureau.

Shechtman, Z., & Halevi, H. (2006). Does ethnicity explain functioning in group counseling? The case of Arab and Jewish counseling trainees in Israel. *Group Dynamics: Theory, Research and Practice, 10,* 181–193.

Simonetta, M., Serpieri, S., Giusti, P., Contarini, R., & Valerio, P. (2005). The Chance Project: Complex interventions with adolescent school dropouts in Naples. *Psychodynamic Practice, 11,* 239–254.

Smith, A., Lalonde, R. N., & Johnson, S. (2004). Serial migration and its implications: A retrospective analysis of the children of Caribbean immigrants. *Cultural Diversity and Ethnic Minority Psychology, 10,* 107–122.

Soresi, S., Nota, L., & Ferrari, L. (2005). Counseling for adolescents and children at-risk in Italy. *Journal of Mental Health Counseling, 27,* 249–265.

Spencer, J., & Le, T. (2006). Parent refugee status, immigration stressors, and Southeast Asian youth violence. *Journal of Immigrant and Minority Health, 8,* 359–368.

Suinn, R., Ahuna, C., & Khoo, G. (1992). The Suinn-Lew Asian Self-Identity Acculturation Scale: An initial report. *Educational and Psychological Measurement, 47,* 401–407.

Strom, R., & Strom, S. (1998). *Parent Success Indicator.* Bensenville, IL: Scholastic Testing Service.

Van de Vijver, F., & Willemse, G. (1991). Are reaction time tasks better suited for ethnic minorities than paper and pencil tests? In N. Bliechrodt & P. Drenth (Eds.), *Contemporary issues in cross-cultural psychology* (pp. 450–464). Lisse, Netherlands: Swets.

Van Ecke, Y. (2005). Immigration from an attachment perspective. *Social Behavior and Personality, 33,* 467–476.

Vasilyeva, A. (2006). The development of Russian psychotherapy as an independent medical discipline in the second half of the twentieth century. *International Journal of Mental Health, 34,* 31–38.

Weine, S., Feetham, S., Kulauzovic, Y., Knafl, K., Besic, S., Klebic, A., et al. (2006). A family beliefs framework for socially and culturally specific preventive interventions with refugee youths and families. *American Journal of Orthopsychiatry, 76*, 1–9.

Weisman, A., Feldman, G., Gruman, C., Rosenberg, R., Chamorro, R., & Belozerksy, I. (2005). Improving mental health services for Latino and Asian immigrant elders. *Professional Psychology: Research and Practice, 36*, 642–648.

Xiong, Z., Eliason, P., Detzner, D., & Cleveland, M. (2005). Southeast Asian immigrants' perceptions of good adolescents and good parents. *The Journal of Psychology, 139*, 159–175.

Yakushko, O., & Chronister, K. (2005). Immigrant women and counseling: The invisible others. *Journal of Counseling and Development, 83*, 292–298.

Yeh, C., & Inose, M. (2003). International students' reported English fluency, social support, satisfaction, and social connectedness as predictors of acculturative stress. *Counseling Psychology Quarterly, 16*, 15–28.

Yeh, C., Ma, P., Madan-Bahel, A., Hunter, C., Jung, S., Kim, A., et al. (2005). The cultural negotiations of Korean immigrant youth. *Journal of Counseling and Development, 83*, 172–182.

Zagelbaum, A., & Carlson, J. (2008). The case of Dalbir: Critical incident reaction. In N. Arthur and P. Pedersen (Eds.), *Case incidents in counseling for international transitions*. Alexandria, VA: American Counseling Association.

12

COUNSELING WITH THE POOR, UNDERSERVED, AND UNDERREPRESENTED

Leon D. Caldwell

Economic disadvantage in the United States of America is considered the root of social economic disparities. Access to quality healthcare, housing, and education has its price. Members of society who have limited financial resources become the most vulnerable and susceptible for being marginalized and alienated by the haves in this false dichotomy. Names, labels, and categories like impoverished, poor, underrepresented, underserved, disadvantaged, underachievers, homeless, and so on, which identify a condition, are given as a means of describing one's humanity. These descriptors and resulting stigmas create barriers, burdens, and ultimately disparities.

Ironically the helping professions have contributed to the creation of those we categorize as underserved and underrepresented. Culturally encapsulating service delivery systems, training models, and research methods perpetuate the experiences of service estrangement by those who are not categorized as status quo. The purpose of this chapter is to describe the global phenomenon of poverty in the context of the United States of America. Then there is a discussion of the public health challenges confronting those below or near the poverty threshold. In addition, there is an explanation of access and utilization as structural and interpersonal concepts that serve as barriers for service delivery. Then strategies for meeting the needs of the underserved and underrepresented are provided for individual counselors, counselor education programs, and the counseling profession. Finally, the Family Potential

Center is provided as an example of how the strategies were implemented in a counselor education program.

POVERTY IN PERSPECTIVE

A competent discussion of poverty must begin by putting it into perspective. Poverty is asserted here as a condition in which a person or community is deprived of or lacks the essentials for a minimum standard of well-being and life. Thus, poverty in a global perspective is dynamic and very relative to economic and monetary standards. As the counseling profession is internationalizing (Marsella & Pedersen, 2004) it is important to contextualize topics with global implications to avoid assumptions of universality. The assertion is that poverty in the United States of America is more distinctly defined and experienced than poverty in a developing country, for example Ghana or India. For the purpose of this chapter the United States is the frame of reference.

The *poverty line* was established in 1964 as part of President Lyndon Johnson's war on poverty. Although there is controversy about the calculations, the measure of poverty is set at approximately 3 times that of a nutritionally adequate diet, varies by family size, and is updated annually (U.S. Census Bureau, 2006). When a household's income falls below this threshold everyone is considered in poverty (U.S. Census Bureau, 2006).

There are now 37 million Americans living under the official poverty line. According to Toldson and Scott (2006), in 2004 the official poverty rate rose for the fourth year in a row to 12.7%, up from 12.5% in 2003. Although there are greater and more rapidly growing numbers of Americans moving toward the threshold of government-defined poverty, public and political attention has been stagnant.

Glasmeir (2007) asserts that the numbers of those in the severely poor category are across several demographics with the largest number of abjectly poor being European Americans (twice as many as African Americans), however, African Americans and Hispanics are disproportionately represented. The poverty statistics illustrate that children and women are at a greater risk than men of being in poverty (Armstrong, 2007). Therefore, ethnicity, gender, and age are risk factors for poverty and its implications. States with the largest rates of growth in poverty are unsuspected places such as Minnesota, New Hampshire, Idaho, Maine, and Wisconsin (Glasmeir, 2007). Racial and regional stereotypes are rapidly being challenged as poverty becomes more prevalent in the suburbs. Armstrong (2007) asserts that although these statistics illustrate those in actual poverty, there are several million more who are near the poverty threshold.

In August of 2005, Hurricane Katrina exposed the fragility of human life and the challenges of those in or near poverty in the United States. For a brief moment in history the nation caught a glimpse of the faces at the "bottom of the well" (Bell, 1992). Substandard housing, corporate exploitation (i.e., insurance companies), basic transportation, a lack of health care, unemployment, environmental pollution, and a failure to respond to the hurricane aftermath by all levels of government exposed the vulnerability of economically disadvantaged citizens across all demographic areas. Poverty's pluralism was captured in international media outlets as the confluence of race/ethnicity; social economic status (SES), educational attainment, and governmental responsibility were displayed as the haves and the have-nots.

POVERTY AND MENTAL HEALTH

Economic disadvantage is in itself a risk factor for health-compromising behaviors, which have a consequence of emotional distress. As a result of poor health care systems and behaviors, low educational attainment, poor nutrition, early and high-risk pregnancy, substandard housing, transportation difficulties, unemployment/underemployment, and limited health insurance, children, women, the elderly, and other vulnerable members of these communities are at risk for psychical and mental illness (World Health Organization [WHO], 2001). The WHO (2001, as cited in Myers & Gill, 2004) reported that the mental health consequences of poverty include higher prevalence of mental disorders, lack of self-care, and more severe mental health symptoms and outcomes. Often below the radar of health assessments is the amount of emotional distress that accompanies poverty. It is important for counselors to make the distinction between diagnosed and undiagnosed symptoms. Given that many in poverty lack access to health care, it is likely their symptoms may go undiagnosed by a professional mental health practitioner. However, the absence of a professional diagnosis does not indicate clinical distress. For this reason it is plausible that mental health prevalence statistics for those in poverty are understated.

As a result of deprivation and uncertainty regarding basic daily needs, economically disadvantaged people are prone to stress-related chronic diseases like hypertension, chronic heart disease, type 2 diabetes, and other diseases that contribute to a diminished lifespan of those in poverty. Furthermore, there are some in poverty who either do meet diagnostic criteria or have a cultural-based aversion to Eurocentric mental health practices. Utilization rates of the poor, especially racial/ethnic minorities, are inadequate indicators of need. Those caught in a cycle of poverty may have developed coping skills or enough real and vicarious-based mistrust of mental health services that these systems are deemed ineffective. The philosophical paradigm that influences mental health service delivery models is important when considering real access for poor people. For example, many community mental health models are designed for individual treatment of severe pathology between the hours of 8 a.m. and 6 p.m. Monday through Friday. The hours of operation and the service delivery model may be problematic for some poor, especially the working poor. Access to goods and services that enhance life and reduce risk is a major disadvantage of poverty. Invisibility to professional helping service providers and systems amplifies the disadvantage.

Prevention and resilience models of culturally responsive community mental health may prove to be more useful for economically disadvantaged populations. The resilience perspective assesses which survival and coping strengths promote a will to live in conditions pathologized by the status quo. For example, what some family therapists might consider enmeshment may be a form of protection for mothers and children in crime-ridden neighborhoods where they are prey. A prevention and resilience model, for example, would conduct a community forum with members of the local police force to discuss ways to protect families from harm and maintain supportive, healthy, and nurturing relationships. Suggestions for maintaining an extended family, exchanges of creative recreational ideas, and developing a child and family safety plan could be the focus of this type of intervention. Counselors working with other helping professionals can help empower families by recognizing their reality.

Harper, Harper, and Stills (2003) contend that counselors consider the needs of client's along Maslow's hierarchy and offer an inventory for assessing needs as a preliminary intervention tool. Individual and community interventions from these paradoxical perspectives can produce very different interventions from oppressive to naive. In truth, counselors must be aware of the potential for pathology and not assume it exists merely as a result of one's economic conditions. Conversely, to ignore the inherent impediments of poverty and establish an unrealistic appraisal of how to overcome them would be negligent. The message is that with empowerment, planning, and successful navigation of the multiple systems involved in the lives of the poor, one can transcend economic status. For example, there are several examples of prominent social and political figures who have poverty in their personal histories.

THE LIMITS OF THE COUNSELING PROFESSION
TO SERVE THOSE IN POVERTY

Although the counseling professional has its historical genesis as a profession of social justice and social action, its modern history has rendered it a vice of the status quo. Arguably, its deviation from Frank Parson's call to protect the exploited to a status quo profession is evident by the dearth of literature proposing adequate theories, interventions, research, and training addressing the need of the economically disadvantaged either globally or in the United States.

Several scholars have called attention to the counseling profession's lack of attention to preparing counselors in training for working with the economically disadvantaged (e.g., Bemak, 1998; Brown, 2002; Lewis & Lewis, 1977; Marsella & Pedersen, 2004; Toporek & Pope-Davis, 2005). A consistent theme throughout the literature on this topic is the need for counselor education programs to include specific courses in such areas as social justice and social action to augment the multicultural counseling course requirements. Accrediting and professional licensure should require such courses from anyone who is serving the public.

The dearth of counseling theory and research in the literature limits the development of service delivery to economically disadvantaged populations. Although integrative models (Brown, 2002) and counseling approaches (Boyd-Franklin, 1989) offer conceptual guidance to service delivery, they are not in the traditional canon of counseling theory covered in textbooks. Literature offering conceptual guidance to practice and research offer promise to swinging the pendulum back toward Frank Parson's pioneering work, which started the field of counseling. However, cultural encapsulation (Wrenn, 1982) limits the counseling profession to effectively serve the poor.

The Western philosophical tenets (e.g., individualism and autonomy) inherent in modern counseling undergird professional ethics and standards, theories, practice, curriculum, and every other facet of the profession (Marsella & Pedersen, 2004). Western values and assumptions offer a limited perspective to effectively treat people in poverty. It might be argued that these very tenets created the underserved and underrepresented. Counselors, as a result of culturally encapsulating training, are often the greatest barriers to serving the underrepresented and poor. A lack of knowledge about the competing values of economically disadvantaged families; interpersonal confrontations with attitudes toward the poor (Toporek & Pope-Davis, 2005); the belief in academic dogma, which discourages interdisciplinary team approaches (Bemak,

1998); and Western values regarding mental health (Marsella & Pedersen, 2004) contribute to underserving those in poverty.

There is nothing more contraindicative to the therapeutic process than inserting an intervention that is fundamentally flawed because it assumes autonomy when in fact, as Lewis and Lewis (1977) assert, counselors work with the whole person and the person's environment. An example of negligent professional behavior is the well-documented disproportionate numbers of economically disadvantaged African American boys in special education classes in school districts across the United States (Graham, 2007). School counselors, school psychologists, psychiatrists, and other helping professionals often interpret the behavior of this vulnerable population irrespective of communal or familial context. Without a holistic assessment of the child and his environment, it is no wonder why boys from low-income, urban neighborhoods are often misdiagnosed, not diagnosed, or medicated by those charged with their development and care. An alternative perspective is that children from neighborhoods with blight, violence, substandard education, a lack of developmental recreational options, and economic underdevelopment have normal reactions to abnormal circumstances. Those in privilege rarely look for alternative explanations that do not assume status quo standards and patterns of behavior.

Counseling interventions that provide a hand out versus a hand up also have limited utility when working with the poor. Myers and Gill (2004) suggest an empowerment approach to the vicious cycle of poverty by acknowledging the complexity in which poverty influences physical, mental, and social health, particularly for women in rural areas. The authors assert that the experience of poverty and near poverty includes economic deprivation, low education, and unemployment, which creates a self-perpetuation that places those in this economic status at greater risk for health-compromising behaviors. Poverty as a self-perpetuating cycle introduces language that offers the possibility of altering the cycle with the appropriate intervention approach. Strength-based assessment of support networks, developing personal wellness plans, family counseling, and advocacy by mental health professionals for fair and just governmental and organizational policies could improve service delivery to those in poverty (Myers & Gill, 2004). Boyd-Franklin (1989) asserts that counselors working with poor families should be empowering agents as families navigate the maze of social services.

Counseling the poor requires an acknowledgment that old pedagogy and approaches need revision. In many ways, the profession must admit that it has contributed to creating the underserved by maintaining methods that only serve the few who fit its parameters. The true challenge to the profession in meeting the counseling needs of the abject poor and others socially and economically marginalized is in recreating itself for the social and economic realities of the 21st century in America. Revising professional language, graduate training, and service-delivery models are given as examples of the needed professional changes to make counseling relevant to the masses.

The growing rate of abject poverty in this country poses several opportunities and challenges for the counseling profession. The opportunity is in returning to the roots of the counseling profession as social-change advocates for the exploited and socially marginalized. The challenge is in embracing an internationalization of counseling (Marsella & Pedersen, 2004) and redefining the counseling profession by confronting status quo counselor educators (Bemak, 1998) who tacitly support the maintenance of the status quo. Professional counselors in the face of the growing chasm between the haves and have-nots in America are poised to serve multiple roles for those in abject poverty. Poverty no longer has a stereotypical face, gender, ethnic group, or location. The challenge for counselors in meeting the diverse needs of this rapidly growing population is gaining the skills to competently serve a population that has historically been underrepresented. This challenge presents an opportunity to engage in professional introspection, address the gaps in training, and develop new strategies for serving the growing number of Americans in poverty.

PREPARING TO SERVE THE UNDERSERVED: ADDRESSING THE LIMITATIONS OF THE PROFESSION

The creation of the underserved by the counseling profession is a result of inadequate training for counselors working with the economically disadvantaged (Hargrove & Breazeale, 1993); inequitable insurance reimbursement policies (DeLeon, Wakefield, Schultz, Williams, & VandenBos, 1989); stigmatization of the poor as lazy, unwilling to individually change, and morally deviant (Brown, 2002); limited and conservative interpretation of professional ethics codes (Caldwell & Tarver, 2003); and a misinterpretation of their value systems as deficient because they are different than the economically advantaged, status quo professional (Human & Wasem, 1991). In addition, professional narcissism may cause some practitioners to perceive working with the poor as a matter for social work or social services professionals. These limitations could be addressed by (a) expanding the theoretical assumptions and (b) language of the professional counselors, (c) modernizing counselor training programs by including specific coursework addressing the needs of the poor and disenfranchised, and (d) creating alternative forms of service delivery to meet the needs of the poor.

Theoretical Assumptions

The cultural encapsulation and ethnocentrism of counseling theories have exposed their limitations for contemporary society, especially ethnic and culturally underrepresented groups. Most major counseling textbooks, if not specific to multicultural counseling, begin with a caveat that the "traditional canon" of counseling theories must be applied with special considerations for these groups. Most textbooks offer a section at the end of each chapter discussing a theory's limitations with minorities, women, and the underserved. Despite these obvious shortcomings—for example, assumptions of economic privilege, autonomy, and individualism—the traditional canon remains as the standard for which even integrative and constructionist theories are derived. Retrofitted theories adapted for application to the poor and underserved perpetuate the rampant cultural encapsulation hindering the appeal of professional counseling to a wider range of those in need.

Even multicultural counseling theorists have been scant in their development of culturally authentic theories describing human behavior, the nature of maladjustment, and intervention approaches from a non-Western perspective. Parham (2005), for example, offers an edited volume of African-centered interpretations of human nature and therapeutic approaches. Yet the work of these scholars is relegated to supplemental reading even in graduate programs where a majority of the counseling services are rendered to African Americans. If the underserved and economically disadvantaged are ever to be served by professional counselors' theories emerging from their experiences, the theories must be mainstream not peripheral. Although many are still being utilized, the language and approaches are applied as an afterthought for ethnic minorities and economically disadvantaged populations.

Language

Lewis and Lewis (1977) describe the devaluing process when the privileged and powerful (e.g., professional counselors) provide the language for labels describing segments of the population in terms of their quality or condition. The labels often carry an assumption of limited worth. Disabled, impoverished, impaired, minority, single mother, homeless, and deviant are examples of labels replete in the literature that conjure an emotional response, which may preemptively establish a dispositional response by counselors serving these populations. Professional counseling jargon can distance counselors from clients by placing stigmatizing labels on people. Creating language that does not stigmatize or pathologize would demonstrate that all people, despite their economic condition, are valuable and deserve dignity. Counselors should adopt and create strength-based language that does not pathologize or dehumanize those in poverty.

Counselors serving the poor have to become professionally multilingual in order to participate in interdisciplinary service delivery teams. Conversing with school, community, and vocational counselors, in addition to social workers and primary health care physicians, is an expected skill for those serving the poor.

Counselor Education

Counselor education programs are the conduits for transmitting the values of the profession. They produce providers of counseling services. If poverty is increasing in prevalence, more diverse in its location, and more complex than in previous generations, it seems prudent to expect graduate programs to adjust to the demands of its consumers—contemporary society. Counselor education must be made relevant beyond the status quo. Thus, counselor education faculty need continuing education in order to spark a revolution of thought and training to revise training models to meet the demands of the changing demographics. Changing programs from traditional and static models (i.e., scientist–practitioner) to contemporary or dynamic models (i.e., scholar–activist) requires an identity transformation for some and a rejuvenation of the spirit for others. The ultimate goal of such a suggestion is to produce culturally confident scholars–activists who can take on the diverse roles of helpers as they participate in the broader public health mission. One example is increasing the presence of the training program in the community, especially in hard-hit economic areas. One of the biggest challenges for academicians is to include this aspect of their professional responsibilities into their service requirement and then develop a personal posture that can appreciate this level of outreach to some of the most deserving members of the community (C. M. Ellis, personal communication, November 19, 2007).

Service Delivery Models

A consequence of cultural encapsulation is counseling intervention methods and models that are consistent with the cultural norms of the status quo. For example, the hours of operation for most community mental health agencies is what is considered a normal work day between the hours of 8 a.m. and 6 p.m. The limitations of these hours for shift workers or low-income families with limited options for child care render these services practically inaccessible. Developing culturally consistent alternatives to status quo service delivery could mitigate the numbers of underserved and increase the likelihood of counseling service utilization by those currently underrepresented. Alternative forms of service delivery include a mobile therapy facilitated in a recreational vehicle parked in a mutually agreeable safe place in proximity to help seekers or altering the counselor time from a 50-minute individual session in an office to a 2-hour support network in naturalistic settings for clients (i.e., around a kitchen table). Creativity can provide opportunities for professional counselors to maintain an ethical standard of care and serve those that require different approaches to match their value systems.

Focus groups of nonusers to assess the appropriateness of policies and practices by agencies will help make the distinction between perceived access (where the agency believes its policies are inclusive) and real access (where the end users have determined that the practices are not culturally consistent). From payment options to interpretations of ethics codes, particularly dual relationships (see Caldwell & Tarver, 2003; Parham & Caldwell, 2006), service providers need to engage in self-scrutiny and dismantle barriers to serving the economically disadvantaged.

Interdisciplinary approaches to service delivery may provide the creative boost needed to develop alternative forms of service delivery to reach the underserved. Bemak (1998) offers 17 guiding principles to promote interdisciplinary collaboration for counselors and asserts that interdisciplinary collaboration is a powerful tool for engaging in social and political change. One such important collaboration is with that of the larger public health community, which is almost rarely mentioned in the counseling literature. The fact is that much of the policy regarding mental health, poverty reduction, and health and human services is more generally addressed in the public health literature (i.e., health promotion, health behavior, human services, etc.). Counseling's exclusion of this language in its theories, training, research, and interventions has marginalized such contributions as multicultural counseling. The issues confronting those in poverty are far more expansive than the culture-bound assumptions of the counseling profession, for example, (a) egocentricity of the self, (b) mind–body dualism, (c) culture is an imposition on biological presuppositions (Lewis-Fernandez & Kleinman, 1994). Because poor families are often in need of several different types of social services, it is important that counselors are willing to learn new professional languages and build information-sharing collaboratives with other professionals that are in the best interests of their clients.

STRATEGIES FOR COUNSELING THOSE IN POVERTY

The following list of strategies are in no way exhaustive but are offered as starting points for introspection and action for counselors. The strategies are organized as points for practitioners, counselor educators, and researchers.

Acknowledge Economic Privilege

The call for self-awareness is consistent throughout the multicultural, social action, and social justice literatures. Awareness of how one's economic status and history influences attitudes and behaviors toward the poor and underrepresented is an essential first step to improving the quality of care to underserved populations. The goals of counseling those in poverty are no different than in counseling the economically privileged. People either are instructed to seek our services to enter into a process to regain balance in their life, change a behavior, or search for a deeper meaning of unconscious experiences; or to protect themselves from being marginalized. However, those with privilege have different access points than those without. The sooner we can see the commonalities between our expression of the human experience beyond behaviors, the better equipped we are to embrace the humanness in all our clients and the communities in which they live.

A constructive acknowledgement of economic privilege will help counselors understand their family history of privilege, oppression, resilience, and transformation. The purpose is not to produce guilt-laden reactionary behaviors but to afford counselors the opportunity to explore and assess their disposition toward those in poverty and the underrepresented. Collison et al. (1998) offer a personal decision-making process for counselors to examine their disposition toward social advocacy. This process can also be very helpful in examining a helping professional's disposition toward the economically disadvantaged. Counselors should always be aware of their biases and assumptions.

Prepare for Multiple Roles

The role of a counselor for those in poverty must be dynamic and flexible. This may test one's interpretation of the professional codes of ethics, but, as Caldwell and Tarver (2003) suggests, conservative reads of the professional guidelines tacitly support status quo interventions and contribute to the increasing numbers of underserved or ill-served.

Economically disadvantaged clients in many cases are saturated with social services that oftentimes conflict or contradict. Boyd-Franklin (1989) suggests that counselors conduct an eco-map, which helps the families navigate the multiple systems. Be prepared to take on roles in which you have no official training, in addition to being flexible enough to learn from your clients and other human service providers. Counselors may find themselves empowering clients by supporting and role-playing communications with social service, governmental, or nonclinical third parties.

Build Interdisciplinary Coalitions and Collaboratives

Rejecting the myth that counselors and psychologists have sole possession of answers to the meaning of life and the end of human suffering is fundamental to building interdisciplinary coalitions and collaborations. The silo approach promoted and perpetuated by academia is not only inefficient, it is also ineffective. As a thought-provoking illustration, imagine if counselors were to agree that the eradication of poverty was a central issue in improving the United State's public health. Who else would need to be at the table to discuss the mental health consequences of substandard housing, poor neonatal care, unemployment, accessibility to quality health care, and so on? Academic tribalism will relegate individual disciplines, even within the helping professions, to irrelevant for real social change.

The critical element is building relationships with other helping professionals. It's amazing that this needs to be a statement, but it is all too common to engage in discipline-based dogma. Counseling practitioners should attend other professional conferences as presenters and students to mutually benefit service delivery to vulnerable populations. Building service delivery coalitions with social workers, the reality of multiple tasks and roles will require relationship-building skills with professional and nonprofessional staff.

Consider the Influence of Gender and Race

Gender, race, and ethnicity are usually somewhere present in our discussion of social issues. This recommendation similar to the aforementioned obligates counselors and counselor educators to be aware of their race- and gender-based attributions of poverty (see Toporek & Pope-Davis, 2005). Research supports that women, particularly minority women, are overrepresented in poverty statistics. Gender is particularly important in treating the underserved because men, particularly minority, have historically been underrepresented in the counseling literature. The multiple oppressions of being poor and of minority status produce several levels of emotional distress with health and behavioral consequences (Bryant-Davis, 2007). For example, a chronically under-employed, economically disadvantaged African American male job searching in the rural South may be experiencing frustration with the lack of career opportunities as a result of an underfunded educational system. In addition, he may feel equally oppressed by a labor market that has historically engaged in discriminatory hiring practices. A counselor must be willing to explore the client's experiences with all forms of oppression.

Demand Nonstatus Quo Training Experiences

Students should demand practical experiences that are inclusive of nonstatus quo clients in interdisciplinary settings. The only way to prepare for the real world is to train in the real world. Although there are programs that have begun to address alternative ways of training their students, counselor education faculty need to continue to develop meaningful and cutting-edge options for their students to gain explor-atory experiences in social justice and action.

Represent the Underserved with Research

The poor and underserved are underrepresented in the literature for the following reasons: (a) status quo faculty orientations; (b) accessing the poor requires full community engagement, which is not the norm for most faculty; (c) they require multiple methods of data collection because of variability in literacy, comfort with researchers, and an assortment of other issues that are not present in gathering information from economically privileged (i.e., computer access); and (d) it takes time to build trusting relationships to gain permission to gather infor-mation. Counselors committed to social action and social justice must be versed in multiple and mixed methodologies. An entire research career can be made of validity studies on popular measures normed and validated on economically privileged samples. In addition, several qualitative studies are warranted to fully understand the phenomenon of poverty and the resulting behaviors. Embarking on such a research agenda fills a large void in the counseling literature.

THE FAMILY POTENTIAL CENTER: SOCIAL ACTION FROM THEORY TO PRAXIS

The Family Potential Center (FPC) was developed to address the skills gap in multicultural and vulnerable population counseling training in an American Psychological Association-accredited program in a small,

Midwestern city. The program offered master's degrees in school and community counseling, in addition to a PhD in counseling psychology. Although faculty of one program developed the FPC, the entire department participated in the training and intervention efforts. The FPC was developed as a partnership with a nonprofit social service organization (SSO) that delivered a range of social services, including English language classes for refugees, a food bank, transportation assistance, utility assistance, youth intervention, head start administration, and computer literacy classes.

Language

The title of the FPC was carefully chosen to demonstrate a nonpathologizing or deficiency-based philosophical foundation. By referencing *family potential* versus clinic, the counseling center alerted the community and service providers that there was a broader range of helping services. The term *potential* was chosen to demonstrate that all families can strive to function better by engaging in potential maximizing and minimizing activities.

Location

The FPC was located on the site of the SSO. Five offices (four small and one large for group and training meetings) were allocated for the FPC, which were fully equipped with audio/videotaping equipment. The A/V equipment was purchased as part of a grant from a local community foundation. The SSO building was over 10,000 square feet and had parking for over 100 vehicles including staff.

Curriculum Infusion

The FPC was infused into the counseling curriculum. In addition to inclusion in the practicum sequence, faculty of the core counseling classes included readings and discussions about counseling the FPC clients. Reading in such areas as social justice, counseling poor, action research, and multicultural counseling were used as foundational knowledge and prerequisites for the FPC practicum.

Service Delivery Model

The FPC utilized a prevention intervention model that sought to meet families and youth in activities in which they were already engaged. Psychoeducational groups were the primary intervention model that would often lead to individual or family counseling interventions. Feedback from case managers, parents, youth, and other stakeholders was used to develop intervention titles, content, and schedules to address issues in psychoeducational groups. The interventions were conducted as workshops and forums. The workshops were the introduction to counseling concepts and a method of relationship building for all stakeholders.

Faculty Engagement

In addition to infusing curriculum content, the counseling program's faculty also provided counseling supervision to students, facilitated workshops, and conducted program evaluations for other programs in the SSO. The counseling faculty program was integrated into the SSO as an advocate and consultant for programs and staff development.

Professional Training

The FPC required students to confront their own biases about underserved and underrepresented community members. It was not uncommon for a student to provide services to a homeless person, a single-parent mother in poverty, a woman in a work release program, a United Nations resettled refugee from the Sudan, or a high school dropout struggling to stay focused on attaining a GED. Students were challenged to take on several roles and work with multiple offices in the city's and county's social service and health communities. Advocacy was a major theme in the training experience. Of importance to the training model was that counseling did not happen in a vacuum. It should also be noted that doctoral-level counseling psychology students also had practicum in the FPC and would serve as supervisors for counseling students.

Research

Two dissertations, several course papers, and professional conference presentations were developed as a result of the FPC experience. An empowerment evaluation approach was utilized with the SSO. Students involved in the program evaluation process were responsible for developing protocols, collecting data, using mixed methods, conducting the analysis, and facilitating an interpretation session with the program staff of the SSO. This model, although laborious, often vetted stronger programs for the SSO staff and eventually its grant proposals.

CONCLUSION

The FPC is a model of infusing social action into counselor and psychologist training. If the counseling profession is to have a *sankofa* (the West African concept of going forward while fetching the past) experience, then it must begin to address its training models. The status quo training that dominates counselor education will continue to perpetuate a counseling profession that underserves and underrepresents the poor. Poverty has its disadvantages and challenges, which should not be invisibile to the counseling profession. Social action and social justice rhetoric in the counseling profession must be moved to deliberate action. Counselors and other mental health professionals are integral parts of the public health of this country. It is our time to acknowledge the faces at the bottom of the well and greet them not with flashlights but with ladders.

REFERENCES

Armstrong, K. L. (2007). Advancing social justice by challenging economic disadvantage. In C. C. Lee (Ed.), *Counseling for social justice* (2nd ed.). Alexandria, VA: American Counseling Association.

Bell, D. (1992). *Faces at the bottom of the well: The permanence of racism.* New York: Basic Books.

Bemak, F. (1998). Interdisciplinary collaboration for social change redefining the counseling profession. In C. C. Lee and G. R. Walz (Eds.), *Social action: A mandate for counselors* (pp. 279–292). Alexandria, VA: American Counseling Association.

Boyd-Franklin, N. (1989). *Black family in therapy: A multisystems approach.* New York: Guildford.

Brown, S. L. (2002). We are, therefore I am: A multisystems approach with families in poverty. *The Family Journal: Counseling and Therapy for Couples and Families, 10*(4), 405–409.

Bryant-Davis, T. (2007). Healing requires recognition: The case for race-based traumatic stress. *The Counseling Psychologist, 35,* 135–143.

Caldwell, L. D., & Tarver, D. D. (2003). An ethical code for racial-cultural practice: Filling gaps and confronting contradictions in existing ethical guidelines. In R. Carter (Ed.), *Handbook of racial-cultural psychology and counseling: Training and practice Volume 2,* 514–527. Hoboken, NJ: Wiley.

Collison, B. B., Osborne, J. L., Gray, L. A., House, R. M., Firth, J., & Lou, M. (1998). Preparing counselors for social change. In C. C. Lee & G. R. Walz (Eds.), *Social action: A mandate for counselors* (pp. 263–277). Alexandria, VA: American Counseling Association.

DeLeon, P. H., Wakefield, M., Schultz, A. J., Williams, J., & VandenBos, G. R. (1989). Rural America: Unique opportunities for health care delivery and health services research. *American Psychologist, 44,* 1298–1306.

Graham, T. S. (2007). *Race and referrals: Teacher attitudes, culturally relevant teaching, and the special education referrals of African American males.* Doctoral dissertation, Cambridge College, Massachusetts.

Hargrove, D. S., & Breazeale, R. L. (1993). Psychologists and rural services: Addressing a new agenda. *Professional Psychology: Research and Practice, 24,* 319–324.

Harper, F. D., Harper, J. A., & Stills, A. B. (2003). Counseling children in crisis based on Maslow's hierarchy of basic needs. *International Journal for the Advancement of Counseling, 23,* 11–24.

Human, J., & Wasem, C. (1991). Rural mental health in America. *American Psychologist, 46,* 232–239.

Lewis, J. A., & Lewis, M. D. (1977). *Community counseling: A human services approach.* New York: Wiley.

Lewis-Fernandez, R., & Kleinman, A. (1994). Culture, personality and psychopathology. *Journal of Abnormal Psychology, 103,* 67–71.

Marsella, A. J., & Pedersen, P. (2004). Internationalizing the counseling psychology curriculum: Toward new values, competencies, and directions. *Counseling Psychology Quarterly, 17,* 413–423.

Myers, J. E., & Gill, C. S. (2004). Poor, rural and female: Under-studied, under-counseled, more at-risk. *Journal of Mental Health Counseling, 26*(3), 225–242.

Myers, J. E., Sweeny, T. J., & Witmer, J. M. (2000). Counseling for wellness: A holistic model for treatment planning. *Journal of Counseling and Development, 78,* 251–266.

Parham, T. A. (2002). *Counseling persons of African descent.* Thousand Oaks, CA: Sage.

Parham, T. A., & Caldwell, L. D. (2006). An African centered perspective on dual relationships: Revisited. In B. Herlihy & G. Corey (Eds.), *Boundary issues in counseling: Multiple roles and responsibilities* (2nd ed.). Alexandria, VA: American Counseling Association.

Toldson, I. A., & Scott, E. L. (2006). *Poverty, race, and Policy: Strategic advancement of a poverty reduction agenda* (Congressional Black Caucus Foundation). Washington, DC: Center for Policy Analysis and Research.

Toporek, R. L., & Pope-Davis, D. (2005). Exploring the relationships between multicultural training, racial attitudes, and attributions of poverty among graduate counseling trainees. *Cultural Diversity and Ethnic Minority Psychology, 11*(3), 259–271.

World Health Organization. (2001). The vicious cycle of poverty and mental disorders. *The World Health Report 2001.* Retrieved June 29, 2002, from http://www.who.int/whr/2001/main/en/figures1.4htm

Wrenn, C. G. (1982). The culturally encapsulated counselor. *Harvard Educational Review, 32,* 444–449.

U.S. Census Bureau (2006). *Poverty: Overview.* Retrieved July 31, 2006, from http://www.census.gov/hhes/www/poverty/overview.html.

13

THE NEXT STEP

Cyrus Marcellus Ellis and Jon Carlson

Like life, racial understanding is not something that we find but something that we must create. And so the ability of Negroes and whites to work together, to understand each other, will not be found readymade; it must be created by the fact of contact.

—Rev. Dr. Martin Luther King, Jr.

Completing a study into cross-cultural awareness and social justice can leave your mind full of a wealth of information. An additional question that can be raised following a study into cross-cultural awareness and social justice is "Now what do I do?" As you read this text, the information that the contributors have provided are not intended to be just words on a page. The professional and scholarly work of each contributor is a call to action for all people who are mentally and communally aligned with being a part of the solution when it comes to basic human liberties. As the information in this text can challenge our thoughts, affirm our posture concerning diversity, or upset our emotions concerning fairness and legitimacy, helping professionals need to be focused and purposeful when engaging in the world as an advocate for societal change. As a next step, we will provide some thoughts that ought to help the intentionality of one's actions based on the awareness and information this text provides.

What often gets missed during this process of examination into cultural and societal differences is how the person is not just becoming a better professional, but the person is becoming an instrument for change. Each helping professional's knowledge and skills concerning cross-culturalism and social justice is an instrument that impacts our world just as a scalpel in the hand of a skilled surgeon impacts the body of a patient. There are three thoughts that need to be presented in order for the helping professional to have closure with our text as well as being able to launch into becoming an social advocate: forming your instrument, perception versus apperception, and understanding culture.

FORMING YOUR INSTRUMENT

Forming your instrument as a cross-culturally competent and socially just counseling professional involves laying a foundation for how you make sense of the world in areas that do not necessarily correspond to your way of thinking, believing, and acting. Many professional helpers are aware of the importance of evaluating the self in relationship to others as well as articulating one's chosen method of counseling, but putting into words your posture of relating to the cultural milieu of the world around you is a different task. Attempting to define your path toward cross-cultural awareness can be difficult. Such a journey requires each individual to "take off the mask" and show the true self.

Kottler (1993) in his text *On Being a Therapist* recognizes that the commitment to becoming a helper is a commitment to change, whether we like it or not. This statement underscores helping professionals' need to grow, but it also implies that we need to grow concerning differences of race, gender, class, and ability. As it is in the Multicultural Counseling Competencies (Arrendondo, 1998; Arrendondo & Arciniega, 2001), the ability to recognize potential biases when working with culturally different clients is paramount to our understanding of how we are able to perceive others' sense of love, family, law and order, and faith and spirituality to name a few. All of us will be tested in our ability to be sincere and authentic as we approach the lived condition of our diverse clients.

The method of qualitative inquiry is a guide for how helping professionals can form their instrument. Patton's (1990) work in developing qualitative research designs underscored the important role that paradigms play in making sense of societal phenomena. Developing your instrument is inclusive of Patton's posture by acknowledging the abundance of paradigms that shape our perceptions of events and people. The key for helping professionals is to first be on familiar terms with the reality that your developed, unfiltered paradigm is not the beginning of your ability to understand and evaluate others. The first step is to know that your "lens" is dependent upon what you hold onto or grow from when you are attempting to prove or disprove a particular phenomenon or attempting to understand the complexity of the phenomenon under investigation (Patton, 1990). The following questions can qualitatively address the formation of your instrument as it relates to cross-cultural information:

1. Where has my information about cultural differences come from?
2. What is my fundamental belief about the problems facing the poor, minorities, and people constantly wanting justice?
3. Do I see diversity as an asset or as a liability?
4. Am I an advocate that prefers to stay out of the limelight and am I willing to share space with the people who have been historically oppressed and shunned?

A sound cross-cultural and socially just instrument involves an accurate knowledge of self, but, more importantly, it involves a conscious effort to expand one's awareness of the murky depths of people existing on the other side of what is accepted as established society (West, 1993). Developing your self as an instrument through the information presented in this text has the ability to integrate your training experiences and substantive study to create a cross-cultural and socially just personal and professional posture concerning the lived experience of people attempting to work through the dissonance of their conditions.

PERCEPTION VERSUS APPERCEPTION

Perception is defined as recognizing and interpreting stimuli based chiefly on your memory of that stimuli; conversely, apperception is a process of understanding new phenomena through your past experiences. Being consciously aware of these two constructs can be the helper's filter to serve as a point of detection when contact is made between the helper and the client. In order to grasp the power of the material of this text and how it is infused into practice and training, the precise nature of these two terms and how they form your cultural outlook regarding the structure and impact of race-based human interaction are very important. Building cross-cultural competence involves the ability to distinguish if your ability to comprehend racial, gender, and other differences is through what you have encountered, or is it by what you understand about people and situations that is understood and acted upon based solely on the wealth or lack of wealth of your past experiences. In order to create a process to uncover if your manner of interpreting cultural awareness is a product of your perceptions or apperceptions, answer the following questions:

1. Do I have direct experiences of race, gender, social class, and other differences?
2. Although I am trained to see differences, do I lack any real connection to people who are different?
3. Do I stop short of investigating the lived experience of people because I make up my mind before I hear another person's narrative?
4. Am I all right with some calls for justice and equity and do I dismiss for others the claim for fairness too quickly based on my core beliefs?
5. How do I understand the structural consequences and corresponding behaviors of the dominant culture to historic inequities in society such as Jim Crow laws, genderism, homophobia, and anti-Semitism that shape the way people respond to the world they live in?
6. If I acknowledge that I may not know or have experienced the "actual" experience of culturally diverse people, am I willing to silence my apperceptive tendencies and begin to develop direct experiences to the myriad of conflicting thoughts, feelings, and beliefs of the culturally diverse?

UNDERSTANDING CULTURE

Many years ago W. E. B. DuBois (1903/1993) wrote a question that has remained a central theme for examining the impact of acculturation and assimilation for people in this land. In DuBois' work *The Souls of Black Folk* he posed a question: "What does it feel like to be a problem?" (p. 7). It is a powerful question that ought to be included in the social justice and cross-cultural literature. The question raised by DuBois is like asking what does it feel like to live inside of an ism (i.e., racism, sexism, genderism, ageism, ableism, etc.). There is a myriad of issues faced by individuals who live inside of a world where their morality, loyalty, patriotism, faith, and fidelity are called into question by their very existence. The answer to DuBois' question of what it feels like to be a problem is somewhat unanswerable. DuBois' answer of what it feels like to be a problem is that those of us who understand this feeling tend not to respond. DuBois did one more thing for us: he understood culture not by race, believe it or not, but by how culture is divided and why we fight over it. DuBois said the following to recognize American culture:

> In the civilized life of to-day the contact of men and their relations to each other fall in a few main lines of action and communication;

there is first physical proximity of homes and dwelling places ... [second] there are economic relations ... [which means] the production of wealth, the meeting of wants ... [third] there are political relations ... [that is to say] the cooperation in social control ... laying and paying the burden of taxation ... [fourth] there are the less tangible but highly important forms of intellectual contact and commerce ... [which is] the interchange of ideas through conversation and conference [in common places]. (p. 118)

Culture, then, is more than just mores and customs. It is how we assemble and share space for the exchange of ideas; it is how we commune with one another; and it is how we share in the development and direction of purpose for ourselves, others, and our public and private institutions.

Alfred Adler was talking about social justice in the early stages of psychotherapy. Somewhere these ideas were lost. He talked about the importance of social interests and equality. He stated that true social interest or community feeling involved a sense of belonging and connectedness to others, empathy, caring, compassion, and acceptance of others. He stated that healthy people have high levels of social interest. Although these ideas are almost 100 years old they are finally coming to fruition.

THE PATH BEFORE YOU

This text has included in it an appendix that lists the organizations and people who have made advocacy their work. We encourage you to call them, speak with them and determine for yourself if you will reach beyond your comfort zone and join them if their cause and your sense of self are aligned. Although these lists were created some time ago, it is sure that they are available to you now. We encourage all of you to reach out to those who are in need of your particular talents. By building a grassroots coalition of those who are like-minded we can begin to impact our communities for the better.

May all people benefit from our help and guidance.

REFERENCES

Arredondo, P. (1998). Integrating multicultural counseling competencies and universal helping conditions in culture-specific contexts: Reconceptualizing multicultural counseling. *Counseling Psychologist, 26,* 592–602.

Arredondo, P., & Arciniega, G. M. (2001). Strategies and techniques for counselor training based on the multicultural counseling competencies. *Journal of Multicultural Counseling & Development, 29*, 263–273.

Du Bois, W. E. B. (1993). *The souls of Black folk.* New York: Everyman's Library. (Original work published 1903)

King, Coretta Scott (1996). *The words of Martin Luther King Jr.* (2nd ed.). New York: Newmarket Press.

Kottler, J. A. (1993). *On being a therapist* (Rev. ed.). San Francisco: Jossey-Bass.

Patton, M. Q. (1990). *Qualitative evaluation and research methods* (2nd ed). Newbury Park, CA: Sage.

West, C. (1993). *Race matters.* Boston: Beacon Press.

APPENDIX: RESOURCES

GAYS AND LESBIANS

Communities United Against Violence (since 1979)
www.cuav.org
info@cuav.org

170 A. Capp Street
San Francisco, CA 94110
415-777-5500
415-333-HELP (24-hour support line)

CUAV offers crisis intervention, counseling, advocacy, and support for gay men and lesbians in abusive relationships.

Families Like Ours, Inc. (since 2000)
www.adoptionfamilycenter.org

David Wing-Kovarik (Executive Director)

PO Box 2311
877-230-3055

Reduce barriers faced mainly by gay and lesbian adoptive/foster families by connecting families and professionals to a network of resources, support, education, and advocacy.

International Lesbian and Gay Association (since 1978)
www.ilga.org

Rosanna Flamer-Caldera (Board Member)

17 Rue de la Charity
1210 Brussels
Belgium
+32-2-502 24 71

Worldwide network of national and local groups dedicated to achieving equal rights for lesbian, gay, bisexual, and transgender and intersex (LGBTI) people everywhere.

Human Rights Campaign (since 1980)
www.hrc.org
hrc@hrc.org

1640 Rhode Island Ave. NW
Washington, DC 20036-3278
202-393-5177

Human Rights Campaign maintains the largest full-time lobbying team in the nation devoted to issues of fairness for lesbian, gay, bisexual, and transgendered Americans.

National Gay and Lesbian Task Force (since 1979)
www.thetaskforce.org
theTaskForce@thetaskforce.org

Mark M. Sexton or Alan T. Acosta
325 Massachusetts Ave. NW
Washington, DC 20009
202-393-5177

Builds the grassroots power of the lesbian, gay, bisexual, and transgender (LGBT) community by training activists, equipping state and local organizations with the skills needed to organize broad-based campaigns to defeat anti-LGBT referenda and advance pro-LGBT legislation, and building the organizational capacity of the movement.

National Youth Advocacy Coalition (since 1997)
www.nyacyouth.org
nyac@nyacyouth.org

Laura Crustsinger-Perry (Director of Health Programs)
lara@nacyouth.org

1638 R Street NW, Ste 300
Washington, DC 20009
202-319-7596
800-541-6922

Social justice organization that advocates for and with young people who are lesbian, gay, bisexual, transgender, or questioning (LGBTQ) in an effort to end discrimination against these youth and to ensure their physical and emotional well-being.

International Gay and Lesbian Human Rights Commission
www.iglhrc.org
iglhrc@iglhrc.org

80 Maiden Lane, Ste. 1505
New York, NY 10038

Secure the full enjoyment of the human rights of all people and communities subject to discrimination or abuse on the basis of sexual orientation or expression, gender identity or expression, and/or HIV/AIDS status.

Gay and Lesbian Advocates and Defenders (since 1978)
www.glad.org
gladlaw@glad.org

Lee Swishlow (Executive Director)

30 Winter Street, Ste 800
Boston, MA 02108
617-426-1350

New England's leading legal rights organization dedicated to ending discrimination based on sexual orientation, HIV status, and gender identity and expression.

THE POOR

Advocacy for the Poor (since 1998)
www.advocacyforthepoor.org

Reverend Ginny N. Britt (Executive Director)
ginny@advocacyforthepoor.org

608 Summit St., Ste. 4
Winston-Salem, NC 27101
336-725-6155

Exists to focus attention on issues related to economic independence for the poor of Forsyth County, representing their interests, and working for systemic change.

National Center for Law and Economic Justice (since 1965)
www.nclej.org
wlc@welfarelaw.org

275 Seventh Ave., Ste 1506
New York, NY 10001-6708
212-633-6967

Advances the cause of economic justice for low-income families, individuals, and communities across the country.

National Coalition for the Homeless (since 1982)
www.nationalhomeless.org
info@nationalhomeless.org

2201 P. St. NW
Washington, DC 20037
202-462-4822

Mission is to end homelessness, by engaging in public education, policy advocacy, and grassroots organizing.

National Housing Institute (since 1975)
www.nhi.org

John Atlas (Board President)

460 Bloomfield Ave., Ste 211
Montclair, NJ 07042-3552
973-509-2888

Examines the issues causing the crisis in housing and community in America. It examines key issues affecting affordable housing and community development practitioners and their supporters.

Poor People's Economic Human Rights Campaign (since 1998)
www.economichumanrights.org
info@economichumanrights.org

C/O KWRU
PO Box 50678
Philadelphia, PA 19132
888-233-1984

Unite the poor across color lines as the leadership base for a broad movement to abolish poverty.

THE DISABLED

American Association for People with Disabilities (since 1995)
www.aapd-dc.org

Andrew J. Imparato (President and CEO)

1629 K Street NW, Ste 503
Washington, DC 20006
800-840-8844

The largest national nonprofit cross-disability member organization in the United States, dedicated to ensuring economic self-sufficiency and political empowerment for the more than 56 million Americans with disabilities.

Americans Disabled for Attendant Programs Today
www.adapt.org
national@adapt.org

Babs Johnson

201 S. Cherokee
Denver, CO 80223
303-733-9324

Fighting so people with disabilities can live in the community with real supports instead of being locked away in nursing homes and other institutions.

The Arc of the United States (since 1950)
www.thearc.org
info@thearc.org

Mary V. Jordan (President)

1010 Wayne Ave., Ste 650
Silver Spring, MD 20910
301-565-3843

Works to include all children and adults with cognitive, intellectual, and developmental disabilities in every community.

Bazelon Center for Mental Health (since 1972)
www.bazelon.org
info@bazelon.org

Robert Bernstein (Executive Director)

1101 15th St. NW, Ste. 1212
Washington, DC 20005-5002
202-467-5730

Protect and advance the rights of adults and children with
mental disabilities to exercise meaningful life choices and
to enjoy the social, recreational, educational, economic,
political, and cultural benefits of community living.

Disability Rights Education and Defense Fund (since 1979)
www.dredf.org
info@dredf.org

Beverly Bertaina (President)

1730 M. St. NW, Ste 801
Washington, DC 20036
800-348-4232

National law and policy center dedicated to protecting and
advancing the civil rights of people with disabilities through
legislation, litigation, advocacy, technical assistance, and
education and training.

National Organization on Disability (since 1981)
www.nod.org
ability@nod.org

Michael R. Deland (President)

910 16th St. NW
Washington, DC 20006
202-293-5960

Expand the participation and contribution of America's 54
million men and women and children with disabilities in
all aspects of life.

TASH (since 1975)
www.tash.org
info@tash.org

Barbara Trader (Executive Director)
btrader@tash.org
202-263-5601

1025 Vermont Ave. NW, 7th Floor
Washington, DC 20005
202-263-5600

Focuses on those at most risk for being excluded from the
mainstream society, are perceived to be the most challenging, and most likely to have their rights abridged.

NATIVE AMERICANS

American Indian Movement (since 1973)
www.aimovement.org
AIMGCC@wrldnett.att

PO Box 13521
Minneapolis, MN 55414
612-721-3914

Pledged to fight White Man's injustice to Indians, his oppression, persecution, discrimination, and malfeasance in the
handling of Indian Affairs. AIM will be there to help the
Native People regain human rights and achieve restitutions
and restorations.

National Congress of American Indians
www.ncai.org
ncai@ncai.org

Joe Garcia (President)
mistylake@cybermesa.com

1301 Connecticut Ave. NW, Ste. 200
Washington, DC 20036
202-466-7767

Inform the public and the federal government on tribal self-
government, treaty rights, and a broad range of federal
policy issues affecting tribal governments.

National Indian Counsel in Aging (since 1976)
www.nicoa.org

10501 Montgomery Blvd. NE, Ste. 210
Albuquerque, NM 87111-3486
505-292-2001

Bring improved comprehensive services for American Indian and Alaska Native Elders.

Native American Rights Fund
www.narf.org
pereiar@narf.org

John E. Echohawk (President)

1506 Broadway
Boulder, CO 80302-6296
303-447-7860

Preservation of tribal existence, protection of tribal natural resources, promotion of Native American human rights, accountability of governments to the Native Americans, development of Indian law, and educating the public about Indian rights, laws, and issues.

ASIAN AMERICANS

Asian American Justice Center (since 1991)
www.advancingequality.org

Karen K. Nagasaki (President)

1140 Connecticut Ave. NW, Ste 1200
Washington, DC 20036
415-954-9988

The mission of the Asian American Justice Center is to advance the human and civil rights of Asian Americans through advocacy, public policy, public education, and litigation.

Asian and Pacific Islander American Health Forum (since 1986)
www.apiahf.org
healthinfo@apaihf.org

Dr. Ho Luong Tran (President and CEO)

450 Sutter St., Ste. 600
San Francisco, CA 94108
415-954-9988

Envisions a multicultural society where Asian and Pacific Islander communities are included and represented in all health, political, social, and economic arenas.

Japanese American Citizens League (since 1929)
www.jacl.org
jacl@jacl.org

T. Larry Oda (President)
President@jacl.org

1765 Sutler St.
San Francisco, CA 94115
415-921-5225

Protecting the rights of all segments of Asian communities.

National Asian Pacific American Women's Forum (since 1995)
www.napawf.org

Koran Ahuja (Executive Director)

6930 Carroll Ave., Ste 506
Takoma Park, MD 20912
202-293-4507 (fax)

Advancing social justice, and addressing the concerns and increasing the rights of APA women and girls.

Organization of Chinese Americans (since 1973)
www.ocanational.org
oca@ocanational.org

Ginny Gong (President)

1322 18th St. NW
Washington, DC 20036-1803
202-223-5500

National and political organization to advance the political, social, and economic well-being of Asian Pacific Americans in the United States.

HISPANIC AMERICANS

Hispanas Organized for Political Equality (since 1989)
www.latinas.org
Latinas@latinas.org

Elmy Bermejo (Chair of the Board)

634 S. Spring St., Ste 920
Los Angeles, CA 90014
213-622-0606

Ensuring political and economic parity for Latinas through leadership, advocacy, and education to benefit all communities and the status of the political process coupled with active participation will fuel a powerful and necessary engine of change.

Mexican American Legal Defense (since 1968)
www.maldef.org
info@maldef.org

John Trasvina

6 S. Spring Street, 11th Floor
Los Angeles, CA 90014
213-629-2512

Protect and promote civil rights of more than 40 million Latinos living in the United States. MALDEF works to secure the rights of Latinos, primarily in the areas of education, employment, immigrants' rights, political access, and public resource equity.

National Counsel of La Raza (since 1968)
www.nclr.org
comments@nclr.org

Janet Marguia (President)

Raul Yzaguirre Building
1126 16th St. NW
Washington DC 20036

Reduce poverty and discrimination and improve the life opportunities for Hispanic Americans.

League of Latin American Citizens (since 1929)
www.lulac.org

Brent Wilkes
bwilkes@lulac.org

2000 L St. NW, Ste 610
Washington, DC 20036
877-LULAC-01

Advance the economic condition, educational attainment, political influence, health, and civil rights of the Hispanic population of the United States.

IMMIGRATION

Center for Immigration Studies (since 1985)
www.cis.org
center@cis.org

1522 K St. NW, Ste 820
Washington, DC 20005-1202
202-466-8185

Expand the base of public knowledge and understanding of the need for an immigration policy that gives first concern to the broad national interest. The center is animated by a pro-immigrant, low-immigration vision, which seeks fewer immigrants but a warmer welcome for those admitted.

Center for Social Advocacy (since 1985)
www.centerforsocialadvocacy.org
info@c4sa.org

Russel Dehnel (Executive Director)

1068 Broadway Street, Ste. 221
El Cajon, CA 92021
800-954-0441

Long an advocate for fair housing and tenant/landlord mediation, the Center for Social Advocacy addresses diverse issues such as hate crimes, the civil rights violations experienced by newly arrived immigrants, human trafficking, youth alienation, and poverty. Through direct client services, field outreach, public education, regional, state and national policy work, and collaboration with organizations with similar missions, the Center for Social Advocacy is becoming a national leader in human and civil rights advocacy.

National Network for Immigrant and Refugee Rights (since 1986)
www.nnirr.org
nnirr@nnirr.org

Catherine Tactaquin (Executive Director)
ctactaquin@nnirr.org

310 8th St., Ste. 303
Oakland, CA 94607
510-465-1984

It serves as a forum to share information and analysis, to educate communities and the general public, and to develop and coordinate plans of action on important immigrant and refugee issues. It works to promote a just immigration and refugee policy in the United States and to defend and expand the rights of all immigrants and refugees, regardless of immigration status.

AFRICAN AMERICANS

Congressional Black Caucus Foundation (since 1976)
www.cbcfinc.org
info@cbcfinc.org

Dr. Elsie Scott (President)

720 Massachusetts Ave. NW
Washington, DC 20036
202-63-2800

The premier organization that creates, identifies, analyzes and disseminates policy-oriented information critical to advancing African Americans and people of African descent toward equity in economics, health, and education.

National Association for the Advancement of Colored People (since 1909)
www.naacp.org

Dennis Courtland Hayes (Interim Vice President and CEO)

4805 Mt. Hope Drive
Baltimore, MD 21215
877-NAACP-98

The mission of the National Association for the Advancement of Colored People is to ensure the political, educational, social, and economic equality of rights of all persons and to eliminate racial hatred and racial discrimination.

National Counsel of Negro Women (since 1935)
www.ncnw.org
ncnwinfo@ncnw.org

Dorothy I. Height (Chair and President Emerita)

633 Pennsylvania Ave. NW
Washington, DC 20004
202-737-0120

Lead, develop, and advocate for women of African descent as they support their families and communities. NCNW fulfills this purpose through research, advocacy, and national and community-based services and programs on issues of health, education, and economic empowerment in the United States and Africa.

National Urban League (since 1910)
www.nul.org
info@nul.org

Mark H. Morial

120 Wall Street
New York, NY 10005
212-558-5300

The mission of the Urban League movement is to enable African Americans to secure economic self-reliance, parity, power, and civil rights.

Rainbow/PUSH Coalition (since 1996)
www.rainbowpush.org
info@rainbowpush.org

930 E. 50th St.
Chicago, IL 60615-2702

773-373-3366

Working to move the nation and the world toward social, racial, and economic justice.

WOMEN

Equal Rights Advocates (since 1974)
www.equalrights.org
info@equalrights.org

Irma Herrera (Executive Director)

1663 Mission St., Ste 250
San Francisco, CA 94103
415-621-0672

Protect and secure equal rights and economic opportunities for women and girls.

Feminist Majority (since 1987)
www.feminist.org
femmaj@feminist.org

Eleanor Smeal (President)

1600 Wilson Blvd., Ste 801
Arlington, VA 22209
703-522-2214

Dedicated to women's equality, reproductive health, and non-violence. FMF engages in research and action to empower women economically, socially, and politically.

Independent Women's Forum (since 1976)
www.iwf.org
info@iwf.org

Michele D. Bernard (President)

1726 M St. NW, 10th Floor
Washington, DC 20005
202-419-1820

Advancing the spirit of enterprise and self-reliance among women, and supporting the principals of political freedom, economic liberty and personal responsibility.

International Center for Research on Women (since 1976)
www.icrw.org
info@icrw.org

Geeta Rao Gupta (President)

1120 20th St. NW, Ste. 500 North
Washington, DC 20036
202-797-0007

Created to fill the gaps in understanding the complex realities
of women's lives and their role in development.

National Committee on Pay Equity (since 1979)
www.pay-equity.org
fairpay@pay-equality.org

Michele Leber (Chair)

555 New Jersey Ave. NW
Washington, DC 20001
703-920-2010

Coalition of women's and civil rights organizations; labor
unions; religious, professional, legal, and education associations, commissions on women, state and local pay equity
coalitions, and individuals working to eliminate sex- and
race-based wage discrimination and to achieve pay equity.

National Organization for Women (since 1966)
www.now.org
now@now.org

Kim Gandy (President)

1100 H Ste. NW, 3rd Floor
Washington, DC 20005
202-628-8669

Works to eliminate discrimination and harassment in the
workplace, schools, the justice system, and all other sectors
of society.

National Partnership for Women and Families (since 1971)
www.nationalpartnership.org
info@nationalpartnership.org

Debra L. Ness (President)

1875 Connecticut Ave. NW, Ste. 650
Washington, DC 20036
202-986-2600

Public education and advocacy to promote fairness in the workplace, quality health care, and policies that help women and
men meet the dual demands of work and family.

National Women's Law Center (since 1987)
www.nwlc.org

Nell Hennessy (President and CEO)

11 Dupont Circle NW, Ste. 800
Washington, DC 20036
202-588-2180

Uses law in all forms and educates the public.

9to5 National Association of Working Women (since 1972)
www.9to5.org
9to5@9to5.org

207 Buffalo St., #211
Milwaukee, WI 53203
800-522-0925 (hotline)
414-272-0925

Organized to end sexual harassment and discrimination and
to win better wages, working conditions, and family-
friendly policies.

MEN

The National Center for Men (since 1987)
www.nationalcenterformen.org
info@nationalcenterformen.org

PO Box 555
Old Bethpage, NY 11804
631-476-2115

Dedicated to the advocacy of men's equal rights. Educates the
public about how men have been hurt by sex discrimination

and also counsels individuals and families who have been damaged by discrimination against men.

National Fatherhood Initiative (since 1993)
www.fatherhood.org
info@fatherhood.org

Roland Warren (President)

101 Lake Forest Blvd., Ste 360
Githersburg, MD 20877
301-948-0599

Improve the well-being of children by increasing the probation of children growing up with involved responsible and committed fathers.

100 Black Men of America Inc. (since 1976)
www.100blackmen.org
info@100bmoa.org

141 Auburn Avenue
Atlanta, Georgia 30303
404-688-5100 (phone)
404-688-1028 (fax)

100 Black Men of America, Inc., seeks to serve as a beacon of leadership by utilizing our diverse talents to create environments where our children are motivated to achieve, and to empower our people to become self-sufficient shareholders in the economic and social fabric of the communities we serve.

INDEX

A

Ableism, 232
Abreu, J., 171
Academic concerns, Asian Americans, 158
Acculturation, 150, 154–156, 304
  Berry's modes of, 174
  Hispanics, 173–174
  immigrant populations, 244–246
  Native Americans, 194–196
  new citizens, 244–246
Addis, M. E., 104
Adler, A., 305
Advocacy, 28–29
  diversity, 25–27
  as a helping role, 24
  key concepts in, 25–29
  oppression, 25
  purpose of, 28
  social justice, 27–28
Advocacy competencies, 29–32
  client/student level, 30–31
  public arena level, 30–31
  resources for, 39–40
  school/community level, 30–31
  six domains of, 237
Advocacy practice, 33–36
  bio-psycho-social model, 36
  client-based factors, 33–34
  power, role in, 34
  qualitative/quantitative research on, 37–39
  self-awareness in, 35
Advocacy traditions
  Beers as pioneer in, 24
  in helping professionals, 23

Affective disorders, 71
African Americans
  community demographic, 121–124
  counseling implications, 140–143
  counseling relationship, 138–140, 143–144
  counseling strategies, 136–138
  cultural values, 130
  earnings, 123
  education, 122–123
  family households, 122
  high-need populations, 123
  historical context of culture, 124–126
  Jim Crow, 128–130
  legislation and, 126–128, 126–130
  multidimensional model of racial identity, 133–134
  occupations, 123
  post traumatic slave syndrome, 124
  poverty rate, 125–126
  psychological nigrescense (Cross model), 132–133
  racial identity development, 130–134
  youths, 134–136
African clients, 269–271
Ageism, 232
Alcoholism, Native Americans and, 196–198, 203
Allport, G. W., 53
American Counseling Association (ACA), 6–8, 13, 29
  Code of Ethics, 33, 36, 46, 227–228, 235
  Counselors for Social Justice (CSJ), 40

W

Ward, E. C., 12
Watson, I., 167
Watts, R. J., 36
We the People: Blacks in the United States, 122
West Indies, 262
What Is Marriage For? The Strange Social History of Our Most Intimate Institution (Graff), 234–235
Williamson, J., 128
Wilson, W. J., 128
Womanist identity model, 76–77
Women
  affective disorders, 71
  barriers faced by, 66–70
  cultural considerations, 70–73
  feminism, 64–65
  feminist multicultural counseling, 77–81
  gender pay gap/career choices, 66–67
  historical context, 62–63
  identity development in, 75–77
  marginalized women, 61
  multiple roles of, 68–70
  relationship status of, 68
  sex and violence, 70
  sexual harassment, 67–68
  single motherhood, 68–69
  standards of attractiveness, 70–71
  substance abuse, 71–73
  suffrage movement, 63–64
  violence against, 73–75
  women's suffrage, 63–64
Women of color, 61, 67, 70
Woodford, M. S., 109
Wrenn, C. G., 46
Wright, K., 218

Y

Young, C., 126

Z

Zagelbaum, A., 243
Zea, M. C., 171